NEW EXPLORATIONS
Critical Notes

ON PRESCRIBED POETRY FOR THE 2006 EXAMINATION
(HIGHER AND ORDINARY LEVEL)

EDITED BY
John G. Fal

GW00728974

CONTRIBUTORS
Carole Scully
Bernard Connolly
John G. Fahy
Martin Wallace
Ann Hyland
Seán Scully
John McCarthy
David Keogh

GILL & MACMILLAN

Gill & Macmillan Ltd
Hume Avenue
Park West
Dublin 12
with associated companies throughout the world
www.gillmacmillan.ie

0 7171 3691 4

Print origination and design in Ireland by O'K Graphic Design, Dublin

*The paper used in this book is made from the wood pulp of managed forests. For every
tree felled, at least one tree is planted, thereby renewing natural resources.*

Acknowledgments

For permission to reproduce copyright material in this book the publishers are grateful
to the following:
Michael Longley and Lucas Alexander Whitley for extracts from *Tuppenny Stung:
Autobiographical Chapters* by Michael Longley;
Penguin Putnam Inc. for an extract from *The Iliad* by Homer, translated by Robert
Eagles, translation copyright © 1990 by Robert Eagles, introduction and notes copyright
© 1990 by Bernard Knox. Used by permission of Viking Penguin, a division of Penguin
Putnam Inc.

CONTENTS

P = POEM ALSO PRESCRIBED FOR ORDINARY LEVEL 2006 EXAM

P = POEM ALSO PRESCRIBED FOR ORDINARY LEVEL 2006 EXAM

P = poem also prescribed for Ordinary Level 2006 Exam

P = POEM ALSO PRESCRIBED FOR ORDINARY LEVEL 2006 EXAM

P = POEM ALSO PRESCRIBED FOR ORDINARY LEVEL 2006 EXAM

1 John DONNE

Carole Scully

The quest for certainty

John Donne was born in 1572 in Bread Street, London, into a family that was prosperous, educated and, as Catholics, part of an unpopular religious minority. He was the third of six children. His father, also called John, was a successful merchant and a prominent member of the Company of Ironmongers. His mother, Elizabeth, a devout Catholic, was the daughter of John Heywood and the granddaughter of John Rastell, both popular writers in their time; even more significantly, she was the grandniece of Sir Thomas More, who had been beheaded by King Henry VIII in 1535 because he would not swear the oath accepting Henry as supreme head of the church. More had famously declared on the scaffold: 'I die the King's good servant, but God's servant first.'

This staunch religious devotion in the face of oppression was very much in evidence in Elizabeth's family. Two of her brothers, Donne's uncles, became members of the Jesuit order – an extremely dangerous choice of career, as Jesuits were considered, with some justification, to be the main leaders of the Catholic revolt against English Protestantism. It was treason, punishable by horrific forms of death, to be a Catholic priest, or even to help a Catholic priest. One of Donne's uncles, Jasper, led a secret Jesuit mission to England between 1581 and 1583; he was caught and sentenced to death, but this sentence was reduced to imprisonment and exile. There have been suggestions that the young Donne accompanied his mother to visit Jasper in the Tower of London, but there is no proof of this. In all likelihood, Donne was fully aware of his uncle's situation, as he was about eleven years old at the time and still living at home with his mother and stepfather.

Donne's father had died when Donne was four years old, leaving about £3,500 to his wife and six children – a large fortune at the time. About six months later Donne's mother, still only in her thirties, had married Dr John Syminges, a wealthy widower with three children. At one time Syminges had been president of the Royal College of Physicians; more significantly, he was a Catholic. Donne continued to live, therefore, in a family where education was valued, affordable, and Catholic.

EDUCATION

Donne was educated at home with his brother Henry for the early years of his life. There are strong indications that the boys' teachers were Jesuits. In later years Donne wrote of these men: 'I had my first breeding and conversation with men of suppressed and afflicted religion, accustomed to the despite of death and hungry of an imagined martyrdom.' This early exposure to religious intensity had a profound effect on Donne and may partly explain his constant intellectual struggle to find some evidence of certainty in existence. Izaak Walton, Donne's first biographer, relates how Donne, at the age of twelve, entered the University of Oxford with his younger brother, Henry. By starting university at a slightly younger age, Catholic boys could finish early; in this way they left before taking a degree, as that involved swearing the Oath of Supremacy, which declared the English monarch, and not the Pope, to be head of the church. The boys attended Hart Hall, a college with Catholic sympathies, for three years. There are suggestions that they then transferred to the other great university town of Cambridge. Even though he was still unable to take a degree, Donne benefited from this time spent in studies and in mixing with the intellectual group that lived around the colleges.

THE WORLD'S PLEASURES

At some time in his youth, most probably between 1589 and 1591, Donne appears to have travelled on the Continent. Travel was very much a part of a young gentleman's education at this time. He seems to have been fluent in Italian and Spanish, and in later years he kept a great many Spanish books in his library; indeed at about this time he chose a Spanish motto for himself, *Antes muerto que mudado* (Sooner dead than changed). The dramatic nature of this motto expresses the type of young man Donne was, or at least wished to be. An early portrait shows him beautifully dressed, with long, dark, curly hair, his intelligent, educated gaze looking into the future while his hand grasps a sword. He is the epitome of the Elizabethan gentleman. Perhaps Donne had discovered, as so many of us do, that there is a comforting certainty in belonging to a recognisable group.

In 1592 Donne was admitted to study law at Lincoln's Inn, London. In this he was following the strong family tradition on his mother's side. However, as the student lawyers were from wealthy families, they spent more of their time pursuing the pleasures of London life than in studying law. A friend of Donne's from this time, Sir Richard Baker, described him as 'not dissolute but very neat: a great visitor of ladies, a great frequenter of plays, a great writer of conceited verses'.

At this point in his life the twenty-year-old Donne was living a life that was radically different from the one he had learnt from his Jesuit teachers and his family. He was Master of the Revels (the title explains his role) for the Christmas celebrations at Lincoln's Inn. His poetry was circulated, with much praise, among the learned of London. He went to the theatre and socialised with fashionable women; he was on the way to becoming a popular celebrity. This may simply have been the natural rebellion of a young man against the beliefs of the older generation, or it may have been a reaction to seeing his younger brother, Henry, die from the plague while imprisoned in Newgate prison for helping a Catholic priest. It could have been another attempt to find the elusive certainty in life. Whatever the reason, Donne gave himself up to living the life of a gentleman about town and expressing his view of the world in bright, clever, sensual poetry:

> Put forth, put forth that warm balm-breathing thigh,
> Which when next time you in these sheets will smother
> There it must meet another.

Gradually, he drifted away from the law. In 1596 he joined a band of volunteers, under the leadership of Robert Devereux, Earl of Essex, and Sir Walter Raleigh and sailed to Cádiz. He experienced a violent sea battle and wrote with grim honesty of the terrible scenes he witnessed: 'They in the sea being burnt, they in the burnt ship drowned.' He returned to England briefly, but in 1597 he joined another expedition under the command of the Earl of Essex, sailing to the Azores with the aim of capturing the Spanish treasure fleet.

It was socially acceptable for young men from the upper classes to take part in these expeditions. At the time relations between England and Spain were uneasy. As recently as 1588 English forces had narrowly defeated the Spanish Armada, more by luck than by design. Queen Elizabeth, though officially disapproving of her subjects' attacks on Spanish vessels and territories, was perfectly happy to receive a share of the booty. Certainly the sense of drama and adventure seems to have appealed to Donne, as can be seen in his poetry:

> Here take my picture, though I bid farewell;
> Thine, in my heart, where my soul dwells, shall dwell.

The trip to the Azores was not a success, with violent storms battering the ships. Donne described the damage vividly:

> And from our tattered sails, rags drop down so,
> As from one hanged in chains, a year ago.

There is a feeling that Donne may have gone on these voyages hoping to find that elusive certainty he craved, but came home with the realisation that it was not to be found in the role of adventurer.

THE WORLD OF POLITICS

On his return to England, Donne, who by now had largely exhausted his finances, became a rather lowly member of Queen Elizabeth's court. He was twenty-five years old, charmingly ambitious, entertainingly educated, and had proved his valour on military expeditions. Not surprisingly, his fortunes soon improved. In 1598 he was offered a post by the father of one of his fellow-volunteers to Cádiz, and he became private secretary to Sir Thomas Egerton, Lord Keeper of the Great Seal. This was a great opportunity for Donne, as he now had steady employment and a clear connection with an important member of the court. The Lord Keeper presided over the House of Lords and the Court of the Star Chamber, where religious trials were conducted, and he organised the Court of Chancery. As was customary, the Lord Keeper lived at York House; so Donne came to live in a large palace with beautiful gardens that swept down to the Thames. He became part of Egerton's extended family group, which included his fourteen-year-old niece Ann More.

There is no doubt that Egerton was very fond of Donne. When his son died of his wounds in Dublin Castle while serving with Essex in Ireland, Egerton asked Donne to carry his son's sword in the funeral procession at Chester Cathedral. In 1601 he made Donne member of Parliament for one of the boroughs that he controlled. It seemed as if John Donne was destined to play an important role in the world of Elizabethan politics. Perhaps he had found his certainty at last.

THE RELIGIOUS DIFFICULTY

In all likelihood it was about this time that Donne began to move towards the Church of England. He had already considerably loosened his connections with the Catholic Church. In his pursuit of certainty he had been drawn to study the religious controversies that abounded at the time, and he seems to have developed the view that the different religions were simply different representations of the one truth:

> As women do in divers countries go
> In divers habits, yet are still one kind,
> So doth, so is religion.

By taking up the post with Sir Thomas Egerton, Donne in effect committed himself to practising the religion of the court: it would have been impossible for a Catholic to act as a private secretary to one of Queen Elizabeth's more senior courtiers. There is no doubt that Donne was fully aware of the opportunity he now had. A man could advance himself at court if he came to the attention of those in power. Donne carried out his duties diligently and enthusiastically.

MARRIAGE AND ITS CONSEQUENCES

In December 1601, in what could be seen as a foolish and impulsive action or as yet another attempt to find certainty, Donne, now twenty-nine years old, eloped with Ann More, who was seventeen. Ann's father, Sir George More, was a man known for his violent temper. When the couple finally confessed the marriage to him he was furious that his daughter had tied herself to a penniless private secretary. Donne was instantly dismissed from his post by Egerton, Ann's uncle, and was for a time imprisoned. Sir George More used his influence to ensure that Donne was unable to find employment to support his new wife. Donne, with his customary honesty, summed up his situation in six words: 'John Donne, Ann Donne, Un-done.'

Luckily, Ann's cousin, Sir Francis Wolley, offered the couple shelter in his home in Surrey. For the next few years Donne struggled to provide for his growing family. By 1608 Ann had given birth to five children. He spent some time assisting Thomas Morton, a chaplain, who was fiercely anti-Catholic. Indeed there are some indications that Donne may have collaborated with Morton on a number of writings against the Catholic Church, though his name does not appear on any of them.

When Morton was made Dean of Gloucester in 1607, he tried to persuade Donne to take holy orders in the Church of England. Donne's letter of refusal expresses a change in his approach to life. He appears to be ashamed of the heady days of his youth:

> . . . Some irregularities of my life have been visible to some men, and though I have, I thank God, made my peace with Him . . . yet this, which God knows to be so, is not so visible to man, as to free me from their censures and it may be that sacred calling from a dishonour.

Donne may have been using his past life as an excuse to avoid taking holy orders, because he was not yet fully convinced of the religious doctrines of the Church of England. Perhaps he still harboured the desire to succeed in Elizabethan politics. Or it could simply have been that Donne was not sure whether he could make an adequate living in the religious world to support his ever-increasing family. Nevertheless, whatever their motive, these are the words of a man who has sought certainty but has yet to find it.

Happily, in 1608 relations between Donne and his father-in-law improved, and Ann finally received her dowry. They were able to move to a small house in

Mitcham that was, to Donne's delight, convenient to London and his old friends.

There has been a great deal of debate about the nature of Donne's relationship with his wife. On the one hand, he seems to have felt extremely guilty about the way in which their marriage changed her life. He wrote to a friend, describing himself sitting

> in the noise of three gamesome children, and by the side of her whom I transplanted into a wretched fortune, I must labour to disguise that from her by all such honest devices, as giving her my company and discourse.

On the other hand, he wanted to escape from the house at Mitcham, calling it a 'prison' and a 'dungeon'.

Donne travelled extensively on the Continent with Sir Robert Drury and his family between 1611 and 1612. Ann remained in England with their seven children. Finally, in 1615, as a result of continual urging from King James I, Donne broke from the Catholic Church when he was ordained deacon and priest at St Paul's Cathedral, London, and became a royal chaplain. He quickly became known for his brilliant and moving sermons.

THE DEATH OF HIS WIFE

In 1617 Ann died, a few days after giving birth to a stillborn child. She had borne twelve children in fifteen years, seven of whom lived; the eldest was fourteen, the youngest only twelve months. Donne was devastated. Walton describes how he 'became crucified to the world . . . a commensurable grief took as full possession of him as joy had done . . . .' When he wrote a sonnet in her memory Donne clearly stated that he intended to channel all his passion into his life as a cleric and his new religion:

> Since she whom I loved hath paid her last debt
> To nature, and to hers, and my good is dead,
> And her soul early into heaven ravished,
> Wholly in heavenly things my mind is set.

He did indeed become extremely successful in his new religion. In 1625 he preached a sermon at the lying in state of King James I, and then another for the new king, Charles I. His sermons were noted for their use of striking metaphors. In the 'Sermon of Valediction' he challenged his parishioners to consider their relationship with God in the following terms:

No man would present a lame horse, a disordered clock, a torn book to a king . . . . Thy body is thy beast; and wilt thou present that to God, when it is lam'd and tir'd with excess of wantonness? When thy clock . . . is disordered with passions . . . when thy book . . . is torn . . . wilt thou then present thy self thus defac'd and mangled to almighty God?

Donne was by this time deeply ashamed of his youthful adventures, and he adjusted his life story so that the biography written by his contemporary, Izaak Walton, largely omits his early years. Nevertheless he was sympathetic towards the extremes of youth:

An old man wonders then how an arrow from an eye could wound him when he was young, and how love could make him do those things which he did then.

He came to believe that his difficulties in supporting his family were part of God's plan for him:

. . . And looking back on my past life, I now plainly see it was his hand that prevented me from all temporal employment; and that it was his will I should never settle nor thrive till I entered into the ministry.

His sermons were popular because they were filled with a sense of the common humanity of mankind:

No man is an island, entire of itself; every man is a piece of the continent, a part of the main . . . . Any man's death diminishes me, because I am involved in mankind. And therefore never send to know for whom the bell tolls. It tolls for thee.

THE FINAL QUEST

In 1631, having got out of his sick-bed, Donne delivered his last sermon, entitled 'Death's Duell'. He spoke of the interconnection of life and death, once again using vivid images to convey his message:

Wee have a winding sheet in our Mother's womb, which grows with us from our conception, and wee come into the world, bound up in that winding sheet, for wee come to seek a grave.

In a gesture that recalls his youthful fondness for the dramatic, Donne ordered a large carved wooden urn to be brought to his room. He stood on it wrapped in his own shroud while an artist made the life-size sketch that was later used for a stone figure.

It is generally agreed that had Donne not died when he did, on 31 March 1631, he would have become a bishop. He was buried in St Paul's Cathedral.

Donne's apostasy

There has been much debate about Donne's apostasy (giving up his religion) and the sincerity of his conversion to the Church of England. Perhaps he was motivated by the desire to succeed in a world where Catholics were definitely second-class citizens. There is no doubt that King James greatly influenced his decision to be ordained by refusing to grant him a secular appointment. Or it may have been that his early experiences led him to rebel against the religion that had caused so much distress in his family. Interestingly, his mother, who was always a staunch Catholic, came to live with Donne and his family in the Deanery at St Paul's. Was his change of religion simply another attempt to find that emotional and intellectual certainty he so badly craved?

Whatever his motivation, Donne's conversion did not end his quest for certainty. His sermons may have expressed an unwavering faith in God, but his poetry still trembled with uncertainty. In his final poem, 'A Hymn to God the Father', Donne begs God for mercy. There is a poignancy in the uncertainty that still haunts his very being after all his years of searching. Yet behind the overwhelming need and the religious language there is still the glimmer of the man who, in spite of the terrible uncertainty he could see, lived life with a passion, the man who was made Master of the Revels, sailed the seas, married impulsively and preached inspiringly, the man who even at the last could not resist punning on his own name:

> But swear by thy self, that at my death thy son
> Shall shine as he shines now, and heretofore;
> And, having done that, thou hast done,
> I fear no more.

Perhaps he did find his certainty after all.

John Donne and metaphysical poetry

John Donne wrote poetry throughout his life. Whether he was on land, at sea, at court, in prison, Catholic or Protestant, single or married, Donne wrote poetry. But, surprising as it may seem, he did not write for publication. For Donne lived at a time when the writing of poetry was considered to be the accomplishment of a true gentleman. Rather like mastering fencing, it was a skill that defined a man's social status. A gentleman wrote to amuse, to impress and even to seduce, but he never wrote to publish. Donne circulated his poetry among a select group of friends and patrons. His point of exhibition and distribution was generally the Mitre, an inn frequented by intellectual gentlemen. He rarely dated his work and all too often did not keep copies of the poems he had written. But although Donne followed the customs of the day in the way he viewed his poetry, he was rigorously individual in the way he wrote.

It is ironic that the term 'metaphysical', applied so often to Donne's style of writing, was first thrown at him as a term of critical abuse. In 1693, some sixty years after Donne's death, John Dryden wrote that he

> affects the metaphysics, not only in his satires, where nature only should reign, but perplexes the minds of the fair sex with nice speculations of philosophy, when he should engage their hearts, and entertain them with the softnesses of love.

In truth, this passage says more about Dryden's expectations of poetry than it does about metaphysical poetry; but his use of the word 'metaphysics' is important, because it captures in one word an essential aspect of Donne's poetry: his desire to go beyond the physical confines of existence. When Donne wrote about love he did not list his beloved's physical qualities, as was customary with traditional poets: instead he ignored these 'softnesses of love' and told her of the ways in which she filled his emotions, his mind and his every waking moment. Donne united the intellect and the emotions in a way that had never been done before. As T. S. Eliot put it, 'a thought to Donne was an experience; it modified his sensibility.'

In an effort to communicate this unified experience of thought and emotion, Donne made use of the *conceit*. Conceits, in the form of far-fetched comparisons, had long been used in traditional love poetry as a device for emphasising the beauty of the poet's beloved. But Donne discarded the traditional in favour of his own unique approach. Once again it is a negative interpretation by a critic that provides the key to what Donne was attempting to do. Samuel Johnson famously commented that in metaphysical poetry 'The most heterogeneous ideas are yoked together by violence; nature and art are ransacked for illustrations, comparisons and illusions . . . .' His use of the words 'violence' and 'ransacked', though intended to be a reproach, suggest the uncompromising way in which Donne combined ideas in his poetry. He disregarded convention, both in thought and taste. He can use the image of a flea in a love poem and urge God to ravish him in a religious one.

Because he was trying to communicate an incredibly complex experience, Donne used the conceit as a device whereby he could connect apparently unconnected images in such a way that the gradual uncovering of a connectedness between them conveys both an intellectual and an emotional message. T. S. Eliot called it a 'telescoping of images and multiplied associations . . .' It is a way of dramatically and rapidly communicating complexity of both feeling and thinking. So Donne could summarise the essence of Elizabeth Drury's being in three words: 'Her body thought.' As readers we can react to this statement on an instinctive level. By combining two images that are accepted as relating to two distinctly different aspects of human existence, Donne succeeds in communicating a unity of message. The three words, and the mental images they carry, amalgamate into a new and complex concept that simultaneously appeals to the intellect, the emotions and the spirit. There is an instinctive quality to our reaction to Donne's conceits that arises out of this challenging combination, a quality all too often lacking in more logical and expected comparisons. In his writing Donne released himself from the accepted norms of appropriateness; in our reading of his work we should endeavour to do the same.

To be able to make these connections, the metaphysical poet had to be finely tuned in every fibre of his being. Here again, those who were suspicious of metaphysical poetry regarded this as a weakness. Johnson rather huffily pronounced that 'The metaphysical poets were men of learning, and to show their learning was their whole endeavour . . . .' In a way, Johnson both hit and missed the point with this statement. The metaphysical poets, and Donne in particular, were indeed men who had benefited from the privilege of education; but instead of simply exhibiting their education by reproducing skilful copies of what they had previously studied, they confronted the very foundations of that education: they questioned the logic they had been taught and tested the substance of the rhetoric they had practised. In this way Donne takes the framework of the traditional Petrarchan sonnet and subjects it to the stresses of unexpected conceits; he fills the dramatic opening, so long the poet's comfortable starting point, with a tension of contradiction, and rejects the conventionally artificial language and rhythm of poetry for the words of everyday speech and the rhythm that comes from the sense of these words.

To be able to do all this, he had to have 'wit' – not in the simplistic sense in which we use that word today but, in the words of the critic Josef Lederer, as 'a brilliant result of long study, a quintessence of deep learning'. Samuel Taylor Coleridge expresses his view in more detail:

> Wonder-exciting vigour, intenseness and peculiarity of thought, using at will the most boundless stores of a capacious memory, and exercised on subjects where we have no right to expect it – this is the wit of Donne!

Of course the fundamental question with Donne is whether his poetry grew out of some inner, inescapable urge that demanded expression or was the calculated posturing of a man who was ambitious for fame and fortune. Did Donne possess a mind that was, in T. S. Eliot's words, 'perfectly equipped for its work' of 'constantly amalgamating disparate experience'? Was this mind tormented by the vision of the uncertainty of existence and forever searching for some evidence of certainty? Do his unconventional conceits and 'wit' simply represent the spiritual, intellectual and emotional insecurity that Donne felt throughout his life? Or was his poetry merely a brilliant exercise in self-advertisement, a cynical publicity stunt to attract the applause and admiration of his peers?

The Flea

Text of poem: New Explorations Anthology page 2

[*Note: This poem is also prescribed for Ordinary Level 2006 exam*]

One of the difficulties with Donne's poetry is that he never made any attempt to keep his poems together, or to organise them in chronological order. Izaak Walton deeply regretted this attitude, commenting that Donne's pieces 'were loosely, God knows too loosely scattered in his youth'. Publication did not appeal to Donne, and on the rare occasion when he allowed the 'Anniversaries' to be printed he wrote to a friend: 'The fault that I acknowledge in myself is to have descended to print anything in verse.' It was not until 1633, two years after his death, that the first collected edition of Donne's verse appeared. The order and grouping of the poems was largely a matter of guesswork on the part of his friends.

It has been said that 'The Flea' was one of Donne's most celebrated and most widely known poems while he was alive. Though there is no definite evidence to support this, there are indications that it was translated into Dutch.

A READING OF THE POEM

Donne opens the poem in a dramatic fashion. He is talking to his lover, but it is definitely a one-sided conversation. It is almost as if he is lecturing her. His use of the image of the flea, though a common poetic device in the seventeenth century, adds to the drama and the tension. There is a feeling that Donne has already tried a number of arguments and has been rejected. Perhaps somewhat at a loss in the face of constant refusal, his eyes wander around the room and suddenly light upon the flea, and inspiration strikes.

The first line appears to be a casual comment on the appearance of a flea. We can imagine how it would catch his lover's attention, how she would probably feel rather puzzled at this sudden change of topic. But the second line quickly undercuts this apparent simplicity. Donne uses the flea to make a very important point to his lover. She is denying him something he wants, but so far he does not specify what it is.

In the next two lines he returns to his comments on the flea. He describes how the flea has bitten both himself and his lover, and their blood is now mixed together in the flea. A basic physicality is suggested in his use of the blood image, which prepares us for the sixth line. Donne's use of the word 'maidenhead', along with 'sin' and 'shame', leaves little doubt about what it is his lover is denying him.

Donne reinforces the connection between himself and the flea in the final three lines of the first stanza. Unlike Donne himself, the flea is able to enjoy an intimate relationship with this woman, even though it has not gone through the rituals of courtship. The use of the word 'pampered' implies a feeling of contentment and satisfaction – two states that Donne most certainly does not feel. The suggestion is that he has played the wooing game according to the rules, and he feels that, in all fairness, his lover should play her part in the game.

It is evident from reading this first stanza that how this poem is interpreted, and what reaction we experience to it, depends on how we view the tone of the piece. Donne would probably have read this poem aloud to a small group and in this way could have coloured the tone. But our interpretation has to develop as a result of careful reading and rereading. If we consider Donne to be approaching his lover in a mock-dramatic or charmingly pathetic manner, we can react with amusement; we can join in the joke that is trembling between Donne and his lady. But if we think he is behaving in a thoroughly unpleasant fashion, exerting considerable emotional blackmail on his lover with his selfish, adolescent whingeing, we are bound to feel anger and annoyance.

Finally, it may be that Donne deliberately wove this ambiguity into the poem as a way of adding a sense of danger. He knows he is skating on thin ice, and so do we. In this way he deliberately moves away from the safety of creating straightforward amusement and into the perils of humour that challenges our preconceptions.

Donne ended the first stanza on an extremely dramatic note, lamenting in mock-heroic terms – evident in the use of the word 'alas' – the fact that he and his lover have not experienced physical intimacy. He continues this approach in the second stanza. His dramatic plea, 'Oh stay,' asking her to not to squash the flea, carries with it a wealth of understated comedy. In an age when fleas and their destruction were commonplace, the drama Donne attaches to this incident can only be interpreted as humorous. He asks that the flea's life be spared, because in killing it his lover will destroy the flea's life and, because it contains their blood, her life and Donne's. He urges her to remember that the mingling of their blood is intimate and special: it is like their 'marriage bed' and their 'marriage temple'. Here again Donne overstates the situation in a humorous way: linking the image of a temple with a flea is patently ridiculous. Donne races on, carried forward by his own eloquence and perhaps by his lover's lack of response despite his best efforts. Nevertheless, in the midst of all these theatricals he produces a stunningly vivid image of their blood within the flea, 'cloistered in these living walls of jet.' Barely pausing for breath, he launches another argument at his lover. If she is unmoved by his death and that of the flea, then she must be concerned about causing her own suicide and thereby committing a sin to add to that of two murders.

Donne uses religious language in this stanza to provide a framework for his argument. His implication is that he regards physical intimacy with his lover as something sacred and special; but there is an undercutting awareness of the humorous incompatibility that lies in linking a flea sucking blood with religion.

Though Donne's lover never speaks, we can clearly visualise her reaction to his arguments in the way that she behaves. She may be verbally inactive but she is far from being passive. The third stanza opens with the death of the flea. Donne is horrified by her action. It is 'cruel and sudden,' perhaps as cruel and sudden as her rejection of his advances. She has spilled the 'blood of innocence'. The clear suggestion is that the woman is callous and cruel in her behaviour towards the innocent flea, just as she is with the innocent Donne. This, of course, is obviously ridiculous. Donne is far from innocent in his desires. He continues this line of thought, stating that she triumphs in the flea's death because she has proved the arguments that Donne put forward in the second stanza to be wrong.

At this point it appears that Donne is completely beaten. He gives the impression that his lover has outwitted him. But he is simply lulling her into a false sense of security. The last three lines of the poem are produced with a magician's flourish. Donne concedes that the woman is absolutely right: she has lost nothing with the death of the flea. But, in a breathtaking reversal of the balance of power, he tells her that, in exactly the same way, her yielding to his advances will not cause her to lose her honour. He is, in effect, using the well-worn argument that he will respect her in the morning!

STYLE

Donne uses a popular device from sixteenth-century love poetry as the framework on which to hang his poem. The linking of a male lover with a flea had been used in Greek, Latin, French, Spanish and Italian poetry. The image was usually developed along very bawdy lines, with the flea wandering over the woman's body; the death of the flea at the hands of the woman was regarded as ultimately blissful.

This poem could be viewed as Donne testing the limitations of the device not simply to achieve a humorous effect, but to challenge the conventionality that the device represented.

Samuel Johnson wrote of the metaphysicals: 'Whatever is improper or vicious is produced from nature in pursuit of something new and strange; the writers fail to give delight by their desire to excite admiration.'

This piece may be nothing more than the poetic equivalent of a dirty joke. It causes a reaction simply because it uses rude images. Donne takes an 'improper' idea in the belief that he will be able to give it a new slant, purely in an attempt to impress his friends at the Mitre. It is neither 'new' nor 'strange', nor does it 'excite admiration' or 'delight'. In short, it is the perfect piece to be read in a dimly lit room filled with immature men.

Song: Go, and catch a falling star

Text of poem: New Explorations Anthology page 4
[*Note: This poem is also prescribed for Ordinary Level 2006 exam*]

This poem appears to have been written during the time Donne spent at Lincoln's Inn, when he was beginning to make a name for himself as a poet. Poetry at this time was one way in which an educated young man on the fringes of the court could bring himself to the attention of those in power.

STYLE

The listing of impossible tasks was popular in Petrarchan poetry. This use of *hyperbole* (an exaggerated statement not meant to be taken literally) was a device to emphasise the poet's devotion to his beloved.

There is a strong element of *satire* in this poem. Broadly speaking, satire is used to expose and ridicule folly and shallowness. It is frequently driven by anger, but it is more refined and sophisticated than an angry outburst. The writer generally expresses a one-sided view of his subject, in order to ensure that the satire works. The use of satire suggests that the writer feels superior to those he is satirising, that he can see the folly while others are unaware of it.

A READING OF THE POEM

The first line of this poem has a magical, fairy-tale quality about it. The catching of a 'falling star' belongs to the romantic world of handsome princes and beautiful princesses. Donne deliberately creates specific expectations in the reader by using this as his opening line. However, the second line introduces a sense of unease, as it is a much darker image. The phrase 'get with child' is brutally unromantic. The mandrake is a plant that people at the time believed had human qualities, such as screaming when it was uprooted. Though this image, like that of catching a falling star, is meant to represent an impossible task, it is very much the stuff of nightmares.

The tone changes again with Donne's rather conventional question about the passing of time. But we return to a darker world of images with the question about 'the Devil's foot'. The 'mermaids singing' could belong to the world of falling stars and passing time; however, Donne appears to be deliberately exploiting the ambiguity that existed around the image of the mermaid at this time: while it could refer to a beautiful half-woman, half-fish creature, it could also be used to denote a prostitute. The final image of 'envy's stinging' has a deeply personal feeling about it.

Donne is deliberately playing with his reader's perception of the nature of this poem. He alternates between images usually connected with the Petrarchan view of love and images that are radically and disturbingly opposed to it. He is consciously confusing his reader in order to create tension. All this tension culminates in the final three lines of the stanza, where Donne uses both the sense of his words and their rhythm in a most unsettling way. There is real vehemence in his statement about the lack of success for the 'honest mind'. Does it reflect the frustrations of an ambitious young man not yet able to break into the powerful world of the court? By interrupting the rhythm of the stanza with two lines of only two words, Donne skilfully emphasises this final image.

The second stanza continues this tension but in a slightly different way. Rather than alternate between pleasant traditional images and more unpleasant unconventional ones, Donne remains in the world of the unpleasant. A series of disquieting images is hurled at the reader: being 'born to strange sights,' able to see 'things invisible', riding 'ten thousand days and nights,' hair turning 'snow white' and returning with stories of 'strange wonders'. It is not accidental that Donne repeats the word 'strange' in this stanza, for it is unsettlingly strange.

In a final flourish Donne ends the stanza on the strangest concept of all: the fact that it is impossible to find 'a woman true and fair.' He has propelled us along a roller-coaster ride of emotions, and we are left gasping at the end of this outburst. Are we speechless from shock at the strength of emotion underlying his opinion of women? Or has the tension that fills every word in the poem become unbearable?

The tone of the final stanza is more controlled; it is as if Donne has been emotionally drained by the first two stanzas. There is a sad vulnerability and longing in the line 'If thou find'st one, let me know,' for, despite his best efforts, Donne still yearns for the 'woman true and fair.' Quickly he changes his mind, asking not to be told of such a woman, not even if she were living next door to him. Once again Donne's bitterness returns, perhaps even more effective now that it is more understated in its expression.

In the last five lines of the poem Donne summarises his attitude to women. He no longer rants and raves: he simply states the fact that even if a 'true' woman were to be found she would inevitably turn 'false' in the length of time it would take for a letter to be sent to him while travelling to meet her. It is a shocking ending to the poem; or is it?

As with 'The Flea', this poem is a mass of unresolved ambiguities. Is Donne being serious or not? Is he expressing his real views, his longing for certainty, or is he simply acting out an attitude? Is the 'me' in the poem Donne, or a persona he has taken on? Did he write this poem as a satire? If he intended it to be a satire, what was he satirising? Was he satirising women, perhaps as a result of something he experienced? Or was he drawing attention to the stupidity of the conventional Petrarchan love poem? Was Donne fighting for women to be treated by men as real human beings? It is up to you to decide.

Alternatively
William Hazlitt commented on the metaphysical poets: 'Their chief aim was to make you wonder at the writer, not interest you in the subject . . . .' This poem could be seen as the work of a self-absorbed man. Donne was determined to gain notoriety by being outrageous and controversial. Though this poem may have been written as the words to a song, it is not pleasantly amusing. His images are deliberately disturbing, his views on women are offensive and his tone is nastily pompous. He may pride himself on having an 'honest mind', but on the evidence of this poem it is little wonder that he was unable 'to advance'.

The Sun Rising

Text of poem: New Explorations Anthology page 6

Donne made no attempt during his lifetime to date the majority of his poems, nor to keep them in any kind of order. As very little of his work was published and the poems were simply distributed in manuscript form, we have few indications of when most of the poems were written. In the first printed edition of his poetry, in 1633, the love poems are scattered through the book. However, in 1635, four years after his death, an edition of Donne's poetry grouped all his love poems together under the title 'Songs and Sonnets'. Generally, later editions have stuck to this arrangement, because not enough definite information is available to organise them in any other way.

STYLE

Donne frequently places himself in a dramatic setting in his love poems. Whether he is attempting to seduce his lover, to remain with her or to leave her behind, the reader is brought into the scene at a very important moment. In this poem Donne uses this drama to give new life and energy to the traditional love-poetry images of royalty and the sun.

A READING OF THE POEM

The opening three lines of this poem are wonderfully dramatic. Donne balances straightforward language and natural speech rhythms to vividly create a sense of immediacy. It is as if we are there with him as he vents his annoyance on the sun. The beams of sun shine in through 'windows' and 'curtains', disturbing Donne and his lover. It is an intrusion into their close intimacy, an unwanted reminder that they will not always be able to exist in this tranquil and contented state. The sun is a reminder to the two lovers of the world outside. Their quietness is emphasised by the frenzied activities, clearly suggested by the rhythm of these lines, of the early morning. In four lines, we see 'late school-boys' and 'sour prentices' reluctantly going on their way, while courtiers scurry around after the king and farm workers, 'country ants', set about the harvesting. All these people are governed by something outside themselves: the schoolboys by the school day, the apprentices by their work, the courtiers by the whims of the king, and the farm workers by the seasons. However, Donne and his lover are freed from such controls by their love. They have transcended time itself.

The second stanza continues this theme of love triumphant. Donne challenges the power of the sun with his beams 'so reverend and strong'. He states that he could easily blot out these beams by simply shutting his eyes. But he will not do this, because he does not want to miss seeing his beloved for one instant. Therefore, for him his lover is stronger than the sun. This links into the following image, where Donne speaks of her eyes being bright enough to blind the sun. This is a traditional image in love poetry, but Donne places it in a context where the comparison seems to occur naturally and spontaneously. As in the first stanza, he sweeps from the close intimacy of the room to the outside world by his use of vivid images. He challenges the sun further by stating that it may spend the day moving across the world, over the evocative 'Indias of spice and mine' or shining on kings, but the real, true world will be in this room with the two lovers. In this way, love transcends the confines of space.

In the third stanza Donne draws together this central theme of love triumphant. His lover is 'all states' and he is 'all princes'. There is an irresistible quality about Donne's enthusiasm, whatever his motivation. Even if he was only driven by the desire to seduce, it is hard not to be swept along with him. He is emphatic in his belief that the two lovers have everything that matters with them in the room: 'Nothing else is.' The trappings of worldly success, considered so important in the external world, are irrelevant in the world of love. The unlimited power wielded by sixteenth-century royalty is but an imitation of the lovers' power; the rewards of 'honour' are simply amusing imitations, and wealth is useless. The sun, which so rudely wakened them, is pitied by Donne, because its movement is across this external world on its own, whereas Donne and his beloved are two people united in a limitless world of love. Momentarily, he has found some certainty.

In the final four lines of the poem Donne slows the rhythm of his words to underpin the alteration in his emotions. His excited and challenging confidence changes to sympathetic concern for the sun. The sun is old and deserves some respect, particularly from two who have such power. Donne comforts the sun by allowing it to enter into their world, so that in shining on them it will be shining on the true world. Is there a touch of humour in these lines? Could Donne be, once again, practising the art of humorous seduction?

Alternatively

The critic John Carey considers the 'vaunting language' used by Donne in this poem to be a clear indication that he did not feel as confident and contented as he said he did. Rather than feeling better than those involved in the court, or richer than those who had wealth, Carey feels that Donne, who had financial difficulties, was deeply envious of the world of the rich and powerful. He was desperately ambitious to make his mark on the world. Carey's view is that Donne regards the 'private world' he inhabits with his beloved as being only an imitation of the 'public' world he so longs to join. No matter how hard he tries to concentrate on the superiority of love, he is 'irascibly conscious of the rest of the world's activities'.

The Anniversarie

Text of poem: New Explorations Anthology page 8

BACKGROUND

See the background notes for 'The Sun Rising', pages 16–18.

STYLE

Donne's poems on love are usually classified as *lyrics*. Though the term 'lyric' is a rather general one, there are certain characteristics that tend to be obvious in a lyrical poem. The nineteenth-century writer John Ruskin defined the lyric as 'the expression by the poet of his own feelings'. There is an undeniable personal quality about the lyric, in that the words are spoken by one person from a personal viewpoint. However, a problem arises regarding exactly who the 'I' of lyrical poetry is. The 'I' could be the poet himself, or it could simply represent a character the poet has created, a persona, to act as a mouthpiece for what he wants to express. Therefore, it is not always clear just how personal 'lyric' poems are.

There has been a great deal of discussion about the reality of the love experiences Donne describes in his love poetry. Some have felt that the 'I' in these poems is not Donne and that the feelings expressed are no more than the wishful thoughts of a frustrated young man. Others believe that Donne based his poems on actual experiences in his life and that the 'I' is very definitely Donne himself. What is undeniable is the fact that when Donne turned to religion he became deeply embarrassed by these poems from his youth.

A READING OF THE POEM

This poem opens on familiar territory, both for the modern reader of Donne and for those few of his contemporaries who were privileged to read his work in manuscript form. The images of the court and the sun were part of the traditional formula of Petrarchan love poetry, which was so popular in Donne's time. For modern readers who have read some of Donne's works these images are familiar because he uses them frequently in his writing. Yet, even though these two groups of readers are separated by more than four hundred years, a common sense of expectancy is stimulated by this opening. Just as Donne's friends might have glanced at each other in anticipation of how Donne was going to follow this beginning, so we are also aware that something will happen in the course of this poem that will not be totally expected.

However, the first stanza continues in a reasonably conservative way. Donne, having noted that everything from the 'kings' to the 'sun' has aged by a year since the lovers first met, states clearly that it is only their shared love that is untouched by time. In the face of 'destruction' and 'decay' their love 'keeps his first, last, everlasting day.'

In the first stanza the concept of time passing is conveyed by fairly unthreatening images. The idea of 'kings', 'beauties', 'wits' and the 'sun itself' ageing by a year is not really disturbing: Donne is simply reproducing the usual formula to suggest the passing of time. Similarly, the line 'Only our love hath no decay' is a common sentiment expressed in love poetry. Love has 'no tomorrow', nor has it a 'yesterday'. This is all fairly unremarkable. But then we meet the line 'Running it never runs from us away,' and the formulaic safety of the opening eight lines begins to tremble slightly. What does Donne mean by this line? He must have felt it was of reasonable importance to use it to interrupt the traditional approach he had followed so far. There is a kind of premeditated intellectualisation in this paradox, a conscious self-awareness that is not present in the previous lines. The verb 'running' is not one that immediately springs to mind in connection with a love affair, yet Donne obviously chose it carefully. Was it simply so that he could construct this clever little paradox to amuse both himself and his friends? Or did he deliberately use 'run' because it was definitely *not* part of the vocabulary of the Petrarchan love poem?

Donne ends this stanza with a line that is beautifully balanced, both in its meaning and its rhythm: 'But truly keeps his first, last, everlasting day.' Love remains untouched by the 'destruction' and 'decay' that haunts everything else.

The second stanza begins with a graphic image of two bodies in separate graves. The threat of death was very real to the Elizabethans, and this would have been a disturbing image, one far removed from the niceties of Petrarchan love poetry. The description of the two lovers lying in the one grave is not totally comforting. Donne continues the royalty image of the first stanza with his comparison between the two lovers and 'princes'. This is an idea that we have met previously with Donne: that mutual love makes two people special, powerful, and set apart – rather like royalty but even better. However, despite their uniqueness the two lovers, along with 'other princes', must inevitably surrender their physical bodies.

It is interesting that there is generally a marked lack of physical details in Donne's poetry: we rarely learn anything about what his lovers look like, even though his love poetry is filled with a sensuous pleasure. Yet here he deliberately writes of the 'eyes' with their 'sweet salt tears' and the 'ears' that were 'oft fed with true oaths'. The first six lines of the second stanza vividly describe the physicality of death, because Donne wants us to feel the overwhelming nature of death, so that love's ability to triumph over it will appear all the more wonderful. For love does triumph. Donne declares that their love has transcended the limitations of mere physical love: it has become a part of their very souls. This spiritual love is able to cheat death: the bodies of the lovers may go 'to their graves,' but the souls will escape to 'there above'. This was provocative stuff in an age when access to Heaven was being fought over by the Catholic and Protestant churches. Both promised eternal life to their followers and damnation to those who rejected them. Yet here is Donne, filled with certainty, saying that love shared between a man and a woman is the way to gain entry into Heaven.

The final stanza opens where the second stanza ends. When the souls of the lovers go up to Heaven they will be 'thoroughly blessed', because their love will be increased by heavenly love. There they will join all the other lovers who have also attained spiritual love, and in this way they will no longer be unique in the way that they are on Earth. However, for the moment they are still here on Earth; they are still 'kings', because their love is true, but they need not fear death. The lovers are safe, because they can be damaged in only one way: by each other. Their love ensures that they are immune to the passing of time and the horrors of death but, ironically, it also makes them profoundly vulnerable to each other. Happily, Donne is so confident in the certainty of their love that he quickly dismisses this possibility. They must simply avoid worrying about 'true and false fears' and live a long life together, secure in the protection of their shared love.

This poem ends in a way that is far removed from the Petrarchan conventions that filled the first stanza. It has travelled from the world of the court to the sun blazing in space, from the darkness of the grave to the light of Heaven. But above all it has declared the power and the certainty of the love that Donne shares with his beloved.

Alternatively

Samuel Taylor Coleridge commented on the metaphysical poets that they 'sacrificed the heart to the head'. Is this poem a sincere expression of Donne's belief in the certainty of his love, or is it simply an intellectual exercise designed to show just how stale and old-fashioned traditional Petrarchan love poetry had become? Did he write from the heart, or did his head make it look as if he was writing from the heart?

Sweetest love, I do not go

Text of poem: New Explorations Anthology page 10

It has been suggested – particularly by Donne's first biographer, Izaak Walton – that Donne wrote this poem, together with 'A Valediction: Forbidding Mourning', to his wife before he left to travel on the Continent in 1611. However, as Donne rarely dated any of his poetry, there is no proof to support this view.

In some manuscripts this poem is in a group entitled 'Songs which were made to certain airs which were made before'. Several seventeenth-century manuscripts contain music for this poem, but again there is no proof that Donne ever intended this poem to be sung.

A READING OF THE POEM

The poem opens in typical Donne style. It is a moment of drama, and we have stumbled upon two people immersed in an intense conversation. But the drama in this poem is far more understated than in much of Donne's other love poetry. There is a sense of true intimacy about the language he uses to express his feelings. He speaks simply and with apparent sincerity. There is little evidence of his sparkling wit and tongue-in-cheek humour; he is simply trying to reassure his beloved. In the very first lines of the poem he emphasises to her that he is not going 'for weariness' of her, nor because he is looking for 'a fitter love'. He then uses gentle humour to try to lighten the moment. After all, he says, he will have to die some time, and he would rather enjoy life than spend it imagining all the dreadful deaths that might happen to him. We can almost see Donne widening his eyes and giving an appealing smile to emphasise this little joke.

In an effort to carry this lighter tone into the second stanza, Donne then compares himself to the sun. The sun, he tells his beloved, set yesterday but was still able to return. So, he must go away, but he will be back. In a simple little hyperbole he tells her that he will be back more speedily than the sun, because he has the motivation to return to her.

The third stanza approaches the main theme of the poem from a slightly different angle. Donne reflects on the ways humankind deals with life experiences. He comments that we tend to accept the good times for what they are, but when it comes to the bad times we tend to exaggerate how bad they are. He is trying to minimise the 'bad chance' of their parting in an effort to comfort and reassure his beloved.

However, in the fourth stanza he returns to the intensely personal tone of the opening stanza. In a series of beautifully constructed images and rhythms he describes just how deeply connected the two lovers are. Her sadness is so real to him that it actually erodes his life force. Her sighs diminish the strength of his soul; her tears are like a loss of blood to him. Her grief is killing him, and he urges her to remember this, to realise that she is 'the best of me'. This stanza vibrates with a level of sincerity and an emotional openness that are in marked contrast to some of Donne's earlier love poetry. There is no sense that Donne is performing or taking up a position in an effort to impress or amuse. For once, it seems that we are seeing John Donne the man as he really is, filled with the certainty that their love is true.

This emotional intensity sweeps into the final stanza. Donne begs his lover not to imagine all the terrible things that could happen to him when they are parted. He admits the possibility of something dreadful occurring, but he reminds her that they really have no control over destiny. Once again he uses a wonderfully evocative image to convey the depth of his feelings. For lovers such as they, the ultimate terror of death is simply a turning 'aside to sleep'. Their true and certain love enables them to triumph over time and space, and even death itself.

STYLE

The structure of this poem is deceptively simple. The very appearance of the printed lines on the page implies that this is a poem that should be easily understood, and in many ways it is. Donne uses the simple language of everyday conversation. There are no dramatic exclamations, no witty constructions: just the desire to express sincerity. His occasional movements away from the deeply personal tone (in the second and third stanzas) are not for the purpose of displaying his intellect, but rather are further attempts to relieve the dreadful emotional turmoil the two lovers are experiencing. His use of a light rhythm and a strong rhyme seems to be a deliberate attempt to lighten the intensity of the situation. Similarly, the five eight-line stanzas impose a definite structure on the scene, a structure that is clearly lacking in the reality of the lovers' imminent separation. However, in spite of his best efforts, Donne cannot control the emotional impact of this moment. His true feelings break through rhyme and rhythm. He cannot hide his own vulnerability. The death that he is suffering in this poem is more real and painful than the one he described in 'The Flea', because love is no longer a game.

Alternatively

'In his poems there is often a perfect equilibrium between their exact truth to mood and feeling and their acute awareness of an audience' (Barbara Everett). Is this poem simply another example of Donne using love as a vehicle for his desire to impress his little group of fans? Is he exploiting his lover, once again using their apparent emotional connection as an opportunity to display his 'wit'?

A Valediction: Forbidding Mourning

Text of poem: New Explorations Anthology page 12

As we have seen, Izaak Walton links this poem with 'Sweetest Love, I Do Not Go', suggesting that they were written just before a trip to the Continent in 1611. He comments: 'I beg leave to tell you, that I have heard some critics . . . say, that none of the Greek or Latin poets did equal them.' However, attractive though it may be to connect them to Donne's life, it should be noted that parting or absence from a loved one were traditional themes in love poetry.

A READING OF THE POEM

Donne opens this poem with a vivid image of a death-bed scene. This, coupled with the title – 'A Valediction: Forbidding Mourning' – creates the expectation that this poem will be about the death of someone. It is certainly not an unpleasant death, as the 'virtuous men' are confident of a life after death in Heaven. The atmosphere is one of dignity and composure, with a group of friends present at the gentle passing.

The second stanza links into this idea of a quiet withdrawal. Donne advises his beloved that they should 'melt, and make no noise'. At this point Donne still seems to be dealing with death in its physical sense. But the following three lines have something odd about them. Donne seems to be suggesting that the two lovers should die peacefully. He emphasises the depth and uniqueness of their love by using such religious phrases as 'profanation of our joys' and 'to tell the laity'. Theirs is a love that is wonderfully special and should not involve others. In the light of this intensity it seems odd that he should be advising her to meet their death with 'no tear-floods, nor sigh-tempests'.

The third stanza makes no attempt to resolve this difficulty. Donne seems to deliberately leave the personal and move to the impersonal. He comments on the custom, popular since classical times, of viewing natural occurrences, such as earthquakes, as signs or portents. He sweeps the focus of the poem up into the skies to see the 'trepidation of the spheres', the very planets moving. Gradually this image connects with those in the opening two stanzas: the death of 'virtuous men', Donne's desire for the two lovers to 'melt', and now the 'trepidation of the spheres'. Each of these images is centred on the idea of movement, movement that is profoundly important but is nevertheless a gentle, quiet and 'innocent' movement.

Donne continues his astronomical imagery in the fourth stanza with his reference to 'sublunary lover's love'. This is the type of love that 'the laity' experience. It is a narrow, earthbound type of love that is dependent on physical presence, a love that cannot endure 'absence'. At this point we begin to realise that Donne is not concerned with death in a physical sense but in an emotional sense.

From the fifth stanza on, Donne slowly reveals the reason for his 'valediction'. He expands on the love he shares with his beloved. It is quite unlike that of the 'sublunary lovers'. It has been 'refined', purified, so that all impurities have been removed. Their love is not confined by physical nearness, the presence of 'eyes, lips, and hands': they have achieved an 'inter-assured' love that is founded on connection of the mind rather than of the body. They are able to be careless of the physical presence of each other because they are so confident in each other.

The sixth stanza reaffirms the special quality of their love. Donne has described it as something close to a religious experience, a moving of planets, a shared emotion without imperfections. Now he draws all these images together to represent theirs as a relationship of 'two souls', where a parting, reluctant though it is, is nothing more than 'an expansion'. The central theme of the poem is revealed. Donne and his beloved must face a separation. He is trying to comfort her, to stop her mourning as if it were a death. For, he tells her, physical separation takes their 'refined' love and refines it still further, so that they achieve a connection of exquisite pureness, 'like gold to aery thinness beat.'

These interwoven images of a perfect love are breathtaking; and yet they are not enough for Donne. He has to go beyond the poetically expected, to explore a dimension of imagery that is neither expected nor accepted. He takes the concept of 'connection' and searches for a way to express it further. In the final three stanzas of the poem he rejects the traditional, the quickly recognised, the easily understood, and finds the world of science. For him, the essence of their relationship is captured by the 'twin compasses'. Just as this instrument of measurement is made up of two metal legs joined at a point, so Donne and his beloved are connected in separation. In Donne's case he is the 'foot' that 'far doth roam,' while his beloved is the 'fixed foot' that 'leans, and hearkens after it'. They are mutually dependent, while being independent. So, Donne can declare that she is the certainty in his life; her 'firmness' ensures that his direction is true, and it is she to whom he will return, just as the compasses must inevitably meet together, 'and makes me end, where I begun'. He reassures his beloved that there is no need for her to mourn this separation, because for them it is no separation at all.

Alternatively

In 1837 Henry Hallam wrote of Donne's poetry: 'Few are good for much; the conceits have not even the merit of being intelligible . . . .' This poem is not only confused, it is also confusing. Donne wanders around the early part of the piece in a kind of intellectual haze. Then, in the later part, he pulls out the conceit of the pair of compasses, rather as a bad magician pulls out a bunch of flowers from a pot. There is no real sense to the trick, but it might just impress the audience!

The Dreame

Text of poem: New Explorations Anthology page 14

The idea of the poet's beloved appearing to him while he is dreaming or daydreaming originated in Classical poetry. It was taken up by Renaissance poets and became a very popular topic. Donald Guss holds the view that Donne was in a direct line of influence from the Renaissance: 'Donne sometimes expresses dramatic emotions through the gallant conceits of the Petrarchans.'

METRE

Donne's approach to metre has been the subject of much debate. Though he frequently employed *iambic pentameter* (each line having five stressed and five unstressed syllables), it is generally agreed that the reading of his poetry is controlled more by the sense of the words than by their metre. Coleridge commented on the poetry of Donne that 'In poems where the writer thinks, and expects the reader to do so, the sense must be understood to ascertain the metre.' This view was echoed by Joan Bennett when she wrote: 'Often the rhythm is as intricate as the thought and only reveals itself when the emphasis has been carefully distributed according to the sense.' Any personalised consideration of 'The Dreame' should include an analysis of the way in which Donne links sense and metre to achieve a deceptively natural rhythm.

A READING OF THE POEM

As we have seen, Donne's poetry frequently begins with a moment of drama, where the reader is swept into the piece by a dramatic statement. So, in 'The Flea' we read:

Mark but this flea, and mark in this,
How little that which thou deny'st me is . . .

Similarly, with 'Sweetest Love, I Do Not Go':

Sweetest love, I do not go,
For weariness of thee . . .

And, perhaps the most dramatic of all openings, that of 'The Sun Rising':

Busy old fool, unruly sun . . .

However, with 'The Dreame' we encounter a slightly different opening technique. The theatrical statement gives way to a remark that is immediately and intensely intimate and, in many ways, even more dramatic. It is as if we have chanced upon Donne at his most open, caught him in those unguarded seconds between sleep and wakefulness. The very rhythm and sounds of the words in the first two lines of the poem are filled with an unexpected gentleness and emotional vulnerability. Donne tells his beloved that she acted 'wisely' in waking him. His lack of irritation at being disturbed is in marked contrast to the last time we saw Donne being awakened, in 'The Sun Rising'. He speaks to his 'dear love' in a quiet and familiar way, welcoming her arrival. His comment that she 'brok'st not' his dream, but rather continued it, is touching in its sincerity. This Donne is certainly not playing at the game of love. He tells her that she is 'so true' that she makes 'dreams truths, and fables histories'; she embodies the idealised perfection of the worlds of dreams and fairy stories. His invitation to her to 'enter these arms' is a million miles away from his attempt in 'The Flea' to entice his lover to yield to him. A desire to possess and dominate has given way to a longing for mutual submission, for them to finish his dream, to 'act the rest.'

This intense intimacy continues in the second stanza. He tells her that she did not wake him by the noise of her movement, but by the light of her eyes. Here Donne expresses a common feeling among lovers, where a meeting of eyes can have the power to set hearts fluttering and pulses racing. He is so aware of her that her very presence is enough to wake him. The level of their closeness becomes even more apparent as the poem continues. Donne tells her that he thought she was 'an angel', adding with a moving vulnerability that he is telling the truth because she 'lov'st truth'. This is not the Donne who used amusing flattery as an aid to seduction. This relationship is much too serious for anything but the truth; it is based on the certainty of mutual understanding, emotional empathy and a sharing of thoughts. It is no wonder that Donne uses the religious words 'angel' and 'profane' in an effort to convey just how special it is.

In the final stanza Donne gradually becomes more wakeful. He now begins to 'doubt'. On one level, this doubting is simply a question whether his beloved is actually there or not. However, on a deeper level it is indicative of the terrible inner doubt that Donne experienced in all aspects of his life, but particularly when it came to love. Previously, when he did not truly love he had been able to hide this doubt beneath sparklingly witty comments. Now that he does love he must lay his soul bare. He is embarrassed by his own insecurity, admitting that the strength of his love is equalled by the strength of his fear. He speaks for all lovers who know the wonder of truly loving and the terror that it will all suddenly disappear. His beloved is as a light in the overwhelming darkness, with her 'lightning' eyes and her ability to know his heart and his thoughts. She comes into his dream 'to kindle,' to set him on fire with her presence. But even more than that, there is a sense that Donne felt she had come to kindle his very life, to light up the gnawing darkness in his soul that craved some certainty.

The poem closes with an expression of the complexity of Donne's emotions. He longs to return to 'dream that hope again' with such intensity that if he cannot do so he will die. This is more than poetic over-dramatisation, or the role of the charmingly pathetic lover. Instead it is an admission of dependence: he needs to experience true love again, he needs to be close to his beloved, he needs to feel that certainty.

Alternatively
Mario Praz felt that Donne's 'sole preoccupation is with the whole effect'. In this poem Donne simply reproduces a popular poetic device so that he can, once again, display himself. For him, the 'whole effect' of this piece rests on his willingness to be the centre of attention, to describe and analyse his emotional viewpoint. To this end he sacrifices coherent structure, disciplined metre and intellectual resolution. It is undeniable that the 'whole effect' of this piece is impressive, but it is equally undeniable that it is based on a structure of shifting sands.

Batter my heart
Text of poem: New Explorations Anthology page 16

As always with Donne, the dating of this poem is the subject of much debate. Some critics like to view Donne's poetic output as occurring in two phases, which represent two distinct parts of his life. The first phase is that of his youth and marriage and traces his growth from a young man desiring adventure and romantic conquests to a mature man, who shares a deep love with his wife but is profoundly frustrated with his position in life. The second phase is seen as occurring in his later life, after his ordination and his wife's death, when Donne gave himself up to his new religion but was still tormented by doubt.

In this scheme the three sonnets 'Batter My Heart', 'At the Round Earth's Imagined Corners' and 'Thou Hast Made Me' would be seen as belonging to the second phase, while the other seven poems under consideration would belong to the first phase.

However, this is a rather simplistic view of both Donne's life and his poetry. Life is not lived in distinct phases, and poetry is more than just a rhyming diary of day-to-day events. Donne was a highly intelligent and complex man, who was fully aware of the limitations of the human condition and the profound uncertainty of existence. His life was spent in a continuous search for some evidence of certainty in the many aspects of his experience. The world of love and the world of religion were always present in the world of John Donne, as was the world of poetry. His poetry was not written for financial gain, since it was rarely published, nor was it stimulated solely by the desire for notoriety, since Donne frequently expressed embarrassment about his writing. Rather, he wrote poetry because he had no choice but to write poetry. It was his way of confronting the worlds that he inhabited. Poetry enabled him to express the very turmoil and desires of his soul, and the soul does not exist in phases.

A READING OF THE POEM

This sonnet in many ways condenses a number of the aspects of Donne's earlier poetry into a tight, fourteen-line structure and a rigorous rhyming scheme of *abba, abba, cdcdee*. It begins with the usual dramatic opening – indeed it is an opening that is spectacularly dramatic. The implied paradox of the 'three-personed God', the representation of the spiritual, being called upon to physically 'batter' Donne's heart, is both stunning and shocking. Before we can recover from it Donne launches us into a list of breathtaking verbs: 'knock, breathe, shine . . . rise, and stand, o'erthrow me . . . bend . . . break, blow, burn . . .' We are left gasping by this combination of action images, the conflict suggested in the paradox 'that I may rise, and stand, o'erthrow me,' and his clever use of the alliterative 'b'. The first quatrain of this sonnet is a challenge not only to God but also to us, the readers.

In the second quatrain, Donne sustains this drama and intensity. He sweeps us into a wonderful conceit, comparing himself to a 'usurped town'. This combination of images to suggest Donne's dilemma enables us to understand intellectually and to empathise emotionally. It is the metaphysical conceit at its very best. Donne is betrayed by reason, God's 'viceroy', and without this support he is unable to surrender himself totally to God. He longs for God, the source of certainty, to dominate him, rather in the way that he hoped his lover might desire his domination in 'The Flea'.

The final six lines of the sonnet, the *sestet,* begin with a change in tone, though the content links to the previous quatrain. The city under siege was a common image in courtly love poetry for the woman who was reluctant to yield to her lover's advances. Violence and frenzied activity give way to courtly phrasing and language. Donne declares his intentions to God: 'Yet dearly I love you, and would be loved fain.' His confession that he is 'betrothed' to God's enemy is filled with the submissiveness and reluctance of the courtly lady; it is as if Donne has changed not only his religion but also his sex. He is trying to communicate his human vulnerability in the face of God's overwhelming power by drawing on the image of the female figure being overwhelmed by her lover's passion. It is a subtle and complex combination of images and ideas, a conceit that is both vivid and unsettling.

Donne develops the image in the following line, where he asks God to free him: 'Divorce me, untie, or break that knot again.' As his sense of fear and panic increases, so his imagery begins to intensify. He begs God to 'Take me to you, imprison me.' He concentrates all his desperation into the paradox: '. . . for I | Except you enthral me, never shall be free.'

Finally, driven to the very edge of his emotions, he grasps at a paradox that is profoundly shocking and deeply disturbing: 'Nor ever chaste, except you ravish me.' We are left reeling from this image and his total disregard for the conventional 'niceties' of expression. Does it represent Donne at his very best, or at his very worst? Only you can decide.

Alternatively

A. J. Smith commented on Donne's poetry: 'There is a calculated offence to decorum in the interests of truth.' Is this true for 'Batter My Heart'? Does Donne shock us in order to make us think? Or is it simply that his search for new and exciting combinations of ideas sometimes led him into lapses of good taste? Is there a place for decorum and good taste in the world of poetry? Or are they only restrictions imposed by those who are afraid to think?

At the round earth's imagined corners

Text of poem: New Explorations Anthology page 18

BACKGROUND

See the notes on 'Batter my heart', pages 27–29

STYLE

Donne's decision to write some of his poetry in *sonnet* form placed a number of restrictions on his writing. His poem had to consist of fourteen lines, as that is the required length of a sonnet. In addition, the Petrarchan form of the sonnet involved the creation of two parts to the poem, the *octet* and the *sestet*. The octet, which comes first, consists of eight lines, the sestet of six lines. A strict rhyming scheme is used to mark the two parts: for the octet *abba, abba,* for the sestet *cdcdee*. It is obvious that this rhyming scheme is quite complicated, and it requires a lot of effort to ensure that the sense and mood of the sonnet fit into the rhyming scheme successfully.

Generally, the octet describes a situation, while the sestet presents a meditation on or a reaction to the octet. The change in rhyme between the octet and the sestet is often mirrored by a similar change in the mood and tone of the poem. The final rhyming couplet, which forms part of the sestet, usually expresses the main theme of the sonnet.

A READING OF THE POEM

Donne daringly uses a paradox to open this sonnet. His image of the 'round earth's imagined corners' is at once completely illogical, since something round has no corners, and wonderfully descriptive, in that it conveys a sense of boundless expanse. Indeed the quatrain creates a scene that is the poetic equivalent of 'Cinemascope'. Rather like the legendary director Cecil B. de Mille, Donne uses a cast of thousands to populate his magnificent backdrop. Angels fill the heavens, and 'numberless infinities' of souls go in search of their 'scattered bodies'. Behind all this activity, heavenly 'trumpets' ring out a clarion call of triumph. For this is a description of triumph: it represents the triumph over death of those saved by God. On the promised Day of Judgment, the souls who have inhabited Heaven may return to their bodies to embark on a life that will stretch to eternity.

The second quatrain expands this concept. Donne uses the device of the 'list' to communicate a feeling of multitudes and to emphasise just how total this triumph over death is. No matter what the cause of death is, whether 'flood', 'fire', 'war, dearth, age, agues, tyrannies,' or 'Despair, law, chance,' those who believe in God are guaranteed eternal life, while those who are alive on the Day of Judgment, provided they believe, can join in this transition to eternal existence 'and never taste death's woes.' This promise of eternal life was a powerful one in an age when death was a real presence in everyday life; but to attain it there had to be a complete act of faith, and it is this that Donne finds difficult.

In one sweeping movement, Donne shifts the focus of his sonnet away from the swarming Earth and the crowded heavens to himself. His concern for the dead – 'But let them sleep, Lord' – may sound compassionate, but it is founded on purely selfish reasons. Donne asks God to put off the Day of Judgment, quite simply because he is afraid. He is afraid that he has so many sins that he has not yet truly repented for them all. He is afraid that he is spiritually unprepared to face the Day of Judgment. Since he understands that ''tis late to ask abundance of thy grace' when he is facing God, he begs God to show him how to repent 'here on this lowly ground'.

Donne knows that the key to his salvation is repentance, and being Donne, he is equally aware of the fact that he is finding it difficult to repent sincerely, because he still doubts the certainty of God. He outlines his predicament with an unswerving honesty to God. If God can help him, Donne knows that he will be saved, just as surely as a condemned man will escape execution by the monarch placing his seal upon a document of pardon. But in Donne's case the seal is absolute, because it will be made not of wax but of blood, the blood of God. Perhaps at last Donne is beginning to grasp the ultimate certainty, or perhaps he is once again simply trying to persuade himself that there is a certainty.

Alternatively

'Donne elaborates and decorates at the expense of theme, sometimes so far that he displaces it altogether' (Michael Schmidt). Is this sonnet an uneasy combination of vivid description and confused intellectualisation? Does Donne become carried away by his own creativity to such an extent that he loses his theme completely? Is Donne claiming to be concerned with repentance and spiritual salvation when all the time he is really interested only in his own descriptive powers?

Thou hast made me

Text of poem: New Explorations Anthology page 20

Religious exploration seems to have played a continuing role in Donne's life. Long before his decision to change his religion he was concerned with forging a personal and independent religious philosophy. This was, perhaps, just another aspect of his quest for certainty that arose from his uncompromising intellectualisation of the experience of human existence. Izaak Walton, probably influenced by Donne himself, characterises Donne's religious struggle as the central force in his life. But this is really only a reflection of Donne's own desire to minimise the importance of his earlier, less religious work.

Whatever their motivation, Donne's religious poems convey the intense religious debate that raged not just within his mind, but also within his very soul. Some critics have suggested that Donne's approach to this debate was influenced by the spiritual exercises of Ignatius Loyola, the founder of the Jesuit order. Given Donne's early education and his family connections with the Jesuits, it is likely that he was familiar with Loyola's work. These exercises encouraged the individual to develop an intensely personal and emotional relationship with God through 'conversations' that were founded on inner debate and private reflection.

STYLE

Coleridge wrote of Donne's poetry: 'We find the most fantastic out-of-the-way thoughts, but in the most pure and genuine mother English . . . .' This sonnet is a wonderful illustration of this comment. Within the strict structural confines of the Petrarchan sonnet (fourteen lines, rhyming scheme, octet and sestet) Donne presents his complex spiritual struggle in a language that is both natural and simple. He is able to communicate the agonising dilemma he faces and the real terror in his soul in such a profound way that it comes as something of a shock to realise that he has written only fourteen lines.

A READING OF THE POEM

The dramatic opening that Donne has used so successfully in all his poetry, both secular and religious, becomes in this sonnet an expression of the essence of his emotional and spiritual turmoil. In one line he captures all the anguished questioning that haunts his soul: 'Thou hast made me, and shall thy work decay?' His lifelong quest for certainty is distilled into this one devastatingly simple question to God. He has left behind the intellectual gymnastics that occupied him in his youth. For Donne those bright, brittle days are past. Now his poetry has a personal intensity that is uncompromising and unaffected.

His description of the state of his life is stunning: 'mine end doth haste'. In an image that is both vivid and disturbing he conveys just what this 'haste' is like: 'I run to death, and death meets me as fast.' There is an inescapable inevitability about this line and a suggestion of a strange intimacy. Rather like two lovers irresistibly drawn together, Donne and Death move towards each other. Donne is completely focused on this inescapable meeting. All his previous life fades away in the face of this ultimate moment: 'all my pleasures are like yesterday'. It is no wonder that Donne's request to God, 'Repair me now,' vibrates with urgency. The time for clever intellectual tricks is over.

The second quatrain maintains this intensity. We see Donne poised, frozen with terror, between despair and death. The inner vision of his soul becomes, for him, a frail rope to cling to in his desperation: 'I dare not move my dim eyes any way.' But his horror increases as he realises that his 'feeble flesh doth waste', that the very hands that grasp this rope, the very eyes that focus on the safe horizon, are rotting away. His physical self, that body that in his youth had seemed to hold the certainty he craved, is now a dead weight, putrefying with sin, which drags him down 'towards hell'.

There is only one means of escape for Donne: his total faith in God. It is a terrible irony that the man who spent his life searching for certainty in the world outside himself should come to understand that the ultimate certainty could only be found within his own soul. The pure existence of God is not the answer; it is Donne's ability to believe in that pure existence that is the final solution. If he is empowered by God, given the strength to focus his 'dim eyes' so that he 'can look,' his state instantly alters. The dead weight melts away and he begins to 'rise again'. But he has to have the faith that God will empower him. Donne sways on the brink of this 'leap of faith'. Doubt, the weapon of their 'old subtle foe', the Devil, constantly tempts him. Doubt has for him such a terrible attraction that he cannot hold himself focused for even 'one hour'. In desperation, he pleads with God to help him escape. God's grace will release him from this terrible struggle, the weight dragging him down will fall away, and like a bird he will fly from the clutches of the Devil's art. God's grace will draw him onwards and upwards as smoothly and as irresistibly as a magnet attracts iron. It is an image of wonderful ease and beautiful certainty. Sadly for Donne, who had lived his life driven by the urge to intellectualise and rationalise, the action of a magnet can be scientifically proved, while the redeeming grace of God depends solely on an unscientific and profoundly irrational act of faith.

Alternatively
William Hazlitt commented on the metaphysical poets: 'The complaint so often made, and here repeated, is not of the want of power in these men, but of the waste of it; not of the absence of genius, but the abuse of it.' Is this the truth that lay behind John Donne? He frittered away his incisive intellect on glittering verses to entertain the crowd; he used his literary skills in a calculated attempt to grasp the trappings of wealth and power. For him, poetic genius was no more than a convenient tool of manipulation. It was a way to make life easier. He used his poetry for seduction, he used his poetry for self-glorification, and finally he used his poetry as a short cut to salvation.

Developing a personal reaction to John Donne

1. Why do you think John Donne wrote poetry?

2. Was his poetry based on the intellect, or on the emotions, or on a combination of the two?

3. What does the term 'metaphysical' stand for? Can John Donne be classed as a metaphysical poet?

4. What is a conceit? How is it used in Donne's poetry? Do you feel that the conceit is a successful poetic device?

5. What themes recur in Donne's poetry? What do they tell you about John Donne himself? Do you think he was a likable man?

6. How did Donne use traditional poetic devices and structures in his work?

7. What is your reaction to the type of language and rhythms found in

Donne's poetry? Are they appealing to a modern reader?

8. Consider what aspects of Donne's poetry appeal to you and what aspects you find unappealing.

9. Has the work of John Donne anything to say to a twenty-first-century reader?

10. Do you think you will ever return to Donne's poetry, or will you be glad to leave it all behind?

Questions

1. Read 'The Flea', then answer the following questions.

   (*a*) (i) What impression of Donne's attitude to love emerges for you from your reading of this poem?

   (ii) Choose *two* phrases from the poem that especially convey that impression, and comment on your choices.

   (*b*) (i) Why does Donne introduce the flea into his poem?

   (ii) How does Donne's lover react to what he says? Support your answer by reference to the words of the poem.

   (*c*) Answer *one* of the following questions:

   (i) How would you describe Donne's tone in this poem? What words or phrases in the poem convey this tone?

   (ii) Would you write such a poem to a person you loved? Explain your view by reference to the words of the poem.

   (iii) Donne seems to have read a great many of his poems aloud to a small group. Choose *two lines or phrases* from this poem that you feel would have caused a reaction among the group, and explain what that reaction might have been in each case.

2. Read 'Song: Go Catch a Falling Star', then answer the following questions.

   (*a*) (i) What do you think is the point of this poem? (ii) Choose *two phrases* from the poem that especially convey this point to you, and comment on your choices.

   (*b*) What have all the strange tasks got to do with the theme of the poem? Illustrate your view by close reference to the text.

   (*c*) Answer *one* of the following questions:

   (i) How does the pattern of the lines in this poem emphasise what

Donne is saying? Support your view by referring to the words of the poem.

(ii) What is the mood of this poem? Refer closely to the text.

(iii) What part does rhyme play in this poem? Explain your answer by reference to the poem.

3. 'Donne's poetry represents an attempt to connect emotions with mental concepts.' Discuss this view, supporting your answer by quotation from or reference to the poems you have studied.

4. 'Donne's deliberate avoidance of poetic language gives his poetry a sense of realism.' In your reading of Donne's poetry, did you find this to be true? Support your answer by reference to or quotation from the poems on your course.

5. 'John Donne: A Personal Response.' Using this title, write an essay on the poetry of Donne, supporting your points by quotation from or reference to the poems on your course.

6. 'Underlying Donne's poetry is a unity of experience that is not immediately apparent.' Discuss this view, supporting your answer by quotation from or reference to the poems you have studied.

7. 'Donne's poetry is generally unpleasant and occasionally disgusting.' Give your response to this point of view, with supporting quotation from or reference to the poems on your course.

8. 'The poetry of Donne is a continuous commentary on the world and on himself.' In your reading of Donne's poetry, did you find this to be true? Support your answer by reference to or quotation from the poems you have studied.

9. 'Though Donne rejected the traditional poetry of his time, he was still greatly influenced by it.' Discuss this view, supporting your answer by quotation from or reference to the poetry on your course.

10. 'The tone of Donne's poetry is often unclear, and as a result the reactions it provokes can be confused.' Give your response to this point of view, with supporting quotation from or reference to the poems on your course.

Bibliography

Bennett, Joan, *Four Metaphysical Poets: Donne, Herbert, Vaughan, Crashaw* (second edition), Cambridge: Cambridge University Press 1953.
Carey, John, *John Donne: Life, Mind and Art*, London: Faber and Faber 1983.

Carey, John (editor), *John Donne: Selected Poetry,* Oxford: Oxford University Press 1998.

Everett, Barbara, *Donne: A London Poet,* London: Oxford University Press 1972.

Gardner, Helen (editor), *John Donne: A Collection of Critical Essays,* Englewood Cliffs (NJ): Prentice-Hall 1962.

Garrod, Heathcote William, *Poetry and Prose of John Donne,* London: Oxford University Press 1972.

Hamilton, Ian, *Keepers of the Flame,* London: Pimlico 1993.

Nutt, Joe, *John Donne: The Poems,* London: Macmillan 1999.

Schmidt, Michael, *Lives of the Poets,* London: Phoenix 1999.

Tamblin, Ronald, *A Preface to T. S. Eliot,* Harlow (Middx): Pearson Education 1988.

Walton, Izaak, *Walton's Lives,* London: Methuen 1895.

Wedgwood, C., *Seventeenth-Century English Literature* (second edition), London: Oxford University Press 1970.

2 *Thomas* HARDY

Bernard Connolly

Biography

Thomas Hardy was born on 2 June 1840 in Higher Bockhampton, near Dorchester. From his father came his love of music, and from his mother his love of books. He was a solitary, introspective child who was frequently ill and did not attend school until he was eight years old. Thomas showed an aptitude for languages and was a very conscientious student, keeping meticulous notebooks. At the age of sixteen he left school to become apprenticed to a Dorchester-based architect. In 1862 he travelled to London to continue his architectural studies. While in London Hardy submitted many poems for publication, but they were invariably rejected. He returned to Bockhampton in 1869 and began to write fiction. Between 1871 and 1897 Hardy published fourteen novels and forty short stories. His first major success, *Far from the Madding Crowd* (1874), allowed him to become a full-time writer and to marry. He met Emma Lavinia Gifford in 1870 when he was working on an architectural project in Cornwall. This meeting is celebrated in 'When I set out for Lyonnesse'. The couple lived in a series of rented houses and flats in London and Dorset, but in 1885 settled at Max Gate, in a house built to Hardy's own design. The relationship with Emma deteriorated; she felt that Thomas was her social inferior and she had literary ambitions of her own, while her conventional morality was outraged by the subject matter of Hardy's later fiction. She tried to have *Jude the Obscure* suppressed by the publisher; in the novel Hardy had referred to marriage as 'a sordid contract based on mutual convenience'. The hostile critical reaction to this novel convinced him to abandon fiction and concentrate on his first love, poetry.

In 1898, at the age of fifty-eight, Hardy published his first volume of poetry, *Wessex Poems*. There would be seven further volumes published, the last one – *Winter Words* – posthumously in 1928. He wrote in a wide variety of poetic forms: love poems, ballad poems, animal poems, war (or anti-war) poems, comic and satirical poems, poems about places, poems about the seasons and the weather, poems about rural life and work and poems about family and friends. Emma's death in 1912 inspired some of his finest poetry. He was filled with guilt and remorse and recreated their courtship in the romantic Cornwall countryside.

Hardy married Florence Dugdale in 1914; he had been close to her since 1905. He had rejected conventional Christianity in his twenties and had written about the 'logicless' nature of the workings of the universe in 'New Year's Eve'; he had characterised any god who existed as being 'unknowing' and 'indifferent'. His agnosticism was influenced by thinkers such as Darwin, Huxley and Mill. Hardy rejected the 'optimism' of Victorian writers like Tennyson, and while not revolutionary in his use of poetic forms, he made more extensive use of colloquial speech and dialect than his contemporaries. Norman Paige wrote: 'For part of Hardy's profound originality as a poet is that, just as almost any and every word is a potential candidate for admission into his poetic vocabulary, he has no prejudices or inhibitions about what constitutes a proper poetic subject.' In his later years he wrote an autobiography, published in 1928 after his death, in the guise of a biography under the name of his second wife, Florence Emily Hardy. Thomas Hardy was buried in Westminster Abbey, but stipulated that his heart should be buried with his first wife Emma in Stinford churchyard.

Drummer Hodge

Text of poem: New Explorations Anthology page 74

A READING OF THE POEM

When this poem was first published on 25 November 1899 it was titled 'The Dead Drummer'; Hardy subsequently personalised the title. Consider the effect of using the soldier's name. The horror of the death in the Boer War (1899–1902) of a young Casterbridge man represents the fate of the ordinary man as a victim of human conflict.

The poem opens directly with the unceremonious burial of Drummer Hodge 'Uncoffined – just as found'. The South African landscape, which is alien to the soldier, is evoked with the use of Afrikaans vocabulary: 'kopje-crest . . . veldt'. Stanza two elaborates on how the drummer 'Fresh from his Wessex home' had no understanding of his African surroundings: he 'never knew . . . The meaning of the broad Karoo' and 'why uprose . . . strange stars amid the gloom'.

Stanza three reflects ironically that the plain is 'unknown' to Hodge, who now lies as part of it, and it echoes the 'uncoffined' of the opening lines. Hardy's sympathy for the common soldier is apparent in 'His homely Northern breast and brain | Grow to some Southern tree'. There is pathos in the 'strange-eyed constellations', which were unfamiliar to the soldier when he was alive, looking down on him 'eternally'. Yet Drummer Hodge is given a dignity in the poem that contrasts with his undignified, callous burial.

THEME

The suffering of the common man who is sent to die in a foreign land is the major concern of this poem. There is a contrast between the impermanence of human life and the permanence of nature.

LANGUAGE

The poet achieves a sense of the foreignness of Africa by his use of Afrikaans vocabulary in a poem that is otherwise marked by the simplicity of its language. There is a direct quality to lines such as 'They throw in Drummer Hodge . . . Uncoffined – just as found'. Three six-line stanzas have alternate lines rhyming, reflecting the plainness of the common soldier.

IMAGERY

Drummer Hodge is buried in foreign soil, in surroundings alien to his 'homely Northern breast and brain'. Images such as 'foreign constellations west', 'strange stars' and 'strange-eyed constellations' emphasise the soldier's eternal exile. Landscape reinforces the sense of an alien land: 'Young Hodge . . . never knew . . . the meaning of the broad Karoo'. The physical environment plays a further symbolic role as Hodge becomes part of the African landscape: 'Yet portion of that unknown plain | Will Hodge for ever be'; and 'His homely Northern breast and brain | Grow into some Southern tree'. Critics have seen some consolation in the drummer becoming one with Nature. Nature and the heavens are permanent, while human life is temporary.

The Darkling Thrush

Text of poem: New Explorations Anthology page 76
[*Note: This poem is also prescribed for Ordinary Level 2006 exam*]

A READING OF THE POEM

This poem's original title was 'By the Century's Deathbed'. The scene described in the first stanza is bleak: 'When Frost was spectre-gray' and 'desolate'. Humans have sought shelter away from the lifeless winter landscape. The 'land's sharp features' represent 'The Century's corpse' laid out; the sky is the roof of its tomb and the wind its funeral hymn. Growth is stunted: 'The ancient pulse of germ and birth | Was shrunken hard and dry'. Hardy explicitly links the external scene with his state of mind, which 'Seemed fervourless as I'. His depression reflects the gloom of the winter scene, devoid of life.

The focus of the poem shifts as the thrush, 'In a full-hearted evensong | Of joy illimited', is entirely at odds with the poet's mood. This bird's joy seems incongruous; it is 'aged . . . frail, gaunt, and small'. Hardy could see 'So little cause for carolings | Of such ecstatic sound'. He surmised that the thrush knew 'Some blessed Hope . . . And I was unaware.' It is as if the bird has an intuitive knowledge of spring, but that Hardy foresees nothing save a spiritual winter that gives him no grounds for optimism.

Thomas Hardy's sensitive rendering of the thrush displays his natural sympathy for living things, which endures despite his apparently pessimistic perspective on life.

THEME

Hardy deals with his 'fervourless' state of mind, and the absence of 'Hope', as he contemplates the end of the nineteenth century. The thrush represents an animating spirit and 'blessed Hope' in Nature that endures despite the harshest environment. Thomas Hardy wrote that 'The mission of poetry is to record impressions, not convictions.' You might consider whether this statement has any relevance to the issues raised in the poem.

IMAGERY

Death is ever present in the opening two stanzas: 'Frost was spectre-gray' and 'The land's sharp features seemed to be | The Century's corpse'. Colour is drained from the scene: 'Winter's dregs made desolate | The weakening eye of day'. The absence of any life force is suggested symbolically: 'The ancient pulse of germ and birth | Was shrunken hard and dry'.

Hardy makes it clear that the bleak winter's scene represents his mood and state of mind: 'And every spirit upon earth | Seemed fervourless as I.' In total contrast, the thrush 'Had chosen thus to fling his soul | Upon the glowing gloom.' The frail bird is animated by 'Some blessed Hope' – a spirit that impels it to celebrate life.

The Self-Unseeing

Text of poem: New Explorations Anthology page 78

A READING OF THE POEM

Hardy deals with the inexorable passage of time and the unreflecting attitudes of youth. The first stanza describes the remains of a dance venue, 'the ancient floor'. 'Here was the former door' introduces Hardy's pain and sense of loss, with the transferred epithet, 'Where the dead feet walked in.' The ruin comes to life in the second stanza with the details 'She sat here in her chair, | Smiling into the fire;' and the ecstatic playing: 'He who played stood there, | Bowing it higher and higher.'

In the final stanza the poem becomes more reflective: 'Childlike, I danced in a dream', and the language is heightened: 'Blessings emblazoned that day', as Hardy laments the lost joy of youth. The exclamation mark in the final line emphasises the intensity of his emotion as the poet's youthful self fails to appreciate the value and rarity of such happiness: 'Yet we were looking away!'

IMAGERY

A sense of the destruction wrought by time is suggested by the evocative image in the fourth line, 'Where the dead feet walked in'. 'Blessings emblazoned that day;' is a metaphor for a charmed moment when joy animates everything, as 'Everything glowed with a gleam'. The 'looking away' symbolises the absence of self-awareness and self-reflection which comes with age and bitter experience.

LANGUAGE

The poem uses the language of the ballad to depict moments from the past. Alternate lines rhyme, as alliteration adds emphasis and momentum. Soft *f* sounds predominate in the first stanza: 'floor', 'footworn', 'former', 'feet'. In the final stanza the more forceful sounds of *d*s and *b*s are repeated: 'Childlike, I danced in a dream' and 'Blessings emblazoned that day'. The simple diction is heightened briefly in line ten, as the day is celebrated. A colloquial effect is reinforced by the choice of words in the final two lines. There is a pained simplicity in the exclamation, 'Yet we were looking away!' The musical sound effects inherent in the ballad form are especially appropriate in a poem that evokes music and dance.

Channel Firing

Text of poem: New Explorations Anthology pages 80–81

A READING OF THE POEM

This poem, which was written in April 1914, is narrated by a dead man who is woken by the boom of the great naval guns protecting the south of England, during a practice firing. To the dead man, the report of the guns sounds like 'the Judgment-day'. The moment is dramatised by the reaction of the dead who 'sat upright', the howl of hounds and the startled response of mouse, worms and 'glebe cow'. God intervenes to announce, 'The world is as it used to be'. Mankind's propensity for violent conduct is unchanged: 'All nations striving strong to make | Red war yet redder.' God's punishment is not yet at hand: 'this is not the judgement-hour', and 'For some of them's a blessed thing . . .' they'd have to scour | Hell's floor for such threatening . . .' There is a mocking humour in God's threat: 'Ha, ha. It will be warmer when | I blow the trumpet'.

The narrator resumes in the seventh stanza as the dead discuss, 'Will the world ever saner be . . . than when He sent us under | In our indifferent century!' The consensus among the deceased is not optimistic: 'And many a skeleton shook his head.' The parson sees the futility of his life inculcating virtue: 'Instead of preaching forty year . . . I wish I had stuck to pipes and beer.'

In the final stanza the poem incorporates a wider historical perspective, as the guns which roar their 'readiness to avenge' are heard in the ancient sites of 'Stourton Tower, | And Camelot, and starlit Stonehenge.' Humanity's essential nature has not changed, despite the passing of time. Hardy's words were especially prescient, coming as they did just months before the calamitous slaughter of the First World War.

THEME

The poem deals with the universal theme of mankind's enduring warlike nature. Human nature is constant in its drive for domination and vengeance: 'All nations striving strong to make | Red war yet redder.' Guns are perpetually 'Roaring their readiness to avenge,'. Hardy's view is profoundly pessimistic. It is interesting to note that the God of this poem offers eternal punishment, not redemption: 'It will be warmer when | I blow the trumpet'.

IMAGERY

Judgment day is the recurring symbol in the poem, as the firing of the guns is mistaken for the end of the world. The effects of war are suggested using colour: 'Red war yet redder.' The fires of Hell are jokingly referred to: 'It will be warmer when | I blow the trumpet', in an image that resonates with the traditional portrayal of judgment day. The personification of the guns, 'Roaring their readiness to avenge', reverberates through the centuries and the historic sites: 'And Camelot, and starlit Stonehenge.'

The Convergence of the Twain

Text of poem: New Explorations Anthology pages 84–85

BACKGROUND NOTE

On 15 April 1912 the SS *Titanic* sank, with the loss of 1,513 lives, after colliding with an iceberg during her maiden voyage. Hardy was recruited as a member of a sub-committee that organised a 'Dramatic and Operatic Matinee in aid of the *Titanic* Disaster Fund' and wrote a poem, later revised and expanded, for recitation as part of a programme at Covent Garden on 24 May 1912.

The poem has an elevated tone appropriate to its subject matter and is a more 'public' poem than much of Hardy's other work, which is highly personal in content and treatment.

A READING OF THE POEM

Stanza I opens with the wrecked liner on the seabed far from 'the human vanity, | And the Pride of Life that planned her'. Water flows through her compartments: 'late the pyres | Of her salamandrine fires' (stanza II). The fires have been quenched forever. There is obvious irony in the description of 'The sea-worm' which 'crawls – grotesque, slimed, dumb, indifferent,' to the mirrors intended to reflect the images of the 'opulent' passengers on a luxury liner (stanza III). Dazzling jewels are now 'bleared and black and blind', an exercise in futility, where human vanity is mocked by the alliterative *b*s (stanza IV). Fish gape and query 'this vaingloriousness down here' (stanza V). Graham Handley has referred to the speaking fish as 'a rare moment of bathos in Hardy'.

There is a change of emphasis in stanza VI when the role of fate is introduced as 'The Immanent Will that stirs and urges everything'. Fate produces 'a sinister mate . . . a Shape of Ice' with which to punish mankind's pride (stanza VII). The construction of the iceberg matches that of the SS *Titanic:* 'in shadowy silent distance grew the Iceberg too.' Sibilant *s* sounds convey the sinister note of threat (stanza VIII). A metallic image, 'The intimate welding of their later history', expresses the conjoined destiny of ship and iceberg (stanza IX). Their 'paths coincident' are described as 'being anon twin halves of one august event' (stanza X). The malign controlling hand of fate is revealed in the final stanza as 'the Spinner of Years | Said "Now!"'; the collision happens, and in an image from Plato 'consummation comes and jars two hemispheres.'

It is interesting that in Hardy's concern to display human vanity, which fate feels compelled to expose, there is no reference to the suffering of individual people.

THEME

Hardy is concerned with 'human vanity' and 'Pride of Life', which are expressed in the opulent style and the 'vaingloriousness' of the ship's construction and decoration. The malevolent power of the 'Immanent Will that stirs and urges everything' is seen as the determinant of 'The intimate welding of their later history'. *Titanic*'s tragedy is seen as vindicating the poet's pessimistic view of the world.

LANGUAGE

Hardy uses an elevated tone, as would be adopted in an ode: 'In a solitude of the sea | Deep from human vanity'. The rigid rhyme scheme is in keeping with such formality, as is the heightened vocabulary: 'salamandrine' and 'this creature of cleaving wing'. Latinate word order is apparent in 'By paths coincident' and 'for the time far and dissociate'. Triplication adds formality: 'In stature, grace, and hue'. The solemnity of the public occasion is reflected in Hardy's diction and mode of expression on a major public event commemorating a national tragedy.

Under the Waterfall
Text of poem: New Explorations Anthology pages 88–89

A READING OF THE POEM

The poem celebrates an incident from Hardy's courtship of Emma Gifford and is set in the Valency valley, near St Juliot in Cornwall. The poem is written from the woman's perspective.

It opens dramatically with the speaker describing the memories triggered by plunging an arm into a basin of cold water with its 'sweet sharp sense of a fugitive day'. This memory is the only love story that does not contain a share of sorrow: 'And real love-rhyme . . . that leaves no smart'. The waterfall is situated 'Over a table of solid rock' and runs into 'a scoop' constantly without interruption, 'the purl of a runlet that never ceases'. It speaks with 'a hollow boiling voice'. A second speaker asks the significance of the waterfall for the narrator. The answer is that 'jammed' under the stone beneath the waterfall is 'a drinking-glass' that the lovers dropped. An August scene is recalled, when the couple 'sat to dine', and how the vessel slipped from the narrator's hand when it was being rinsed. There it has remained: 'There lies intact that chalice of ours, | And its presence adds to the rhyme of love | Persistently sung by the fall above'. It is an enduring monument to love; 'No lip has touched it since his and mine | In turns therefrom sipped lovers' wine.'

IMAGERY

The waterfall is associated with a moment of perfect happiness, recalling 'a fugitive day' that is 'Fetched back from its thickening shroud of gray.' This recollected moment is compared to a unique 'love-rhyme . . . that leaves no smart' of pain to accompany the bliss. The fall is seen as eternal, 'a runlet that never ceases', and is personified as speaking 'With a hollow boiling voice . . . And has spoken since hills were turfless peaks.' The weather and scenery are described in idyllic terms on the memorable day: 'a sky | Of blue with a leaf-wove awning of green, | In the burn of August'. Basins now recall the scene: 'The basin seems the pool . . . leafy patterns of china-ware | The hanging plants that were bathing there.' An almost sacramental quality is suggested by the metaphor of 'There lies intact that chalice of ours' and its presence 'adds to the rhyme of love' as the fall is personified: 'Persistently sung by the fall above.' This perfect memory of lovers' bliss endures 'intact' and untouched.

The Oxen

Text of poem: New Explorations Anthology page 91

A READING OF THE POEM

The Christmas Eve setting is significant, as Hardy reflects on religious faith and the poet's doubts in a poignant and nostalgic poem. A homely fireside scene 'in hearthside ease' is depicted in the opening stanza as the 'elder', a word rich in biblical associations, tells the children a Nativity story. The second stanza describes how the author, as a child, visualised the scene in the stable in Bethlehem with total faith and credulity: 'Nor did it occur . . . To doubt they were kneeling then'. Such simple faith is not a feature of the poet's age: 'So fair a fancy few would weave | In these years!' (third stanza). Nonetheless, Hardy is attracted to such an innocent belief: 'Yet, I feel, . . .' as his 'childhood used to know'; he would be 'Hoping it might be so.' There is a deep sense of loss at the disappearance of childhood certainty, which has been replaced by adult 'doubt' and uncertainty. Nostalgia is suggested by the archaic language 'barton by yonder coomb', which gives the poem a sense of being rooted in the past.

IMAGERY

The poem's title refers to oxen kneeling in adoration in a children's Christmas story. The 'meek mild creatures' represent a childlike faith, free from 'doubt'. It is the adult who doubts 'they were kneeling then'. To a sceptical adult the story is 'So fair a fancy'. Hardy's pained nostalgia is represented by his wish that 'it might be so' and his mood, 'in the gloom'.

During Wind and Rain

Text of poem: New Explorations Anthology page 93

[Note: This poem is also prescribed for the Ordinary Level 2006 exam]

A READING OF THE POEM

Hardy evokes the atmosphere of a family musical evening: 'They sing their dearest songs – | He, she, all of them – yea'. Musical sound effects echo in the language, as in the assonance 'They', 'their', 'yea'; 'dearest', 'He', 'she'; and the sibilant s sounds, rhyme and sing-song rhythm. Domestic harmony is suggested by 'Treble and tenor and bass | And one to play' in the flickering candlelight. The rapturous mood is interrupted by the dramatically abrupt exclamation 'Ah, no'. The damage inflicted by the inexorable passage of time is suggested by the refrain 'the years O!', with its mournful tones. The stanza culminates in the powerful metaphor of the 'sick leaves' which ironically 'reel down', contrasting starkly with the joyful domestic scene. 'Sick' is a word with many malign connotations and associations of illness and decay.

Another happy domestic scene is presented in the second stanza as the family works cheerfully in the garden, making it attractive, 'and they build a shady seat . . .' Alliteration suggests the energy of workers: 'clear the creeping moss . . . garden gay' as does the repetition of 'And' in lines 11 and 12. The pleasant atmosphere is disrupted by the refrain 'Ah, no' with a variation emphasising 'the years, the years'. A sense of immediacy is communicated by the imperative 'See, the white storm-birds wing across!' The work of the gardeners will inevitably be destroyed by the forces of nature.

The scene described in the third stanza is arguably the happiest, as the people were 'blithely breakfasting all' on a summer's morning. Details bring this blissful picture to life: 'With a glimpse of the bay | While pet fowl come to the knee . . .' After the refrain comes the ferocity of 'And the rotten rose is ript from the wall', where the alliterating *r* sounds convey the violence of the action.

In the final stanza, the family's affluence and material comfort is suggested by their move to 'a high new house' with their 'Clocks and carpets and chairs'; but prosperity and possessions do not protect against the progress of time. In the final image, even the details engraved on tombstones are eroded by time: 'Down their carved names the rain-drop ploughs.' The significance of the poem's title is made explicit in the last line, with its terrible reflection on the impermanence of human life.

IMAGERY

The poem is constructed around a series of contrasts between the happy scenes of domestic life and the succession of images suggesting inevitable decay and impermanence. It is significant that the four images are taken from the natural world, suggesting the relentless action of Nature: 'sick leaves', 'storm-birds', 'rotten rose', 'rain-drop ploughs'.

Afterwards

Text of poem: New Explorations Anthology page 96

A READING OF THE POEM

Hardy wrote this poem in 1917, when he was seventy-seven years old. It begins with a roundabout reference to death as the closing of a garden-gate 'postern' behind the poet's life. Hardy uses the beautifully suggestive adjective 'tremulous' to highlight the fragility of human existence. The subtle beauty of leaf veins is evoked in the simile 'Delicate-filmed as new spun silk'. He wonders if he will be remembered as 'a man who used to notice such things'. The detachment of the poet's reflection is emphasised by the slow rhythm of the long lines.

Hardy maintains his mood in the second stanza, as he uses another euphemism for death as the blink of an eyelid, and describes another scene from country life. The 'dewfall-hawk' alights in a simile suggesting grace, power and menace, 'like an eyelid's soundless blink'. Hardy does not have a sentimentalised view of Nature; he appreciates the role of the predator in the scheme of things. He wonders whether he will be remembered as an observer of the natural world.

In stanza three, Hardy uses another euphemism for death: 'If I pass'. There is a wonderfully tactile description of the night as 'mothy and warm'. His concern for 'innocent creatures' is apparent, as is a modesty regarding his effectiveness in protecting them: 'But he could do little for them; and now he is gone'.

In the penultimate stanza, death is referred to as being 'stilled'; attention is focused on the night sky, 'the full-starred heavens'. Hardy had a lifelong interest in astronomy – 'such mysteries'.

The final image suggesting death is most appropriate: 'my bell of quittance', which is heard 'in the gloom'. The sound reverberates and echoes through the landscape affected by the wind: 'a crossing breeze cuts a pause in its outrollings'. Hardy had no faith in an afterlife and is resigned to death being the end of existence: 'He hears it not now'. There is no mention in the poem of Hardy's position as a successful writer; rather, he wants to be remembered as a countryman 'who used to notice such things' as leaves in May, the prowess of a hawk alighting, and the mysteries of the skies.

MOOD

Hardy contemplates his death with remarkable detachment and acceptance, using a series of non-threatening circumlocutions for death: 'When the Present has latched its postern behind my tremulous stay'. The long lines suggest control and dignity. There is an obvious regard for the countryside and its creatures, and a joy in observing the sights and sounds of Nature: 'but used to notice such things'. It is significant that there is no sense of self-pity or self-regard from one of the world's most famous men of letters.

LANGUAGE

Hardy uses rhythm to suggest a calm detachment, as can be seen in the sixteen syllables of the opening line. The beauty of the summer countryside is evoked in the melodious language of lines two and three, with *l*, *m*, *n* and *s* sounds echoing. Assonance combines with the alliteration to enhance the verbal music: 'And the May month flaps its glad green leaves like wings, | Delicate-filmed as new-spun silk'. Hardy's characteristic use of compound words (associating ideas more closely) is evident here. His acute observation of Nature is brought to life sensuously in the tactile description of the night as 'mothy and warm'.

Alliteration conveys elemental power in 'the wind-warped upland thorn'. Sound reflects sense in the final stanza, as the echoing tolling of the bell with its 'boom' pauses in the breeze. The effect of the rhyme scheme is softened by the informality of the direct speech concluding each stanza: 'To him this must have been a familiar sight'.

When I set out for Lyonnesse

Text of poem: New Explorations Anthology page 98

A READING OF THE POEM

On 7 March 1870 Hardy travelled from his home in Dorset to St Juliot in Cornwall on architectural business, and there he met Emma Gifford, who later became his wife. Lyonnesse is a fabled kingdom in Cornwall associated with King Arthur and Merlin, the magician. The form of the medieval ballad is used to give this highly autobiographical poem a universal resonance. Hardy was a great observer of anniversaries and revisited Cornwall in March 1913, in an act of atonement after his wife Emma's death. He recalled the blissful early days of his marriage before estrangement and disillusionment set in. This journey proved to be the inspiration for many fine poems.

Stanza one describes the hero's journey; he travelled 'a hundred miles', in bad weather: 'the rime was on the spray'. The narrator is lonely as he travels by night: 'And starlight lit my lonesomeness'. In the second stanza there is an air of mystery and enchantment: 'What would bechance at Lyonnesse . . . No prophet durst declare'. The archaic language, 'durst', 'bechance', 'sojourn', adds to the magical mood suggested by: 'Nor did the wisest wizard guess'. No detail is elaborated, nor is any explanation given of what occurred.

In the final stanza the poet's mood is transformed: 'When I came back from Lyonnesse | With magic in my eyes'. There is now an aura associated with the narrator: 'My radiance rare and fathomless'; he has been transformed by the magical and mysterious power of love. The poet has been like the heroes of medieval romances – a knight on a quest, who overcomes difficulties along his journey and wins the love of his lady.

LANGUAGE

The poem is written in short ballad format with stanzas six lines long, rhyming *abbaab*. Repetition and alliteration are used frequently: 'wisest wizard', 'radiance rare', and contribute to the poem's characteristic rhythm. Repetition also emphasises key points in each stanza; the reiteration of line two highlights the nature of the journey: 'A hundred miles away'. In stanza three, the enchanting power of love is reinforced by the repeated 'With magic in my eyes'.

Simple diction such as 'lonesomeness' is blended with archaic vocabulary: 'durst', 'bechance', to give the poem a historical flavour. The reference to 'wizard' evokes the Arthurian legend, as does the melodic name of the place, 'Lyonnesse'.

Overview of Hardy's work

Thomas Hardy writes in a wide range of poetic styles and genres. Traditional short ballad forms such as 'When I set out for Lyonnesse' are present, with elegiac poems like 'Afterwards' and 'The Oxen' and dramatic pieces like 'Channel Firing'. The simple diction of 'The Self-Unseeing' is very different from the elevated rhetorical language of 'The Convergence of the Twain' and the intensity of 'The Darkling Thrush'.

For the purpose of acquiring an overview, it might be useful to re-read the poems in thematic groupings rather than in chronological order.

- 'Afterwards'; 'During Wind and Rain'; 'The Self-Unseeing' deal with the inexorable effects of time and the reality of death.
- 'Channel Firing'; 'Drummer Hodge' are anti-war poems; one takes a dramatic approach, while the second is elegiac.
- 'When I set out for Lyonnesse'; 'Under the Waterfall' are love poems.
- 'The Convergence of the Twain' deals with fate and human vanity.
- 'The Oxen' is a nostalgic evocation of innocence and faith.
- 'The Darkling Thrush' is more than just a nature poem; it is a philosophical questioning of the poet's outlook at the end of the nineteenth century.

THE INEXORABLE PASSAGE OF TIME

Time is seen as destructive of human happiness in 'During Wind and Rain': 'Ah, no; the years O!' The final line is stark in its pessimism: 'Down their carved names the rain-drop ploughs'. The transient joy of youth is presented in 'The Self-Unseeing', but is not appreciated by the young: 'Blessings emblazoned that day | Yet we were looking away!' The inevitability of death is confronted with stoic acceptance in 'Afterwards': 'When the Present has latched its postern behind my tremulous stay'. Hardy has no expectation of an afterlife: 'He hears it not now,' and in that sense shares the pessimistic world-view of 'During Wind and Rain'.

WAR; MAN'S BLOODTHIRSTY VIOLENT NATURE; THE ORDINARY MAN IS THE VICTIM OF WAR

Hardy uses the practice firing of naval guns to explore the age-old propensity for war: 'Roaring their readiness to avenge, | As far inland as . . . Camelot and starlit Stonehenge'. At the notion that human nature will ever change 'many a skeleton shook his head.' When 'All nations' make 'Red war yet redder' it is the common soldier, the 'hero' of 'Drummer Hodge', whose blood must be shed. The treatment of his body as he is thrown 'Uncoffined – just as found' is an indictment of the callous indifference shown to the fate of the ordinary man. His resting place, far from home, is alien to him as 'foreign constellations west | Each night above his mound.' Hardy's sympathy is with the drummer: 'His homely Northern breast and brain | Grow to some Southern tree'.

LOVE

The magical transforming power of love is celebrated in 'When I set out for Lyonnesse': 'All marked with mute surmise | My radiance rare and fathomless . . . with magic in my eyes'. The traditional format and language help to universalise the experience, and at the same time do not detract from the authenticity of the emotion. Love is celebrated in 'Under the Waterfall' as 'The sweet sharp sense of a fugitive day' is recalled. The idyllic moment of bliss is the only love-song that 'leaves no smart'. A 'chalice' as the symbol of love 'lies intact', preserving the moment – the glass 'No lip has touched since his and mine | In turns therefrom sipped lovers' wine.' The woman's viewpoint is explored in this poem, as the man's was in the previous poem. Two speakers chat over household chores: 'And why does plunging your arm in a bowl | Full of spring water, bring throbs to your soul'; the ordinary detail is juxtaposed with the poetry of 'its presence adds to the rhyme of love | Persistently sung by the fall above.'

THE OPERATION OF FATE AND HUMAN VANITY

Hardy interprets the *Titanic* disaster as being the product of 'human vanity' and 'the Pride of Life that planned her,'. This hubris is punished by 'The Immanent Will that stirs and urges everything', as 'the Spinner of the Years' says 'Now!' and 'consummation comes'. This pessimistic world-view is apparent in 'During Wind and Rain' and to an extent in 'The Darkling Thrush'.

NOSTALGIA FOR LOST INNOCENCE AND FAITH

A simple, childlike, religious faith is evoked in 'The Oxen': 'We pictured the meek mild creatures where | They dwelt in their strawy pen'. Scepticism and the adult world have changed the poet's view: 'So fair a fancy few would weave | In these years!' Yet there is a tone of regret, with Hardy 'Hoping it might be so'. Nostalgia plays a significant role in 'The Self-Unseeing', as the poet realises that he did not appreciate the all-too-brief happiness he glimpsed in his youth: 'Childlike, I danced in a dream'. Unfortunately, 'Yet we were looking away!' There is deep loss evident in 'During Wind and Rain', as vignettes of happy family life are shattered by the series of increasingly powerful images: 'How the sick leaves reel down in throngs!', and the very final 'Down their carved names the rain-drop ploughs.' Human happiness is fleeting, as are youth and innocence.

<small>NATURE AND A REFLECTION ON THE END OF THE NINETEENTH CENTURY</small>

On one level 'The Darkling Thrush' is a poem about a songbird in winter, but it is so much more than that. The 'ecstatic sound' of the little thrush represents 'Some blessed Hope' of which the poet was 'unaware'. Hardy looks on the 'Century's corpse' and sees no grounds for optimism. Like the winter scene described, he feels 'fervourless', in total contrast to the 'joy illimited' of the bird's song. Hardy gives no definitive answer, but reflects on the meaning of life and the power of Nature. His concern for 'innocent creatures' is also apparent in 'The Oxen', with his reference to 'the meek mild creatures'; and in 'Afterwards', with its description of the 'When the hedgehog travels furtively over the lawn'. Hardy does not sentimentalise Nature; he is aware of the predatory prowess of the 'dewfall-hawk'.

- Music played a significant role in Hardy's life. He recreates the time in his youth when he played the violin (so intensely that he frequently burst into tears) in 'During Wind and Rain'. A family musical evening is lovingly portrayed: 'They sing their dearest songs – | He, she, all of them – yea'. Hardy's language has its verbal music with his blend of rhyme, alliteration, sibilance and assonance. Another example of musical sound effects can be found in 'The Darkling Thrush', with the assonance and rhyme of 'At once a voice arose among . . . In full-hearted evensong.'
- Close observation of Nature is another feature of Hardy's work: 'He was a man who used to notice such things' as 'The May month flaps its glad green leaves like wings', and 'some nocturnal darkness mothy and warm', which has such sensual appeal. A totally different effect is achieved in 'The tangled bine-stems scored the sky | Like strings of broken lyres'. Hardy is an aural as well as a visual poet, as the following three lines from 'Afterwards' attest: 'And will any say when the bell of my quittance is heard in the gloom, | And a crossing breeze cuts a pause in its outrollings, | Till they rise again, as they were a new bell's boom'.
- Philip Larkin remarked that, 'The dominant emotion in Hardy is sadness.' Hardy rejected the criticism that his poems were overly pessimistic: 'What is alleged to be pessimism . . . is in truth, only such questionings in the exploration of reality, and is the first step to the soul's betterment.' Form your own opinion based on the evidence of the poems you have studied.
- Hardy wrote, 'I have no philosophy, merely . . . a confused heap of impressions like those of a bewildered child at a conjuring show.' Do you think this is an accurate summing up of how Hardy views the world in the poems you have studied?

- Examine how Hardy's two literary careers overlap in that he is a master storyteller in his poems, with an acute ear for common speech. Look at 'Under the Waterfall', 'The Self-Unseeing', 'The Oxen' and 'During Wind and Rain'.

Forging a Personal Reaction
Think about the following points:
- Which poems made the deepest impression on you and why?
- Which images have stayed in your mind?
- What are Hardy's main preoccupations – love, the past, Nature, etc.? What did you like or dislike about how he treated these main themes?
- Look at the variety of poetic language used by Hardy. Identify those features of his style that work well for you.
- Do any of Hardy's poems touch on your own life experience?
- What do you think of Thomas Hardy the man?
- What is the value of studying Thomas Hardy's poetry?
- What have you noticed about the people in Hardy's poems? How does he feel about them?
- Think about the places and landscapes Hardy describes. What is his attitude to them?
- If you had to choose two poems of his to include in an anthology of poetry, which two would you choose? Why?

General questions
1. 'The poems of Thomas Hardy are sensitive, lyrical creations of exquisite concentration, craftsmanship and feeling.' Discuss, supporting your response with quotation and reference from the poems by Thomas Hardy on your course.
2. 'What is remarkable about Thomas Hardy is his variety, his range of poetic forms and subjects.' Respond to this point of view, with supporting quotations or references to the poems on your course.
3. 'Hardy embraces the permanent truths of life as we know it.' Comment.
4. In what ways is nostalgia an important element in Hardy's poetry?
5. 'Repeatedly, in reading a Hardy poem, we have a sense of intrusion – of gaining access, almost illicitly and improperly, to secret feelings.' Discuss.
6. 'Hardy has the quality of relating the particular to the universal, often through strong and sharply observed visual images.' Consider this statement in the light of the poems you have studied.
7. 'Thomas Hardy is a master of the close-up, writing of the natural scene with informed sensitivity.' Discuss.
8. How far do you consider Hardy a pessimistic poet?

9. 'Many of Hardy's poems reflect, in subject matter and sometimes also in form, different facets of his love of music.' Discuss this view, supporting your answer by quotation from or reference to the poems by Thomas Hardy on your course.

10. Hardy wrote, 'The mission of poetry is to record impressions, not convictions.' Discuss.

11. 'Thomas Hardy – A Personal Response'.
    Using the above title, write an essay on the poetry of Hardy, supporting your points by quotations from or references to the poems on your course.

12. 'Historical events, times past and the passing of time are preoccupations in the poems of Thomas Hardy.' Consider this statement, referring to the poems on your course.

Short critical bibliography

Bailey, J. O., *The Poetry of Thomas Hardy*, Durham NC: University of North Carolina Press 1970.

Bloom, H., *Thomas Hardy (Modern Critical Views)*, New York: Chelsea House, 1999.

Davie, D. and C. Wilner (editors), *With the Grain: Essays on Thomas Hardy and Modern British Poetry*, Manchester: Carcanet 1998.

Gibson, J., *The Complete Poems of Thomas Hardy*, London: Macmillan 1976.

Gittings, R., *Young Thomas Hardy* and *The Older Thomas Hardy*, London: Heinemann 1975, 1980.

Kramer, D., *The Cambridge Companion to Thomas Hardy*, Cambridge: Cambridge University Press 1999.

Paulin, T., *Thomas Hardy: The Poetry of Perception*, Palgrave.

Patil, M., *Thomas Hardy the Poet*, Atlantic 1998.

Pinion, F. B., *A Commentary on the Poetry of Thomas Hardy*, London: Palgrave 1976.

Turner, P. D. L., *The Life of Thomas Hardy*, Blackwell 1998.

3 *Gerard Manley* HOPKINS

Martin Wallace

Introduction

> Haslemere, Surrey: December 1918. Into the hands of a bedridden lady
> of nearly ninety-eight, twenty years a widow, was placed one of the first
> copies of a small edition of poems written by her eldest son, who had
> been dead for twenty-nine years. (Norman White, *Hopkins: A Literary
> Biography*)

Norman White's dramatic opening to his excellent biography of Hopkins
draws attention to some of the ironies of the poet's life and work. His
devotion to poetry came second only to his devotion to God, yet he
died an unpublished poet. The closest friends who had access to his poetry while
he was alive were dubious about the value of his work. His experimentation
with language and prosody were considered too outrageous for nineteenth-
century readers; yet his centenary was marked by a multitude of publications
acknowledging him as the most important poet of his time. He had a deep faith
in God and his mysterious ways, but he could never have imagined that his verse
would be familiar to the majority of students who now attend the university
where he taught and was sometimes the victim of ridicule. How amazed he
would have been to read Sunday columnists referring to his works with the
familiarity that comes from being on the course for the Leaving Certificate!
Perhaps the eccentric little priest would have been horrified to find himself
ranked with the great writers of English poetry; but then again he held a great
conviction that his poetry was a service to the greater glory of God and that it
would eventually find its place.

Hopkins can be a difficult poet. His arrangement of words is sometimes
complex and concentrated; his diction and imagery can be demanding; yet if we
just listen to the poems often enough, many of the difficulties disappear. If the
primary purpose of poetry were to communicate meaning, a poet would be
better employed writing in prose. The *way* in which a poem communicates
meaning is what makes it beautiful and worthwhile. Part of the meaning, or
truth, of a poem is in the beauty, and part of the beauty is in the meaning, just
as a song pleases because of its combination of words and music.

The purpose of these notes, therefore, is to provide useful (and some useless!) background information, to provide some guidance through the difficulties of Hopkins's poetry, and to offer, for what they are worth, some perspectives on the poems. These notes are intended as an aid to the development of, *not a substitute for,* your own personal response. Don't read on until you have *spent time* with the poems.

FAMILY

Gerard Manley Hopkins was the first of nine children born on 28 July 1844 into a prosperous middle-class family near London. His father, Manley Hopkins, was a marine insurance broker, who wrote two books on marine insurance, a history of Hawaii (of which he was Consul-General in England), a book on cardinal numbers, an unpublished novel, literary criticism, newsletters, and three volumes of poetry. He also had a great interest in architecture, which he passed on to his son; when Gerard was thirteen his father presented him with a copy of Parker's *Introduction to the Study of Gothic Architecture.* Manley Hopkins had an intense dislike of priests, because of their attempts to convert the people of Hawaii to Catholicism.

Hopkins's mother was an affectionate person who loved music and poetry. Her father had studied medicine with John Keats. Hopkins's aunt, Annie, lived with them; she taught Gerard how to draw and paint. The family used to take holidays in Shanklin, on the Isle of Wight, where Gerard and his brother would spend much of their time sketching the surrounding landscapes.

EDUCATION

When the family moved to Hampstead in 1854, Gerard's father decided that he should attend Highgate School as a boarder. It was important to belong to the right church and attend the right school if one wished to climb the social ladder. At the age of ten Gerard was quite small and delicate; he preferred cricket and swimming to more physical activities such as football. He was an excellent student, with a lively sense of humour; 'he was full of fun, rippling over with jokes, and chaff, facile with pencil and pen, with rhyming jibe or cartoon.' However, the headmaster, Dr Dyne, was a whip-loving authoritarian whom Hopkins disliked intensely.

On one occasion Hopkins made a bet of ten shillings against sixpence (63c to 2.5c – a lot of pocket-money in those days) that he would abstain from liquids for three weeks. His real aim was to show his powers of endurance. When he collapsed in the classroom the truth came out, but not before Hopkins had won his bet. When Dyne found out about the bet he swooped immediately and decided to punish both gamblers, compelling Hopkins to return the money.

In vain [Hopkins] pointed out that such a decision really rewarded the other boy, and only punished him, who had endured the suffering and exhaustion of the effort. Dyne was obdurate and Gerard . . . only heaped up to himself further punishment.

This anecdote gives a good insight into Hopkins's stubborn nature. But he disapproved strongly of this rebelliousness in his own personality and felt that it should be kept under control.

One of the junior masters in the school, a clergyman by the name of R. W. Dixon, later became a poet and a friend of Hopkins. At the age of fifteen Gerard won the school poetry prize. Two years later one of his poems was published in a periodical, one of the very few poems published in his lifetime.

Oxford

In 1863 Hopkins was awarded an exhibition (scholarship) to study Classics at Balliol College, Oxford. From the moment he arrived there he loved Oxford. His quick wit, openness and spontaneity made him many friends, one of whom was to be the man who would save his poetry from oblivion and would make the presentation of his poems to Hopkins's mother fifty-five years later: Robert Bridges. In a letter home, Hopkins wrote: 'Everything is delightful . . . I have met with much attention and am perfectly comfortable. Balliol is the friendliest and snuggest of colleges.'

The artist

At this time Hopkins was more interested in painting than in writing. He kept journals containing extremely detailed descriptions of observed phenomena.

> Round holes are scooped in the rocks smooth and true like turning: they look like the hollow of a vault or bowl. I saw and sketched . . . One of them was in the making: a blade of water played on it and shaping to it spun off making a bold big white bow coiling its edge over and splaying into ribs.

He was fascinated by the teachings of John Ruskin, whose books *Modern Painters* and *The Elements of Drawing* advocated an intense concentration on the individuality of natural objects. Drawing was of secondary importance to seeing and appreciating the subtlety of nature. 'If leaves are intricate, so is moss, so is foam, so is rock cleavage, so are fur and hair, and texture of drapery, and of clouds.'

Pattern and contrast were important features, according to Ruskin. Hopkins loved 'dappled' things – contrasting colours or variations between light and shade. In his later writing he formulated the 'law of contrasts': 'every form and line may be made more striking to the eye by an opponent form or line near them.' The aesthetic principles that would govern his poetry later on were already beginning to take shape in his mind.

THE OXFORD MOVEMENT

During his time in Oxford, Hopkins's personality seemed to change. He became bad-tempered in his relationship with his family. Perhaps he was asserting his independence from them, especially from his overwhelming father. He seemed to lose a good deal of his humour, and he began to become preoccupied with some very serious issues.

The Oxford Movement was a debate taking place within the Church of England between the liberal 'Broad Church' and the Anglo-Catholic 'High Church'. Hopkins was attracted at first towards the liberal wing, which was identified very much with Balliol College, but after a very difficult period of internal conflict he decided to follow the path of the man who was to become a kind of spiritual father, John Henry Newman. Newman had converted to Catholicism and then become a priest (later a cardinal). Hopkins's decision to follow the same path was the most momentous decision in his short life. Whether this decision was based on theology and doctrine or, as Robert Bernard Martin seems to imply, an act of rebellion against his father and the 'upwardly mobile' life that he had planned for his son, it is difficult to say. Certainly Hopkins's writings at this time are preoccupied with matters of doctrine. In a letter to a friend he declared his conviction in 'the Real Presence in the Blessed Sacrament of the Altar. Religion without that is sombre, dangerous, illogical . . .' He came to doubt the historical right of the Church of England to consecrate the Blessed Sacrament.

He also showed a remarkable interest in the life of Savonarola, the fifteenth-century Italian ascetic martyr.

> I must tell you he is the only person in history . . . about whom I have a real feeling, and I felt such an enthusiasm about Savonarola that I can conceive what it must have been to have been of his followers. I feel this the more because he was followed by the painters, architects and other artists of his day, and he is the prophet of Christian art, and it is easy to imagine oneself a painter of his following.

Even at this stage Hopkins was concerned about the dichotomy, as he saw it, between the role of the artist and the role of the priest.

By the time he was in his second year he had become self-denying and ascetic. He sometimes wore a flannel girdle, and walked for a while with downcast eyes – quite a torture for one who delighted in the observation of natural beauty. He became obsessive about sin and personal purity, keeping detailed accounts of his indiscretions, such as time-wasting and inattention at chapel. Sins of the flesh, involving 'temptations' and stolen glances at fellow-students, were a great concern to him. We might laugh at his scrupulousness today from our liberal perspective, but such puritanical obsession was commonplace in the nineteenth century. Purity was associated with sensual deprivation and self-inflicted punishment, which would yield the reward of spiritual ecstasy.

Hopkins decided to give up the idea of being a painter, because it provoked 'evil thoughts'. Clearly he feared his own passionate and sensuous nature, which manifested itself later in his poetry; 'he was in love with the phenomenal world and aflame with fear of it' (R. B. Martin).

His obsession with sexual temptation and the despondency caused by it may have been a contributory factor in his decision to become a Catholic and a priest: he wished to leave behind that person who had begun to disgust him. That Christmas he wrote:

> To the sight of Him who freed me
> From the self that I have been.

CONVERSION

'A man was shaken loose from his position in the rigid English social structure if he became a Catholic' (R. B. Martin). Hopkins informed his family of his intentions by letter on 13 October 1865, and on 21 October he was received into the Catholic Church by his mentor, John Henry Newman. His mother wrote back: 'O, Gerard, my darling boy, are you indeed gone from me?' But although it was a devastating blow for the family, they did not ostracise him. He, however, distanced himself from them. The first they saw of their converted son was the following Christmas, when he adopted a somewhat aloof manner with them.

With the trauma of his decision behind him, Hopkins got on with the business of preparing for his degree. His double first (first-class honours) meant that, were he still an Anglican, he would probably have received a fellowship at one of the Oxford colleges. But he had given up that and other avenues of success when he made his decision to become a Catholic.

THE SOLDIERS OF CHRIST

When his brother heard that Gerard was to become a Jesuit he wondered why he could not become an 'ordinary Catholic'. The Jesuits were regarded as the men of action within the Catholic Church. When a candidate entered the novitiate he faced nine years of rigorous preparation before ordination –

provided he had already completed his primary degree. The perception of Jesuits in England was of devious villains with 'bland smile, insinuating voice, diplomatic skills, noiseless velvet step'.

Unquestioning obedience, self-denial and the 'suppression of aesthetic pleasure' were demanded, especially within the nineteenth-century English Jesuit regime. There was an obsessive preoccupation with sexual temptation. Novices, allowed one bath per month, were given 'modesty powder' to make the bath water opaque. Wearing a chain of barbed wire around the legs was an optional extra. It was typical of Hopkins that he chose the most arduous route to his desired goal.

In 1869 he decided to destroy the poems he had written; it was a decision made without much conviction. In his journal he wrote: 'This day, I think, I resolved.' Some time later he simply noted: 'Slaughter of the innocents.' Three months later, in a letter to Bridges, he explained that 'They would interfere with my state and vocation.'

STONYHURST

On 8 September 1870 Hopkins took his first vows and was sent to Stonyhurst College, Lancashire, an exclusive Jesuit boarding school. It was his first time to live away from the city, and he was immediately entranced by the 'sublimity' of the moors and fells. About this time he began to record detailed descriptions of the natural world. His preoccupation with the observation of detail drew some attention from a local workman: 'Ay, a strange yoong man, crouching down that gate to stare at some wet sand. A fair natural [simpleton] 'e seemed to us, that Mr 'Opkins.' His disregard for conventional behaviour would become more evident later on in his approach to the writing of poetry.

He began to develop some important theories during his time at Stonyhurst. 'What you look hard at seems to look hard at you.' This remark hints at one of the crucial ideas behind Hopkins's world view, namely that humans and nature are united by the fact that they are both aspects of the one divine creation.

During the seven years when Hopkins refrained from writing poetry, his ideas about the composition of poetry and the language he later used were being developed in his mind, so that when they were finally written they had a surprisingly finished quality to them.

INSCAPE AND DUNS SCOTTUS

One of the ideas that is central to the work of Hopkins features regularly in his journals around this time. It concerns the notion that everything in creation is unique and has its own individuality. Scrupulous observation of an object, idea or person would reveal its 'inscape' – its meaning, its essence: 'It is the expression of the inner core of individuality, perceived in moments of insight by an onlooker who is in full harmony with the being he is observing' (Norman MacKenzie).

The part of Hopkins's personality that had caused him to burn his early poems was suspicious of the part that adored the material world so much. Surely the spirit is more important than matter, he thought! Hopkins was unable to reconcile the poet with the priest until he read the work of Johannes Duns Scottus, a mediaeval Franciscan theologian. Duns Scottus argued that the material world is an incarnation of God, a revelation of God to humanity through the senses. Hopkins now felt justified in his preoccupation with the beauty of the world, because it had a sacramental value – in other words, the beauty of the world brings us closer to God. Therefore the senses, which could be the stimulus for sin, could also be the stimulus for religious experience.

Hopkins's appreciation of nature was so intense that he felt its wounds. When an ash tree was cut down in the college he

> heard the sound and looking out and seeing it maimed there came at that moment a great pang and I wished to die and not to see the inscapes of the world destroyed any more.

About this time Hopkins suffered frequently from ill-health and had a morbid fascination with death. He was also lonely, as he had ceased corresponding with his father and with his good friend Robert Bridges.

In 1873 Hopkins was sent to the Jesuit college at Roehampton, near London, to teach Greek and Latin to those who had finished their novitiate. It had become almost a pattern for Hopkins to lose energy as the academic year drew to a close; even though his work was not taxing, as his energy declined, depression took hold. He expected to spend a second year at Roehampton, but his superior decided to send him to St Beuno's College in Wales, where he would study theology.

This was Hopkins's first experience of living in the countryside. St Beuno's overlooked the beautiful Elwy valley, not far from Llanelwy and Rhyl. He developed an immediate affection for the Welsh people and their language, which he studied for a while. His health and state of mind were better than they had been for some time. Later in his life he referred to his time in Wales as his 'salad days'.

'THE WRECK OF THE DEUTSCHLAND'

In December 1875 a ship travelling between Bremen and New York, the *Deutschland,* foundered at the mouth of the Thames. The shipwreck received substantial coverage in the newspapers, because there were claims that the crew of an English boat had watched the disaster happen and made no effort to help.

Among the passengers were five Franciscan nuns, exiled from Prussia by Bismarck's anti-Catholic laws. The *Times* provided a vivid account of their fate:

> Five German nuns . . . clasped hands and were drowned together, the chief sister, a gaunt woman 6 ft. high, calling out loudly and often 'O Christ, come quickly!' till the end came.

The fact that the nuns died on the eve of the Feast of the Immaculate Conception, and that they had been made homeless because of their religion, sparked an immediate empathy in Hopkins. He felt that he too had been 'exiled' as a result of his conversion to Catholicism. He identified particularly with the tall nun. In a conversation with his rector he mentioned how he had been affected by the tragedy. The rector remarked that someone should write a poem to commemorate the nuns.

This was the moment that ended Hopkins's seven-year silence as a poet. By the end of the following May (1876) he had completed an ode of 280 lines, 'The Wreck of the Deutschland', a poem 'of tortuous diction and revolutionary rhythm that had become a glittering and resplendent meditation on the place in the world of suffering' (R. B. Martin). It was really an autobiographical poem about the poet's own tortuous struggle for salvation.

He submitted it to the editor of a Jesuit magazine, the *Month*. The editor could not make sense of the poem, so he consulted another, who deemed it 'unreadable'. The poem remained unpublished.

One of the striking innovations of the poem was its use of 'sprung rhythm'.

> I had long had haunting my ear the echo of a new rhythm which I now realised on paper . . . . To speak shortly, it consists in scanning by accents or stresses alone, without any account of the number of syllables, so that a foot may be one strong syllable or it may be many light and one strong.

The common rhythm of traditional English poetry is measured in *feet* of two or three syllables. Feet of two syllables can be either *iambic* (an unstressed syllable followed by a stressed syllable, as for example 'resígn') or *trochaic* (a stressed syllable followed by an unstressed syllable, as for example 'thúnder').

Three-syllable feet can be either *anapaestic* (unstressed-unstressed-stressed, as for example 'brigadíer') or *dactylic* (stressed-unstressed-unstressed, as for example 'métrical').

Traditionally, English poetry was written in some metrical arrangement involving a fixed number of syllables per line. The sonnet is a good example: each line consists of ten syllables, which can be divided into five feet, as follows:

That tíme of yéar thou máyst in mé behóld (Shakespeare)

This perfectly regular iambic line provides the basic rhythm of the poem. The poet will not persist with exactly the same rhythm, because to do so would create a monotonous effect; however, when the rhythm is varied the basic rhythm is like a drumbeat or a ghost rhythm in the back of the reader's mind.

A feature of 'sprung rhythm' is the rejection of the traditional metrical pattern. Firstly, the number of syllables in a line is not fixed. Secondly, feet need not conform to any iambic, trochaic, anapaestic or dactylic pattern. Thirdly, the scansion of a line continues that of the preceding line, so that if one line is a few syllables too long, the next line may be a few syllables shorter.

The *purpose* of sprung rhythm is more important than a precise technical understanding of its mechanics. Hopkins wanted to make poetry more like natural speech; he wanted to allow for a more 'abrupt' and versatile rhythm:

> For why if it is forcible in prose to say 'lashed: rod', am I obliged to weaken this in verse, which ought to be stronger, not weaker, into 'lashed birchrod' or something?

'AFTER WRITING THIS, I HELD MYSELF FREE TO COMPOSE'

'The Wreck of the Deutschland' marked the beginning of a remarkable flood of poems. Within two years Hopkins had written approximately a third of his mature poetry. The year 1877 concerns us in particular, for in the space of six months (March to August), despite the fact that he was busy preparing for his exams, Hopkins wrote the first five poems in the selection.

The 'bright sonnets'

With his masterpiece, 'The Wreck of the Deutschland', and several other poems already completed, Hopkins took an even keener delight in the beautiful natural landscape of the Clwyd valley, which was overlooked by St Beuno's College. However, he had much to occupy him at this time. In the spring of 1877 he was deep in preparation for his final examinations in moral theology which, he said, 'covers the whole of life and to know it it is best to begin by knowing everything, as medicine, law, history, banking'. He found it 'the most wearisome work', but, as he told his mother in a birthday letter, he had managed to write two sonnets, which he was sending to her as a present. The second of these was 'God's Grandeur'. It is a poem that resonates richly for a modern audience or readership worried by the dangers of global warming and ecological disaster; it has a particular relevance to an Ireland that is being 'developed' at a frightening pace. One wonders, however, whether modern readers can share the poet's confidence that comes from a deep-seated faith.

God's Grandeur

Text of poem: New Explorations Anthology page 104

THEME

Since his time at Oxford, Hopkins was convinced that the world of nature was, in a sense, the incarnation of God. It is not just that when we look at nature we admire his creation: nature is 'charged' with the presence of God; his presence pulses through everything in the world. Hopkins would have been familiar with Psalm 71, which states: 'The whole earth shall be filled with his majesty.' The word 'filled' suggests a substance, but 'charged' implies energy: it argues that God is actively present in the world.

Even though humankind seems oblivious to the sacramental value of nature, and even though the Industrial Revolution has led to widespread pollution and destruction of the landscape, nature is held lovingly in the hands of the Holy Spirit and will never be diminished. The splendour and freshness of nature are contrasted throughout the octet with the stale and sordid influence of humankind.

DEVELOPMENT

The first section of the poem begins with a beautifully direct statement of the theme of the poem. Apart from the obvious meaning of 'charged', meaning 'powered', it can also mean that the people of the world have been given the charge, or responsibility, of looking after this planet.

Taking the main interpretation, Hopkins proceeds to illustrate the different ways in which this grandeur manifests itself. Sometimes it 'flames out'. This image is in keeping with the imagery in 'charged'. It catches our attention in a flash, like a sudden glittering light emanating from foil that catches the rays of the sun when it is shaken. At other times its presence dawns upon us slowly, like the oil oozing from the fruit that has been gathered and stored. Hopkins may well have had in mind the contrast between St Paul's conversion on the road to Damascus and St Augustine's gradual conversion as recorded in his Confessions. There is a reference to them in stanza 10 of 'The Wreck of the Deutschland' that supports this interpretation. Hopkins was fascinated by contrast. Here he contrasts the sudden and the gradual, the dramatic blinding light and the slowly evolving realisation.

The position of the word 'crushed' is dramatic; the full stop after it makes it stand out even more. The fact that the syllable is stressed also draws attention to the word; this is because it is an important word in Hopkins's world-picture. Human beings' free will is in conflict with God's intention for them. If they are to fulfil their destiny they must submit their will to the will of God. They must allow their 'self-will' to be crushed so that they may become an agent of God's will. In a later poem, 'The Windhover', we will see the same idea expressed in the word 'buckle', and we will observe the same techniques used to draw attention to the word.

The question seems to interrupt the first quatrain, as if the poet were impatient to complain of people's lack of interest in God's plan. The link between 'foil', 'oil' and 'men' is not so difficult to make if 'crushed' is understood as the process whereby everything is subject to the will of God. Humankind neither obeys God's authority ('reck his rod') nor heeds his sacrifice for us (rod = rood = cross). Humankind is seen as the rebel, 'wild, wilful and wanton' (Peter Milward), who will not 'bend the knee' in humble obedience.

The second quatrain conveys a picture of humankind as bestial creatures, lacking in intelligence and awareness, clumsily obscuring the sparkle of nature with their grubby activities. Life without God is monotonous and dreary. It reminds us of the fate of Adam and Eve when they were evicted from Paradise and had to learn to labour. The repetition of 'trod' conveys the monotony of industrial labour. The dull repetition of the heavy monosyllabic verb makes an impressive thud in the ears. It has inevitable associations with the treadmill, a byword for monotonous activity. It may even be an echo of Keats's line in 'Ode to a Nightingale', 'No hungry generations tread thee down.'

The result of trade has been to 'sear', to scorch nature. It is typical of Hopkins's word-play to move from 'seared' to 'bleared' and 'smeared', all of which convey the idea that humankind's toil, instead of exercising a respectful dominion over the earth, has damaged and sullied God's creation. The beautiful masterpiece has been 'smudged' and has the smell of sweat from it. This line is quite clever in its technique: 'wears' rhymes with 'shares'; 'man's' balances the line by appearing in each of the two clauses to create a pleasant antithesis; and the alliteration and dissonance of 'smudge' and 'smell' complete the effect. The final image of the bare soil suggests that humankind has exhausted the earth – a prophetic image in many ways. Humankind is incapable of noticing the damage that it has done because it is 'shod' – in other words, people wear shoes, which remove them from the soil and desensitise them. This idea – that by removing people from their natural environment we deprive them of sensitivity – is very much a Romantic one. (Incidentally, Hopkins had a particular dislike of shoes.) 'Thus man is punished for his insensitivity to "God's grandeur" by becoming correspondingly insensitive to the beauty of the natural world' (Peter Milward).

The second quatrain is quite depressing. It is even more depressing for a modern audience, because we know how much more damage has been done to the environment since the poem was written. However, this poem is not an eco-warrior's battle-cry; nor is it a cry of despair: it is a religious poem. Far from wishing to depress, Hopkins's intention was to assert confidently that no matter how sinful and stupid humankind may be, the world is safe, because the Holy Ghost, like a female bird protecting its fledgling, sits protectively over the world. Why is it that 'Nature is never spent'? It is because the spirit of God, the Holy Ghost, is active in renewing the world. It is from him that there comes 'the dearest freshness deep down things;' like a spring that brings fresh water to the surface constantly. Therefore, the earth will never be 'spent', or exhausted. On the contrary: when one looks carefully one sees the freshness of new creation 'deep down (in) things'. Even though the sun sets in the west, it rises again in the east – a powerful image of the death and resurrection of Christ. For this reason, God's creation is safe.

The exclamations in the last three lines ('Oh' and 'ah') convey the immediacy of the poet's excitement as he contemplates with confidence the everlastingness of all things in God's creation, God's grandeur.

> The poet feels the warmth of the divine breast and glimpses the brightness of the divine wings. This is far from a notional recognition on his part, based on an abstract faith in the presence and providence of God. Rather, it seems to rise, in the climax of this poem, to the level of a mystical experience, as he first feels the warmth of the breast, and then sees – with an 'ah!' of ecstatic wonder – the brightness of the wings, at least in a momentary glimpse which is all that this world can afford. (Peter Milward)

Norman White has a different and interesting view on this poem. In the octet, 'There is a vivid sense of Hopkins's urgency to communicate his state of perceptual excitement and the qualities of the natural things which have excited him,' but in the sestet, 'It appears to me as if a different authoritarian voice, representative of tradition, has superimposed an alien framework onto the novel and personal emotions and sights.' The critic is suggesting that the priest is hijacking the poem from the poet and using the poet's perceptions to further his religious doctrine. Perhaps White is disappointed that Hopkins is not a Romantic poet instead of a religious poet. But the tension between the two aspects of the poet's personality is intrinsic to his poetry.

As kingfishers catch fire
Text of poem: New Explorations Anthology page 108

At the end of April 1877 Hopkins was asked to write a poem to commemorate the visit of Father Thomas Burke, a Dominican preacher and well-known advocate of Thomism. Hopkins took his visit as an opportunity to reopen the debate between Thomists and Scotists (followers of the teaching of St Thomas

Aquinas and Duns Scottus). The debate between these two philosophies had been lively before the nineteenth century. There were few supporters of Scottus left; Hopkins was one of them. He expressed his views on this debate most openly in the poem 'As kingfishers catch fire', which he wrote at this time. One of the differences between Aquinas and Scottus is that Aquinas strongly advocated reason as the means whereby we come to know something, whereas Scottus believed that we come to know things through intuition, which involves the whole being, especially the senses, in the process of knowing. The poem asserts the value of the senses and that physical beauty has a moral value. 'All things therefore are charged with love, are charged with God, and if we know how to touch them give off sparks and take fire, yield drops and flow, ring and tell of him' (Hopkins). Indirectly, he is arguing that poetry is a valid occupation for a priest.

Hopkins was not happy with the poem, and did not send it to Bridges.

THEME

The poet argues that everything in creation has its own individuality and unique place in the world (what Duns Scottus called *haeccitas* or 'thisness'). Every created object or person has a purpose or mission, that is, to be itself ('Acts in God's eye what in God's eye he is – Christ'). Our intuition can perceive Christ in the objects around us and in the actions of humankind ('For Christ plays in ten thousand places . . . through the features of men's faces').

DEVELOPMENT

The opening line does not engage our thoughts as readily as the opening lines of the other 'bright sonnets', but it may arouse the curiosity of those who enjoy cryptic crosswords. We have seen in the previous poem how the world is 'charged' with God's grandeur, which will 'flame out'. Here again the poet associates the presence of God in the world with fire. The kingfisher and dragonfly reflect the light of the sun and, metaphorically, of God.

The poet goes on to give examples of everyday actions that are characteristic of themselves. If a stone falls over the rim of a circular well it will give off a ringing sound, presumably when it makes contact with the sides of the well. (Note the difference between the bland paraphrase and the vibrant rhythm of Hopkins's line!) Pluck the string of a musical instrument and it will give off a particular sound; swing a bell and it will emit a characteristic bell sound. Hopkins concludes that 'each mortal thing' has its unique presence in the world and displays this unique identity. He invents a most unusual verb to express this idea: he declares that each individual thing 'selves', or engages in the act of being itself. The individual 'speaks and spells' and is 'crying' out what he is.

The content of the octet is summed up in the final line, which asserts the individuality of all things and that all things have a mission to fulfil.

The sestet takes the idea further ('I say more'). In the octet the poet concentrates on human experience from a secular point of view: in other words, there is no explicit religious significance in the ideas he expresses. In the sestet, however, he introduces theology, 'celebrating the unity of God and the world and affirming the divinization of all creatures in Christ' (Joseph Feeney). The just man 'justices'. Hopkins again invents a verb – not a particularly attractive one but one that is full of emphasis and intensity. The second line has a similarly intense and unattractive feel to it. The third line, which has a modicum of style to it, asserts the same point as the previous two lines, that a man is doing God's will when he is 'himself'. That entails being a flawed creature, born with original sin, redeemed through baptism by Christ and sharing in Christ's being; but, as John Henry Newman put it, 'It is his gift to be the creator of his own sufficiency, and to be emphatically self-made.' In other words, it is the nature of humankind to undertake a journey that can lead it to God or elsewhere.

Joseph Mary Plunkett wrote that he saw Christ's blood 'upon the rose'; Hopkins sees Christ in 'men's faces' (not in women's, however!).

This sonnet is written in sprung rhythm. As an exercise, compare this poem with one of Shakespeare's sonnets, and notice how frequently Hopkins's poem uses stressed syllables.

Spring

Text of poem: New Explorations Anthology page 111
[Note: This poem is also prescribed for Ordinary Level 2006 exam]

Hopkins spent the Whit weekend holiday (mid-May) walking and writing poetry in the beautiful Clwyd valley. Before this he had had a five-day break in Rhyl and was now quite relaxed. May was the month devoted to Mary, the Queen of Heaven, for whom he had a special devotion. The charming poem 'Spring' was written during this time.

THEME

The opening sentence, beautiful in its simplicity, expresses the key idea in the octet. The sestet suggests that spring is a 'strain' or a 'taste' of what the Garden of Eden must have been like before sin deprived humankind of it. The poem ends with an exhortation to Christ to harvest the innocence and beauty of May before corruption takes hold.

DEVELOPMENT

> 'Spring' starts with a burgeoning sound, a hyperbole, which is followed
> by an ecstatic scene of movements, shapes, sounds, textures, and colour.
> (Norman White)

The octet begins with an emphatic statement, which is supported by the evidence
that follows. It is not surprising, when one gets to know a little of Hopkins's
character, that he begins with weeds. For the poet, weeds are wild flowers that
are all the more attractive for being so natural and uncontrolled, as it were, by
humans. The weeds are in 'wheels' – one of many architectural terms employed
by the poet. A wheel window is a circular window whose mullions divide it in
the same way that spokes divide a wheel. The verb 'shoot' adds to the energy of
the scene, as does the tripping alliteration of 'long and lovely and lush'.

How did the poet move from weeds to thrush's eggs? The answer lies in the
sound of the words: 'lush' leads to 'thrush'. This is a technique often employed
by Hopkins, especially in poems where there seems to be a rush of energy, as if
one word sprouts from the other. The breathless excitement of the poet is
captured in the *ellipsis* (omission of words):

> Thrush's eggs look little low heavens.

'The omission of "like" saves the phrase from being merely a pretty simile'
(Walford Davies). The eggs are like the heavens, or skies, because they have the
same dappled pattern of blue and white. Hopkins loved the dappled design
because of the beauty that he found in contrasting colours and shapes.

The song of the thrush echoing through the trees 'does so rinse and wring
the ear'. Another one of Hopkins's fascinating and original images! The song in
its purity, passing through the ear of the listener, cleanses it as if it were rinsed
and wrung dry; 'wring' is also a pun on 'ring'.

When we come to the word 'lightning' we must recall 'charged', 'flame' and
'fire' from previous poems. All these words relate to the startling beauty of
divine nature – God's fire. The song of the bird thrills the poet as if it were an
angelic sound.

The bird in the tree leads on to the 'glassy peartree', 'glassy' because it is
radiant in the sunlight, which 'leaves and blooms' – the nouns 'leaf' and 'bloom'
are used first as verbs and then become nouns and the subject ('they') of 'brush'.
Such experimentation with language contributes to the strangeness of Hopkins's
poetry. In the nineteenth century it would have been regarded even more
strangely. The word 'blooms' connects by alliteration to 'brush'. The tree
brushes against the sky, which descends to meet it ('the descending blue').
Perhaps Hopkins has the painter's brush in mind here; he had ambitions to be

an artist before he became a priest. The 'richness' of the blue sky probably refers to the effect created by a smattering of white, unthreatening clouds, enough of them to create a beautiful dappled effect. The poet's eyes descend to ground level to notice the lambs having 'their fling'. Some years earlier, in his journals, Hopkins wrote: 'It is as if it were the earth that flung them [the lambs], not themselves.'

There is very little to be done with the octet other than to enjoy its sound, colour, and movement, the sheer pleasure that can be taken in the physical world.

The sestet becomes more reflective as the poet wonders 'What is it all about?' He has enjoyed the experience of the physical world; now he wishes to meditate on its meaning. Immediately the tone, pace and imagery have changed. Now, at a distance from the wonderful scene in the octet, the poet declares that this is 'a strain', like a fleeting snatch of a melody, of the Garden of Eden, of the perfect world that existed before sin and corruption took over. He urges 'Christ, lord' to

> Have, get, before it cloy
> Before it cloud . . . and sour with sinning.

He wants Christ to intervene now, seize the world in its momentary perfect state and preserve it for evermore. It is as if the poet, overwhelmed by the perfect beauty of the scene he has just witnessed, cannot bear the thought of returning to the real world, with all its imperfections.

'Innocent mind and Mayday in girl and boy' seems to be the object of the verbs 'cloud' and 'sour'. May, because of its associations with the Blessed Virgin, is identified with purity and innocence. This state of innocence is 'Most . . . choice' or most precious and 'Most . . . worthy' of being won. 'O maid's child' is, of course, Christ.

The poem is written in standard sonnet form with elements of sprung rhythm.

The Windhover

Text of poem: New Explorations Anthology page 114

A week later, at the end of May 1877, Hopkins composed 'The Windhover'. He had already composed four poems that month. It was his day off; the weather was lovely; he had been successful in his examinations, and the next one was a long way off. He described this poem as 'the best thing I ever wrote'. It is also one of his more difficult poems.

The kestrel, a kind of falcon, was very common in the Clwyd area and was known locally as the windhover, a name that Hopkins thought exotic. It is remarkable for its habit of remaining suspended in the air while scanning the ground for its prey.

THEME

'The Windhover' is perhaps the most complex of Hopkins's poems in this anthology, but it can be enjoyed on different levels. At one level the poem is about a bird in flight and the poet's response to its beauty. At a deeper level the hawk, with its outstretched wings, represents Jesus Christ, and the poem is about the relationship between humankind and God. In essence, the poet believes that the greatest beauty is revealed when we subdue our personal ego and ambitions, submit to the will of God, and live our lives in a Christ-like manner.

DEVELOPMENT

It is very difficult to subdivide the octet. There is no clear division into quatrains, and there are no end-stopped lines; the whole is fluid, fast-moving, and graceful, like the bird. For convenience we will take the octet in four segments.

> I caught . . . Falcon

The ellipsis in 'I caught [sight of]' is very effective. It emphasises the dramatic moment of perception. The poet did not just see a bird: his spirit was arrested by a sudden flash of magnificence. This is the moment when he perceives the 'inscape' of the bird. The word 'caught' may also refer to the artist who 'catches' the shape, the movement or the moment of the bird's flight. One of the reasons that Hopkins moved from art to poetry was that he found it impossible to capture movement in a painting or sketch; and it was the energy of movement that fascinated him most.

The phrase 'this morning' adds a tingling freshness to the moment. There follows a procession of titles, 'as in some royal proclamation of medieval pageantry' (Peter Milward). The bird is the 'minion' or favourite of the morning. The French word already adds a certain grace to this creature; it is the 'dauphin' or heir-apparent to the kingdom of daylight. The regal imagery invests the bird with a majestic quality. The capitalisation of 'Falcon' adds to its dignity, as if it were a royal person with a title. The Falcon is 'dapple-dawn-drawn', a coined adjective that throws up two possible interpretations: the falcon has been drawn or attracted by the dappled dawn, or it looks as if it has been drawn or sketched against the dappled sky in the background.

> in his riding . . . ecstasy.

The mediaeval chivalric imagery in the first part of the poem seems to inspire the comparing of the bird to a horse in a show ring. The bird is 'riding' the 'rolling level' – in other words, it is riding the air. Even though the air is 'rolling', the bird remains 'level' and 'steady', because of its control and poise. The word 'striding' suggests the ease and mastery of the bird as it hovers 'high there'. Then it begins to swivel on the tip of its wing. The predicate 'rung upon the rein' is a technical term of the riding-school to describe a horse circling at the end of a rein held by its trainer. The verb 'to ring' in falconry means to rise in spirals. Hopkins would have been familiar with both terms and would have intended the two meanings.

> There is a combination of physical power and intellectual skill in his momentary motionlessness, as he hovers in the wind – like an expert trainer pulling on the rein of a fierce, untamed animal in a ring and forcing it to keep within the limits of the rein he holds. (Peter Milward)

Why does the bird make these movements? For the sheer pleasure of it! This bird is being what it is, exulting in its control, power and victory over the air, exulting in its own self. The bird is a majestic, graceful creature totally in harmony with its environment and its own self.

Then off . . . the big wind

The dramatic exclamation that concludes with the word 'ecstasy' is followed by the even more dramatic elliptical 'then off'. It is so much more abrupt and startling than 'then the bird flew off'. The repetition of 'off' and the fluidity of 'off forth' add to the energy of the line. The poet uses the simile of a skater taking a corner to describe the dramatic, energetic yet elegant manner in which the bird suddenly changes direction. The alliteration of 's' evokes the sound of the skate against the ice.

'The hurl and gliding' conveys two paradoxical qualities of the bird. The verb 'hurl' suggests strength and power, vehement effort; 'gliding' suggests grace and easeful action. The bird seems to unite these qualities in its victory over the 'big wind'.

My heart . . . mastery of the thing

From 'I caught' to 'big wind' the focus has been exclusively on the magnificence of the bird. The attention now shifts to the poet, his heart, which is in 'hiding'. It is impossible to say with certainty what the poet intended with this line. Why is his heart 'in hiding'? Why for 'a bird' rather than *the* bird that he has been describing? What we can say with a degree of confidence is that the poet feels somewhat humbled by the majesty of the falcon. He is overwhelmed by admiration for this creature. This bird has the qualities that he lacks: power, self-assurance, grace.

The octet concludes with the climactic 'the achieve of, the mastery of the thing!' The word 'achieve' is an abbreviation of 'achievement', the shorter version adding to the sense of breathless awe as the octet draws to a close. The poet spends his time studying and praying, 'obscure, constrained, unsuccessful', as he said himself. Perhaps he envies the bird its sense of purpose and its activity, in contrast to his own lack of it.

Why does he call it a 'thing'? Is it not something of an anti-climax after such a majestic description? Yes, it is. Hopkins may be reminding us that this bird is, after all, merely a bird. How much more wonderful then would a human being be, if he (or she) were to reflect the same sense of activity and purpose!

If we ignore for a moment the dedication of the poem, 'To Christ our Lord', we could say that the octet deals with a secular experience; it is a nature poem.

> I believe that the proper and perfect symbol is the natural object, that if a man uses 'symbols' he must so use them that their symbolic function does not obtrude; so that a sense, and the poetic quality of the passage, is not lost to those who do not understand the symbol as such, to whom, for instance, a hawk is a hawk. (Ezra Pound)

We can enjoy the description of the falcon for what it is, independent of the symbolic significance of the bird.

As we have seen so often in Hopkins's poetry, the religious dimension is introduced in the sestet. This is divided into two tercets, which, again for convenience, we will subdivide.

> Brute beauty . . . Buckle!

This continues the thought of the previous line with a list of the bird's qualities. Hopkins had great admiration for 'brute beauty', especially stallions. For him, beauty and virility were closely connected.

The concepts of 'valour and act' are interdependent: courage manifests itself in action, not in contemplation. The word 'air' perhaps refers to disposition. We speak of someone having an 'air', or of 'airs and graces'. The nouns 'pride, plume' (plumage) suggest majesty but also a certain vanity, which seems at odds with the clearly admirable qualities of the first half of this line. Suddenly the line is not as simple as it appeared to be. The words 'here | Buckle' provide us with the greatest difficulty. We have reached the heart of the controversy that surrounds this poem.

The word 'here' may refer to (a) his heart in hiding, (b) the bird in his ecstasy, or (c) the situation as a whole. The verb 'buckle' may mean (a) clasp together (like a belt buckle), (b) come to grips, or (c) collapse. Perhaps he wants these qualities to be united in him, like a coat of armour that is buckled on in preparation for doing battle with the forces of evil, just as the bird joins combat with the wind.

A more difficult interpretation – and a more likely one – is to take 'buckle' to mean 'collapse'. Remember the word 'crushed' in 'God's Grandeur' and how it was emphasised by being placed at the beginning of a line, succeeded by a full stop and heavily stressed by its position. Here we have another word with all the same features.

> Well may the bird . . . take pride in its mastery, and plume itself on its achievement, allowing for its wild and wanton condition. But as for himself he now recognises a far wider possibility of mastery and achievement open to him as man, even as his human nature is far nobler than the animal nature of the bird. There is, after all, no need of envy; his is a far higher vocation. Paradoxically, it is to be achieved not by mastery, but by service: not by the exertion of physical strength, or even of intellectual skill, in the eyes of an admiring multitude, but by the renunciation of merely natural powers in obedience to a higher, supernatural ideal, the service of 'Christ our Lord'. (Peter Milward)

Our earthly glory must be crushed so that our heavenly glory may be released. The paradox at the centre of this interpretation is the paradox of Christ's mission. The crucifixion of Christ, on a physical level, was a kind of failure; on a spiritual level it was a triumph, because it was through the crucifixion that Christ rescued humankind from death. The resurrection could not have taken place without the crucifixion. Likewise, for humankind to realise its glorious destiny it must be crushed physically, it must buckle or bend in the service of God's will. The argument in favour of this interpretation is strengthened immeasurably by the three images that conclude the poem.

The copulative 'AND' may be (a) simply connecting or (b) consequential, that is, meaning 'and as a result' (the capitalisation suggests that this interpretation is more appropriate). The word 'thee' may refer to (a) his heart, (b) the bird, or (c) Christ. Taking 'AND' to mean 'and as a result' of this collapse, the fire (a word that should trigger some measure of recognition after we have read the previous poems) that is unleashed should be 'a billion times told lovelier, more dangerous'. When the self-will is subdued and harnessed in the service of Christ, its power is magnified and more dangerous in effecting change. The phrase 'O my chevalier' is an address to Christ. The mediaeval chivalric imagery of the octet has become more explicit.

The last two images describe how something brilliant and wonderful can come from something ordinary or from an apparent collapse. The dull earth (sillion) when ploughed shines in the sun (or perhaps it is the plough that reflects the sun after it emerges from the earth – a symbolic resurrection). If the poet 'ploughs' in the service of God, the light of grace will shine forth from his work.

The dying embers of a fire, 'blue-bleak' in the sense that they appear to be losing their heat and brightness, collapse onto the hearth, crack open, and reveal a beautiful glowing interior. The unglamorous life of the priest, and the suffering endured in the service of God, will reveal the 'gold-vermilion' of divine love. This interpretation is strongly supported by the study of Hopkins's major work, 'The Wreck of the Deutschland'.

> The poet has in fact seen two aspects of the bird in flight. On one view, its controlling mastery; on another, the bird 'buckled', spreadeagled, crucified on the wind. It is that latter moment that is 'a billion times told lovelier, more dangerous.' Of course, the martial imagery, the zeal of the new Jesuit, gives other meanings to that word 'Buckle': the sense of 'buckling on armour', for example, or 'buckling down' to a deed. But the deepest emphasis of the sestet is that sense of buckling under stress and being broken. The full meaning, therefore, makes Christ present not only in princely aggrandisement but in the paradox of his suffering on the cross. That is the realisation that explodes in the pain ('gall'), the spear-wound ('gash'), and the blood ('vermilion') of the final line. (Walford Davies)

Norman White takes a different view:

> In the sestet, the constituents of the falcon's performances are metamorphosed into parts of armour, which the chivalric lord Christ is entreated to buckle on, that he may appear in his glory, the windhover's qualities being merely one minute, exemplary part of the infinitely greater glory of God ('Ad maiorem Dei gloriam'). The two images of the last three lines form a magnificent ending.

The sestet may be seen as a conversation with his own heart, arising out of the experience described in the octet. He then dedicates this meditation 'To Christ our Lord' as a gesture of submission to his will.

Pied Beauty
Text of poem: New Explorations Anthology page 118

In July 1877 Hopkins sat an oral examination in dogmatic theology. It did not go well; his passionate advocacy of Scotism did not meet with the favour of the examiners. His low pass marks may have been responsible for the decision not to allow him to complete a fourth year of theology; poor performances in the pulpit may have been a factor also. 'Much against my inclination I shall have to leave Wales.' Before he left he composed the curtal sonnet 'Pied Beauty'. (A *curtal sonnet* has 6 + 4 lines rather than 8 + 6. It is essentially a shortened sonnet with a very brief coda at the end.)

Beauty in all its variety of appearances is a central part of the poet's vision. In another poem he argued that mortal beauty, despite its short-lived nature, serves to keep warm 'men's wits to the things that are'; in other words, beauty keeps humankind in touch with the essential goodness of creation. For Hopkins this beauty was to be found in nature, especially in the wild and the wilderness, rather than in art or in the manicured gardens of a stately home. He loved 'brute' or 'barbarous' beauty because of its variety and contrasts, 'Earth's dapple', 'pied' beauty. He believed that contrast helped to bring out the distinctive quality of each object, just as light and dark, day and night, winter and summer accentuate each other. If Hopkins were alive today he would be dismayed by the manner in which the media in particular standardise our notions of beauty.

'Pied Beauty' seems an innocuous poem, but there may be a hint of defiance in Hopkins's determination to admire what is 'counter, original, spare, strange'.

THEME

The opening line expresses the theme of the poem: glory be to God for dappled things – in other words for contrast, variety, whatever is unusual – for these are God's gifts to us.

DEVELOPMENT

The simple opening echoes the Jesuit motto, *Ad maiorem Dei gloriam* (For the greater glory of God); likewise the ending echoes *Laus Deo semper* (Praise to God always). A student in a Jesuit school would begin and conclude his written work with these two mottoes. By framing the poem thus the poet makes it a prayer of praise and a meditation on the glory of God as seen in His creation.

After the general opening statement the poet gives the reader a list of examples of dappled things. Skies are dappled by the effect of white clouds against blue 'like a brinded cow'. The blue and white of the sky are like the brown and white of the 'brinded cow' in that both are 'dappled'. The phrase 'couple-colour' is one of five compound words used in the poem. It is as if the poet is trying to invent a new language in order to convey his experience of nature in a fresh and exciting way.

The eye, which has moved from the sky to the meadow, now moves on to the river. The time spent fishing in the Elwy afforded Hopkins the opportunity to observe the patterns on the various fish. He notices the dappled appearance of their skin. Beside the river, lying on the ground beneath the trees, are chestnuts. Hopkins invented the word 'chestnut-falls' (from 'windfalls', meaning fruit that has fallen from the trees). The chestnuts that have fallen and opened, exposing the gleaming brown nuts, remind him of fresh coal. The dapple exists between the tan colour of the husk and the brown kernel. Hopkins's descriptive phrase is worth revisiting to appreciate the concentration of meaning he has achieved: 'Fresh-firecoal chestnut-falls'.

Next the eye moves from beneath the tree to the birds on the tree. He may have chosen finches for their song, or perhaps because the word creates alliteration with the rest of the line. The wings of finches – chaffinches, bullfinches, goldfinches – have the same contrast in colour.

The poet expands the vista to the landscape around St Beuno's, which is like a patchwork quilt: 'fold' is used for grazing sheep; 'fallow' lies unused; and 'plough' refers to the land that is sown with crops. The three together form 'the dappled panoramic inscape of the Vale of Clwyd'. As he looked out over the valley he would have seen not only the evidence of agricultural labour but also some evidence of industrial works from the nearby towns of Denbigh, Llanelwy and Rhyl. Therefore, the last lines refer to the variety of human activities – agricultural and industrial – and the variety of equipment used in these trades (perhaps he is thinking of fishing tackle).

Having provided examples, the poet moves on to a more general view of the subject. He gives a series of descriptive adjectives: all things that stand in contrast with other things are 'counter'; all things that have a unique blend or contrast are 'original'; all things that one rarely sees are 'spare'; all things that by their rarity are startling are 'strange'. He likes what is eccentric, perhaps because he is eccentric himself.

Whatever is 'fickle' is changeable. The adjective 'freckled' brings us back to humankind, just as 'trades' did in the first part of the poem. Humankind shares in this dappled glory. The next line contains a series of contrasts: swift/slow, sweet/sour, adazzle/dim, referring to time, taste, and light, respectively. These contrasts are bound together by alliteration. It is as if language itself demonstrates this dappled pattern.

His conclusion is simple: God, whose beauty is not subject to change, made this wonderful variety, which is subject to change. Earthly beauty therefore is a fleeting glimpse of the eternal beauty of God; therefore we must praise God.

The interplay of consonantal sounds, alliteration, rhythm and rhyme contributes to the energy of the lines. It is a very simple poem, but the veiled attack on orthodoxy and convention reveals an interesting shift from the perspective of the other poems written in 1877.

This poem is similar to 'As Kingfishers Catch Fire' in its promotion of the philosophy of Duns Scottus and in its concentration on intense detail.

Teacher and curate

From Wales, Hopkins went to teach in Chesterfield, then back to Stonyhurst. While there he resumed correspondence with Robert Bridges and began writing to R. W. Dixon, who had been a junior master at Highgate and who proved an invaluable support to Hopkins in his writing. He moved from there to parish work in a fashionable part of London, followed by a short time in Bristol and Oxford. The frequency of transfer must have undermined his self-confidence, since it appeared that he was unfit for the roles he undertook.

Back in Oxford, Hopkins was dismayed to find that the beautiful town was becoming a rail hub and business centre and would soon become a manufacturing city. He found that his parishioners didn't particularly trust converts and the Anglican community didn't trust Catholics, especially Jesuits. He found the people 'stiff, stand-off and depressed'. He himself, of course, was not the most affable of people.

> It was probably difficult to warm to the slight, somewhat vehement young priest with an effeminate manner and the disconcerting habit of waving a large red handkerchief to punctuate his conversation. Those who persevered, however, found him loveable. (R. B. Martin)
>
> Hopkins, it seems, was a man who in his shyness felt enormously awkward when he had to perform any public task. (Joseph Feeney)

BEDFORD LEIGH AND LIVERPOOL

In October 1879 Hopkins was sent for three months to Bedford Leigh, between Manchester and Liverpool. He expressed great satisfaction with his transfer from Oxford to this grimy, red-brick town:

> a darksome place, with pits and mills and foundries . . . I am far more at home with the Lancashire people . . . . The air is charged with smoke as well as damp, but the people are hearty.

However, he complained that the workers were 'too fond of frequenting the public houses.'

His new parishioners were more welcoming and respectful towards him than those in Oxford or London had been. The feeling of being accepted brought the best out of him in the pulpit. At St Beuno's his fellow-Jesuits were sometimes reduced to tears of laughter at the awkwardness of his sermons. His comparing of the church to a cow full of milk with seven udders – the sacraments, through which grace flowed – went down poorly with the refined ladies of London; the same analogy was received more favourably by the simple folk of Bedford Leigh. Even when his sermons became obscure and academic the flock dutifully listened, or slept, but never criticised. Hopkins was now convinced that his calling was to minister to the poor and uneducated.

That Christmas he had a short stay at St Beuno's before moving on to St Francis Xavier's Church in the heart of Liverpool.

BACKGROUND TO 'FELIX RANDAL'

The population of Liverpool had increased dramatically as a result of the Great Famine in Ireland. Thousands of immigrants had settled where the ships landed, flooding the stinking slums with even more unemployed and helpless victims. There were nine priests and ten thousand parishioners. Hopkins's romantic aspiration to serve the lowest in society was put to the test. In letters to A. M. Baillie (an old friend from Oxford) and Dixon he wrote:

> My Liverpool work is very harassing and makes it hard to write . . . . The parish work of Liverpool is very wearying to mind and body and leaves me nothing but odds and ends of time . . . . I do not think I can be long here; I have been long nowhere yet. I am brought face to face with the deepest poverty and misery in my district.

He felt an intense sympathy for the poor. In one famous letter to Bridges, written eight years before his time in Liverpool, he expressed anger at the manner in which the rulers of England ignored the plight of the poor:

> Horrible to say, in a manner, I am a Communist . . . . It is a dreadful thing for the greatest and most necessary part of a very rich nation to live a hard life without dignity, knowledge, comforts, delight, or hopes in the midst of plenty – which plenty they make . . . . England has grown hugely wealthy but this wealth has not reached the working classes; I expect it has made their condition worse.

Much later, in another letter, he wrote:

> My Liverpool and Glasgow experience laid upon my mind a conviction, a truly crushing conviction, of the misery of town life to the poor and more than to the poor, of the misery of the poor in general, of the degradation even of our race, of the hollowness of this century's civilisation: it made even life a burden to me to have daily thrust upon me the things I saw.

Despite his romantic admiration for the nobility of the poor, he found the experience of working in such depressing conditions too much of a strain for his physical and mental well-being. As so often happened when he was unhappy, he fell ill. His poetry suffered too.

> There is merit in it [his parish work], but little Muse, and indeed 26 lines is the whole I have writ in more than half a year.

Felix Randal
Text of poem: New Explorations Anthology page 120

'Felix Randal' was one of two poems composed during this time. It was written about one of his parishioners, a 31-year-old farrier, Felix Spencer, who died on 21 April 1880 from TB, an illness that was common wherever living conditions were bad.

Why did Hopkins change the man's name from Spencer to Randal? Perhaps he wished to maintain the man's anonymity. Since he had no immediate intention of publishing his poetry, this seems an unlikely explanation. It is much easier to believe that the name has a special significance. 'Felix' is the Latin for 'happy' or 'fortunate'. Hopkins believed that all human beings are fortunate, because they have been saved from Hell by Christ's sacrifice on the cross. 'Randal' is more problematic. A 'rand' is a strip of leather between the shoe and heel. 'Randal' rhymes with 'sandal', which links with the shoe image in 'rand'. Hopkins was fond of making such clever word associations. But to what purpose? Just for the sake of rhyme? He would never be that casual in his choice of word. A 'rand-al' is a lowly thing, something trodden on, insignificant and unseen, like a farrier in a slum in Everton. This interpretation is not as fanciful as it seems: in another of his poems, 'That Nature Is a Heraclitean Fire', he conveys a similar idea in a similar way:

> This Jack, joke, poor potsherd, patch, matchwood, immortal diamond,
> Is immortal diamond.

Once again the suggestion is that man is an insignificant thing (Jack . . . matchwood) who is given a glorious destiny (immortal diamond) through the agency of Christ. So the name 'Felix Randal' conveys the paradoxical nature of humankind as insignificant creatures who have been exalted and given everlasting life as a result of the death and resurrection of Christ. The theme of the poem, in a sense, is 'hidden' in the title.

There is another possibility. 'Rand' is the Old English word for the boss of a shield – often used to represent the shield itself. Perhaps Hopkins is suggesting that the farrier's faith acted as a shield when confronted by the terror of dying. As a keen student of etymology Hopkins would have consciously tried to enrich his poetry by giving words such layered meanings.

THEME

On a superficial level, the poem is about the death of a parishioner. On a deeper level it is a celebration of his existence. At the deepest level it is about the relationship between God and humankind, a celebration of God's creation.

DEVELOPMENT

Octet

In the first quatrain the physical power of the man is emphasised by the repeated alliteration in the line.

> his mould of man, big boned and hardy-handsome.

The same technique is used to show the rapid decline in his condition:

> Pining, pining, till time when reason rambled in it.

The personification of his illness fighting over the physical body of the poor man, like ravenous animals, gives an awful vividness to the process that destroyed him. However, it is the reaction of the priest-poet to the news of Randal's death that intrigues us:

> Felix Randal the farrier, O is he dead then? My duty all ended . . .

Is the tone one of relief that his role as comforter is no longer needed? Is he disappointed that his services are no longer required? Perhaps the question mark simply conveys the surprise on hearing of his death. It is also possible that the blacksmith's death is an anti-climax, in that the real moment of significance was before his death. It is difficult to be sure. Hopkins was a relative newcomer to parish work, and his attitude to it was somewhat ambivalent. He was delighted to be active in the service of God, but he had great doubts about his suitability for the role.

The short dramatic statement at the beginning of the second quatrain is worthy of note. The image of being 'broken' is appropriate, since the man worked with horses. Horses are broken when they are trained to serve people's purpose; now this man has been broken by sickness, perhaps part of God's purpose. It is noteworthy that the sentence begins with the farrier being 'broken' and ends with him being 'mended'. The word 'broke' also emphasises the physicality and sensuousness of Hopkins's poetry. Such metaphysical cleverness is typical of him. However, there is something very ordinary about the statement as well. Similarly, the comments 'Being anointed and all' and 'Ah well, God rest him all road ever he offended' illustrate the poet's desire to use the everyday speech of the community in his poetry.

The second quatrain traces the changes in the farrier's attitude to his illness. His first reaction, a very human response, is to curse his misfortune. The word 'impatient' must be understood in its Latin sense, 'unable to endure'. This man was in no hurry to experience the kingdom of God; one could well imagine him being happy to continue with his impoverished life, enjoying a few drinks in the local pub and chatting with his neighbours – the simple pleasures that make even the poorest existence tolerable. Between his curse and his mending there is an untold story of how a man faces up to the inevitable. Hopkins's ministry and God's sacraments brought about a change of heart: he became attuned to God's will. While his physical body suffered, his mind 'mended'. He acquired a 'heavenlier heart', in the sense that he began to turn his thoughts towards his inevitable destination and made peace with his fate.

The image of 'sweet reprieve and ransom' probably refers to Confession and Communion. The sinner is reprieved in the confessional, and Christ has already paid the ransom for us by suffering on the cross on our behalf. The final line is quaintly colloquial: sure, the man never did much harm to anyone in his life, and may God forgive him if he did.

Sestet (first tercet)

Petrarchan sonnets usually divide into *octet* and *sestet*. The sestet provides us with a reflection on the situation presented in the octet. The change of mood is evident in the first line. The central concern of this section is the reciprocity of the relationship between priest and farrier. In other words, not only did the blacksmith benefit from the priest's ministry but the priest, too, received grace of a kind from his contact with the sick man. The priest comforted him verbally (tongue) with the word of God; he soothed his troubled soul by anointing him (touch). In turn, the tears of the farrier evoked an emotional response from the priest. The childlike simplicity and vulnerability of this 'big-boned and hardy-handsome' man moved the heart of the little priest. Hopkins may have had in mind the biblical advice that 'unless ye are as little children, ye shall not enter the Kingdom of Heaven.'

Second tercet

In the last three lines the focus changes again. It seems as if the poet is looking back through time to the days when the farrier was in his prime – 'thy more boisterous years,' 'powerful amidst peers' – and how distant the thought of death seemed then: 'how far from then forethought of'. There is also a sense in which the poet is presenting us with a kind of *apotheosis* or divine glorification: here is the image of the farrier in Heaven enjoying eternal glory. Just as the blacksmith beat the metal into horseshoes, God has fashioned a new Felix, stronger in heart, brighter in spirit. It was a painful process. The man suffered and grew spiritually.

Once again the theme of 'The Wreck of the Deutschland' (the role of suffering in our world) echoes throughout all Hopkins's poetry. The sense of triumph is conveyed by energetic words such as 'boisterous', 'powerful', 'great grey drayhorse', the luminous 'bright and battering sandal', and the rising rhythm of the lines, which convey the tone of triumph. In this way the poet 'inscapes' the blacksmith by capturing the life force of this man as well as his glorious destiny. The conclusion of the poem provides us with an image of the resurrected farrier.

Sprung rhythm

The length of the lines in this poem varies between twelve and nineteen syllables, unlike the typical sonnet line, which has ten. Hopkins doesn't count the unstressed syllables; the inclusion of a large number of these unstressed syllables adds greatly to the energy of the poem. There are six stresses in each line of the poem; this is usually known as an *Alexandrine* line.

Diction

The poem reflects Hopkins's belief that the language of poetry should stay close to ordinary speech and – equally clearly – his realisation that poetry is not conversation and so can be heightened and rhetorical without falling into artificiality. These two principles working together give the poem its contrapuntal flavour [contrasting melody]: 'all road' is a Northernism for 'in whatever way' and would not come naturally from Hopkins in propria persona [as his natural way of expressing himself]; it seems natural because the poem is saturated with the earthy and demotic presence of the smith himself; whereas a colloquialism like 'This seeing the sick' would be quite normal in educated speech and does, in fact, occur in one of Hopkins's letters. (John Wain)

Glasgow

In August 1881 Hopkins was sent to St Joseph's Church in Glasgow. From there he wrote to Baillie:

Though Glasgow is repulsive to live in yet there are alleviations: the streets and buildings are fine and the people lively. The poor Irish,

among whom my duties lay, are mostly from the North of Ireland . . . .
They are found by all who have to deal with them very attractive; for,
though always very drunken and at present very Fenian, they are warm-
hearted and give a far heartier welcome than those of Liverpool. I found
myself very much at home with them.

Before leaving Scotland he made a trip to Inversnaid on Loch Lomond, inspired
probably by Wordsworth's poem 'To a Highland Girl'. There he wrote the poem
'Inversnaid', his only composition in the space of a year.

Inversnaid

Text of poem: New Explorations Anthology page 124
[*Note: This poem is also prescribed for Ordinary Level 2006 exam*]

The Inversnaid Falls feature prominently in Hopkins's poem.

> The day was dark and partly hid the lake, yet it did not altogether
> disfigure it but gave a pensive or solemn beauty which left a deep
> impression on me.

Hopkins often complained that cities seemed to dry him up, physically and
spiritually. Imagine therefore the pleasure he must have taken from the energetic
waters of Inversnaid Falls! This is a simple poem, consisting of three verses that
describe the progress of Arklet Water, with its

> peaty-brown waters . . . through narrow valleys of heather and ladder-
> fern to oak forests, with the occasional birch, ash and, hanging over the
> water, rowan, gradually steepened and quickened. There were smaller
> falls and side pools, with froth, foam, bubbles, and whirls, in rocky
> basins, before the final, magnificent, high but broken fall into a larger
> pool just before it entered Loch Lomond. (Norman White)

The fourth verse expresses a heartfelt plea for the preservation of natural
environments.

Hopkins was not happy with the poem, and it remained unseen until after
his death.

THEME
The poem celebrates the beauty and inscape of the natural world.

Stanza 1

The brown water, high above the lake, rolls over rocks and develops white foamy patches before it falls noisily into the lake. How much more evocative and 'noisy' the poet's words are! The adjectives contribute immensely, not only because of the visual images they create but also because of their sound. This is Hopkins's only Scottish poem. He succeeds in capturing the flavour of the Glaswegian accent by his frequent use of *l* and especially *r* (together with Scots words like 'burn', 'brae' and 'bonny' in later verses).

If you look at particular examples of his choice of adjective you can gain an insight into his attention to detail. The word 'darksome' attracts and frightens at the same time, emphasising the Romantic credentials of the poet. The adjective 'horseback' is used to qualify 'brown'. When one thinks of 'horseback brown' one thinks of a glossy, textured brown that catches the light. But the real merit in the word is not so much its description of the colour as the association the word has with horses. This is not a static brown, it is imbued with the energy associated with horses. In this way the poet infuses his description of the water with the energy the water displays as it 'roars' down into the lake. In the second line his use of alliteration and harsh consonants achieves the same energetic effect. He has coined another word, 'rollrock', to add to this energy. Imagine how a Scot would deliver this line! In lines 3 and 4 alliteration combines very well with the four stresses of the *iambic tetrameter* to create a melodic effect:

> coop – comb – fleece – foam
> Flutes – low – lake – home

Stanza 2

The froth is described as fawn-coloured. Once again Hopkins has chosen a word that (*a*) creates alliteration with 'froth', (*b*) describes a yellow-brown colour, and (*c*) describes a young deer. This froth is like a bonnet that has been puffed up by the wind. Hopkins is very sensitive to the contrast between the light-coloured froth and the pitch-black pool. Also, there is a contrast in sound between the light beat of the first two lines and the heavy, sombre rhythm of the last two lines of the stanza. The words 'broth', 'pitch-black' and 'fell-frowning' and the phrase 'Despair to drowning' create a somewhat sinister atmosphere. The image is of an eddy or whirlpool that is very dark, which the poet seems to associate with the descent into Hell.

Stanza 3

So far, the movement of the poem has been downwards. In this verse the attention is drawn upwards to the terrain through which the stream flows. The stream runs through 'the groins of the braes', a phrase that perfectly evokes the rough Highland landscape. It refers to the steep banks of the river, which are 'degged' or sprinkled with dew. The guttural 'g' sounds are complemented by the 'b' and 'd' sounds to create a cacophonous melody not unlike the music of the bagpipes. The river now 'treads' carefully, whereas in the first verse it roared and galloped. The banks are covered in heath and fern, but to make these seem more fearsome he uses the harsh-sounding 'packs' and 'flitches'. The final line is almost tranquil by comparison.

Stanza 4

The rhetorical question gives way to a plea on behalf of unspoilt natural scenes as the poet takes us from this particular place to a contemplation of the natural world. Two-and-a-half years earlier, in Oxford, Hopkins had written the germ of an idea for which he had now found a place:

> O where is it, the wilderness,
> The wildness of the wilderness?
> Where is it, the wilderness?

The weeds, wetness and wilderness of the scene represent the essential purity of nature, in contrast to the 'sordid selfishness of man'. The weeds and wilderness are God's creation, untouched by human hand, still perfect and therefore sacramental. His plea is for the Earth that has no tongue.

> Yet his plea is not a hopeless one. He looks not to the likelihood of ruin, but to the certainty of resurrection. In his poem as a whole there is a structural contrast between the downward fall of the stream, to the drowning of Despair at the end of the second stanza, and the upward rising of the banks on either side, sprinkled as they are with bright dew and looking up to the sky through the branches of the 'beadbonny ash'. This rising movement culminates in the 'long live' of the final line, which is not just a ceremonial 'Viva!' or an outburst of forced enthusiasm, but the poet's confession of his faith in eternal life. Thus in the end of the poem we may discern theological undertones of Baptism and Resurrection. (Peter Milward)

METRE

This poem is written in *iambic tetrameter* (in imitation of Wordsworth's poem) but with elements of 'sprung rhythm'. The iambic tetrameter normally has four stresses in a line with eight syllables: 'de-*dum* de-*dum* de-*dum* de-*dum*'.

It is possible for a tetrameter to gain or lose a syllable. However, this poem has between seven and twelve syllables per line. The extra syllables are unstressed:

Are the groins of the braes that the brook treads through . . .
'de-de-*dum* de-de-*dum* de-de-*dum* de-*dum*.'

THE INFLUENCE OF RUSKIN

A glance at the poem by Wordsworth that drew Hopkins to Inversnaid serves to illustrate the difference between the two poets as well as an important characteristic of Hopkins's poetry.

> . . . these grey rocks; that household lawn;
> Those trees, a veil just half withdrawn;
> This fall of water that doth make
> A murmur near the silent lake . . .

This is very tame by comparison with Hopkins's poem. The rocks are just 'grey', and the water makes a 'murmur'. Hopkins described the Lake poets as 'faithful but not rich observers of nature'. They were not disciples of John Ruskin. In *Modern Painters* and *The Elements of Drawing,* Ruskin advocated an almost scientific attention to the observation of detail: 'If you can paint one leaf, you can paint the world.' His journals illustrate this way of looking at natural objects:

> I have particular periods of admiration for particular things in Nature; for a certain time I am astonished at the beauty of a tree, shape, effects etc.

There is a page of studies of ash-twigs. Ruskin wrote:

> Each has a curve and a path to take . . . and each terminates all its minor branches at its outer extremity, so as to form a great outer curve. Choose rough, worn, and clumsy-looking things as much as possible.

His readers were warned to avoid 'all very neat things.' Is it any wonder that Hopkins would proclaim: 'Long live the weeds and the wilderness!'

GAIA: A MODERN PERSPECTIVE?

An English scientist, James Lovelock, put forward the 'Gaia hypothesis'. Gaia in Greek mythology was the goddess of the earth. In Lovelock's theory the Earth is a living organism, of which humankind is a part. In a lecture he said:

> I sometimes wonder if the loss of soul from science could be the result of sensory deprivation – a consequence of the fact that the majority of

us now live in cities. How can you love the living world if you can no longer hear a bird song through the noise of traffic, or smell the sweetness of fresh air? How can we wonder about God and the universe if we never see the stars because of the city lights?

The attraction of the city is seductive. Socrates said that nothing of interest happened outside its city walls, and that was two thousand years ago. But city life – the soap opera that never ends – reinforces and strengthens the heresy of humanism, the narcissistic belief that nothing important happens that is not a human interest.

City living corrupts: it gives a false sense of priority over environmental hazards. We become inordinately obsessed with personal mortality – especially death from cancer.

When we read 'Inversnaid' we cannot avoid thinking of the destruction of the Amazon rainforests, the extinction of species, and the disappearance of our own green fields under a concrete jungle.

Final vows and Dublin

ROEHAMPTON

When he returned to Roehampton for his *tertianship*, the final stage of his training (1881–82), Hopkins wrote to Bridges that he intended to give up writing poetry for the ten months leading up to his final vows. This excuse would have been plausible if he had been in the habit of writing, but he was not. The absence of inspiration and general listlessness he wrote about before his death was already a problem for him: 'I therefore want to get things done first, but fear I never shall.'

Despite the fact that tertianship was like a second novitiate and the candidates were treated like schoolboys again (Hopkins was now thirty-seven) he delighted in the opportunity and time for meditation, prayer and seclusion. Significantly, his health was robust during his time there.

On 15 August 1882, after fourteen years of training, Hopkins took his final vows. A week later he left for Stonyhurst, where he would teach Greek, Latin and a little English to the 'Philosophers' – the academic elite who were preparing to take their B.A. The order was not yet sure how best to use Gerard Manley Hopkins.

1882–84: STONYHURST

I like my pupils and do not wholly dislike the work, but I fall into or continue in a heavy weary state of body and mind in which my go is gone . . . make no way with what I read, and seem but half a man . . .

I find myself so tired or so harassed I fear they [books he proposed to write] will never be written.

It is clear that Hopkins had more to contend with than a lack of inspiration. The listlessness he describes seems to have been frequent and cyclical – perhaps a form of manic depression. The feelings of guilt that accompanied his lack of endeavour served to depress him even further.

His Provincial (superior) liked Hopkins but was not sure what to do with him. 'I am trying him this year in coaching the B.A.s at Stonyhurst, but with fear and trembling.'

During his two years at Stonyhurst, Hopkins wrote three poems of any merit, all concerned with the destruction of beauty. He worried about being moved again:

It seems likely that I shall be moved; where I have no notion. But I have long been Fortune's football and am blowing up the bladder of resolution big and buxom for another kick of her foot. I shall be sorry to leave Stonyhurst; but go or stay, there is no likelihood of my ever doing anything to last. And I do not know how it is, I have no disease, but I am always tired, always jaded, though work is not heavy, and the impulse to do anything fails me or has in it no continuance.

To his surprise, he was not moved that year, and shortly after this letter he went on holiday with his family. When he returned he became acquainted with the poet Coventry Patmore. They corresponded frequently and acted as critics of each other's poetry. Patmore's comments on Hopkins's poetry are worth quoting.

It seems to me that the thought and feeling of these poems, if expressed without any obscuring novelty of mode, are such as often to require the whole attention to apprehend and digest them; and are therefore of a kind to appeal only to a few. But to the already sufficiently arduous character of such poetry you seem to me to have added the difficulty of following several entirely novel and simultaneous experiments in versification and construction, together with an altogether unprecedented system of alliteration and compound words – any one of which novelties would be startling and productive of distraction from the poetic matter to be expressed.

In a letter to Bridges, Patmore described the effect of Hopkins's poetry as 'of pure gold imbedded in masses of unpracticable quartz'.

At the end of January 1884 Hopkins was invited to become professor of Greek and Latin at University College in Dublin and a fellow of the Royal University of Ireland.

1884–89: DUBLIN

Hopkins was somewhat apprehensive about the honour that had been bestowed on him. He would have been even more anxious if he had known the circumstances of his appointment.

The Catholic University, founded by Newman a quarter of a century earlier, had been so unsuccessful that the hierarchy was only too happy when the Jesuits offered to take over the running of the college. Father William Delany was put in charge of the operation. His chief aim was 'by hook or by crook to put our College in front of Belfast' – not the loftiest of educational aspirations and one that Hopkins would have found utterly distasteful. Father Delany looked to the Jesuit order in England for highly qualified Jesuits who would raise the academic standards of the college, but the English Provincial was unwilling to lose those men, with the exception of Fr Hopkins. 'Fr Hopkins is very clever and a good scholar – but I should be doing you no kindness in sending you a man so eccentric.'

Delany offered the job to Hopkins, not least because his salary of £400 a year would be available for the running of the college (as Jesuits were not allowed to retain their salary or have money). The fact that he was English, and a convert, did not sit well with many of the influential figures in the clergy; but the appointment was made.

Hopkins was conscious of the fact that he was, once again, following in the footsteps of his mentor, John Henry Newman. 'I have been warmly welcomed and most kindly treated. But Dublin itself is a joyless place . . . I had fancied it quite different.'

Indeed it had been quite different a century earlier, when the aristocratic Anglo-Irish families presided over one of the finest cities in Europe. By the time of Hopkins's arrival they had moved to the suburbs, and the rising Catholic merchant class were putting their stamp on the city. It became as smoky as London; the Georgian town-houses were evolving rapidly into overcrowded tenements; and the Liffey provided the chief public sewer. The high death rate was due mainly to poor sanitation and a thriving rat population. At 85–86 St Stephen's Green, where Hopkins lived with his fellow-Jesuits, two rats were found in the stew-pot in the kitchen.

Hopkins had to set and correct six examinations for the whole university each year – between 1,300 and 1,800 scripts. Of the examinations he wrote:

I can not of course say that it is wholly useless, but I believe that most of it is and that I bear a burden which crushes me and does little to help any good end.

The physical and mental effort he put into these examinations contributed significantly to the deterioration in his state of mind during his time in Dublin.

He had to teach about a hundred arts undergraduates, most of whom had a utilitarian attitude to education, seeing it as a means to an end rather than an end in itself. Hopkins's style of teaching was based on the Oxford model, which encouraged students to enquire and to think for themselves. Not for the first time, Hopkins was subjected to ridicule. Admittedly he drew some of it upon himself. He declared that he would not examine any topic that he had taught in lecture; this, of course, meant that his lectures were 'not of much marketable value' (Humphry House). His declaration of disappointment at never having seen a naked woman produced a predictable response from his young students – predictable by everyone, perhaps, except Hopkins himself. There is the famous story of how a colleague entered the classroom and found Hopkins on the flat of his back, being dragged around the room by his students as he demonstrated how Hector had been dragged around the walls of Troy.

Hopkins's fellow-Jesuits found his frequent complaints, his Englishness and his eccentricities less than endearing. He was 'thought by most to be more or less crazy'.

He had one good friend in the community, Robert Curtis, a scholastic, who was not allowed to take final vows because of his epilepsy. His friendship was valuable at a time when his other two friends, Dixon and Bridges, were getting married – a reminder to Hopkins of his own isolated state.

> The reason of course why I like men to marry is that a single life is a difficult, not altogether a natural life; to make it easily manageable special provision, such as we [Jesuits] have, is needed, and most people cannot have this.

His letters to Bridges became more desperate. He felt that his life was wasting away, and that there was little enough to show for it. (The average life span of a Jesuit in the nineteenth century was forty-four.)

1885: THE 'TERRIBLE SONNETS'

> I think that my fits of sadness, though they do not affect my judgment, resemble madness . . . . I must absolutely have encouragement as much as crops rain . . . . I have after long silence written two sonnets, which I am touching: if ever anything was written in blood one of these was.

The 'Terrible Sonnets' or 'Sonnets of Desolation' are completely different from Hopkins's earlier religious poetry, because they are written by one who seemed to believe that God had abandoned him. Whether he had undergone a breakdown and had concealed his inner torment from colleagues it is difficult to know. The poems, however, provide an insight as no other poems do into what St John of the Cross called 'the dark night of the soul'.

One of these sonnets (not included in the anthology) is 'To Seem the Stranger Lies My Lot'. In this poem he laments the fact that he and his family have been separated by religion; that he and his nation have also been divided by his conversion to Catholicism; and that the division between him and his Irish colleagues has alienated him further.

> To seem the stranger lies my lot, my life
> Among strangers. Father and mother dear,
> Brothers and sisters are in Christ not near
> And he my peace/my parting, sword and strife.
> England, whose honour O all my heart woos, wife
> To my creating thought, would neither hear
> Me, were I pleading, plead nor do I; I wear-
> y of idle a being but by where wars are rife.
> I am in Ireland now; now I am at a third
> Remove. Not but in all removes I can
> Kind love both give and get. Only what word
> Wisest my heart breeds dark heaven's baffling ban
> Bars or hell's spell thwarts. This to hoard unheard,
> Heard unheeded, leaves me a lonely began.

It would seem that this was the first of the sonnets written and was followed by the two in the anthology.

No worst, there is none

Text of poem: New Explorations Anthology page 128

THEME

There is no known limit to suffering. There is no such thing as the 'worst', because the abyss of suffering has never been 'fathomed'; it is a bottomless pit.

DEVELOPMENT

The opening statement is dramatic, because of its brevity and its startling declaration that suffering has no boundary or limit. The poet feels that he has been 'pitched' or thrown beyond the limit of suffering. To make matters worse, he imagines the torments or 'pangs' as living creatures capable of giving instruction to the next generation of torments on how to inflict even more pain.

The violent impact of the imagery is strikingly supported by the use of alliteration and monosyllabic words. The suffering is not solely physical, however. The word 'pitch' is a richly suggestive one: it can refer to sound or colour. In the first instance the impression is created that mental torment manifests itself through a hypersensitivity to noise: in other words, every sound is magnified, as it seems to be when one has a headache. With this in mind, the echoing sounds of the first two lines ('p' and 'ng') convey a sense of the aural torment that accompanies mental suffering. In her poem 'I Felt a Funeral in My Brain', Emily Dickinson provides magnificent images of the aural dimension to nervous breakdown:

> And when they all were seated,
> A Service, like a Drum –
> Kept beating – beating – till I thought
> My Mind was going numb –

'Pitch' can also describe a type of blackness, a colour – or rather a non-colour – associated with a mood of despair. Hopkins was fascinated with words and their possible meanings. He showed great ingenuity in using words that had an impact on several levels. Here one word, 'pitch', appeals to three different senses: touch, hearing and sight.

The abrupt change from description to address adds to the drama of the poem. He challenges the Holy Ghost, who is supposed to bring comfort to those who are afflicted by suffering. The accusatory tone is heightened by the repetition of 'where'.

In the fourth line he turns to the Blessed Virgin and, again, implies that she has been a neglectful 'mother'. With the exception of the metaphysical religious poets of the seventeenth century, nowhere does one find such daring communication between humankind and God.

In the second quatrain the poet returns to description. He imagines his cries of pain, or perhaps cries for help, as a herd of cattle. Imagine for a moment the lopy, lugubrious appearance of cattle as they trundle home to the milking-parlour. What characteristics do they share with his cries? Are they pitiful? helpless? indistinguishable from each other? No person can declare with authority what Hopkins meant. You are invited to engage imaginatively with the poem and arrive at an intelligent conclusion. (To suggest that the common characteristic between the cries and the cattle is that they are both covered in mud would not be an *intelligent* conclusion. There may be no such thing as a right answer, but there are many wrong answers!)

'Heave' is an *onomatopoeic* word; its sound suggests the enormous physical effort involved in uttering the cries. 'Herds-long' emphasises the frequency. They 'huddle' together like cattle. If there is one particular source of grief it is 'world-sorrow'. The poet leaves it at that. His concern in this poem is not to deal with the causes of his suffering but rather to document the experience of suffering.

The image of sorrows beating against an anvil emphasises again the aural dimension of suffering. 'Wince and sing' is onomatopoeic. The anvil is presumably God's discipline, and on it lies the poet as a piece of metal.

> The two verbs ['wince and sing'], the first with its sense of human suffering combined with metallic vibration, the second with its sense of metallic vibration combined perhaps with human triumph, make the metal suffer as metal under the hammer, and the suffering metal is terribly vivid. We suffer with the metal under the blow, and we forget that the literal metal does not suffer, that metal and blow are figurative. (Yvor Winters)

When there comes a respite, a 'lull', Fury, the personification of punishment – probably a personification of guilt – denies him the opportunity for rest. In classical mythology the Furies were grotesque women whose purpose it was to torment the sinful. In other words, if the poet escapes from the suffering that comes from 'world-sorrow', he is set upon by the suffering that comes from within his own conscience. There is no 'lingering', no respite – no rest for the wicked, as we sometimes glibly say.

As one would expect from a Petrarchan sonnet, the tone of the sestet changes to one of reflection. The image of the mind as dramatic landscape, with high mountains and deep ravines, is vivid. It is quite common for people to speak of feeling 'high' or 'low'. Life is sometimes described as a 'valley of tears', or a 'roller-coaster ride'. Sometimes one can be 'on top of the world'. For a manic depressive the imagery would be particularly apt. Hopkins's cyclical moods would have brought him many 'highs' and 'lows'.

The ellipsis in the third quatrain is very effective in increasing the intensity of the statement. Compare it with a prose rendition: 'Oh, the mind, the mind has mountains. It has cliffs of falling that are frightful, sheer, and no-man-fathomed. Those who have never hung there may hold them cheaply.'

The inversion of the natural word order also serves to create a dramatic impact. One is reminded of Michael Paul Gallagher's reference at the Centenary Mass to 'his wrenching of words into unheard-of collusions, into compressions that echoed his own wrenched self.'

When one is suffering mental anguish, one does not worry about correct syntax. Hopkins reminds us that if we have never hung by the fingernails from the edge of a cliff with an abyss gaping below, we will not appreciate the sheer terror involved or, as Hopkins sparingly put it, 'Hold them cheap may who ne'er hung there.'

People cannot survive for long in this mental state; our 'durance' (endurance) cannot 'deal' with it. The only refuge is death or, more immediately, sleep. Hopkins seems to be grasping at any consolation he can find so as to escape from despair. The image he uses is of a lowly creature crawling under a rock during a whirlwind. The unrelieved bleakness of the poem is emphasised by the fact that the only hope lies with the suspension or obliteration of consciousness.

The poem is written in standard sonnet form, with strong 'sprung rhythm' effects.

I wake and feel the fell of dark

Text of poem: New Explorations Anthology page 130

No sooner does one read the title than one recognises that this acts as a sequel to the previous poem. The only consolation that could be found in the previous poem was in sleep; now the poet lies awake in the depths and darkness of the night.

'Fell' is another one of those words with several meanings. Darkness is like a wild animal whose fell, or hide, the poet feels – an eerie image. Darkness is a landscape in whose fell, or mountainous region, the poet wanders. Darkness is a mood whose fell, or cruelty and ruthlessness, torments him. Darkness is a creature whose fell, or blow, strikes the poet. All these readings of the word 'fell' combine to create a horrifying impression of the poet's experience of darkness. From his experience of daylight in the previous poem, we know that 'day' has its own 'fell' qualities.

In his discussion of this poem, F. R. Leavis wrote:

> This is characteristic Hopkins in its methods of compression and its elimination of all inessential words. There is the familiar use of assonance: 'feel' becomes 'fell', i.e. feeling becomes an obsessing sense of the overwhelming darkness . . . and the sequence 'night,' 'sights,' 'lights' suggest the obsessing horror of the night.

The poet makes dramatic use of exclamation and repetition in the second and third lines. The long vowel sounds and dragging repetition also contribute to the sense of anguish in 'What hours, O what black hours.' The address to his own heart serves to emphasise his loneliness and desolation as he waits for dawn to break. The heart is the witness that can be trusted: 'The heart is what rises towards good, shrinks from evil, recognising the good or evil first by some eye of its own' (Hopkins). The 'sights' and 'ways' undertaken during the night suggest the waking nightmares that he has experienced.

The opening statement of the second quatrain almost challenges the reader to dispute the authenticity of his account. It is a curious sentence, yet it adds to the manic quality in the poem. This torment that he is enduring has not just been the experience of a few hours, it has been going on for years; in fact his whole life has been cruel. His cries have been 'countless' and like 'dead letters sent to dearest him that lives, alas! away.' It is customary to read 'him' as a reference to God; however, it would seem natural for the poet to capitalise the word if this is what he meant. R. B. Martin has suggested that 'him' is a reference to Digby Dolben, a friend from Oxford, for whom Hopkins felt unmanageable emotions. 'I have written letters without end, without a whiff of answer,' he wrote regarding his attempts to correspond with Dolben. Not long after, Dolben died in a drowning accident.

> Here, and occasionally elsewhere in his poems, Hopkins seems deliberately to blur the dividing line between persons and Deity . . . as if to indicate the difficulty of distinguishing between his feelings for other men and those for Christ; we are inevitably reminded of Dolben, who often followed the same practice in his poems to Gosselin/Christ. (R. B. Martin)

The sestet is astonishing. It divides into two *tercets*. The poet gives a description of himself that seethes with self-disgust. He changed the phrase 'God's most deep decree' to 'God's most just decree', and then changed it back again. What is the difference? 'Just decree' expresses confidence that God knows what he is doing; 'deep decree' suggests that the poet has no understanding of God's purpose. His suffering is caused by having to live with himself. He is a vile 'curse', a sinful, slothful creature who has failed in his mission. It is the nature of damnation to have one's own senses torment one; here the torment is described in physical terms: tasting, scourging.

In the final tercet the 'Selfyeast of spirit' may refer to his will, which 'sours' a 'dull dough', which may refer to the body. He identifies himself with the 'lost' in Hell, because he feels he has been condemned; but there is the possibility of consolation in the final two words if we take it to mean that, unlike those in Hell, he is not condemned for eternity.

The fourth sonnet, 'Carrion Comfort', was probably written during a retreat at Clongowes Wood College in Co. Kildare. It strongly suggests that Hopkins battled with the thought of suicide. The fifth sonnet, 'My Own Heart Let Me More Have Pity On', reveals his acceptance of his lot. These five sonnets seem to chart an extraordinary mental journey, through profoundest torment and self-disgust to an eventual acceptance of life as it is lived. There is, of course, a possibility that these poems are not so much autobiographical as imaginary, some kind of Ignatian exercise. But their rawness and intensity makes that an unlikely possibility.

> The melancholy I have all my life been subject to has become of late years not indeed more intense in its fits but rather more distributed, constant, and crippling.
>
> One, the lightest but a very inconvenient form of it, is daily anxiety about work to be done, which makes me break off or never finish all that lies outside that work . . .
>
> All impulse fails me: I can give myself no sufficient reason for going on. Nothing comes: I am a eunuch – but it is for the kingdom of heaven's sake.

He declined an invitation to spend that Christmas at home with his family, preferring to stay at Clongowes Wood, in the hope that he would write. However, he did manage to visit his family in the summers of the next two years.

In September 1886 his spirits were so low that he was allowed a holiday in Wales with his friend Robert Curtis. These were the happiest two weeks of his time in Dublin. He also loved to escape from Dublin to Monasterevin, Co. Kildare, where he was a frequent guest of the Cassidy family. The suburb (then village) of Donnybrook was a short walk from Dublin and another refuge for Hopkins from the claustrophobic effect of city, colleagues and self.

Thou art indeed just, Lord
Text of poem: New Explorations Anthology page 132

Hopkins began the last New Year of his life at a retreat in Tullabeg, near Tullamore. His thoughts were preoccupied with the sense of being tired and useless.

> What is my wretched life? Five wasted years almost have passed in Ireland. I am ashamed of the little I have done, of my waste of time, although my helplessness and weakness is such that I could scarcely do otherwise . . . . All my undertakings miscarry: I am like a straining eunuch. I wish then for death: yet if I died now I should die imperfect, no master of myself, and that is the worst failure of all. O my God, look down on me.

It was customary for a Jesuit to repeat *'Justus es, Domine, et rectum judicium tuum'* (You are just, O Lord, and your judgment is right). This was intended to fortify one's spirits when life was difficult; it signifies that the individual accepts his cross and is offering it up to God. These thoughts and feelings evolved into the final poem in the anthology. It was written the following St Patrick's Day, a day on which an Englishman might feel particularly isolated in an Ireland that was looking for its independence. When he sent the poem to Bridges he suggested that it be read *'adagio molto'* – that is, very slowly and with great stress.

One preparation for St Ignatius's Spiritual Exercises is called a 'composition of person', in which one is expected to put oneself into the mind of another. In this case Hopkins is imagining himself to be the exiled Jeremiah of the Psalms. There is a dramatic quality in the impression created that the poet is like an advocate before a judge. The poem begins formally with the quotation from the Bible, but it quickly loses its formality, and the intensity of a real voice bursts through.

THEME

In the poem, Hopkins challenges God in a most humble yet provocative manner. God may be just, but the poet has justifiable cause for complaint. Why is it that the wicked seem to prosper, while those who devote their lives to God meet with nothing but obstacles and frustration? It is a universal and timeless complaint. The poem then moves from a concern with the prosperity of the wicked, in contrast to his lack of success, to a desperate plea for poetic inspiration, the absence of which is emphasised by the fruitfulness of the natural world that surrounds him. The first part of the poem is concerned with morality and justice, the second part with creativity.

DEVELOPMENT

The first quatrain is simply a translation from Jeremiah in the Vulgate (the Latin version of the Bible). It opens the argument in a formal manner. Yet the poet manages to invest some tension in the clipped monosyllabic diction of the second line and the inversion of natural word order that places the verb 'end' at the end of the line instead of after 'Disappointment'. The polysyllabic word 'disappointment' stands out from the words that precede it. There is a hint of frustration, despite the humility of the address to 'Lord' and 'sir'. The poet might well have had in mind the 'sinners' who surrounded him, rebellious and nationalistic Jesuits – to his way of thinking – deviously and unlawfully plotting against the government of England.

One can almost imagine the poet's voice rising in the second quatrain as he struggles to restrain his anger. The rhetorical use of antithesis in the line

> Wert thou my enemy, O thou my friend

cleverly illustrates the tension that exists between the servant's loyalty and the feeling that he is being abused.

The struggle between the two emotions becomes less manageable as the poem progresses. The exclamations and run-on lines build up the intensity of the poem. The extra syllable in line 7, the emphatic monosyllables and the 'spill' of octet into sestet serve to convey the idea that his frustration is bursting out of the sonnet straitjacket. 'Sir' at the beginning of the sestet acts almost as a temporary brake on his feelings. But the imperatives 'see' and 'look' heighten the sense of exasperation again as he points out that even vegetation and birds, which would have been in full flourish in mid-March, can enjoy the fruits of creation, while he exerts every sinew without anything to show for it.

The image of the eunuch is very powerful, precisely because of its sexual association, which is continued in the phrase 'not breed one work that wakes'. Not only was a eunuch incapable of breeding but he was a slave, usually employed in a harem. As an image of frustration it is most appropriate. The word 'work' most probably refers to poetic work, but he may also have in mind the academic projects that he never finished; or perhaps it applies more generally to anything that would mark his existence. Most people leave behind children; what will he have to show for his life?

> So with me, if I could but get on, if I could but produce work I should not mind its being buried, silenced, and going no further; but it kills me to be time's eunuch and never to beget. (Letter to Bridges, September 1885)

The final line of the poem is probably inspired by Jeremiah 17, which had been the Epistle for the Mass of the previous Sunday:

> Blessed be the man that trusted in the Lord and the Lord shall be his confidence. And he shall be as a tree that is planted by the waters, that spreadeth out his roots towards moisture and it shall not fear when the heat cometh.

The poet now prays for the 'waters' that God had promised.

What is fascinating about this poem is the fact that a man and priest of such great faith can speak so directly to God and become so angry with him. Never was the use of the sonnet form, with its highly disciplined format, more needed to restrain the intensely felt emotions that strain to become wild and irreverent. It is ironic that in fact he left behind quite a monument in the form of his poetry.

The end

'I am ill today, but no matter for that as my spirits are good,' Hopkins mentioned in passing in a letter to Bridges on 29 April 1885. Two days later he informed his mother that he thought he had rheumatic fever. On 8 May he told her it was 'a sort of typhoid'. No one else in the house caught the disease; in fact there was no typhoid at that time in the vicinity of St Stephen's Green. Six days later his family was notified of an improvement in his condition. On 5 June he took a turn for the worse, and his family was summoned. Having complained virulently over minor ailments, Hopkins was 'the placidest soul in the world' when faced with terminal illness.

His dying words were 'I am so happy, I am so happy.' Norman White suggests that this exclamation of joy in the face of death was a tradition among the Jesuits, rather than a sincere expression of happiness at the prospect of leaving this life and meeting his maker. We will never know for certain what Hopkins intended with these words.

The obituary read: '1889. On the eighth day of June, the vigil of Pentecost, weakened by a fever, he rested. May he rest in peace. He had a most subtle mind, which too quickly wore out the fragile strength of his body.' He was buried in Glasnevin Cemetery in a plot reserved for Jesuits.

The death column of the *Nation* made reference to Hopkins's scholarship in classics, philology, literature and art but of course made no reference to his poetry, because, outside a small coterie of friends, he was unknown as a poet. Hopkins had told Bridges that he was content to leave the fate of his poems in the hands of God, but the immediate responsibility lay with Bridges himself, since he was in possession of them. Bridges, however, was not yet wholly convinced of their quality; he felt they were too strange for public tastes. He decided to print privately a small collection, for family and friends; but the idea never materialised. In 1893 he submitted eight of the poems for an anthology of nineteenth-century poetry. A review of the book in the *Manchester Guardian* read: 'Curiosities like the verses of the late Gerard Hopkins should be excluded.'

In 1909 Katherine Bregy wrote a favourable essay on his poetry in *Catholic World*; three years later the essay was reprinted in *The Poet's Chantry*.

> [His] exceedingly delicate and intricate craftsmanship – and not less the singularity of his mental processes – must, indeed, produce in many minds an impression of artificiality. Yet . . . in all the poems of his manhood there is a poignant, even a passionate sincerity . . . his chances of survival are excellent.

Others began to reassess Hopkins's work in the light of Bregy's comments. In 1916 Bridges included a further six poems in *The Spirit of Man*, an anthology designed to lift spirits during the Great War. The response was very positive. Bridges decided it was time to publish all the poems. The book, he told A. E. Housman, 'will be one of the queerest in the world, but it is full of genius and poetic beauty and will find its place'.

Thus the poems of Gerard Manley Hopkins came to public knowledge at a time when originality and technical experimentation were becoming fashionable; and they found their place.

Critical comments on Hopkins

INSCAPE, HAECCITAS, INSTRESS

(It is not essential to have an understanding of these concepts to appreciate the poetry of Hopkins. If your reading of this section enhances your understanding of the poet's work, then it is worth reading; otherwise, it is a hindrance.)

What you look hard at seems to look hard at you.

When Hopkins was at Oxford he began to explore theories of perception. He copied into his notebook an extract from an essay on Wordsworth by J. C. Shairp:

Each scene in nature has in it a power of awakening, in every beholder of sensibility, an impression peculiar to itself, such as no other scene can exactly call up. This may be called the 'heart' or 'character' of that scene.

In our modern world we are familiar with the idea of each human being having a unique genetic code. Hopkins's theory was that everything in God's creation had its own unique characteristics. If an onlooker observes an object intensely and has the sensitivity to recognise its unique character, *haeccitas* or 'this-ness' – that which makes it itself – the object will reveal its 'inscape' or, if you like, its inner landscape. The observer reaches a point of intimacy with the object so that he feels as if he is within it, becoming both the observer and the observed. Finding the object's form and shape, both external and internal, is the same as finding its inscape. One of the reasons Hopkins abandoned the idea of being an artist was that he found that he could not 'capture' the inscape of things in his drawings.

'Instress' is the energy of God pulsating through all created things ('The world is charged with the grandeur of God'). It is a coherent force, coherent because it comes from a single source. He sees the inscape and feels the instress. 'All things are upheld by instress and are meaningless without it.'

Essentially, what Hopkins was attempting to do with the words 'instress' and 'inscape' was to provide a theory on the way in which objects, natural or human, create a reaction in the person who is looking at them. He believed that what he saw was contained in the object rather than a result of his imaginative interpretation of that object. He believed that the impact of that object on him was due to the object rather than to his subjective response to it. 'I thought how sadly beauty of inscape was unknown and buried away from simple people and yet how near at hand it was if they had eyes to see it.'

As a Jesuit he would have been taught to distinguish between the natural and the supernatural. Emboldened by the teachings of Duns Scottus, he saw the two as one. In his journals he described a bluebell:

> I do not think I have ever seen anything more beautiful than the bluebell I have been looking at. I know the beauty of our Lord by it. It is strength and grace, like an ash.

(The passage continues with a detailed description of the unique characteristics of the bluebell.)

This is its inscape. The impact of the bluebell on the poet is its instress. Even if there is no impact on the viewer, the object still possesses its inscape, because it is not dependent on being seen. In other words, in Hopkins's mind it has an objective reality. There lies behind his theory the Platonic idea that this world is an imperfect reflection of an ideal world, and that we are sometimes blessed with glimpses of that ideal world. It was the duty of the artist to give to the work of art that 'life' that exists in the original subject. The purpose of poetry was to 'carry the inscape', or to capture it.

'The Windhover' provides an excellent example of these concepts. The effort to describe the bird goes beyond mere description of its physical form or appearance ('wimpling wing'): there is almost a scientific attempt to 'capture' its movements ('Of the rolling level underneath him steady air'). This, however, is only part of the process. The inner form of the bird, its virtues or strengths, are identified ('Brute beauty and valour and act, oh, air, pride, plume'). There is more. The hidden 'meaning' or symbolic significance of the falcon is uncovered in a moment of mystical recognition that Joyce would call an 'epiphany'. T. S. Eliot called it 'the intersection of the timeless with time.' It is the moment when the observer recognises God's plan for humankind in the actions of a bird in flight.

When he was at Roehampton, Hopkins became quite emotional over the felling of an ash tree. He wrote: 'I heard the sound and looking out and seeing it maimed there came at that moment a great pang and I wished to die and not see the inscapes of the world destroyed any more.' Individuality is irreplaceable.

Can you imagine, therefore, what Hopkins thought of the Industrial Revolution, with its emphasis on mass production and the reduction of people to cogs in a machine on an assembly line? Can you imagine what he would think of a world where species of animals and plants are becoming extinct at a frightening rate?

SPRUNG RHYTHM

> His prosodic account in terms of Logaoedic Rhythm, Counterpoint Rhythm, Sprung Rhythm, Rocking Feet and Outriders will help no one to read his verse. (F. R. Leavis)

It is important to have a grasp of poetic rhythm; but it is not essential to have a detailed understanding of sprung rhythm. Pupils have in the past memorised pages of notes on the complexities of it in the misguided notion that it was 'required for the exam'. Poetic rhythm attempts to impose regularity on the rhythm of language. For example, a sonnet is normally written in *iambic pentameters* – that is, it has ten syllables per line, divided into five *feet*. Each foot consists of two syllables. The standard rhythm of the iambic pentameter is: de-*dum* | de-*dum* | de-*dum* | de-*dum* | de-*dum* – for example, 'That time | of year | thou mayst | in me | behold' (Shakespeare).

If the whole poem were to be written in exactly the same rhythm the effect would become extremely monotonous. Therefore, poets vary the combination of stressed and unstressed syllables. In the same poem by Shakespeare the line

> Bare rulined choirs | where late | the sweet | birds sang
> (*dum-dum* | de-*dum* | de-*dum* | de-*dum* | *dum-dum*)

startles the reader, because it diverges so much from the standard rhythm of the previous lines. In this way a poet can use variations from the standard rhythm to achieve certain effects. In the line above, the frequent stresses make the line seem 'heavy', adding to the pathos of the image.

Poetic rhythm is 'an adjustment between a yearning for repetition and regularity, and a need to work variations upon them' (R. B. Martin). If there is no regularity there is no scope for improvisation ('like playing tennis without a net' in the words of Robert Frost). Sprung rhythm is an attempt to 'loosen' the rules further in order to allow the poet a greater freedom.

By the time Hopkins's poetry was published, many poets had already begun to dispense with regularity and rules anyway; nevertheless Hopkins's revolutionary experiments with rhythm inspired many modern poets to be more daring and unconventional in their approach to composition. Of 'The Wreck of the Deutschland' Hopkins wrote: 'I had long had haunting my ear the echo of a new rhythm which now I realised on paper.' He called this new rhythm 'sprung rhythm', because it springs naturally. It has the following characteristics:

1. There is a fixed number of *feet* (rhythmic units) per line.

2. Each foot has one stressed syllable.

3. The stressed syllable may stand on its own, or may be accompanied by any number of slack (unstressed) syllables.

Hopkins summed it up concisely when he wrote: 'One stress makes one foot, no matter how many or how few the syllables.'

He employed sprung rhythm because 'It is the nearest to the rhythm of prose, that is the native and natural rhythm of speech.' He added that 'My verse is less to be read than heard . . . . It is oratorical, that is the rhythm is so.'

One of the most important consequences of allowing any number of unstressed syllables in a line is that it generates energy. Unstressed syllables must be uttered quickly. The more there are in a line, the more energetic the line will be. This has a clear value for a poet who sees the world of nature as charged with the energy of God.

Sprung rhythm is used most blatantly in 'As Kingfishers Catch Fire' and 'The Windhover', both of which vibrate with the energy of the natural world.

> I caught this morning morning's minion, king-
> (de-*dum* de-*dum* de-*dum* de-*dum* de-*dum*)
> dom of daylight's dauphin, dapple-dawn-drawn Falcon, in
> (de-de-*dum* de-*dum* de-de-de-*dum* de-*dum* de-de)
> his riding
> (de-*dum*-de)

'Felix Randal' also employs sprung rhythm extensively; other poems contain elements of it.

The complexities of the explanations above can be simplified as follows: Hopkins believed in the idea of incarnation. Christ was both man and God; so, too, the world is a combination of the material and the divine. Seeing the divine in the world is the same as seeing its inscape. Feeling the divine presence is the same as feeling its instress. Sprung rhythm is a poetic device used to reveal the energy of God that pulses through the world. *Haeccitas* is the uniqueness of every object's way of revealing God.

ON HIS OBSCURITY

> The blemishes [of Hopkins's style] . . . may be called Oddity and Obscurity; and since the first may provoke laughter when a writer is serious (and this poet is always serious), while the latter must prevent him from being understood (and this poet has always something to say), it may be assumed that they were not a part of his intention. Here, then, is

another source of the poet's obscurity; that in aiming at condensation he neglects the need that there is for care in the placing of words that are grammatically ambiguous. English swarms with words that have one identical form for substantive [noun], adjective, and verb; and such a word should never be so placed as to allow of any doubt as to what part of speech it is used for; because such ambiguity or momentary uncertainty destroys the force of the sentence. Now our author not only neglects this essential propriety but he would seem even to welcome and seek artistic effect in the consequent confusion; and he will sometimes so arrange such words that a reader looking for a verb may find that he has two or three ambiguous monosyllables from which to select, and must be in doubt as to which promises best to give any meaning that he can welcome; and then, after his choice is made, he may be left with some homeless monosyllables still on his hands. (Robert Bridges)

F. R. Leavis, in a commentary on the passage quoted above, wrote:

A great deal is too readily assumed here: it is possible to put the readers of Hopkins too much at their ease. The 'obscurity' is . . . intended. The 'oddity' . . . Hopkins was aware of; but he felt that too big a price might be paid for the approval of [traditional readers]. What Dr. Bridges calls 'blemishes' are essential to Hopkins's aim and achievement . . . . He aimed to get out of his words as much as possible unhampered by the rules of grammar, syntax, and common usage. But to the late Dr. Bridges, as to so many people, these rules were ends in themselves.

. . . He had positive uses for ambiguity, and he presumed to expect from the reader prolonged and repeated intellectual effort . . . .

If we could deceive ourselves into believing that we were reading easily, his purpose would be defeated; for every word in one of his important poems is doing a great deal more work than almost any word in a poem of Robert Bridges. [Ouch!]

No doubt my poetry errs on the side of oddness . . . but as air, melody, is what strikes me most of all in music and design in painting, so design, pattern, or what I am in the habit of calling inscape, is what I above all aim at in poetry. Now it is the virtue of design, pattern, or inscape to be distinctive and it is the vice of distinctiveness to become queer. This vice I cannot have escaped . . . but take breath and read it with the ears, as I always wish to be read, and my verse becomes all right . . .

I had long had haunting my ear the echo of a new rhythm which now [in 'The Wreck of the Deutschland'] I realised on paper . . . . I do not say the idea is altogether new . . . but no one has professedly used it and made it the principle throughout, that I know of . . . . However, I had to mark the stresses . . . and a great many more oddnesses could but dismay an editor's eye, so that when I offered it to our magazine, The Month . . . . They dared not print it . . .

The effect of studying masterpieces is to make me admire and do otherwise. So it must be on every original artist to some degree, on me to a marked degree. (Gerard Manley Hopkins)

The prescription he gives when warm from reading his verse – 'take breath and read it with the ears' . . . – is a great deal more to the point, and if we add 'and with the brains and the body' it suffices.

His words and phrases are actions as well as sounds, ideas and images, and must, as I have said, be read with the body as well as with the eye: that is the force of his concern to be read aloud. (F. R. Leavis)

The poem which is absolutely original is absolutely bad; it is in the bad sense, 'subjective' with no relation to the world to which it appeals . . .

Originality, in other words, is by no means a simple idea in the criticism of poetry. True originality is merely development. (T. S. Eliot)

An overview of Hopkins's poetry

THEMES AND ISSUES: MAIN POINTS

Nature
• The world of Nature pulses with energy because it is charged with the grandeur of God.
• Spring is a glimpse of what the Garden of Eden must have been like.
• Everything in existence has its own unique identity and inscape. It is possible to recognise God's design in every natural object.
• The Ruskinian method of observing natural objects in minute detail establishes a way of seeing and consequently a way of relating to the natural object.
• Contrast (dappled things) and variety set off the beauty of things.
• Unspoilt nature (the weeds and the wilderness) is a precious resource.
• Humankind's sinfulness and the Industrial Revolution have made us insensitive to the beauty and preciousness of the natural world.
• Despite the destructive activities of humankind, the Holy Ghost protects and renews the natural world.

Suffering and alienation
• Humankind's sinfulness brings it suffering and toil.
• Acceptance of God's will brings comfort and relief from pain.

- Spiritual desolation is a bottomless pit of suffering.
- The worst form of suffering, outside of Hell, is the desolation caused by self-disgust.
- Suffering is a mystery understood fully by God alone.

Relationship between people and God
- God makes himself known to us through the world of nature and in the faces of people.
- He is the 'dearest freshness' that permeates the natural world.
- Only through the submission of our own will to the will of God can we truly reveal our inner beauty.
- God has given us the gift of natural beauty, with all its variety.
- Humans are insignificant beings who have been rescued from death and oblivion by the sacrifice by Christ on the cross.
- God's will is a mystery to us.

STYLE

In order to have a full appreciation of a poet's work one must have some sense of how the poet communicates *theme*. There are two aspects to understanding style: (*a*) the poetic devices employed by the poet, and (*b*) the effect achieved by the use of these devices.

> It is not as mere musical effects (if such were possible in poetry) – melody, harmony, counterpoint – that these devices are important; they are capable of use for expressing complexities of feeling, the movement of consciousness, difficult and urgent states of mind. (F. R. Leavis)

SUMMARY OF POETIC DEVICES
Sprung rhythm
– allows greater freedom
– adds energy
– is closer to ordinary speech.

Ellipsis
– creates a greater concentration of meaning
– conveys an intensity of emotion (excitement or suffering)
– creates energy.

Inversion
– makes demands on the reader's concentration
– contributes to originality of expression and freshness of language

– allows for dramatic juxtaposition of words, phrases, images
– conveys intensity of emotion
– creates energy.

Alliteration and assonance
– produce characteristic sound patterns (influenced by the *cynghanedd* tradition
in Welsh literature)
– link words together
– create energy.

Coined words: nouns, adjectives, verbs
– contribute to originality of expression, freshness of language
– create a greater concentration of meaning
– create the dramatic impact of the unfamiliar.

Exclamations
– convey emotional intensity
– add dramatic quality.

Condensation of meaning
– creates obscurity
– makes demands on the reader's concentration
– creates intensity.

Colloquialisms
– contribute to originality and freshness of language
– add local colour.

Variety of language and imagery
– provides pleasure!
– emphasises the startling originality of the poet.

Onomatopoeia
– contributes to the wonderful sound patterns
– adds energy
– emphasises the aural quality of the poems.

*Tension between restrictions of the sonnet form and the poet's liberal
interpretation of it*
– points to the central tension in his life and work.

Energetic, intense, concentrated in meaning, obscure, tortuous, original, musical, dramatic, oratorical, erudite, demanding . . .

Developing a personal response

1. What impression of Hopkins the man do you get from his poetry?
2. Is it necessary to admire the author to admire his work?
3. Does the poet's profound faith make it easier or more difficult for you to relate to his work?
4. If you had the opportunity to interview Hopkins, what questions would you ask him?
5. Does biographical knowledge enhance your enjoyment of Hopkins's poetry, or is it of no significance?
6. What do you like or dislike about the way Hopkins writes poetry?
7. Do you think that the themes of his poetry have relevance in the modern world?
8. Which lines, images or phrases from Hopkins's poems do you remember most? Explain why they are memorable for you.
9. Put together an argument as to why Hopkins's poetry should be retained on, or removed from, the Leaving Certificate course.

The Gerard Manley Hopkins International Summer School takes place every year in Monasterevin, Co. Kildare, in the last week of July (website: http://www.iol.ie/~Hopkins).

Questions

1. What are the central themes of Hopkins's poetry?
2. What are the central features of his poetic style?
3. 'Extremes of emotion, from ecstasy to despair, are what make Hopkins's poetry so interesting.' Do you agree?
4. Hopkins has been called 'the poet of energy'. How does the poet create this energy in his poems?
5. 'The language of Hopkins's poetry is vigorous, sensuous, and intensely spiritual.' Discuss.
6. 'In a Hopkins poem, every word has a stringent part to play in the creation of meaning.' Discuss.
7. 'No doubt my poetry errs on the side of oddness.' Is Hopkins's poetry too 'odd' to be enjoyable?

8. 'This is a poet who celebrates unique identities and experiences, their meaning and their value.' Discuss.
9. 'To be a "devotional poet" is a limitation: a saint limits himself by writing poetry, and a poet who confines himself to even this subject matter is limiting himself too.' Do you agree?
10. 'Hopkins's poetry presents us with a deeply personal and passionate response to the world and its creator.' Discuss.
11. 'Complexity of thought and novelty in the use of language sometimes create an apparent obscurity in the poetry of Hopkins.' Discuss.
12. 'Hopkins does not allow the brevity of the sonnet form to hinder the expression of his complex themes, and he uses its intimacy to give effective expression to all his moods.' Discuss
13. 'Language, rhythm and imagery are forged into an exciting mode of expression in the poetry of Hopkins.' Discuss.

Bibliography

Davies, Walford (editor), *Poetry and Prose: Gerard Manley Hopkins,* London: J. M. Dent 1998.

Gardner, W. (editor), *Gerard Manley Hopkins: Poems and Prose,* Harmondsworth (Middx): Penguin Books 1971.

Hartman, Geoffrey (editor), *Twentieth-Century Views: Hopkins,* New York: Prentice Hall 1966.

House, Humphry, and Storey, Graham (editors), *The Journals and Papers of Gerard Manley Hopkins,* London: Oxford University Press 1959.

Martin, Graham, and Furbank, P. N. (editors), *Twentieth-Century Poetry: Critical Essays and Documents,* Milton Keynes: Open University Press 1975.

Martin, Robert Bernard, *Gerard Manley Hopkins: A Very Private Life,* London: Fontana 1992.

Milward, Peter, and Schoder, Raymond, *Landscape and Inscape: Vision and Inspiration in Hopkins's Poetry,* London: Elek 1975.

Studies (annual G. M. Hopkins issues), summer 1995, 1996, 1997.

Sundermeier, Michael (editor), *Hopkins Annual, 1992.*

Weyand, Norman (editor), *Immortal Diamond: Studies in Gerard Manley Hopkins,* New York: Octagon Books 1969.

White, Norman, *Hopkins: A Literary Biography,* Oxford: Clarendon Press 1992.

4   *William Butler* YEATS

John G. Fahy

A *literary life*

Williamilliam Butler Yeats was born on 13 June 1865 at number 1
Sandymount Avenue, Dublin, a son of John Butler Yeats and Susan
Pollexfen. John Butler Yeats originated from Co. Down, where his
father was Church of Ireland rector and whose father before him had been
rector at Drumcliff, Co. Sligo. The Butler part of the family name came from an
eighteenth-century marriage to a relative of the Butlers of Ormonde, one of the
oldest Anglo-Irish families. That marriage brought with it the more tangible
asset of a few hundred acres of land in Co. Kildare, the rents from which
continued to provide a measure of financial support for the family until the land
had to be sold in 1886.

John Butler Yeats had trained as a barrister before his marriage but decided
to become an artist instead, and in 1867 the family moved to London so that he
could study painting. This was the first move of a peripatetic childhood and
youth for the young William, as the family moved from one house to another in
London or between London and Dublin in pursuit of the father's artistic career,
which never really became financially viable.

William was the eldest surviving child, followed by Susan Mary (called Lily),
Elizabeth Corbet (called Lollie), and John Butler (Jack) – all born within six
years of each other. Their mother, Susan Pollexfen, was the daughter of a
wealthy merchant and shipping family from Co. Sligo; and when John Butler
Yeats got into financial difficulties the family spent a good deal of time there,
which the poet remembered with great affection. So a good deal of Yeats's
childhood and youth was spent in an atmosphere of genteel poverty, supported
by better-off relatives.

He was educated at the Godolphin School, London, 1875–80; the High
School, Dublin, 1880–83; and the Metropolitan School of Art, Dublin, 1884–
86. At first the young Yeats found it difficult to learn to read, and when by the
age of seven or eight he still could not distinguish all the letters of the alphabet,
his father is reputed to have thrown the reading book at him in a rage. In later
life Yeats's spelling continued to be idiosyncratic, supporting the later conclusion
that he suffered from dyslexia. As it was unlikely that he would pass the
entrance examination for Trinity College, his father's old university, he was

tutored to some extent by his father, who regarded himself as the young man's chief mentor, and was therefore largely self-educated. Consequently his acquaintances and readings assumed a very significant role in his development.

Among the people introduced to him by his father was the old Fenian John O'Leary, and this sparked off an interest in nationalism, particularly as a subject for poetry. He was influenced also by the writings of Douglas Hyde, Katherine Tynan and Samuel Ferguson, as well as James Clarence Mangan's versions of Irish poems. But it was probably the histories and the fiction of Standish O'Grady that most impelled Yeats to investigate Irish mythology. At this time he was fascinated by the folk tales, fairy tales and supernatural beliefs found in Co. Sligo and Co. Galway, which resulted in the collection *Fairy and Folk Tales of the Irish Peasantry* (1888). He also wanted to reformulate in English the old Irish legends and so re-create Ireland's lost intellectual and cultural heritage. This found expression in his collection of poetry *The Wanderings of Oisín* (1889).

At this time also Yeats began to search for alternative philosophies to Christianity, such as Buddhism, magic, spiritualism and astrology. Influenced to some degree no doubt by his discussions with his friend George Russell, the poet, he began to explore mysticism and the occult, often through the practices of esoteric groups and cults. Among these were the theosophists (through whom he encountered the notorious Elena Blavatsky), who believed that knowledge of God could be achieved through spiritual ecstasy and direct intuition. He became involved also with the 'Hermetic Order of the Golden Dawn', a Rosicrucian order that practised ritual demonstrations of psychic power, which he joined in 1890. The Golden Dawn was based on the desire for alchemical change – the transformation of people into gods, the possibility of transforming the world. Yeats became quite dedicated to the practice of magic, believed in the evocation of spirits, and indeed was convinced that he himself was a magician.

Among the principal beliefs that he subscribed to were:
• that the borders of our minds are ever shifting and that minds can melt and flow into each other, creating a single entity or 'Great Mind';
• that there is a 'World Soul' or shared memory in nature;
• that the Great Mind can be evoked by symbols, which Yeats introduced into poetry in order to access truths.

He learnt a great deal about symbolism from Shelley and Blake. Symbols reveal themselves in a state of trance. He felt that the purpose of rhythm in poetry is to create meditative rhythms in which the mind is lulled into a state of trance. So, when poetry is working well it operates like a mantra or chant, helping us to see past the ordinary. Yeats believed that 'simple' people (those who were considered fools), ascetics and women can see beyond modern culture into the world of magical truths.

Yeats also believed that Celticism was the remnant of a former world religion, that the occult is really the remnant of this old religion or magic, and that Ireland is the place where it can best be contacted. So Celticism and the occult are important and connected twin pillars of his poetic philosophy.

During the 1890s Yeats's poetry developed from simple pastoral poetry and verses about fairy tales to the use of cycles of mythology of Ulster and the Fianna. He introduced heroes from these tales into his poetry: Cú Chulainn, Méabh, Deirdre and others. He began to use the Celtic material in a visionary way to create mystical poetry, which culminated in the volume *The Wind Among the Reeds* (1899).

Women were important in Yeats's life, and he had a number of troublesome and tempestuous love affairs. Of all the women he encountered two were to be most influential: Maud Gonne and Lady Augusta Gregory. The former, whom he met in the late 1880s, was the source of passionate romantic involvement and disappointment for him over the succeeding three decades; but she was also the inspiration for some of his work, such as the play *The Countess Kathleen*, was a frequent reference point in his poetry, and was the focus for some of his ideas on nationalism, women in politics, the aesthetic, ageing and others.

He first met Lady Gregory in 1894, and from 1897 onwards her home, Coole Park, near Gort, Co. Galway, was a summer refuge from his somewhat nomadic life. As well as helping him collect folk tales she provided both psychological and financial support and the opportunity to meet other writers, such as George Russell, George Bernard Shaw, George Moore and Edward Martyn.

Lady Gregory, Yeats and Martyn were the principal co-founders of the Irish Literary Theatre. Their manifesto clearly outlines the driving philosophy and ambition of the movement.

> We propose to have performed in Dublin in the spring of every year certain Celtic and Irish plays, which whatever be their degree of excellence will be written with a high ambition, and so to build up a Celtic and Irish school of dramatic literature. We hope to find in Ireland an uncorrupted and imaginative audience trained to listen by its passion for oratory, and believe that our desire to bring upon the stage the deeper thoughts and emotions of Ireland will ensure for us a tolerant welcome, and that freedom to experiment which is not found in the theatres of England, and without which no new movement in art or literature can succeed. We will show that Ireland is not the home of buffoonery and of easy sentiment, as it has been represented, but the home of an ancient idealism. We are confident of the support of all Irish people, who are weary of misrepresentation, in carrying out a work that is outside all the political questions that divide us.

Eventually this movement led to the founding of the Abbey Theatre,

Dublin, in 1904, where Yeats was manager from 1904 to 1910. But the public did not always appreciate the movement's artistic vision. There was adverse reaction to Yeats's play *The Countess Kathleen*; and in 1907 John Millington Synge's play *The Playboy of the Western World* sparked off riots in the theatre. Yeats was deeply disillusioned by this lack of understanding and aesthetic appreciation, a feeling that was deepened by the controversy over the Hugh Lane proposal. This disillusionment is reflected in his poetry *The Green Helmet* (1910), *Responsibilities* (1914) and *The Wild Swans at Coole* (1917). In contrast, his visit to Italy in 1907 with Lady Gregory and her son, Robert, pointed up the difference between the mob in Ireland and what it had been possible to create through aristocratic patronage in Florence and Ravenna.

The Easter Rising of 1916 forced Yeats to rethink his view of Irish society, as we see in the poem 'Easter 1916'. These years ushered in other decisive changes for Yeats. After a final round of marriage proposals to Maud Gonne and then to her adopted daughter, Iseult, he settled into marriage with Georgina Hyde-Lees on 20 October 1917. The marriage produced two children and much-needed domestic stability for Yeats. And, whether by chance or design, it also produced the 'automatic writing' created by his wife, who, while in a sort of trance, transcribed the words of certain spirit guides or instructors. This seemed to offer a new system of thought to Yeats, incorporating themes of change within a new view of history, which he developed in his book *A Vision* (1925).

The central idea of his philosophy was that civilisation was about to reverse itself and a new era of anti-civilisation was about to be ushered in. The signs of this were everywhere: in mass movements in Europe, in the rise of communism, fascism, etc. Yeats examined change against the backdrop of world history. In his review of history he noticed that certain eras favoured the development of human excellence in art and learning and also produced social harmony: Athens of the fifth century BC, Byzantium, the Italian Renaissance – all of which developed political culture and artistic culture and in general fostered human achievement, creating what Yeats termed 'unity of being'. These eras were separated by a thousand years, each reaching its peak about five hundred years after it replaced the previous 'millennium'. There were two main forces at work: what Yeats called 'anti-thetical' energies, which created this unity of being, and the opposite force, which he termed 'primary' energy. These two energies grew or waned in their turn over the course of each millennium.

Yeats represented this theory of change by the symbolism of the 'gyres', two interpenetrating cones (see page 131), one primary and the other anti-thetical, each growing or decreasing in strength as the centuries pass. He felt that his own time was now reaching the end of the primary gyre and that the growing violence on the Continent and in Ireland was an indicator of its imminent collapse, to be replaced by a new anti-thetical gyre. This is the philosophical background to the bleak view he took of the current fractious age in the volumes *Michael Robartes and the Dancer* (1921) and, in particular, *The Tower* (1928). See in particular his poems 'The Second Coming', 'Sailing to Byzantium' and 'Meditations in Time of Civil War'.

This philosophy, which had as its central belief the notion that the times were out of joint and that cataclysmic changes were about to happen, may help to explain Yeats's flirtation with extreme political philosophies and movements: for example, his consideration of fascism, his exploration of the place of violence in politics, his scepticism about democracy and his preference for the political model of Renaissance prince–ruler (a model that cast the Anglo-Irish gentry in a similar role), and his engagement with theories of eugenics.

This search for solutions, for paradigms of thought and models for living, continued into the poet's old age, but it took more conventional forms in his volume *The Winding Stair and Other Poems* (1933). Here we find many elegies – to dead friends, to past times and to other more unified eras, such as the eighteenth century, from which Yeats took his chief model, Jonathan Swift, whom he wished to emulate as poet–statesman.

Indeed, he was pursuing that ideal in his role as a senator in the new Irish Free State. He devoted much energy to his work in the new senate, which first sat on 11 December 1922 and of which he was a member until 1928. During 1923, for instance, he spoke nineteen times on such subjects as law enforcement, manuscripts, the Lane pictures, film censorship and Irish, and he continued over the years to contribute on issues such as partition, divorce and the new coinage. In 1922 the University of Dublin conferred an honorary doctorate on him, and he was similarly honoured by the Universities of Oxford and Cambridge in 1931 and 1933, respectively. But the crowning international recognition was the award of the Nobel Prize for Literature in 1923.

In the late 1920s and early 1930s Yeats experienced a number of health problems, and the family began to spend more time in the sunnier regions of southern Europe. The house at 82 Merrion Square, Dublin, was sold and exchanged for a flat in Fitzwilliam Square. In 1933 Yeats took himself out of the city altogether when the family took a long lease on a house, 'Riversdale', in Rathfarnham, 'just too far from Dublin to go there without good reason and too far, I hope, for most interviewers and the less determined travelling bores'. (See 'An Acre of Grass'.) But he continued to write, indeed with renewed vigour, and *New Poems* was published in 1938. His last public appearance was at the Abbey Theatre in August 1938. He died on 28 January 1939 at Roquebrune in the south of France; in 1948 his body was re-interred, as he had wished, in Drumcliff churchyard.

PRINCIPAL VOLUMES OF POETRY	**Poems in this selection**
The Wanderings of Oisín (1889)	
Crossways (1889)	
The Rose (1893)	– 'The Lake Isle of Innisfree'
The Wind Among the Reeds (1899)	
The Green Helmet and Other Poems (1910)	
Responsibilities (1914)	– 'September 1913'
The Wild Swans at Coole (1917; second edition 1919)	– 'The Wild Swans at Coole'
	– 'An Irish Airman Foresees His Death'
Michael Robartes and the Dancer (1921)	– 'Easter 1916'
	– 'The Second Coming'
The Tower (1928)	– 'Sailing to Byzantium'
	– 'Meditations in Time of Civil War'
The Winding Stair and Other Poems (1933)	– 'In Memory of Eva Gore-Booth and Con Markiewicz'
	– 'Swift's Epitaph'
A Full Moon in March (1935)	
New Poems (1938)	– 'An Acre of Grass'
Last Poems (1939)	– 'Under Ben Bulben'
	– 'Politics'

Note: The edition of the poems used in this anthology is *Yeats's Poems*, edited by A. Norman Jeffares (Basingstoke: Macmillan, 1989).

The Lake Isle of Innisfree

Text of poem: New Explorations Anthology page 137

[*Note: This poem is also prescribed for Ordinary Level 2006 exam*]

This poem was written in 1888, when Yeats was living in London, where he was unhappy and homesick for Ireland. A somewhat altered version was first published in the *National Observer* in December 1890, to much acclaim; this really was the poem that first made Yeats's name. It is included in the collection *The Rose* (1893).

Yeats had been greatly influenced by the vision of self-sufficiency in nature found in Henry David Thoreau's book *Walden* (1854), which his father had read to him. And he too dreamed of living alone in nature in a quest for wisdom. This was a theme he explored not just in verse but in his prose writings also, an indication of the pervasive autobiographical nature of the quest. For instance, there are close similarities between this poem and the scenario in *John Sherman*, a novel Yeats had written in 1887–88, in which a young Sligo man who had left home in search of a fortune and was now homesick in London recalls an island on a lake where he used to pick blackberries. He dreams of returning there, building a wooden hut, and listening to the ripple of the water.

YEATS'S VISION AND QUEST

The vision of self-sufficiency in nature obviously pervades this whole poem. However unlikely a scene, it shows the poet as rustic woodsman and gardener, writing in the first person, actually planning to build a simple, crude dwelling and attempting agricultural self-sufficiency. 'Clay and wattles' were the traditional rural building materials for centuries past. The hive and the bees suggest the simple sweetness and richness of life, as well as providing a natural musical ambience. Altogether the vision is one of idyllic rural primitiveness, with a hint of the hermit's ascetic: a life 'alone in the bee-loud glade'.

This is a romantic view of the human being in perfect harmony with nature, at one with its sights and sounds. It is an alluring picture, sensual even, where the feminised morning is draped in veils. But there is also a strange, slightly unreal quality about it. The light is different: noon is a 'purple glow'. The archaic language in the expression of 'midnight's all a glimmer' reinforces the strange, even magical nature of the atmosphere. For representative sounds Yeats chooses the simple, rhythmic, calming sound of lake water lapping and also the repetitive rustic sounds of the cricket on the hearth, a common feature of rural stories and tales. Co. Sligo is one of the few places in the country that provides an all-year-round habitat for the linnet, a small unspectacular bird that likes rough hillsides and uncultivated lands near the sea. With accurate recall, Yeats is celebrating the indigenous wildlife of the area. His vision of happiness is a romantic one – a simple, unsophisticated lifestyle in an unspoilt habitat, surrounded by the sights and music of nature. It is a picture full of the rich textures of colour, sound and movement, in total contrast to his present environment, that of the cold, colourless and lifeless 'pavements grey'. So in one sense the poem can be read as an expression of Yeats's romanticised and nostalgic yearning for his native countryside.

But it is also more than this. For it is no frivolous weekend in the woods that he is planning: it is rather a quest for wisdom, for deep, eternal truths – an attempt to see into the heart of things. This is the sentiment that comes across in the first line. The sound of water, one of the essential elements and a life force, haunts him and seems to suggest that only in nature will he find the truths of the heart. The ambiguity about whose heart is in question here further strengthens the connection between the poet's heart and the heart of the earth. This is a move he feels compelled to make, a compulsion. We can sense the strength of his resolve in the verbs 'I will arise' and 'I shall have'. But the biblical allusions underlying this expose even more complex layers of compulsion. The repeated 'I will arise' echoes the words of the Prodigal Son, who has wasted his inheritance, led a profligate few years in exile, and finally resolves to go home: 'I will arise and go to my father.' So the words of the poem carry great unhappiness, a sense of failure and loss, the loneliness of exile and separation and perhaps even a feeling of guilt or remorse. The phrase 'always night and day' could also be a Biblical allusion. St Mark's gospel (5:5) refers to a man possessed by an evil spirit who was freed from his torment by Christ: 'Night and day among the tombs and on the mountains he was always crying out and bruising himself with stones.' This allusion, if intended, hints at a somewhat manic compulsion and mental and spiritual turmoil, or at the very least a great discontent.

The music of the verse

The poet's feelings of unease and discontent and of being driven to take this course of action are hidden by the musical quality of the verse. Apart from the obvious repetitions of the end rhymes in alternate lines, there are subtle musical vowel repetitions throughout the poem. For example, there is a profusion of long 'i' sounds in the first stanza ('I', 'arise', 'Nine', 'I', 'hive') and a repetition of long 'o' and 'a' sounds in the final stanza ('go', 'low', 'shore', 'roadway', 'core' and 'day', 'lake', 'pavements', 'grey'). The repetition, particularly of long broad vowels, gives this a languidness and soporific calmness that belies the tension at the heart of it.

Issues

Among the issues that preoccupy the poet here we might emphasise:

- the yearning for self-sufficiency in natural surroundings
- the search for truth, wisdom and peace
- the poet's discontent, which impels him on this quest.

September 1913

Text of poem: New Explorations Anthology page 139

This poem was written in September 1913 and was first published on 8 September in the *Irish Times,* where it was entitled 'Romance in Ireland (on reading much of the correspondence against the Art Gallery)'. It was included in the volume *Responsibilities* (1914) under its present title.

YEATS AND POLITICS: SOME OF HIS VIEWS ON SOCIETY

At one level of reading this is just a political poem – an angry poetical response to a particular event in which Yeats was passionately involved. Sir Hugh Lane, a wealthy art collector (and Lady Gregory's nephew), had presented to the city of Dublin a unique collection of modern paintings, with the proviso that the city build a suitable gallery to house them. There were various suggestions for building a gallery, such as one on a bridge over the River Liffey; but the entire project became entangled in increasingly bitter public disputes about the location, the architecture, and particularly the cost. Yeats was furious about what seemed a mean-spirited, penny-pinching and anti-cultural response to Lane's generous offer. The opponents of the project drew attention to the poverty and slum living conditions that many Dubliners endured at the time and accused the proponents of the gallery of putting art before bread and also of an elitist arrogance typical of the Ascendancy class. The controversy developed strong overtones of class conflict and set Yeats thinking about the recent changes in Irish society.

The make-up of society, the need for particular kinds of people in a cultured society, and the responsibilities of particular classes – these were issues that had long preoccupied Yeats. In 1907, on the death of the old Fenian John O'Leary, Yeats wrote an essay entitled 'Poetry and tradition', in which he talks about the ideals that he and O'Leary had discussed and shared. Though the primary emphasis in the essay is on poetry and culture, the views reflect Yeats's notions of the ideal society.

> Three types of men have made all beautiful things. Aristocracies have made beautiful manners, because their place in the world puts them above the fear of life, and the countrymen have made beautiful stories and beliefs, because they have nothing to lose and so do not fear, and

the artists have made all the rest, because Providence has filled them with recklessness. All these look backward to a long tradition, for, being without fear, they have held to whatever pleases them.

So for Yeats, the really important constituents of society were the aristocracy, country people and artists. It should not surprise us that Yeats was bitterly disillusioned with the changes in society that were proceeding apace from the end of the nineteenth century and into the twentieth: changes in land ownership hastened the demise of the aristocracy; a new upper and lower middle class emerged. Yeats saw only a new Ireland of small shopkeepers, clerks and traders; and it is at this section of the new society that he directs his wrath in the poem.

In the main he makes two accusations. Firstly, their only preoccupations are making money and practising religion, as he ironically says:

> For men were born to pray and save.

They are a money-grubbing and fearful people, tyrannised by their religion. And Yeats is revolted by this combination of materialism and religious serfdom; it is the antithesis of his Renaissance model of a cultured society, where art and literature are valued. Secondly, these small-minded, self-regarding, blinkered people are incapable of understanding the generosity of spirit and the self-sacrifice that motivated the patriots of old. Lines 25–30 can be read in this way. The selfless patriotism of the heroes of past time would now be misinterpreted by this unenlightened generation as love-crazed emotion merely to impress a woman.

> You'd cry, 'Some woman's yellow hair
> Has maddened every mother's son'

So the present generation and society are contrasted, most unfavourably, with previous generations.

It is worth exploring Yeats's notion of the heroic past and his view of the influential figures of romantic Ireland. They all were political rebels, risk takers who tried and failed gloriously to free Ireland. They all were men of action, soldiers who willingly gave liberty or life for the cause: 'They weighed so lightly what they gave.' They were hugely energetic, forceful characters:

> They have gone about the world like wind,
> But little time had they to pray.

In particular, Yeats seems to admire their extraordinary selflessness and courage, their almost manic bravery: 'All that delirium of the brave'.

Yeats's thinking accommodated two sometimes conflicting notions of the heroic: the hero as representative leader of a people, and the hero as a solitary figure, often even in opposition to the people. There are elements of both notions here. There are some hints of their popular influence ('the names that stilled your childish play') and perhaps also in their willing sacrifice ('all that blood was shed'). But the overwhelming impression is that of the solitary figure, apart, different: 'they were of a different kind'; 'the wild geese spread | The grey wing upon every tide'; 'those exiles as they were | In all their loneliness and pain.' And it is this difference that gives them status in the poem. And, by implication, the present generation lack their qualities of nobility, courage, selflessness, and self-sacrifice for an ideal.

TONE

This poem is built on contrast – an extreme, somewhat simplistic contrast between a present and a past generation, or what Yeats sees as representative figures from these generations. The heroic past he idolises in tones of reverence and awe. There is a suggestion of their strange power in 'the names that stilled your childish play' and in the reference to their going 'about the world like wind'. He empathises with their loneliness and pain and inevitable fate:

> But little time had they to pray
> For whom the hangman's rope was spun,
> And what, God help us, could they save?

His undoubted admiration for their selfless courage is carried in 'They weighed so lightly what they gave' and in that 'delirium of the brave'.

In contrast, the new middle class is lampooned in the caricature of the shopkeeper as a kind of sub-human creature, fumbling, shivering, and certainly not capable of understanding more noble motives. The tone of savage mockery is often achieved by the use of irony – for example the perverse irony of 'What need you, being come to sense' – or the ironic statement of philosophy, 'For men were born to pray and save.' The bitter contempt is hammered home through the repetition of 'For this . . . for this . . . for this.' The sneer of disdain rings through these lines.

Altogether this is a poem exhibiting passionate but contrasting emotions.

SOME THEMES AND ISSUES

- Bitter disillusion with recent social changes
- Contempt for the perceived materialism and religious serfdom of the new middle class of business people

- Concerns for the well-being of a cultured society; concern for its lack of altruistic principles and generosity of spirit
- A particular view of Irish history as a history of courageous failure in the struggle for independence
- A nostalgic, romanticised view of Irish history
- Thoughts on patriotism and the notion of the heroic.

The Wild Swans at Coole

Text of poem: New Explorations Anthology page 142
[Note: This poem is also prescribed for the Ordinary Level 2006 exam]

The poem was written in 1916 and first published in the *Little Review* in 1917, and it is the title poem of the volume *The Wild Swans at Coole* (1917).

This poem is structured as a retrospection by Yeats as he records how his life has changed since he first stayed at Coole Park during the summer and autumn of 1897 ('the nineteenth autumn'). It is important to be aware that this is an artistic construction, because in reality his state of mind had changed very little. Though he chooses to say that he was more carefree ('trod with a lighter tread') at that earlier period, probably for aesthetic purposes and to set up a contrast, in fact he had been in a state of mental and nervous exhaustion during that visit in 1897. His love affair with Diana Vernon had just ended. He was 'tortured with sexual desire and disappointed love', and, as his diaries reveal, 'It would have been a relief to have screamed aloud.'

In the summer of 1916, the year the poem was written, Yeats went to France to Maud Gonne, the great, omnipresent, passionate love of his life for the previous quarter of a century. Her husband, Major John MacBride, had been shot for his part in the Easter Rising. She was working as a volunteer nurse with the war wounded, and Yeats once again proposed marriage to her. On her refusing for the last time he contemplated the possibility of marriage with her adopted daughter, Iseult. Possibly it was this turmoil and the disparity in their ages that set him thinking of time, age and immortality, the death of love or the possibility of its being eternal. But this is one instance where a biographical approach does not help very much, as the poet orders and alters events and ideals to suit an artistic construction rather than any actual reality.

When Iseult finally refused him in 1917 he married Georgina Hyde-Lees and bought a tower-house, Thoor Ballylee, not far from Coole in Co. Galway.

THEMES AND ISSUES

This poem, as Yeats's literary biographer Terence Brown says, 'sets a mood of autumnal introspection'. In a certain sense it is quite a personal poem, in which Yeats, at fifty-one, unmarried and alone despite many passionate love affairs, takes stock of his emotional situation. Primarily he laments the loss of youth, passion and love. He regrets the loss of his carefree youth, 'trod with a lighter tread', however inaccurate this nostalgia is. Now his 'heart is sore'; he is a man broken-hearted, discontented, emotionally unsatisfied. He no longer has what the swans appear to have – youthful passion.

> Unwearied still, lover by lover . . .
> Passion or conquest . . .
> Attend upon them still.

And he has not got unchanging or constant love, while 'their hearts have not grown old'. Above all else, the poet seems to resent the loss of passionate love in his life; we cannot mistake this yearning in the many references to hearts, lovers, passion and conquests.

The loss of love is just one aspect of Yeats's general sense of regret here, which concerns ageing and the passage of time. Indeed he seems to have been ambushed by time – the nineteenth autumn 'has come upon me' – and is forced to accept that 'all's changed'. His awareness of this and his resentment are accentuated by the seeming immortality of the swans: 'Their hearts have not grown old'. By implication we sense the poet's yearning for changelessness, for immortality.

Yet another kind of loss is hinted at here: the possible loss or diminution of the poetic gift, insight or vision. Perhaps that is what he fears at the end of the poem, in that final plaintive image: that the poetic sight or vision will have deserted him and passed to others. For him, the swans are in some way a manifestation of his poetic vision. So we can see that he explores
- the personal loss of youth, passion, and love
- the consequences of ageing
- the passage of time and the yearning for changelessness and immortality
- the loss of poetic power and vision – the sense of failure.

IMAGERY AND SYMBOLISM

The entire poem is structured around the swans, real and symbolic, which have particular significance because they appear to have defied time for the past nineteen years. They give the illusion of immortality: 'Unwearied still . . . Passion or conquest . . . attend upon them still.' Our rational mind tells us that of course they may not be exactly the same swans; but the poet glosses over and even builds further on this poetic illusion. He concentrates our attention on the patterns they establish, patterns that will survive even though they may die. These 'great broken rings', the spiral imagery they create, are similar to the 'gyres' or cones of time (see pages 113–14) that Yeats saw as the cyclical pattern behind all things, time and eternity. So there is a hint of the eternal about the spiral imagery the swans establish. Also, they link the water to the sky, link earth and heaven; and so in a way they are both mortal and immortal. The swans provide an exciting, vibrant, multi-layered symbolism, but they are also hauntingly and accurately described as real creatures. The real power and energy of the movement is evoked by the breathless enjambment of the lines and by the use of sinuous and muscular verbs and adverbs:

> All suddenly mount
> And scatter wheeling in great broken rings
> Upon their clamorous wings.

The swan imagery carries great resonances and symbolic value in the poem; but there are other images also that add to the richness of texture. The 'woodland paths' can be either the straight paths of the intellect or the winding paths of intuition. Whatever symbolic weight they carry they are dry here, in keeping with the themes – lack of passion and creativity. The trees, a great symbol of permanence for Yeats, are in the ageing cycle of their lives, as is the poet.

Three of the four symbolic elements are used in the poem: earth, air and water. Only fire is not used, indeed is conspicuously absent. The suggestion is that this is more than just a poem, that it carries elements of magical divination. Even the musical image 'The bell-beat of their wings above my head' reinforces this sense of the magical. And of course Yeats believed in and practised magic. Our sense of this is strengthened further by an exploration of the degree of patterning in the poem. Notice how the swans on the lake take to the air and finish by drifting on the still water again – creating a perfect round or circular pattern. Consider the pattern of antitheses in the poem – between the swans and the speaker and between the poet now and the poet nineteen years ago. And, as the critic Donald Stauffer points out, the essential pattern is a contrast of moods, something experienced only by humans. The essential contrast in the poem is that between transient humanity and eternity.

All in all, there is a richness of imagery and symbolism here that can be enjoyed and appreciated at many levels.

STRUCTURE

There is a gradual opening out of both the voice and the vista as this poem progresses. Stanza 1 just paints the picture, unemotionally and accurately, as any ornithologist or naturalist might do. From this very anchored and particular opening we go to the poet's personal reminiscences in the second and third stanzas, before moving on to more generalised speculative philosophising in the fourth stanza. The final stanza opens up unanswerable questions, speculating on the future, leaving us with the possibility of a completely empty final scene, a blank canvas. The future is as unclear and ungraspable as that final question – incidentally the only question in the poem.

The poem goes from the particular to the general and then to the entirely speculative. Beneath the tranquillity of the imagery, the languidness of language and the sounds of the words, the ideas of the poem are tightly linked and structured. Notice how images or ideas are picked up from one stanza to the next, and so the stanzas are chain-linked.

The first stanza ends with the enumeration of 'nine-and-fifty swans', and the second stanza takes up the count.

> The nineteenth autumn has come upon me
> Since I first made my count;

Stanzas 2 and 3 are linked by the poet's looking: 'I saw . . . I have looked'. At the end of stanza 3 he remembers or fancies his carefree 'lighter treat' of nineteen years earlier. Stanza 4 opens with the still 'unwearied' creatures.

The fifth stanza picks up phonetically on the word 'still', and, though semantically different, it provides a phonic linkage. There is of course the imagery link also, where swans 'paddling in the cold | Companionable streams' of the fourth stanza are picked up in the fifth stanza as they 'drift on the still water'.

An Irish Airman Foresees his Death

Text of poem: New Explorations Anthology page 145

This poem was one of a number written by the poet for Robert Gregory, Lady Gregory's son, including 'Shepherd and Goatherd' and 'In Memory of Major Robert Gregory'. Yeats saw Gregory as an educated aristocrat and all-round Renaissance man ('Soldier, scholar, horseman, he'). He was also an energetic boxer and hunter and a painter who designed sets for Yeats's own plays. The poem was written in 1918 and first published in the second edition of *The Wild Swans at Coole* (1919).

CRITICAL COMMENTARY

At one obvious level of reading, this is a type of elegy in memory of the dead man. But it is a variation on the form, in that it is structured as a monologue by the dead man rather than the more usual direct lament by a poet, praising the person's good qualities and showing how he is much missed, and so on.

It makes an interesting contribution to war poetry in its attempt to chart the motivation and psychological state of the volunteer. What strikes one immediately is not just the fatalism – he knows his death is imminent – but the bleakness of his outlook on life, his disenchantment with living, despite his privileged background.

> The years to come seemed waste of breath,
> A waste of breath the years behind . . .

In contrast, the war seemed an adventure, an 'impulse of delight', a 'tumult in the clouds'. The poem captures well the excitement and exhilaration felt by many a volunteer. As Ulick O'Connor put it (in *The Yeats Companion*, 1990), 'There can seldom have been a better summing up of the sense of elation which the freedom to roam the uncharted skies brought to the young men of Gregory's pre-1914 generation.'

Yet the decision to volunteer was not a heady, emotional one. The poem stresses the thought and calculation brought to the decision. The concept of balance is repeatedly stressed:

> I balanced all, brought all to mind . . .
> In balance with this life, this death.

He was not carried away by the emotion of enlistment meetings ('Nor public men, nor cheering crowds'). He was not moved by any sense of 'duty' or 'patriotism'; neither was there conscription in Ireland ('Nor law, nor duty bade me fight'). These 'nor – nor' negatives of the rejected motives are balanced against the excitement of action. The general picture is of a young man who has chosen, after careful consideration, this path of action, almost indeed chosen his death.

This heavy sense of fatalism is most obvious in the opening lines. But there is never a sense in which this fatalism is merely weak surrender or opting out. He accepts his fate, he goes consenting to his death, but more like one of Homer's heroes. Yeats gives Gregory Homeric stature by allowing him to choose a heroic death; and this gives meaning to an otherwise meaningless conflict. The airman feels none of the great passions of war, neither patriotic love nor hatred of the foe:

> Those that I fight I do not hate,
> Those that I guard I do not love;

Further, he does not think the war will make a whit of difference to his own countrymen:

> No likely end could bring them loss
> Or leave them happier than before.

But it is the self-sacrificing death, 'this death' freely chosen, that raises the young man above the events of his time and confers particular significance on him. The awareness of impending death also brings this moment of insight, this clearness of vision that allowed him to evaluate his past life and contemplate a possible future as a country landowner – all of which he rejects for the 'tumult' of action.

So, as a war poem, this is an interesting, personal, even intimate approach, charting the thoughts and motivation of this young man. But it has a more general aspect also. Gregory may be seen as representative of all those young men of talent who were cheated of their promise by the slaughter of the First World War.

We have already mentioned that Yeats saw Gregory as the all-round Renaissance man – in other words, an educated man and person of culture as well as a man of action. Yeats had felt that the 'lonely impulse of delight' was what differentiated the artist from others, that the artistic impulse was essentially lonely and solitary. Here we see this artistic impulse motivating a man of action, who is essentially instinctive rather than intellectual. Yeats felt that the impulse was sometimes hampered in the artist, who often thought too much. So the later Yeats began to champion the non-intellectual hero and the instinctive man; the sportsman and the adventurer are given the status of mythic figures. The airman Gregory is essentially a solitary figure, like other mythic figures created by Yeats, such as the 'Fisherman'.

Some critics read this poem as a classic statement of Anglo-Irishness as Yeats saw it. In later life Yeats used to talk about the 'Anglo-Irish solitude'. Is there a sense here of not quite fully belonging to either side, of being neither fully committed English nor unreservedly Irish? There is certainly a sense of emotional distance on the part of the subject, both from those he guards and those he fights. Though he has an affinity with Kiltartan's poor ('my countrymen'), he is aware that the war and his involvement in it will have no impact on their lives. In general, the feeling one gets is of some detachment from the events in which he participates, and this could be read as a metaphor for 'Anglo-Irish solitude'.

Easter 1916

Text of poem: New Explorations Anthology page 148

On Monday 24 April 1916 a force of about seven hundred members of the Irish Volunteers and the Irish Citizen Army took over the centre of Dublin in a military revolution and held out for six days against the British army.

At first the rising did not receive widespread support; but the British military authorities regarded it as high treason in time of war, and the subsequent systematic executions of fifteen of the leaders between 3 and 12 May brought a wave of public sympathy and created heroes and martyrs for the republican cause.

Though Yeats's poem was finished by September 1916 and a number of copies had been printed privately, it was not published until October 1920, when it appeared in the *New Statesman*. It is included in the volume *Michael Robartes and the Dancer* (1921).

THE NATIONAL QUESTION: YEATS'S POLITICAL VIEWS

Yeats spent a good deal of his time in England during his early life, but he felt that the English understanding of the Irish was stereotypical and condescending. One of his main ambitions was to help change Ireland's view of itself through a revival of its unique cultural identity. He had denounced the English government of Ireland, and his refusal of a knighthood in 1915 is a statement of his political stance. Yet his view did not prevent him living there, and indeed he was in England when the Easter Rising took place.

This ambiguity was further complicated by Yeats's arrogant and scathing dismissal of the current generation of Irish people as ignoble, self-focused, materialistic and priest-controlled, who were totally incapable of the idealism or courage necessary for heroic leadership and personal sacrifice. These views he had expressed very trenchantly in 'September 1913'.

The Rising took Yeats by surprise and blew some serious holes in his thinking. Firstly, he now had to rethink his public stance and views on the new Irish middle class. These people had been prepared to give their lives for an ideal. Yeats had been quite wrong. Secondly, though he was disgusted, like most people, at the savagery of the executions, he began to realise that the establishment's brutality had created martyrs, had transformed ordinary men into patriots with a strange new unchallengeable power. Perhaps Pearse's idea of a blood sacrifice was correct. Yeats had to rethink the place and value of revolutionary determination. So Yeats had to work out how this cataclysmic change had occurred in Irish society – 'all changed, changed utterly'.

A READING OF THE POEM

Though it may not appear on the surface to be a questioning poem, this work is really an attempt to answer or clarify a great number of questions that the 1916 Rising stirred up in Yeats's mind, an attempt to come to terms with:
- how everything had changed
- how wrong he had been
- how ordinary people had been changed into heroes
- the deep structure of change in society, the mysterious process, a kind of fate that directed and powered change (Terence Brown puts it eloquently: 'It seeks to penetrate beneath the appearance of history to comprehend the

mysteries of destiny.')
- the place and functioning of revolutionary violence in the process
- the change in his own position: how to resolve his own complex and contradictory feelings towards this violent process.

The diplomatic difficulty of having to recant his views on Irish society Yeats faced honestly and generously in the first section of this poem. Technically he achieved this by structuring the poem as a *palinode* or recantation of his opinions in the earlier 'September 1913'. Re-creating the drab, unexciting milieu of pre-revolution evenings, the poet acknowledges his own blindness and failure to engage with these people in any depth:

> I have passed with a nod of the head
> Or polite meaningless words,
> Or have lingered a while and said
> Polite meaningless words,

He confesses to his own unpleasant, condescending mockery ('a mocking tale or a gibe . . .') and his belief that all the pre-1916 organising was mere comical posturing:

> Being certain that they and I
> But lived where motley is worn . . .

He includes himself ('they and I') in this attempt at identification.

He spends the second section looking again at these people that he knew, as he needs to understand how they have changed. They are still the flawed characters he remembers: Constance Markievicz wasted her time in misplaced volunteer work ('ignorant good-will') and became a shrill fanatic ('nights in argument . . . voice grew shrill'); MacBride he thought 'a drunken vainglorious lout' who 'had done most bitter wrong' to Maud Gonne and Iseult. These are very ordinary, fallible, flawed and unlikely heroes.

Furthermore, the impression Yeats perceives is not one of energetically active heroes, but rather the passive recipients of this mysterious change. MacDonagh 'might have won fame in the end'. MacBride 'has resigned his part | In the casual comedy'. This smacks of an unknown actor giving up his part in an inconsequential work. The impression given is of relatively insignificant lives, out of which MacBride 'has been changed in his turn'. Note the passive voice: the change was effected on him, rather than by something he did, and it happened 'in his turn'. He waited his turn – perhaps a reference to the executions. Is Yeats saying that it was the executions that effected this change, transformed everyone utterly, and gave birth to this terrible beauty? That it was not due to the nature or any action of heroes?

Another aspect of these patriots that Yeats refers to is their feminine qualities. 'What voice more sweet' than Constance Gore-Booth's (in younger days)? MacDonagh's thought is 'daring and sweet'. Even MacBride has his passive side. So there is a sensitivity about these people that balances their more aggressive and masculine qualities, also referred to.

It is this softer, feminine quality in man and woman that is destroyed by fanaticism, something Yeats explores in the third and fourth sections. But first it is worth noticing the feminine aspect of the new order. This utter transformation of the social and historical reality is imagined as a new birth; but Yeats is so disturbed and confused by it that he can only describe it in paradoxical terms as a 'terrible beauty' – something that is partly feminine, aesthetically pleasing, sexually alluring even, but also carries suggestions of terror and of destructive power. This magnificent image carries all Yeats's confusions and contradictory feelings about the dramatic change.

In the third section he explores how change is effected. Only a stone, usually taken as a metaphor for the fanatical heart, can change or trouble the course of a stream, and it can achieve this only at a price. The heart will lose its humanness:

> Too long a sacrifice
> Can make a stone of the heart.

In the 1909 *Journals* Yeats had already written about the effects of political fanaticism on Maud Gonne, in metaphors akin to those used here:

> Women, because the main event of their lives has been a giving of themselves, give themselves to an opinion as if it were some terrible stone doll . . . They grow cruel, as if in defence of lover or child and all this is done for something other than human life. At last the opinion becomes so much a part of them that it is as though a part of their flesh becomes, as it were, stone, and much of their being passes out of life.

In this third section Yeats is exploring the dangers of fanatical devotion to a cause or ideal, and he represents this metaphorically as the conflicting forces between a stone and a stream.

The living stream is marvellously evoked. It is a picture of constant change, the flux of natural life and bursting with energy. The seasons are changing 'through summer and winter'; the skies change 'from cloud to tumbling cloud'; all is life and regeneration, as 'hens to moor-cocks call'. It is full of transient animal and human appearances, as they slide or plash or dive. And all this activity happens 'minute by minute'. Against this stream of ever-changing energy and life is set the unmoving stone, the fanatical heart. It is not difficult to conclude that the weight of the poet's sentiment is with the living stream rather than the unmoving stone. And yet out of this confrontation is born the 'terrible beauty'.

There is no easy answer to the conflicts posed by the poet. And indeed he seems to weary of the dialogue and of this dialectic in the fourth section. Having concluded that prolonged devotion to an ideal is dehumanising –

> Too long a sacrifice
> Can make a stone of the heart.

– he seems to accept the necessity of it and at the same time wishes for an end, in that sighing plea: 'O when may it suffice?'

The first seventeen lines of this fourth section are structured in questions – rhetorical questions, or questions that cannot be answered – thereby revealing the poet's uncertainties about the validity of the entire process of revolution and change. There is a kind of shocked vulnerability about the poetic voice here, a realisation of helplessness as all the doubts flood in with the questions: Are they really dead? Was it necessary if England intended to grant home rule after the war? What if they were just confused and bewildered by an excess of patriotism? There is an awareness that some things cannot be answered, that some of this mysterious dynamic of change cannot be understood – 'That is Heaven's part.' And the poet adopts a soothing mother's voice and persona, murmuring 'As a mother names her child'.

But then he seems to shake off the uncertain and shocked voice and finds a new assurance for that very definite confident ending. Why is this? Terence Brown believes it has to do with the magical significance of the poem, deliberately created by Yeats. He suggests that the poem is a 'numerological artefact', based on the date when the rising began: 24 April 1916. There are four movements or sections, with the following numbers of lines in each: 16, 24, 16, 24. It is suggested also that Yeats intended this to be a verse of power, a magical recitation, seen in for example 'I number him in the song'; 'I write it out in a verse.' Certainly there is a surge of powerful assurance in those final lines, whether we read them as a litany of respectful remembrance or an occult incantation.

> I write it out in a verse –
> MacDonagh and MacBride
> And Connolly and Pearse
> Now and in time to be,
> Wherever green is worn,
> Are changed, changed utterly:
> A terrible beauty is born.

The Second Coming

Text of poem: New Explorations Anthology page 154

This poem was finished in January 1919, to a background of great political upheaval in Europe: the disintegration of the Austro-Hungarian, German and Russian empires, and uprisings and revolution in Germany and Russia. The events in Europe are most likely to have prompted the speculation that 'mere anarchy is loosed upon the world'; but as the poem was not published for twenty-two months, in the *Dial* of November 1920, it came to be read as a reaction to the atrocities of the War of Independence in Ireland. It is included in the volume *Michael Robartes and the Dancer* (1921).

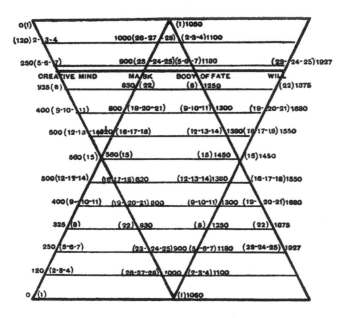

YEATS'S OCCULT PHILOSOPHY AND THEORIES OF HISTORY

Yeats was deeply interested in the patterns of history. He was also engaged in the study and practice of the occult and maintained regular contact with the spirits. These 'spirit communicators' helped him develop a cyclical theory of change in history, which is outlined in *A Vision* (1925). He used geometrical forms to express abstract ideas; and the concept of 'gyres' or cones representing time zones is one of these. In this poem the reference is to a single gyre or inverted cone. But the full representation of the gyres consists of two interpenetrating cones, expanding and contracting on a single axis. These represent the contrary forces, always changing, that determine the character of a person or the culture of a particular phase in history. There are particularly significant moments both for individuals and in historical time when the dominant influence passes from one gyre to its contrary. In history, he believed, this can happen every two thousand years. Hence the reference to 'twenty centuries of stony sleep' that preceded the Christian era, which is now waning and giving way to a new and antithetical era.

In its Christian interpretation, the 'Second Coming' refers to the prediction of the second coming of Christ; in Yeats's occult and magical philosophy it might also refer to the second birth of the Avatar or great antithetical spirit, which Yeats and his wife felt certain would be reincarnated as their baby son, whose birth was imminent. In fact the child turned out to be a girl, dashing that theory.

In this poem the hideous 'rough beast' that 'slouches towards Bethlehem to be born' is suggestive of the Anti-Christ, that legendary personal opponent of Christ and his kingdom expected to appear before the end of the world. See, for example, the Book of Revelations (chapter 13) on the portents for the end of the world:

> And I saw a beast rising out of the sea, with ten horns and seven heads, with ten diadems upon its horns and a blasphemous name upon its heads. And the beast that I saw was like a leopard, its feet were like a bear's, and its mouth was like a lion's mouth. And to it the dragon gave his power and his throne and great authority. One of its heads seemed to have a mortal wound, but its mortal wound was healed, and the whole earth followed the beast with wonder. Men worshipped the dragon, for he had given his authority to the beast, and they worshipped the beast, saying, 'Who is like the beast and who can fight against it?'

A READING OF THE POEM

This poem reflects Yeats's interest in historical change and his real fear that civilisation would break down and be replaced by an anti-civilisation or an era of anarchy. This was sparked off in part by his disgust and revulsion at what was happening in European politics and history around this time (1919). But, as we have seen, he was also preoccupied with patterns in history and immersed himself in the occult, with signs, portents, astrological charts and spirit communicators, and had developed a cyclical theory of change in history, which was represented graphically by the 'gyre' symbol.

So this poem deals with the turbulence of historical change; but what is particularly exciting is the enormous perspective that the poet takes. Time is not counted in years or decades but in millennia; and it is this vast perspective that is both exhilarating and terrifying.

First section

Essentially what is happening here is that Yeats is exploring the breakup of civilisation in metaphorical language. The falcon, that trained bird of prey, cannot hear the falconer and is reverting to its wild state. The falconer has also been interpreted as a representation of Christ, and so the image has been read as representing the movement of civilisation away from Christ. This dissipation is happening within the framework of its allotted time span, at a point within the gyre, representing the present. Yeats is bringing a critical philosophical viewpoint to bear on the social and political structures. He suggests that there is failure at the very heart of society, presumably in human beings themselves: 'things fall apart; the centre cannot hold. Instead of clear-sighted vision and forward progress there is this confusing circular movement, an out-of-control centrifugal force that threatens to send everything spinning away in disorder. In this chaos human beings are changing, becoming ignoble and destroying innocence: 'The ceremony of innocence is drowned.' People either have no convictions at all or are irrationally and passionately committed to causes; they have become either cynics or fanatics.

> The best lack all conviction, while the worst
> Are full of passionate intensity.

This first section embodies this very tension in its structure. Consider how the ideas are set up as opposites: centre – fall apart; falcon – falconer; indifference – intensity; innocence – anarchy. This polar oppositional tension is seen in the terrifying image of 'the blood-dimmed tide . . . loosed . . . innocence is drowned.' This sinister image has connotations of the great flood and its destruction of the world, but might also suggest a ruthless cleansing or purging. The repetition of 'loosed upon' and 'loosed' might suggest a savage wild animal, at the very least the 'dogs of war'. The circular imagery creates a sense of continuous swirling movement. Look at the repetition of -ing: 'turning, turning, widening'. There is a sense of a world out of control, of inevitable disaster.

Really it is the force of the imagery that carries the ideas in this section. Consider the falconry image. This was the pastime of kings and lords, so the image carries associations of an aristocratic life, civilised living, affluence. We know how much Yeats valued civilised living. Falconry was a 'noble' pastime, requiring skill and patience. Now this trained bird of prey is reverting to its wild state – a metaphor for the destruction of civilised living. It would also carry religious overtones and signal the breakdown of ordered religious systems. The falcon has also been interpreted as symbolic of the active or intellectual mind, so the breakdown of intellectual order might be signalled as well. Either way the image suggests dissolution in a number of different spheres and levels.

The second graphic image, of the 'blood-dimmed tide', has already been explored for its layers of suggestiveness. Its general impact is powerful, both visually and intellectually: innocence is drowned in a sea of blood. This is the ultimate nihilism, a world without justice, reason or order. Note Yeats's emphasis on the 'ceremony' of innocence. The rituals of civilised living will also be destroyed, of course.

The final image of the section, though somewhat ill defined, is a political one, suggesting that fanatical people have now got all the influence and are in power. The general impact of the imagery is one of frightening and irrational disorder and breakup in life and society.

Second section

Yeats begins by casting around for a reason for the breakdown of civilisation, and the possibility of a second coming together with the end of the world suggests itself as the only one great enough to cause this. 'Surely the Second Coming is at hand.' But it turns out not to be the Second Coming of Christ as foretold in the Gospels but rather the emergence of the Anti-Christ that Yeats imagines, an Anti-Christ who embodies the absolute reverse of the Christian era, which is now drawing to its end in the gyre of time. This rough beast, a nightmare symbol of the coming times, signals the end of this era, with its values and order.

Again, the image of this rough beast carries all the ideas about the new era. It is a 'vast image', overwhelming and troubling. It is a horrific hybrid of human and animal – suggesting unnatural times, such as foretold in the Book of Revelations. Its blank gaze suggests no intelligent sight or understanding; indeed it is as 'pitiless as the sun', incapable of empathy or feeling. The qualities it conjures up are gracelessness and brutishness: 'moving its slow thighs . . . Slouches towards Bethlehem to be born'. The final paradox is explained by the fact that its era has already begun, overlapping with the demise of the Christian era, so it is moving into position to initiate the new age or be born. The paradox further emphasises the antithetical nature of the coming age: how totally contradictory or opposite it is. There is something blasphemously shocking in the idea of the beast being born at Bethlehem. The nugget of insight gained by the poet out of this horrific vision concerns the nature of time and changing eras. He realises that eras have come and gone before, and that the advent of the Christian era must have been as troubling to the previous age.

> Now I know
> That twenty centuries of stony sleep
> Were vexed to nightmare by a rocking cradle.

Sailing to Byzantium

Text of poem: New Explorations Anthology page 156

This poem was written some time in the autumn of 1926 and is the opening poem in the collection *The Tower* (1928).

A READING OF THE POEM

Writing for a radio programme in 1931, Yeats outlined some of the preoccupations of his poetry at that time, in particular the spiritual quest of 'Sailing to Byzantium':

> Now I am trying to write about the state of my soul, for it is right for an old man to make his soul [an expression meaning to prepare for death], and some of my thoughts upon that subject I have put into a poem called 'Sailing to Byzantium'. When Irishmen were illuminating the Book of Kells and making the jewelled crosiers of the National Museum, Byzantium was the centre of European civilisation and the source of its spiritual philosophy, so I symbolise the search for the spiritual life by a journey to that city.

So this poem is structured, as he says, in the shape of a journey – more of a quest, really – with a tightly argued personal commentary by the poet. The main theme surfaces immediately in the first stanza. With that strong, declamatory opening he renounces the world of the senses for that of the spirit and the intellect, the timeless.

> That is no country for old men. The young
> In one another's arms . . .

Notice the perspective ('that'): he has already departed and is looking back, not without a little nostalgic yearning for the sensuality of youth. The sensual imagery of lovers and the teeming rich life of trees and seas, the athletic vigour of the hyphenated words ('the salmon-falls, the mackerel-crowded seas') and the sensual *'f'* and *'s'* sounds of 'fish, flesh or fowl' – all used to describe the cycle of life in the flesh – would strongly suggest that he does not renounce it easily. Indeed this ambiguity is carried in the paradox of 'those dying generations', with its linking of death and regeneration.

The importance of the spirit is re-emphasised in the second stanza as the poet asserts that it is the soul that gives meaning to a person: 'An aged man is but a paltry thing . . . unless I Soul clap its hands and sing.' And art enriches the soul, teaches it to sing: 'studying I Monuments of its own magnificence,' i.e. works of art inspired by the spirit. Byzantium, as a centre of religion, philosophy and learning and also of a highly formalised art, is the ideal destination for the intellectual and spiritual person. In 'A Vision' (1925) Yeats wrote about the harmoniousness of life in fifth-century Byzantium: 'I think that in early Byzantium, maybe never before or since in recorded history, religious, aesthetic and practical life were one.' He had visited Ravenna in 1907 and when he composed the third stanza probably had in mind a mosaic on the wall of S. Apollinore Nuova showing martyrs being burnt in a fire.

Addressing these sages or martyrs directly in the third stanza, he entreats them to traverse history in the gyre of time, come to him and teach his soul to sing. He wants them to 'make' his soul, as he said, to purify it, separate it from emotions and desires and help it transcend the ageing physical body:

> Consume my heart away; sick with desire
> And fastened to a dying animal
> It knows not what it is . . .

These lines betray a seriously troubled state of mind. Central to the conflict is a dualist view of the human being as composed of two radically different and warring elements: body, and soul or spirit. Yeats values one element – the soul – imaged as singer and bird but is filled with self-disgust and loathing for his ageing body, imaged as a dying animal, not even dignified as human, that has entrapped the soul.

This confusion is evident even in the ambiguity of language here, in for example 'sick with desire'. Is he sick because of the desires of the flesh he cannot shake off, or does the desire refer to his spiritual aspiration, which continues to elude him? This acute existential conflict has led to a loss of spiritual identity: 'It knows not what it is'; hence his emotional entreaty to the sages to 'gather me | Into the artifice of eternity'.

It is worth exploring the richness of this ordinary language here. By using 'gather me' the poet is acknowledging how fragmented and scattered his condition is and how he needs both direction and comfort; it is as if he needs to be embraced, gathered in arms. Ironically, he wants to be gathered into the coherence and timelessness of art – 'the artifice of eternity'. It is through this transition that he will find immortality. But the language carries hints of ambiguity, even about this much-desired goal. 'Artifice' refers primarily to a work of art, but it can also mean 'artificiality'. Is this the first hint that this great quest might be flawed?

Still he begins the fourth stanza with great confidence that art holds the answer to the problem of mortality. 'Once out of nature' he will be transformed into the perfect work of art and so live on. The golden bird is ageless and incorruptible and will sing the song of the soul. The final irony, though, is that the song it sings is about the flux of time, 'what is past, or passing, or to come'.

There is no perfect solution after all.

Discuss these and see if you can justify each from the evidence of the poem.
- Yeats in old age is attempting to develop his spiritual side. It is a poem about the values of the soul as against the world of the senses.
- It is an attempt to escape the harsh reality of old age and death through the immortality of spiritual things and of art.
- The view of the human being portrayed is that of a fractured, divided entity in an uncomfortable state of war between the spiritual and the physical.
- It is a meditation on the nature of art and its importance to humanity.
- It delivers fine insights into the nature of Byzantine imagination and culture.

STRUCTURE

As befits the theme of conflict, the ideas and images in this poem are developed in a series of *antinomies* or contrasts. In the very first line youth and age are set opposite each other: 'That is no country for old men . . .' While youth is imaged in those wonderful scenes of sensuous life in the first stanza, age is realised in the scarecrow image – 'a tattered coat upon a stick' – with all its suggestions of fake outward show, a grotesque parody of the human being and the sense of powerlessness and indignity. The body is imaged as a dying animal, while the soul is imaged as a priceless golden bird, singing.

The mortality of life is contrasted with the timelessness of art. The teeming sensuality of Ireland is set against the culture of Byzantium, with its religious ethos ('holy city'; 'God's holy fire'), its reputation for learning and philosophical thought ('O sages'), and its artistic achievement ('artifice'; 'a form as Grecian goldsmiths make | Of hammered gold and gold enamelling', etc.). These conflicts reflect the internal struggle, the yearnings and the reality within the poetic persona here.

Yet the struggle is smoothed over by the grace and elegance of the language used. There is a regular pattern of end-rhymes or sometimes half-rhymes, which gives the verses a musical ease. Yeats also uses a rhythmic phrasing, often grouping in lists of three, which has magical significance as well as producing a rhythmic rise and fall: 'fish, flesh, or fowl'; 'Whatever is begotten, born, and dies'; 'unless | Soul clap its hands and sing, and louder sing'; 'Of what is past, or passing, or to come'. We might also notice other rhetorical qualities, such as the strong, declamatory opening, the rhetorical plea to the sages, indeed the strong, confident, first-person voice of the poet all through. These sometimes belie the conflicts and uncertainties at the heart of the work.

The Stare's Nest By My Window

Text of poem: New Explorations Anthology page 160

FROM 'MEDITATIONS IN TIME OF CIVIL WAR'

'Meditations in Time of Civil War' is quite a lengthy poem, structured in seven sections. Apart from the first, composed in England in 1921, it was written in Ireland during the Civil War of 1922–23 and was first published in the *Dell* in January 1923. It is included in the volume *The Tower* (1928).

In the poem as a whole, Yeats explores aspects of the Anglo-Irish ascendancy tradition: its origins and heritage and his own sense of sharing in the values of that tradition, particularly those of continuity, culture and family line. Conflict too was a necessary element of that planter culture, and now he is brought face to face with the violence of the Civil War and must re-evaluate his own role in the continuing tradition of history.

Images of houses and building provide one of the unifying metaphors and themes throughout this poem. Yeats acknowledges the violence out of which the great Anglo-Irish culture was built:

> Some violent bitter man, some powerful man
> Called architect and artist in, that they,
> Bitter and violent men, might rear in stone
> The sweetness that all longed for night and day.

His own house in Co. Galway, Thoor Ballylee, was originally a defensive fifteenth-century tower. He acknowledges proudly that conflict is part of his tradition; he wishes that his descendants too will find 'befitting emblems of adversity'. So in section V, when a band of Irregulars calls to his door, he experiences a certain envy of the men of action. Perhaps it is the graphic details of that war in section VI that led to a reappraisal. The terrifying vision of the nightmarish destruction of civilisation in section VII throws him back to thinking on his own role as poet in his isolated tower.

Yeats wrote the following description of the genesis and context of section VI:

> I was in my Galway house during the first months of civil war, the railway bridges blown up and the roads blocked with stones and trees. For the first week there were no newspapers, no reliable news, we did not know who had won nor who had lost, and even after newspapers came, one never knew what was happening on the other side of the hill or of the line of trees. Ford cars passed the house from time to time with coffins standing upon end between the seats, and sometimes at night we heard an explosion, and once by day saw the smoke made by the

burning of a great neighbouring house. Men must have lived so through many tumultuous centuries. One felt an overmastering desire not to grow unhappy or embittered, not to lose all sense of the beauty of nature. A stare (our West of Ireland name for a starling) had built in a hole beside my window and I made these verses out of the feeling of the moment . . . [here he quoted from 'The bees build in the crevices' to 'Yet no clear fact to be discerned: come build in the empty house of the stare.'] . . . That is only the beginning but it runs on in the same mood. Presently a strange thing happened. I began to smell honey in places where honey could not be, at the end of a stone passage or at some windy turn of the road, and it came always with certain thoughts. When I got back to Dublin I was with angry people who argued over everything or were eager to know the exact facts: in the midst of the mood that makes realistic drama. (From *The Bounty of Sweden*)

A READING OF THE POEM

At one level, this poem is an attempt to balance the horrors of war with the healing sweetness and regenerative power of nature. As Yeats himself saw it, 'Men must have lived so through many tumultuous centuries. One felt an overmastering desire not to grow unhappy or embittered, not to lose all sense of the beauty of nature.' The brutality of war is graphically represented here:

> Last night they trundled down the road
> That dead young soldier in his blood . . .

The onomatopoeic sound of 'trundled' carries suggestions of some primitive war machine or evokes the tumbrels and savage excess of the French Revolution. There is none of the traditional respect for a dead enemy here, but rather the ferocity of civil war enmity in the indignity with which the dead solder was treated – 'trundled . . . in his blood'. The bees are evoked as an antidote to this savagery. They may symbolise patience and creative force, as opposed to the destructive forces round about. They bring sweetness, healing and the richness of life. These may also be a classical allusion to Pomphyry's bees, who visited the world to perform tasks for the gods. So the bees could be seen as a manifestation of the divine in the world. Whether they evoked for Yeats the simple beauty of nature or carried more complex connotations, his plea to them is a desperate plaintive cry. That cry for healing and for natural regeneration of life echoes through that repeated refrain at the end of each stanza, culminating in the final direct personal address, 'O honey-bees'. There is honest emotion here.

But this is more than simply a reaction to a specific event. Taken in the context of the poem as a whole, we could read this section as a metaphor for Yeats's own life situation and that of his traditional class, the Anglo-Irish ascendancy. The tower-house, once a fortified planter house, used as a place of both safety and dominance, is now a place of 'loosening masonry'; the structures of that colonial past are crumbling. The Yeats' isolation in the tower during that particular fortnight is symptomatic of the isolation and uncertain future of the entire minority but once-powerful class.

> We are closed in, and the key is turned
> On our uncertainty.

This is not just physical imprisonment but a mental segregation, a way of viewing themselves as different, distinct and separate – a cultivated isolation. The key has been turned from the inside. The physical barriers of stone or wood accord with the mental barriers created by class and outlook, so that we are acutely aware of how introverted and cut off the poet is. Yet there is a hint in the first stanza that some sweetness can come with the ending of his self-isolation:

> My wall is loosening; honey-bees,
> Come build in the empty house of the stare,

Or is this just a vain hope?

In the final stanza he faces up to the illusions on which his philosophy is based and which are explored in the rest of the poem: that sweetness and beauty might grow out of bitter and violent conquest, that conflict and a life of adversity could be a glorious thing. These are the fantasies that sustain his class outlook and for which he now indicts himself. The consequence has not been beauty but self-brutalisation.

> The heart's grown brutal from the fare.

He strips away any delusions of superiority or righteousness as he admits that negative emotions are strongest.

> More substance in our enmities
> Than in our love.

It is as if the violence outside has forced him to confront the past violence of his own class, in an honest moment of shared guilt. This is a critical moment of bleak insight, yet one that he attempts to balance with the final plea: 'O honey-bees' – a plea for sweetness and healing at a time of pain, for order in a time of chaos.

Imagery

Images of houses and buildings dominate this poem; but they are either abandoned, like the house of stone, or destroyed by violence ('a house burned'), or are gradually crumbling away in time ('loosening masonry'; 'My wall is crumbling'). They are symbols of a way of life being destroyed; or else they are isolating and self-imprisoning:

> We are closed in, the key is turned
> On our uncertainty.

Any building done is for destructive and disorderly purpose: 'A barricade of stone or wood'. So the poet's plea, while romantic and positive in outlook, is rather pathetic in the context. Only the bees and birds may build where the once-powerful colonising class raised great edifices.

In Memory of Eva Gore-Booth and Con Markiewicz

Text of poem: New Explorations Anthology page 162

This poem was written in the autumn of 1927, was first published in 1929, and is included in *The Winding Stair and Other Poems* (1933). Constance Markievicz had died in August 1927, her sister Eva the previous year.

A reading of the poem

This is one of Yeats's poems of age, the reverie of an old man addressing the now-dead companions of his youth: 'Dear shadows . . .' It is very much a retrospective piece, viewing life from the perspective of the end. Yeats avoids sentimentality, opting instead for retrospective judgments, assessing the significance of their lives. He felt that they had wasted their lives. Constance Markievicz's years of political agitation for socialist and republican ideals he dismisses as dragging out lonely years – 'Conspiring among the ignorant' – while Eva's social and women's suffrage work is merely 'some vague Utopia'.

To understand this harsh condemnation of what to us seem idealistic and committed lives we need to take the poet's value system into account. His view was that the Anglo-Irish ascendancy class, with its wealth and great houses, had a duty to set an example of gracious and cultured living; this was its value for society. As the critic Alasdair MacRae says, 'The graciousness of accustomed affluence, the unostentatiousness of inherited furnishings and family traditions, what he saw culminating in courtesy, appealed to Yeats and he considered Eva and Con along with Maud Gonne as betraying something precious and feminine.' Yeats's idea of beauty is linked to the feminine. The image of feminine beauty he creates here is exotic. The silk kimonos give a hint of eastern mysteriousness, while the comparison with a gazelle suggests both a natural elegance and a certain wild, unknowable quality. And the two sisters are a decorative part of the big-house scene, a house that is elegant, imposing, a symbol of Anglo-Irish achievement and cultured way of life. It is primarily this image and what it symbolised that Yeats is nostalgic for: it is not the people he missed in the first instance, but the house and the cultured dinner-table conversation!

> Many a time I think to seek
> One or the other out and speak
> Of that old Georgian mansion, mix
> Pictures of the mind, recall
> That table and the talk of youth . . .

Yeats's negative retrospective judgments are not so much the bitter rantings of an old man, but rather what he saw as a failure to fulfil an inherited role in society.

But this has some of the more usual features of an 'age' poem – the contrast of youth and age. The 'two girls in silk kimonos . . . one a gazelle' become 'withered old and skeleton-gaunt'. It is interesting that old bodies are rarely beautiful for Yeats: he is repelled and disgusted by physical ageing. We are made aware of the ravages of time very early on in the poem, right after the first four lines of that beautiful limpid opening, and it comes as quite a shocking contrast:

> But a raving autumn shears
> Blossom from the summer's wreath.

Autumn is 'raving', mad, hysterical, out of control, and the sharp-edged onomatopoeic sound of 'shears' conveys its deadly potential. Even summer carries the seeds of death in its 'wreath'.

Out of this retrospection Yeats attempts to distil a certain wisdom about life. This philosophy he sets down in the second section. In a more kindly address to the 'dear shadows' he presumes they now agree with him about the vanity of all causes and all zeal, irrespective of rightness:

> All the folly of a fight
> With a common wrong or right.

And, secondly, he knows that the great quarrel is with time, destroyer of innocence and beauty. He reflects on the vanity of it all, as it will end in a great apocalyptic conflagration, which will consume not just all they've built – great houses or mere gazebos – but all the anguished decisions of their lives. All is vanity before the end.

TONE

At times he manages to be gently nostalgic, such as at the beginning and end of the first section. But he can be very censorious about lives wasted in political agitation. And he seems quite excited by the possibility of the great final conflagration. This is communicated by the energy and repetition of strong verbs (strike, strike, climb, run) and by the repetition of phrases ('strike a match').

THEMES AND ISSUES

- What is a worthwhile way to live life?
- The vagaries of life, the imperfections
- Is it all vanity? What is the point of it all?
- The real enemy is time.
- Contrasting youth and age.

RHYMES AND RHYTHMS

Though Yeats imposes a quatrain rhyming scheme, *abba*, on the poem, he does not structure the thought in quatrains, apart from the first four lines. The first section, for instance, is structured periodically in groups of 4, 5, 4, 7. So the thought structure provides a sort of counter-rhythm to the rhyming structure and gives it a conversational naturalness.

This naturalness is emphasised by the use of off-rhymes rather than full rhymes, for example south – both, wreath – death, ignorant – gaunt, recall – gazelle. Some could argue that the imperfect rhyme befits the theme – the imperfections of life. The rhythmic quality of the language is achieved partly through repetitions: repetitions of phrases such as 'And bid me strike a match', but more obviously with the repetition of the well-known refrain 'Two girls . . .' However, the tone of the second repetition differs markedly from the first, because of the context, where it now carries all the bleak irony and the disappointment of hindsight.

STRUCTURE

The structure of this poem is almost unnoticed, so deftly is it done. It opens with 'The light of evening', proceeds to the darkness of 'Dear Shadows', and erupts again into the final apocalyptic inferno of the end of time. It begins with youth and ends with death; it opens with the great house of Lissadell and ends with a fragile gazebo.

Swift's Epitaph

Text of poem: New Explorations Anthology page 166

[*Note: This poem is also prescribed for Ordinary Level 2006 exam*]

Begun in 1929 and finished in September 1930, this was first published in the *Dublin Magazine* in the winter of 1931. It is included in the volume *The Winding Stair and Other Poems* (1933). The poem is essentially a translation, with some alterations, of the Latin epitaph on Jonathan Swift's memorial in St Patrick's Cathedral, Dublin.

Hic depositum est Corpus
JONATHAN SWIFT S.T.D.
Hujus Ecclesiae Cathedralis
Decani,
Ubi saeva Indignatio
Ulterius
Cor lacerare nequit.
Abi Viator
Et imitare, si poteris,
Strenuum pro virili
Libertatis vindicatorem.
Obiit 19º Die Mensis Octobris
A.D. 1745. Anno Aetatis 78º.

Here is laid the body of
JONATHAN SWIFT, doctor of sacred theology,
dean of this cathedral church,
where savage indignation
can no longer
rend his heart.
Go, traveller,
and imitate, if you can,
an earnest and dedicated
champion of liberty.
He died on the nineteenth day of October
AD 1745, in the year of his age 78.

Jonathan Swift (1667–1745) was dean of St Patrick's Cathedral, Dublin. Poet, political pamphleteer and satirist, he was the author of such famous works as *The Drapier's Letters, A Modest Proposal, A Tale of a Tub* and *Gulliver's Travels*. Politically conservative, Swift voiced the concerns and values of Protestant Ireland with an independence of spirit and a courage that Yeats admired greatly. Swift's writing made him enemies on all sides, but this isolation endeared him even further to Yeats, who often spoke admiringly of 'Anglo-Irish solitude'. Yeats thought of Swift as a heroic figure, an artist–philosopher who, despite the conflicts of his personal life, served liberty by speaking out in his writings and freeing the artist from the tyranny of the mob. He ranked Swift together with Berkeley, Goldsmith and Burke as one of the intellectual founders of the Anglo-Irish tradition.

Yeats's play *The Words upon the Window Pane* (1930) explores some of the conflicts of Swift's life.

A FREE TRANSLATION

Among the chief interests of the Yeats poem are the significance of the changes he made. For instance, 'Swift has sailed into his rest' is much more confident, energetic and vigorous than the original. It sounds more like a victorious progress, while being at the same time a gentle and graceful journey. There are also clearer overtones of a spiritual afterlife – 'his rest' – where the original merely notes the depositing of the body!

He retains the famous reference to *'saeva indignatio'* (savage indignation), which was the driving force of Swift's satirical work, and the reference to his capacity for empathy and for being affected by the injustices and miseries he encountered ('cannot lacerate his breast'). The challenge to the observer is stronger than in the original – to imitate him 'if you dare' rather than 'if you can'. And the traveller is described as 'world-besotted', worldly, lacking in spiritual values and outlook. The implication may be to enhance, by contrast, the unworldly qualities of Swift (which would be somewhat at variance with the facts). Yeats also retains the epithet noting Swift's defence of liberty, a philosophy they shared.

In general it might be said that Yeats has nudged the epitaph more in the direction of a eulogy. And there is more transparent emotion and admiration in the Yeats version.

An Acre of Grass

Text of poem: New Explorations Anthology page 168

This poem was written in November 1936 and first published in *New Poems* (1938).

A READING OF THE POEM

This poem is quite a remarkable response to old age and thoughts of death. The first stanza captures the shrinkage of an old person's physical world in the twilight years. With the ebbing of physical strength his world is reduced to the gardens of his house, 'an acre of green grass | For air and exercise'. The final two lines of the stanza are a marvellous evocation of the stillness, isolation and sense of emptiness that can be experienced at night by the wakeful elderly, a feeling carried in part by the broad vowel rhymes 'house – mouse':

> Midnight, an old house
> Where nothing stirs but a mouse.

He could easily resign himself to restfulness and silence. 'My temptation is quiet.'

But this old man, this poet, needs to write, to continue to find new truths, and he knows that neither a 'loose imagination' – an imagination that is not disciplined by the structure of writing – nor any ordinary observation of everyday occurrences will deliver up any significant truths.

> Nor the mill of the mind
> Consuming its rag and bone,
> Can make truth known.

Real creativity needs something more, like mystical insight; and that comes only through really passionate endeavour or frenzy. Hence his prayer, 'Grant me an old man's frenzy.' That frenzy or madness produced insight and truth for King Lear at the end of his life; and mystical visions, which some interpret as madness, produced the beautiful wisdom of William Blake's poetry. Even at the end of his life, Yeats knows the huge transforming energy necessary to forge new insights and truths, and he faces up to it.

> Myself I must remake

What courage for a person in his seventies!

Yeats had been reading Nietzsche's *The Dawn of Day*, about people of genius who can distance themselves from character and temperament and rise above the weight of personality like a winged creature. Yeats had used Nietzsche's ideas to develop his theory of the Mask: he felt the need to continually transform himself. And this is the ideology driving this poem – the need for transformation in order to achieve new insights and truths. So the poet must discard the persona of dignified old man and remake himself as a wild, mad prophet-like figure, such as Timon or Lear or Blake, and that will bring the searing vision, the 'eagle mind' 'that can pierce the clouds'. This is a poet's fighting response to old age and approaching death. It may remind us of Dylan Thomas's later 'Rage, rage against the dying of the light.'

Explore the following ideas, and expand on each with reference to what you find in the poem.

- A response to ageing: refusing to accept a quiet retirement; summoning reserves of energy to continue working; aware of the huge demands, yet praying for the chance.
- The process of creativity: the ordinary imagination processing or milling everyday events is not sufficient; a frenzy or madness is necessary in order to see things differently or see into things; the after-truths or insights are all-consuming; the power of that insight can 'pierce the clouds' and 'shake the dead'.
- The poet's need for continued transformation. Is it comfortable being a poet? Is it worth it?

Politics

Text of poem: New Explorations Anthology page 170

A READING OF THE POEM

We know that Yeats had intended that the volume *Last Poems* should end with 'Politics'. It is suggested that it was written as an answer to an article that had praised Yeats for his public language but suggested that he should use it more on political subjects. If so, then this is written as a mocking, ironic, tongue-in-cheek response. The speaker affects the pose of a distracted lover who is too preoccupied with the woman to give any attention to the political chaos of European politics of the mid-1930s: Franco, Mussolini, etc. He is little concerned for these earth-shattering events, dismissing them casually in a throw-away comment:

> And maybe what they say is true
> Of war and war's alarms . . .

We can almost see the shrug of indifference.

But the mask of the dispassionate observer slips in the final two lines as his passionate yearning breaks through and we realise that the 'she' is probably 'Caitlín Ní Uallacháin' – Ireland. So we understand Yeats's mocking response to those who have not understood one of his major poetical preoccupations.

The regularity of the four-stress lines alternating with three-stress lines and the simplicity of alternative end-line rhymes, together with the simplicity of the language, give the impression that this is lightweight verse. But, as with all good satire, we are lulled into a false sense of security until the final punch is thrown.

From 'Under Ben Bulben'

Text of poem: New Explorations Anthology page 172

SECTIONS V AND VI

The final draft of this poem is dated 4 September 1938, about five months before the poet's death. Parts of it were published in 1939.

BACKGROUND AND CONTEXT

Some acquaintance with the poem as a whole is necessary for an understanding of the context of sections V and VI. It is recommended that you read through all six sections.

'Under Ben Bulben' can be seen as Yeats's poetic testimony, an elegy for himself, defining his convictions and the poetical and social philosophies that motivated his life's work.

Section I incorporates the two main belief systems that informed his poetry: the occult philosophy, and folk beliefs and traditions.

Section II features another aspect of his belief system: reincarnation.

Section III suggests that poetic insight is born out of moments of violence; that violence and conflict can be invigorating.

Section IV outlines what he considers the great tradition in art, from Pythagoras through Egyptian and Greek sculpture to Michelangelo's Renaissance.

In Sections IV and V Yeats urges all artists, poets, painters and sculptors to do their work in this great tradition of art, to promote the necessary heroic images that nourish civilisation. Specifically, he had in mind the forms of the perfected human body as the necessary poetic inspiration, a concept linked to his ideas on eugenics (the pseudo-science of improving the human race through selective breeding). Yeats had joined the Eugenics Society in London in 1936 and became interested in research on intelligence testing. During 1938 he worked on a verse tract on this topic, published as *On the Boiler* (1939). Convinced that eugenics was crucial to the future of civilisation, he wrote: 'Sooner or later we must limit the families of the unintelligent classes and if our government cannot send them doctor and clinic it must, till it gets tired of it, send monk and confession box.'

Section VI of 'Under Ben Bulben' rounds his life to its close and moves from the mythologies associated with the top of Benbulbin to the real earth at its foot, in Drumcliff churchyard.

A READING OF THE POEM

Section V

This is Yeats's advice to Irish poets concerning the model or tradition they should follow. And the model he recommends is a new, composite one, attempting to fuse together two cultural traditions, those of peasant and aristocratic cultures.

> Sing the peasantry and then
> Hard-riding country gentlemen . . .

The former is the Irish tradition of folk and fairy tales and fantastical mythology; the latter is the Anglo-Irish cultural tradition, which Yeats traced back to the 'other days' referred to, the eighteenth century and the intellectual contribution of Swift, Berkeley, Goldsmith and Burke. He valued this tradition for its spirit of free enquiry, its sense of order and the example of gracious living it produced in Georgian mansions and fine estates. To this fusion he adds the religious tradition as worthy of celebration ('The holiness of monks'), followed immediately by 'Porter-drinkers' randy laughter', which rather devalues the former. Perhaps it's meant to be ironic. The Irish nobility are worthy of celebration, even though they 'were beaten into the clay | Through seven heroic centuries'. So heroic defeat is a fitting subject.

But once again Yeats scorns the present generation. Physically they do not conform to the traditional model of aesthetic beauty ('All out of shape from top to toe'). With an arrogance derived from the reprehensible theories of eugenics, he scorns their low intelligence and inferior lineage:

> Their unremembering hearts and heads
> Base-born products of base beds.

That arrogant tone continues, to end in that triumphant note – 'Still the indomitable Irishry.' The trouble with this poem is that it is so 'well made' – the rhythms of the language, the regular metre, the alliterative repetitions, the graphically grotesque imagery, etc. – that it can distract us from the seriously questionable class and racist attitudes.

Section VI

This section is beautifully structured, like a film shot. Opening with a long shot of the mountain, the camera draws back and focuses on the churchyard, panning by the church and the ancient cross until it finishes with a close-up of the epitaph cut in limestone. The effect is of a closing down of Yeats's life, a narrowing in to death. Many of the important elements of Yeats's life are here: the mythology and folklore associated with Benbulbin; the sense of ancestry, family and continuity provided by the rector; and the continuity of cultural tradition in the 'ancient cross'. No ostentatious marble tomb or conventional tired phrases are permitted, but rather a piece of indigenous material, local stone, to carry his epitaph.

This is a curiously impersonal epitaph, neither celebrating the person's virtues nor asking remembrance or recommending the soul to God: rather it is a stark piece of advice that the challenges of life and death should not be taken too seriously but should be regarded with a certain detachment. It is his final summation, that all the great issues merely come to this.

Developing a personal understanding

1. Select the poem by Yeats that made the greatest impact on you, and write about your reaction to it.
2. What issues raised by the poet did you think significant?
3. On reading this selection, what did you find surprising or interesting?
4. What impressions of Yeats as a person did you form?
5. What questions would you like to ask him?
6. Do you think it important for Irish pupils to study Yeats?
7. What do you find difficult about the poetry of Yeats?
8. What do you like about his poetry?

Overview

On each point, return to the poem for reference and further exploration.

YEATS AND THE NATIONAL QUESTION

Among the issues explored by the poet under this heading are the following:

- the heroic past; patriots are risk-takers, rebels, self-sacrificing idealists who are capable of all that 'delirium of the brave' (see 'September 1913')
- how heroes are created, how ordinary people are changed ('Easter 1916')
- the place of violence in the process of political change; the paradox of the 'terrible beauty' (see 'September 1913', 'Easter 1916', and 'Meditations in Time of Civil War')
- the place of 'fanaticism' and the human effects of it – the 'stone of the heart' (see 'Easter 1916', 'September 1913', 'In Memory of Eva Gore-Booth and Con Markiewicz')
- the force of political passion (see 'Easter 1916', 'Politics').

YEATS'S NOTIONS OF THE IDEAL SOCIETY

- The vital contribution that both the aristocracy and artists make to society; the importance of the Anglo-Irish tradition in Irish society (see 'September 1913', 'In Memory of Eva Gore-Booth and Con Markiewicz', 'Meditations in Time of Civil War', 'Swift's Epitaph', 'Under Ben Bulben')
- His contempt for the new middle class and the new materialism (see 'September 1913')

- Aesthetic values and the place of art in society (see 'Sailing to Byzantium', 'Under Ben Bulben')
- The yearnings for order and the fear of anarchy (see 'Meditations in Time of Civil War', 'The Second Coming')
- His views on the proper contribution of women to society (see 'In Memory of Eva Gore-Booth and Con Markiewicz', 'Easter 1916').

THEORIES OF HISTORY, TIME AND CHANGE

- His notion of thousand-year eras, 'gyres', etc. (see 'The Second Coming')
- The world and people in constant change and flux (see 'The Second Coming', 'Easter 1916')
- Personal ageing, the transience of humanity (see 'The Wild Swans at Coole', 'An Acre of Grass')
- The yearning for changelessness and immortality (see 'The Wild Swans at Coole', 'Sailing to Byzantium')
- The timelessness of art, or the possibility of it (see 'Sailing to Byzantium').

CONFLICTS AT THE CENTRE OF THE HUMAN BEING

- The conflict between physical desires and spiritual aspirations (see 'Sailing to Byzantium')
- The quest for aesthetic satisfaction (see 'Sailing to Byzantium')
- The search for wisdom and peace, which is not satisfied here (see 'The Lake Isle of Innisfree')
- A persistent sense of loss or failure; loss of youth and passion (see 'The Wild Swans at Coole'); the loss of poetic vision and insight (see 'An Acre of Grass').

General questions

1. Select any major theme explored by Yeats and outline his treatment of it.
2. Review critically any poem by Yeats that you considered interesting.
3. 'Yeats displayed great reverence for the past but little respect for his own time.' Consider the truth of this statement in the light of the poems you have examined.
4. 'W.B. Yeats explored complex issues of national identity with great honesty.' Discuss.
5. Having read his poetry, what do you think Yeats chiefly valued in life?
6. 'Yeats's poetry is fuelled by conflict – conflict between past and present, youth and age, mind and body.' Explore this view of his poetry.

Bibliography

Brown, Terence, *The Life of W.B. Yeats,* Dublin: Gill and Macmillan 1999.

Cullingford, Elizabeth Butler, *Yeats: Poems, 1919–1935* (Casebook Series) Basingstoke: Macmillan 1984.

Cullingford, Elizabeth Butler, *Gender and History in Yeats's Love Poetry,* Cambridge: Cambridge University Press 1993.

Donoghue, Denis (editor), *W.B. Yeats: Memoirs,* London: Macmillan 1972.

Ellman, Richard, *The Identity of Yeats,* London: Faber and Faber 1968.

Ellman, Richard, *Yeats: The Man and the Masks,* Oxford: Oxford University Press 1979.

Foster, R.F., *W.B. Yeats: A Life, vol. 1: The Apprentice Mage,* Oxford: Oxford University Press 1997.

Harwood, John, *Olivia Shakespear and W.B. Yeats,* Basingstoke: Macmillan 1989.

Hone, Joseph, *W.B. Yeats,* Harmondsworth (Middx): Pelican Books 1971.

Jeffares, A.Norman, *W.B. Yeats: Man and Poet,* London: Routledge and Kegan Paul 1966.

Jeffares, A.Norman, *W.B. Yeats: The Poems,* London: Edward Arnold 1979.

Jeffares, A.Norman, *W.B. Yeats: A New Biography,* London: Hutchinson 1988.

Jeffares, A.Norman (editor), *Yeats's Poems,* Basingstoke: Macmillan 1989.

Jeffares, A.Norman, and MacBride White, Anna (editors), *The Gonne–Yeats Letters, 1893–1938,* London: Hutchinson 1992.

Kelly, John (editor), *The Collected Letters of W.B. Yeats* (three vols.), Oxford: Clarendon Press 1986, 1997, 1994.

Kinahan, Frank, *Yeats, Folklore and Occultism,* Boston: Unwin Hyman 1988.

MacRae, Alasdair, *W.B. Yeats: A Literary Life,* Dublin: Gill and Macmillan 1995.

Martin, Augustine, *W.B. Yeats,* Gerrards Cross (Bucks): Colin Smythe 1983.

Smith, Stan, *W.B. Yeats: A Critical Introduction,* Dublin: Gill and Macmillan 1990.

Tuohy, Frank, *Yeats,* London: Macmillan 1976.

Yeats, W.B., *A Vision* [1925], London: Macmillan 1937.

Yeats, W.B., *Autobiographies: Memoirs and Reflections,* London: Macmillan 1955.

Yeats, W.B., *Mythologies,* London: Macmillan 1959.

Yeats, W.B., *Essays and Introductions,* New York: Macmillan 1961.

5 *Thomas Stearns* ELIOT

Seán Scully

Timeline

September 26, 1888	Thomas Stearns Eliot is born in St. Louis, Missouri.
1906–1909	Undergraduate at Harvard. Becomes interested in the symbolists and Laforgue.
1909–1910	Graduate student at Harvard. Studies in France and Germany. 'Prufrock' is completed but not published.
1911–1914	Graduate student at Harvard. Begins work on the philosophy of Francis Herbert Bradley.
1914–1915	Study in Germany stopped by war. Moves to Oxford. Short satiric poems. 'Prufrock' is published in Chicago, June 1915. Marriage to Vivienne Haigh-Wood, July 1915.
1915–1919	Eliot has many different jobs, including teaching, bank clerk and assistant editor of the literary magazine *Egoist*.
1915–1916	Teaching and doing book reviews in London. Bradley thesis is finished.
1915	Eliot moves to London.
June 1917	*Prufrock and Other Observations* is published.
1917–1920	Works in Lloyd's Bank. Many editorials and reviews. Writing of French poems, quatrain poems.
1921–1922	London correspondent for *The Dial*.
1922–1939	Founder and editor of *The Criterion*.
1922	'The Waste Land'. Eliot wins Dial Award for *The Waste Land*. London correspondent for *Revue Française*.
1925	Senior position with publisher Faber & Faber.
1927	Eliot is confirmed in the Church of England and becomes a British citizen.
1927–1930	*Ariel Poems*.

1940–1942	'East Coker', 'The Dry Salvages' and 'Little Gidding'.
1943	'The Four Quartets'.
1947	Death of Eliot's first wife, Vivienne Haigh-Wood, after long illness.
1948	King George VI awards the Order of Merit to T.S. Eliot. Eliot is awarded the Nobel Prize in Literature.
1957	Marries Valerie Fletcher.
1958	*The Elder Statesman.*
January 4, 1965	T.S. Eliot dies.

The Love Song of J. Alfred Prufrock (1917)
Text of poem: New Explorations Anthology page 204

THEMES/ISSUES AND IMAGERY

Title

This is, perhaps, one of Eliot's most striking titles. Yet the poem is neither a song nor a traditional, conventional expression of love. Neither is J. Alfred Prufrock a conventional name for a love poet. It is more evocative of a respectable small-town businessman. (In fact, there was a furniture dealer named Prufrock in St Louis when Eliot lived there.)

The name can be seen as mock-heroic, if not comically ridiculous, in the circumstances of the poem. Indeed 'Prufrockian' has entered the language as an adjective indicative of a kind of archaic idealism which is paralysed by self-consciousness. The rather self-conscious 'J.' before Alfred recalls Mark Twain's distrust of men who 'part their names in the middle'.

Overall the incongruity of associations between the two halves of the title prepares us for the tension developed in the poem.

Epigraph

A literal translation of the epigraph reads:

> *'If I thought that my answer were to one who might ever return to the world, this flame should shake no more; but since no-one ever did return from this depth alive, if what I hear is true, without fear of infamy I answer you.'*

The passage is from Dante's *Inferno*, XXVII, lines 61–66, in which Guido de Montefeltro, tortured in hell for the sin of fraud, is willing to expose himself to Dante because he believes that the poet can never return from the pit of hell to the world. In Eliot's poem, too, the speaker tells of himself, because he feels his audience is also trapped in a hell of its own making. This is so since he is speaking to himself.

The use of the extract from Dante's *Inferno* also suggests that the lovesong is not sung in the real world, but in a 'hell' which is the consequence of being divided between passion and timidity.

Lines 1–12

Most critics agree that the 'you and I' of the first line are two sides of the same personality, the ego and alter ego, as it were. Thus the poem is an interior monologue, an exposure of the self to the self. However, the reader is, of course, free to think that it is he who is being addressed, as the self he addresses may be in all of us.

At any rate, the character Prufrock is struggling with the idea of asking the 'overwhelming question' of line 10.

The poem opens with a command to accompany him, presumably to the room of line 13. However the air of decisiveness collapses immediately with the simile of describing the evening (line 3). This image may be quite striking but it does not give us an immediate visual image. Rather, it reveals a great deal about Prufrock's psychological state. He is helpless – 'etherised'.

The setting of these opening lines is evening or twilight – a sort of halfway period, neither night nor day. This enhances the theme of indecision.

The description of what appears to be the seedy side of the city in the next four lines is presented in a series of quite sordid images. They may indicate the pointlessness of Prufrock's search. His emotional numbness would appear to have led him to unsatisfactory, sordid sexual relations in the past, in 'one-night cheap hotels'. The image of the 'sawdust restaurants with oyster-shells' suggests the vulgarity of these encounters, while also introducing sea imagery, which is a feature of the poem.

These seedy retreats show the tiresome, weary nature of city life. So the streets are compared to 'a tedious argument | Of insidious intent'. Thus Prufrock's encounters and perhaps life itself are seen as mechanical and repetitive and characteristic of an inner sickness. Such an area and such a lifestyle naturally lead to 'an overwhelming question'.

Prufrock is unwilling to face this question. It remains isolated and hidden within, and the 'you' is told not to ask. Thus we are beginning to see the depiction of a melancholic character who cannot satisfy his desires.

Lines 13–14

This room would appear to be Prufrock's destination. The women are satirised and seen as quite pretentious. Their 'talking of Michelangelo' as they 'come and go' is made to seem quite trivial and empty-headed. This is suggested by the jingling rhythm and rhyme.

The subject of their conversation, Michelangelo, is the great sculptor of heroic figures. This is a figure to whose magnanimity and greatness Prufrock could not possibly aspire. So how could the women find him (Prufrock) interesting, even if their knowledge is limited and their talk pretentious? Prufrock is a most unheroic figure.

Lines 15–22

There is a fusion of imagery here. The fog which surrounds the house (presumably the house which contains the room) is described in terms of a cat. This essentially metaphysical concept suggests the theme of unfulfilled promise. This is seen in particular by the fact that the action leads to sleep.

Cats, it must be noted, have been traditionally associated with sexuality and so much of the imagery here may also suggest unsatisfied desire.

The image of the fog serves another purpose. It may convey blurred consciousness or vision, a constant theme in Eliot's poetry. Thus on a wider note, through the imagery of the poem and the character of Prufrock, Eliot is speaking of the degenerated vision and soul of humanity in the twentieth century.

Lines 23–34

Time is one of the important themes, not only of this poem, but also of Eliot's poetry generally. Prufrock takes great comfort in time, repeating rather hypnotically, 'there will be time'.

There will be time to 'prepare a face' against the exposure of the true self, or 'To prepare a face' to make small talk over 'a toast and tea', and to 'murder and create' reputations or characters in a gossipy fashion, perhaps.

This unexciting prospect, with its mundane 'works and days of hands' merely leads him back to the question, which he puts off because of his timidity and hesitancy. The sarcasm of lines 32–33 emphasises the avoidance of decision. The play on the words 'vision' and 'revision' adds further emphasis to this.

And all this anxiety and procrastination doesn't lead to some momentous event, but merely to taking 'toast and tea'. The element of mock-heroic is clear.

Lines 35–36

The repetition of lines 13–14 here underscores the tediousness of the women's talk. It further emphasises Prufrock's limitations and how he is inhibited and perhaps intimidated by so-called social discourse. It, together with the reference to Hamlet later, represents the greatness of the past in contrast to the modern world.

Lines 37–48

Here Prufrock speculates on the women's view of his physical self. The 'prepared face' is no protection against the pitiless gaze of the women. The time for decisive action may be at hand, yet he wonders if he dares. He fears a rebuff and even if he retreats – 'turn back and descend the stair' – he may still seem absurd. He is aware of his unheroic appearance. He is growing bald and 'his arms and legs are thin!' He dresses well – albeit in a very conventional manner – possibly to compensate for these physical shortcomings, and indeed his attractive clothes may be part of his mask – his need to make an appearance.

His doubts are expressed in obvious hyperbole – 'Do I dare | Disturb the universe?' How could *he* possibly disturb the universe? The possibility may lie in the immediate sense of the 'universe' of his own world or in his realisation that even trivial human actions may have immeasurable consequences. This self-conscious awareness precludes his taking any decisive action. Emotionally, at least, Prufrock is impotent.

Lines 49–54

Here Prufrock puts forward the first of three arguments against deciding the overwhelming question. Again, Prufrock is hesitant to act due to the limitations of his inner self. He lacks self-confidence due to the sterility and meaninglessness of his life – which is merely an endless round of 'evenings, mornings, afternoons'. The line 'I have measured out my life with coffee spoons' not only epitomises the repetitive tedium of his everyday existence, but may also suggest a desire to escape the pain of living via the use of a stimulant.

How could he, Prufrock, challenge the meaninglessness of such a life? Such a challenge would be presumptuous.

Lines 55–61

His second argument is presented here. He is afraid of being classified and stereotyped 'in a formulated phrase' by the perhaps contemptuous looks of the women. He recoils from the absolute horror of being pinned down and dissected like an insect in some biological experiment. He has a phobia of being restricted, linked perhaps to a fear of emasculation. So how could a man with such fears risk, or presume, to expose himself to further ridicule? The image of the 'butt-end' of a cigarette to which he compares his life suggests further self-disgust.

Lines 62–69

His third argument against deciding the overwhelming question is presented here. He cannot ask the question because he is simultaneously attracted and revolted by the physicality of women.

The ideal perfection of 'Arms that are braceleted and white and bare' develops into the physicality of '(But in the lamplight, downed with light brown hair!).' The sense of the ideal becoming real reflects his being overwhelmed at the prospect of turning desire into action.

The altered but effectively repeated question of 'And should I then presume?', reflecting his insecurity, suggests an apparent increase in tension towards a sense of impending climax. Yet he cannot conceive any formula for his proposal – 'And how should I begin?'

Lines 70–74

Prufrock offers a possible preface or preamble to his question. He wonders if he should mention that he is aware of a different type of world from that known by the women in the room – the seedy world of lines 4–9 recalled in the imagery here. This awareness may be his justification for asking the question. He knows more, but the fact that he poses the preamble in the form of a question suggests uncertainty as to its relevance.

Again the imagery suggests he is a passive observer, not an active participant. Failure to address the overwhelming question leads, as in line 10, to a trailing off into silence indicated by the three dots.

This section ends with his wish to be something like a crab. This sea imagery in fact is reduced to 'claws'. Thus Prufrock seems to wish to dehumanise himself completely, to become a thing of pure action without self-awareness – living, yet mentally inanimate; to be in a place where he can survive in the depths and yet avoid the pain of living. Obviously this is the very opposite of Prufrock's true situation.

Lines 75–88

This section must be seen as a form of reverie. It is also the turning point of the poem.

Having previously seen the fog as a cat (lines 15–22), Prufrock now sees the afternoon as such. All the tensions up to now are resolved, not in action but in images of inaction and weakness. The afternoon/evening/cat 'sleeps', 'malingers', 'Stretched on the floor'. The sense of being etherised (line 3) is recalled.

The triviality of Prufrock's existence is seen in the mock-heroic rhyming of 'ices' and 'crisis'. This prepares us for Prufrock's efforts to put himself in a heroic perspective. However, his greater sense of personal inadequacy won't permit him to sustain the comparison with St John the Baptist. The ironic discrepancy between John the Baptist and Prufrock is heightened by the self-mockery of '(grown slightly bald)'. Prufrock's head would simply look absurd. He is aware of this and immediately denies the possibility of heroic status for himself – 'I am no prophet' (line 84). The continuation of this line can be read as 'it doesn't really matter' or 'I'm not important.' Either way it is an acknowledgement of his own inadequacy.

The final image in this section is of the eternal Footman. This is Death personified. Even death is laughing at him, but the image also suggests that the servants of the polite society hosts whom he visits do not take him seriously. He feels he is the butt of their jokes. To both death and the ridicule of servants, the profound and the trivial, Prufrock admits his fear. It is too late for him to act. Fear is his reality.

Lines 89–115

Prufrock's speculation on whether forcing the crisis, asking the overwhelming question, would have been worthwhile reads like an excuse for inaction. He is rationalising his failure.

He names again the trivial aspects of his polite environment, recalling earlier lines (49–51, 79). However, now the 'you and I' of line 1 are very much part of the trivia of this environment. They are 'Among the porcelain, among some talk of you and me'. Perhaps he cannot accept that any significant action can take place in this type of environment. He is afraid of being misunderstood. What would he do if his 'overwhelming question' should meet with an offhand rejection like:

'That is not what I meant at all.
That is not it, at all.'

The fact that these lines are repeated shows the extent of his fear.

Two references in this section suggest that Prufrock continues to compare himself to those of heroic status.

Line 94 is a reference to Andrew Marvell's poem 'To His Coy Mistress' in which the poet urges his beloved to enjoy immediate sexual union with him as a sort of victory over time. Prufrock's inaction is the antithesis of this.

Both men by the name of Lazarus in the Gospels were figures of triumph over death: one, the brother of Martha and Mary, by being recalled to life by Jesus; the other, a poor man, by gaining Heaven – unlike the rich man, Dives.

Prufrock fears that even the most profound knowledge may be decorously, but casually, rejected.

Essentially Prufrock's fear here is of never being able to connect emotionally with another person. The gulf between human beings inner selves cannot be bridged. This has him cry out in frustration:

It is impossible to say just what I mean!
(line 108)

The possibility of the insensitive comprehension of the other exposes his own sensitivity. It is 'as if a magic lantern threw the nerves in patterns on a screen' (lines 109–110). Thus throughout this section women again appear as catalysts to Prufrock's inadequacy and inferiority.

Lines 116–124
Here Prufrock settles for a less than heroic version of himself. He recognises that any further heroic action would be absurd. He may have something in common with Shakespeare's Prince Hamlet, for he too was indecisive, but any direct identification would be ridiculous.

Rather, he sees himself as a Polonius figure – an advisor to kings – or even a lesser person. The theatrical imagery of lines 117–119 suggests a bit player. Prufrock has become consciously unheroic. In lines 119–124 he is quite self-deprecating, reducing himself eventually to the level of a wise Fool. A passage that begins with 'Hamlet' ends with 'the Fool'.

However, there is the possibility, with the capitalisation of 'the Fool', that Prufrock does not see himself as any old fool, but perhaps akin to the Fool in Shakespeare's *King Lear* – a wise fool who utters uncomfortable truths, which powerful people would prefer not to hear. Maybe this is Prufrock's final fantasy.

Lines 125–136
A world-weariness introduces this section. This in effect becomes a process of dying, until 'we drown' in the last line.

He does, however, make a decision in line 126 – to 'wear the bottoms of my trousers rolled'. The triviality of the decision, in contrast to the 'overwhelming question', suggests his resignation to a trivial existence. This decision is followed by two further trivial questions, which underscore the point. Parting his hair may hide his bald spot. Eating a peach may be the riskiest behaviour he will ever again indulge in.

This hopeless, empty existence has him resort to the beach. Sea imagery throughout the poem (lines 7, 73–74) has suggested some alternative lifestyle – some hope of avoiding the pain of consciousness.

The mermaids of line 129 symbolise a sort of idealised erotic beauty similar to the arms in line 63. But Prufrock realises that this is only a fantasy, a dream. He has been deluding himself. His realisation of this is expressed in the simple bathos of line 130: 'I do not think that they will sing to me.'

Yet delusions are hard to let go and he asserts the existence of the mermaids, of the erotic ideal, in a defiant final cry (lines 131–133).

But he has 'lingered in the chambers' of his world of ideal relationships and heroic actions for too long, perhaps. The dream is unattainable. The use of 'we' here is not just the 'you and I' of line 1, but also the universal plural. All of us can get lost in our reveries, until we are called to reality by other human voices – a reality where 'we drown'. All struggle is ended and we accept the death of our inner selves.

The irony inherent in the title has already been described. It is the self-irony of Laforgue, adapted to a dreadful seriousness. The poem is a tragic comedy, the epitaph sets the mood.

The lyricism of the opening is appropriate to a love-song, but it collapses almost immediately in the simile of Line 3. The simile is quite comically inappropriate for a love-song but is tragically appropriate for the hapless Prufrock and his situation.

The repetition of 'Let us go' suggests that he is already faltering.

The sibilant sounds which dominate the opening sequence underscore the seedy imagery and the sense of being 'etherised'. This is continued into the simile of 'like a tedious argument'. These sounds combined with the rhyming couplets do give a lyrical or musical effect, but also enhance the sense of ennui.

The dramatic pause indicated by the three dots in line 10 emphasises Prufrock's tragic flow and reinforces the bathos.

This bathos is further felt in the jingling rhythm and rhyme of lines 13–14: 'In the room the women come and go | Talking of Michelangelo.'

The fog/cat passage (lines 15–22) is also dominated by sibilant sounds which enhance the tone. These sounds are in contrast with the more cacophonous lines 23–34 which follow.

The fog/cat metaphor is in effect a metaphysical conceit. It is a flight of fancy, a sort of *jeu d'esprit*. Adding to the sensual sibilant sounds is the use of the letter 'L', often seen as the liquid letter, enhancing the sinuous movement of the fog.

The solemn incantatory tone of lines 23–34, echoing the Old Testament speaker in Ecclesiastes, contributes to the mock-heroic element of the poem, which is further added to by the pun on 'revisions' (lines 34 and 48).

Unlike the contrasts in the Book of Ecclesiastes, the opposing forces here do not show a sense of balance or equilibrium, but add to the confusion. The repetition of lines 13–14, which are in danger of becoming a refrain, emphasises the sterility and shallowness of the modern human condition, as mentioned above.

The constant repetition of rhetorical questions is a feature of the next several sections:

> 'Do I dare?'
> So how should I presume?
> And how should I begin?

These suggest a tone of uncertainty and underscore the sense of inaction.

The dominant verbs of lines 58–61 – 'formulated', 'sprawling', 'pinned', 'wriggling' – suggest not only the fear of individual inadequacy, but also a sense of being a victim.

His self-contempt, and possibly anger, are seen in the mixture of sibilants and cacophonous consonants in lines 73–74:

> I should have been a pair of ragged claws
> Scuttling across the floors of silent seas.

The ridiculous rhyming of 'ices' and 'crisis' (lines 79–80) has already been alluded to for its mock-heroic, satiric effect. The same effect is achieved with the rhyming of 'flicker' and 'snicker' in lines 85 and 87. The pathetic admission of:

> I am no prophet – and here's no great matter;
> I have seen the moment of my greatness flicker,

is reduced to a snort of mockery with the word 'snicker'.

The note of tragic satire is also in the bathetic joke on his 'head (grown slightly bald)' and the prophetic Biblical echoes of:

> 'I am Lazarus, come from the dead,
> Come back to tell you all, I shall tell you all' –
> (lines 96–97)

The broad vowels here remind us of one crying in the wilderness and being ignored.

The tone changes in the last section. Now that he acknowledges that 'It is impossible to say just what I mean!', and the 'overwhelming question' is gone, the poem settles down to a lyricism which merely flickered earlier. The use of alliteration, assonance and onomatopoeia in lines 131–136 both intensifies the description and underscores the tone and mood:

> I have seen them riding seaward on the waves
> Combing the white hair of the waves blown back
> When the wind blows the water white and black.
>
> We have lingered in the chambers of the sea
> By sea-girls wreathed with seaweed red and brown
> Till human voices wake us, and we drown.

The reference to Prince Hamlet does not seem pedantic, given the tone of this section. The rather comic bewilderment of:

> Shall I part my hair behind? Do I dare to eat a peach?

helps to raise our sympathy for him. Thus both the 'serious' references and the mocking tone serve to emphasise the comic-tragedy of Prufrock's situation.

Overall, the poem is quite fragmented, full of quickly changing images – aural, visual and tactile – presented in a cinematic, stream-of-consciousness style, reflecting both his character and situation.

THE CHARACTER OF PRUFROCK

- He is consciously unheroic.
- Melancholic and contemplative
- Feels inferior, inadequate and inhibited
- Fears rejection
- Both attracted to and threatened by women
- Women fall short of his idealised vision.
- Cannot find a language in which to express himself
- Indulges in escapist fantasies to avoid despair
- Indecisive, self-contemptuous and sees himself as a victim
- In a 'hell' – the consequence of being divided between passion and timidity – his tragic flaw
- A sensitive man in a psychological impasse
- An ageing romantic, incapable of action
- Tormented by unsatisfied desire
- A comic figure made tragic by his acute self-awareness
- The poem gives us not only the thoughts and feelings of Prufrock, but also the actual experience of his feeling and thinking.

PRUFROCK'S PROBLEMS WITH LANGUAGE

- Much of the meaning of the poem arises from its form: the digressions, hesitations, references, all suggest Prufrock's inability to express himself.
- Language regularly fails him. The first section never arrives at the question.
- Prufrock struggles with his own inarticulateness – 'Shall I say?' 'It is impossible to say just what I mean!'
- The failure of his love-song is also a failure to find a language in which to express himself.
- The fragments that make up the poem are essentially a collection of potential poems, which collapse because Prufrock cannot express his 'overwhelming question'.
- He is not included in the mermaids' song.
- Human voices suffocate and drown him.

MAIN THEMES

- Indecision
- Confronting the difficulty of action
- Time
- Emotional impotence
- The obduracy of language
- Superficiality and emptiness

- The hidden and isolated inner self
- The limitations of the real world
- Dying – spiritually, mentally, physically – death in life
- The movement in the mind.

MAIN IMAGES
- Sordid, seedy city life
- Fog/cat
- The room of pseudo-gentility
- Sea imagery – shells, crab, mermaids
- Cultural imagery – Michelangelo, John the Baptist, Lazarus, Hamlet
- Hair, clothes
- Coffee, tea, cakes and ices.

Preludes (1917)

Text of poem: New Explorations Anthology page 212

[*Note: This poem is also prescribed for the Ordinary Level 2006 exam*]

INTRODUCTION

The 'Preludes' present us with urban scenes where what is seen reflects a particular state of mind. For the deeply disillusioned young poet they illustrate the ugliness, decline, emptiness and boredom of modern life.

The city here is effectively the same as that described by Prufrock in the 'Love Song of J. Alfred Prufrock'. It is a sordid world of deadening monotony and empty routine. The time-sets of the poem – evening, morning, night and day – reinforce the feeling of tedious monotony.

The title 'Preludes' can be seen as a reference to this sequence of evening, morning, night and day. They, as it were, are a 'prelude' to more sameness in the purposeless cycle of life.

'Preludes' could also point to the musical or lyrical effects in the poems.

As is usual with Eliot the poetry here is fragmented, full of quickly changing images – visual, aural, tactile and olfactory – in what is often described as a cinematic style. In what is essentially also a stream-of-consciousness style, Eliot takes us on a journey through the senses and the minds of his observers.

A READING OF THE POEM

Section I

Here the 'winter evening' is personified as it 'settles down' in a way reminiscent of the fog/cat in 'The Love Song of J. Alfred Prufrock'.

Olfactory images and tactile images abound – 'smell of steaks', 'burnt-out', 'smoky', 'grimy', 'withered leaves about your feet', the showers 'wrap' and 'beat' – leaving a sense of staleness and decay. This is compounded by the image of cramped apartments in 'passageways'.

'The burnt-out ends of smoky days' is a visual image that reminds us of Prufrock's 'butt-ends of my days and ways' and also evokes a sense of weariness and disgust.

Adjectives such as 'withered', 'broken', 'lonely' and 'vacant' suggest the decay and isolation of city life, while the insistent beating of the rain adds to the misery. The visual image of the uncomfortable and impatient cab-horse completes the picture of dreariness.

The isolated last line of this section: 'And then the lighting of the lamps', suggests that something dramatic might be about to happen. But nothing does. The opening words 'And then' are not a prelude to drama, but rather a closing in of the night.

Thus the imagery of the section evokes the speaker's mood. The reader can imagine him trudging home through the wet misery of a winter's evening, surrounded by withered leaves and discarded newspapers and inhaling the burnt and musty smells of his living quarters. What else could he be but depressed by it all? The feeling of a numb, aimless, struggle in an ugly, sterile environment suggests a mood of spiritual and mental decay.

Section II

Like 'evening' in the first section, 'morning' is here personified. It is as if the monotonous time-sets were living an independent life from the actors in this tedious drama of life.

Olfactory and tactile images – 'smells of beer', 'sawdust-trampled street', 'muddy feet that press', 'coffee-stands' – again suggest a sense of staleness and decay. Words such as 'trampled' and 'press' add to the mood of oppressiveness.

Individual life is submerged in the city and by the onward march of time and what emerges is a mass conformity and uniformity:

> One thinks of all the hands
> That are raising dingy shades
> In a thousand furnished rooms.

This sense of sameness and monotony is also suggested by:

> all its muddy feet that press
> To early coffee-stands.

Eliot regularly depersonalises the character of individuals to show the mechanical nature of their lives. Here people are reduced to 'hands' and 'feet', invoking something living yet spiritually inanimate. Life has become an enslavement to pressure – the pressure of time, crowds and gulped-down coffee.

For Eliot this morning rush to work is a masquerade. It is an act put on by all the 'feet' and 'hands' to give their lives some meaning. The poet is suggesting that behind all the mad masquerade of activity there is a paralysis of the metaphysical, as people's lives are constituted solely by their mundane masquerades.

Section III

The third section illustrates physical inaction as a woman (the 'you' of the poem) struggles to wake and sluggishly prepares to get out of bed, where during the night she fitfully dozed.

Her uncomfortable sleepless night is caught in the verbs of the first three lines – 'tossed', 'lay', 'waited', 'dozed', 'watched'. She is trapped between sleep and wakefulness which allows her imagination to wander randomly:

> . . . revealing
> The thousand sordid images
> Of which your soul was constituted;

Thus her paralysis, just like the city's, is also a paralysis of the metaphysical. She is quite inert, apart from throwing the blanket from her bed.

As is typical of Eliot, we are again presented with a character's state of mind. The woman cannot sleep and when she dozes her semi-conscious mind projects, like a film on a screen, her interior self which 'flickered against the ceiling'. These 'sordid' images reflect not only her degradation, but are symbolic of the degenerated consciousness and spirit of mankind in the twentieth century. As a projection of the twentieth century she is more passive and vulgar than the woman in 'A Game of Chess'.

When morning arrived, its light 'crept up between the shutters', almost as if it were an unwelcome intruder, while the sparrows are stripped of all beauty by being heard 'in the gutters'. Her vision of the street is not clarified. It is again blurred – a vision that is hardly understood. Both woman and street appear earthbound – she is supine in bed, while the personified street is 'trampled' in both Sections II and IV.

The feeling of degradation and disgust is continued in the last four lines of this section. Eliot again depersonalises the character of the woman to portray this. She is dehumanised into bodily parts – 'hair', 'feet', 'hands' – to evoke the image of a living person who is spiritually inanimate, just as in Section II.

The sense of disgust is more intense here, however. Her hair is artificially curled with paper, her feet are unhealthily 'yellow' and her hands are 'soiled'. This is quite unlike the meticulous image of Prufrock in the 'Love Song of J.

Alfred Prufrock'. He may be ridiculous. She is repulsive. The capacity for spiritual growth is non-existent.

Section IV
This final section in this poetic sequence reveals the speaker more fully. Like the woman in Section III whose soul's images are 'flickered against the ceiling', his soul is also mirrored upwards. But the skies on which it is stretched are not attractive. They 'fade behind a city block'. Indeed, the image is rather tortured – 'His soul [is] stretched tight', reflecting the tension and strain of urban life. The passing of the hours – 'At four and five and six o'clock' – merely reflects the tense tedium and emptiness of his existence.

Eliot again dehumanises and depersonalises individuals to show the mechanical nature of city life – 'trampled . . . feet', 'short square fingers', 'and eyes'. Their daily routine consists of 'newspapers' and 'pipes' and being 'Assured of certain certainties'. Thus the human reality of the street reveals itself as neither conscious nor aware of its own insecurities and sordid dilapidation. The poet sees these people as living lives of drudgery, whose 'conscience' has been 'blackened'. This is a valueless, dreary society, which is now menacingly seen as being 'Impatient to assume the world.'

In one of those abrupt shifts for which he is famous, Eliot suddenly reveals himself in a moving, pathos-filled quatrain:

> I am moved by fancies that are curled
> Around these images, and cling:
> The notion of some infinitely gentle
> Infinitely suffering thing.

What saves the poet from being swamped by his disgust for modern life is his clinging to a belief in 'some infinitely gentle | Infinitely suffering thing.' This is, perhaps, indicating his move towards Christianity as a source of order and veneration.

However, in an equally abrupt shift he returns to cynicism and encourages us to laugh at, and not sympathise with, the human condition:

> Wipe your hand across your mouth, and laugh

The emptiness in life and the struggle for survival is suggested in a simile which underscores the horrific drudgery of deprivation:

> The worlds revolve like ancient women
> Gathering fuel in vacant lots.

The process of dying, which is prevalent among most, if not all, of the characters in Eliot's poetry, is dramatically evident here also.

Language and Mood

Lyrical devices are common throughout.

The monotonous metre of the first section emphasises the drudgery and oppression of these mean streets. Most lines have four iambic stresses, while the others have two. This is in keeping with the image of trampling feet in Sections II and III and, matched by the inexorable flow of time, emphasises the general weariness of moods.

The emphatic rhymes equally convey the sense of oppression. This is particularly the case with the rhyming couplets – 'wraps – scraps' and 'stamps – lamps'.

The insistent beating of the rain is further emphasised by the use of alliteration:

> The showers beat
> On broken blinds . . .

while the impatience of the horse is intensified by alliteration and the strong iambic rhythm:

> And at the corner of the street
> A lonely cab-horse steams and stamps.

Earlier in this section the use of alliteration and consonance furthers the sense of decay and staleness. The use of sibilant 's' sounds is particularly effective in this:

> The winter evening settles down
> With smell of steaks in passageways.

Thus, in keeping with the musical note of its title, the poet uses lyrical devices to emphasise his themes and underscore imagery and mood.

While Section I is generally composed of end-stopped lines, Section II is composed of lines which run on. This use of enjambment serves to convey a sense of movement – the movement of 'muddy feet' on a 'trampled street'. It also emphasises the pressure of time.

The use of synecdoche, in which a part is substituted for the whole, has been alluded to earlier for the way in which it depersonalises individuals and emphasises monotonous conformity:

> One thinks of all the hands
> That are raising dingy shades
> In a thousand furnished rooms.

While Eliot favoured 'vers libre', he does use rhyme to draw attention to or satirise a situation, as we saw in Section I. The rhyming of 'consciousness' with 'press' and 'masquerades' with 'shades' here underscores the theme of pretence; the desire to put on an act to give life some meaning. It also intensifies the mood of oppression.

Overall in this section there is a strong sense of contrast between the descriptions of movement and the sense of spiritual paralysis.

The essentially passive nature of the verbs used at the beginning of Section III reflects her supine state and degenerated consciousness.

The repetition of 'And', which introduces three lines, intensifies the experience of dull monotony, while the almost onomatopoeic effect of the rhyming couplet, 'shutters . . . gutters', reflects the lack of lyricism in the perceived sound of the sparrows. The result is particularly satiric.

The monotonous metre evident in the earlier part of Section IV emphasises the drudgery and oppression of this city's life, just as in Section I. The movement of these first nine lines underscores the repetitive routine. They go on and on.

The abrupt shift from the third to the first person in the tenth line dramatises the poet's revelation of himself and his feelings. The strong iambic metre is also relaxed, suggesting a sense of release from tension and strain.

The sense of pathos inherent in these lines is lost in another abrupt shift in the last three lines to a mood of deep cynicism. The simile is intensified by the word choice – 'ancient', 'vacant' – and the slowing down of the rhythm.

MAIN THEMES
- Incessant toil and suffering
- The decay and isolation of twentieth-century life
- Time
- Death-in-life
- Life is mundane, monotonous, repetitive, mechanical.
- Paralysis of the soul/consciousness
- A journey through the mind and senses.

MAIN IMAGES
- The street
- The woman
- Food and drink
- Body parts
- The detritus of the street
- Masquerades
- Rapidly changing images – visual, oral, tactile, olfactory – cinematic style.

Aunt Helen (1915)

Text of poem: New Explorations Anthology page 216

INTRODUCTION

This is one of those poems in which Eliot outlines his impressions of genteel society in Boston, to the inner circle of which he was introduced through his uncle.

What the philosopher Santayana referred to as its cultural deadness and smug righteousness left this society open to satire. In this poem Eliot comments on its manners and mores, while also suggesting the emotional and spiritual shallowness behind its conventional beliefs and culture. Aunt Helen is a symbol of a world that ought to be mocked. Eliot himself called it a world 'quite uncivilised, but refined beyond the point of civilisation'.

A READING OF THE POEM

The poem is written in the imagist style. The satiric meaning of the poem, therefore, has to be inferred from the few concise detailed images.

The personal note of the first line is quickly dropped in favour of Eliot's usual device of the detached observer. The banal tone borders on that of a newspaper reporter as a series of apparently objective details are given.

She lived 'in a small house' – a large one would have been vulgar. 'Near a fashionable square' further suggests a genteel refinement. Living *in* the square would be too ostentatious.

The rather contrived and archaic-sounding line 3 conveys the fastidious nature of Miss Helen Slingsby and her self-contained little world: 'Cared for by servants to the number of four.'

Lines 4 and 5 have a satiric edge, which is devastating in its implications. The 'silence at her end of the street' is what is expected out of respect for the dead person. However, the 'silence in heaven' conveys the full contempt of the poet for Aunt Helen's self-serving lifestyle. Faced with this, Heaven has nothing to say. Eliot's contempt is not surprising when one considers how he was raised in a religious environment that promoted unselfish service to the wider community's needs.

The observance of conventions that indicate respect for the dead is also seen in line 6: 'The shutters were drawn and the undertaker wiped his feet –'

However, the dash at the end of the line is almost a challenge to the reader to see the gesture as one of rejection. The reader is reminded of Christ's advice to followers concerning those who reject His and their values – to shake the dust of their towns from their sandals.

The deadpan sarcasm of line 7:

He was aware that this sort of thing had occurred before

reduces the death of this privileged lady to the commonplace. Aunt Helen's death is being dismissed as 'this sort of thing'.

Her decorous but distorted sense of values is seen in the next line:

The dogs were handsomely provided for,

The implied criticism of such values controls our response to line 9, which evokes laughter rather than sympathy. Perhaps the poet is also implying that her values don't survive her any longer than the life of a parrot.

The lifeless, artificial, materialistic world in which she lived is seen in:

The Dresden clock continued ticking on the mantelpiece,

and when we read that the servants resort to behaviour which Aunt Helen would not have tolerated, disregarding both her property and her values, laughter entirely replaces sympathy. The servants' behaviour is not a perversion of ancient values, but a release from their artificial confines.

However, even though we do laugh at and reject Aunt Helen's self-centred values, we are also left with a slight sense of distaste at the vulgarity of the final lines. Satire has not entirely reversed our sense of pathos.

The student may wish to compare Miss Helen Slingsby with the portrayal of women in 'A Game of Chess' and in 'Preludes'.

LANGUAGE AND TONE

The flat, banal tone has been alluded to already. This banal style of narration undermines the seriousness with which Aunt Helen viewed herself and the trivialities that surrounded her.

However, the reader might declare the ultimate tone of the narrator to be quite serious and reject its apparent levity; but, as F.R. Leavis has pointed out, 'It is as necessary to revise the traditional idea of the distinction between seriousness and levity in approaching this poetry as in approaching the metaphysical poetry of the seventeenth century.'

A few random rhymes do little but emphasise the overall absence of lyricism, thus reflecting the general dullness of Aunt Helen's life. Indeed, some lines read almost as prose. This is particularly so of lines 6 and 7. This adds to the sense of boredom and staleness.

The reader could not be blamed for believing initially that this poem is a sonnet. It has the general appearance of one. However, if it does then Eliot is perhaps mocking the attitudes and expectations of the reader, for this is a very distorted 'sonnet', being 13 lines long, with little rhyme and varying rhythm patterns. Thus, this distortion may reflect not only Aunt Helen's distorted values but the reader's also. Satire works in a number of ways.

The contrast between the behaviour of the footman and housemaid and that of Aunt Helen might also be said to add to the humour and introduces a slightly risqué, if not entirely vulgar element.

Finally, Eliot the dramatist is very much in evidence in this poem. Apart from his ability to create a comic type with a few strokes of his pen, he has also created a time and place and most especially, perhaps, he has mimicked the pompous tone of Aunt Helen. Thus quite ordinary words and phrases, such as 'a fashionable square', and 'this sort of thing' echo the bourgeois speech of Miss Helen Slingsby.

The reader will have to decide whether Aunt Helen's life was a tragedy or a comedy.

MAIN THEMES

- Criticism of cultural deadness and self-righteousness
- Emotional and spiritual shallowness
- Distorted values
- Time.

MAIN IMAGES

- Silence
- The undertaker
- The dog and the parrot
- The Dresden clock
- The servants.

A *Game of Chess (extract from* The Waste Land II, *1922)*

Text of poem: New Explorations Anthology page 218

THEMES, ISSUES AND IMAGERY

'A Game of Chess' is section II of Eliot's best-known long poem, 'The Waste Land'. This was first published in 1922 and quickly and enduringly became synonymous with the poet himself.

Just like the full poem, 'A Game of Chess' can be read on the level of a narrative or in its more complicated form, when an understanding of the many references helps to universalise the themes and issues. This use of references concurs with Eliot's belief, expressed in an essay published in 1919 called 'Tradition and the Individual Talent', that literary tradition does not just belong to the past but should be used by the poet to express himself more completely.

This allows Eliot to overtly contrast the marvels of the past with the squalid nature of the present. 'A Game of Chess' is an example of this, where the first 33 lines describe, amongst other things, past grandeur, while the rest of the poem depicts the present.

'A Game of Chess' describes the stunting effects of improperly directed love or of lust confused with love. The poem is constructed as an apparent contrast between the class, wealth and education of the characters in the first part and the lower-class female characters in a pub at closing time. A closer reading will suggest that the differences are superficial in comparison with the fundamental similarities.

The title of the poem is taken from a play by Thomas Middleton (1580–1627), where the action is played out like moves in a game of chess. This play is a political satire which created a furore at the time and which Eliot has described as 'a perfect piece of literary political art'. Middleton's greatest tragedy, *Women beware Women*, is also in Eliot's mind here. In this play a young woman is raped while her mother, downstairs and quite unaware of what is happening, plays a game of chess. The allusion to the rape of Philomel by Tereus, as told in Greek legend, is symbolised later in the poem. All of this is related to the principal theme of the section: the theme of lust without love.

The opening lines place a woman in a room that has been described as full of 'splendid clutter'. This room, or more precisely a rich lady's boudoir, is surrounded by symbols of our cultural heritage. The extreme lavishness of the boudoir is stressed by evoking the opulence of legendary queens like Cleopatra, Cassiopeia, Dido and Philomel.

These opening lines also reflect Enoborbus's description of Cleopatra's ceremonial barge in Shakespeare's *Antony and Cleopatra*. Cleopatra is famous for her love affairs with powerful Roman generals such as Julius Caesar and Mark Antony. However, Eliot substitutes 'chair' for 'barge', thus evoking the Andromeda legend and the story of Cassiopeia, which are also 'waste-land' tales. Lavish wealth is suggested by 'burnished throne', 'marble', 'golden'. The carved Cupidons on the glass standards suggest possible shameful love affairs.

The 'sevenbranched candelabra' (line 6) adds to the richness of the room while evoking further historical and cultural references. The seven-branched candelabra suggests the Jewish Menorah, which in turn reflects a religious sanctuary and the laying waste of much of Judaic culture over the centuries. The candelabra may also be a reference to the constellation of the Seven Sisters (the Pleiades), which is next to the Cassiopeia constellation. Thus the richness of description also becomes a richness of reference.

This superabundance of rich visual details continues. There are glittering jewels, 'satin cases', 'ivory and coloured glass'. However, the greater the accumulation, the greater the confusion in the reader and the less sure we are of what we are seeing or sensing. The woman's perfumes are strange and synthetic (line 11) and they 'lurked' in her vials, suggesting perhaps something illicit or at least decadent. Words such as 'unstoppered' and 'unguent' add to the sense of decadence, as does a phrase like 'drowned the sense in odours' (line 13) and thus the reader also is left 'troubled, confused'.

'The air | That freshened from the window' (line 13–14) doesn't really freshen the room, but stirs the odours into 'fattening the prolonged candle-flames'. Thus the sense of a stifling, decadent sensuality, or indeed sexuality, is further enhanced.

The 'laquearia' (line 16), which is a panelled ceiling, also holds a reference to Virgil's Aeneid, to the scene in Carthage where Queen Dido gives a banquet for her beloved Aeneas. He will eventually desert her. This reinforces the theme of misplaced love.

The patterns on the ceiling continue the notion of almost divine decadence. The colours are rich; the scale is huge and the associations are deliberate. The 'sea-wood' can be linked with the dolphin, which in early Christian times was a symbol of diligence in love, and the word 'framed' prepares us for the pictorial representation of the Philomel story. Even as he introduces the story, Eliot reinforces the theme and tone with a reference to Milton's 'Paradise Lost'. The picture was like a window opening upon 'a sylvan scene', but this sylvan scene is the one which lay before Satan when he first arrived at the Garden of Eden. Thus sexual corruption is introduced in a deceptively beautiful scene. 'The change of Philomel' is a euphemism for what really happens – the violent rape of this girl. The reader is troubled by such violence occurring in such a beautiful place. The story of Philomel, which Eliot takes from Ovid's *Metamorphoses*, is continued in lines 24–27. The barbarity of the sexual violence done to Philomel by King Tereus of Thrace (who was married to Philomel's sister Procne) is compounded by the cutting off of her tongue. Zeus, the king of the gods, took pity on Philomel and turned her into a nightingale – the 'nightingale' of line 24. This classic tragic story is given further voice in this room of the present. The theme of rape, the most immoral and improperly directed love/lust, forces us to react and to see its significance in the 'present' of the poem.

The violated Philomel, her tongue cut out, still manages to express her sorrow in inviolable voice when, as the nightingale, she fills all the desert with song. Perhaps this expresses Eliot's own wish to fill the wasteland, or desert, with song.

However, this may not be possible, for even the sound of the nightingale – the 'Jug Jug' of line 27 was a conventional Elizabethan method of expressing birdsong – becomes merely salacious in the modern world 'to dirty ears'. The move in line 26 from the past tense 'cried' to the present tense of 'pursues' underscores this more prurient perspective.

Lines 28–31 return to a description of the room. The other decorations, presumably outlining scenes from our cultural inheritance, are dismissed as 'withered stumps of time'. The poet is scornful of those who possess but do not appreciate such riches. This further suggests modern people's failure to come to terms with this same cultural inheritance. These 'stumps of time' then, ironically, no longer speak to us, despite being 'told upon the walls'. Perhaps, the 'stumps of time' may also evoke Philomel's stump of a tongue.

The image of the woman brushing her hair in lines 32–34 suggests a nervous person under considerable emotional strain. The rather surreal image of her hair glowing into words suggests her hypersensitivity and her tense speech, while 'savagely still' suggests a truly neurotic silence.

Lines 35–62 are made up of a dialogue between this woman and a male protagonist. The lines between the quotation marks represent the woman's words. The man's are not given quotation marks. Perhaps he is silent, his answers to her questions being unspoken thoughts. Thus the episode is not, perhaps, a full dialogue: just an exchange of sorts, indicating an emotional and communicative stalemate.

While the staccato rhythm of the woman's utterances reveals her nervous tension, the substance suggests her state of purposelessness. The dialogue, if such it be, pivots around aimless questions and nervous imperatives. The answers of the protagonist indicate that his is as desperate a situation as hers is. However, his is a calmer, more resigned despair. He may be in a psychological Hell ('rats' alley') but he is aware of alternatives. He quotes from Shakespeare's *Tempest*: 'Those are pearls that were his eyes.' This suggests the possibility of transformation. Indeed, in *The Tempest* two lovers play a game of chess that may be linked with genuine love.

However, the sardonic counter-perspective immediately intrudes with 'that Shakespeherian Rag' of line 52, an American hit tune of 1912. The words 'elegant' and 'intelligent' deny in this context both true elegance and true intelligence, and perhaps the possibility of finding the true nature of either in this room with these people, despite the grandeur of the room itself.

The overall sense of purposelessness is reinforced by the woman's final questions and the answers to them. Water, which is normally a symbol of life giving, is here without potency. In fact it must be avoided by using a closed car.

The pub scene, apparently set in a working-class urban area from the tone of the narrative, opens in line 63. Much of the essential nature of this scene is its vocalness. We, the readers, have the experience of eavesdropping on a bar-side monologue. The speaker of the narrative is a woman. The difference in class between her and the woman of the earlier lines is quite apparent. There is a sense of immediacy in the setting, with the woman recounting a dialogue between herself and another woman, Lil, some time earlier. The barman's words, in capitals, break into the narrative contributing meanings to the narrative not recognised by its narrator.

The theme of the past haunting the present is again immediately identifiable, as are those of sterility, lust without love, spiritual/emotional illness and emptiness and intimations of mortality and the role of women. The sense of a Waste Land is acute: not the waste of war's destruction, but the emotional and spiritual sterility of modern man.

In a society where appearance means everything, Lil is told to smarten herself up for her husband Albert, who is returning from war. Lil is criticised for looking old before her time (line 82). Indeed Albert had criticised her some time earlier, presumably when he was on leave, and had given her money to get a new set of teeth. She, however, had used the money to procure an abortion (line 85).

The sympathy of the narrator lies with Albert – the 'poor Albert' of line 73 who will want 'a good time' after his four years in the army. Albert may even 'make off' with those who will give him a good time if Lil doesn't.

Lil, meanwhile, is told to smarten up; that she 'ought to be ashamed . . . to look so antique' and that she is 'a proper fool'. Little sympathy is had for her nearly dying in pregnancy (line 86) and a fatalistic attitude is held towards the sexual demands of her husband (lines 90–91). The vulgar insensitivity of it all can be compared to the fate of Philomel in the first section, while the use of the word 'antique' (line 82) also reminds us of the imagery of the first section. In this outline of Lil's life, social satire is in effect evoking sympathy.

The narrative is not concluded. It is disrupted by closing time and there is the suggestion of the speaker leaving the pub (line 98). Time is running out for the characters in the narrative, reinforced by the urgent, constant calling of 'Hurry Up Please It's Time'. Their farewells fade into the Shakespearian final line, drawing us back to one of those stumps of time – Ophelia's madness and her drowning. This reference adds a sense of dignity to the narrative, while also universalising the themes of misplaced love and destruction.

LANGUAGE, TONE AND MOOD

As said, Eliot's poetry is essentially dramatic – from conflict to characterisation, from action to dialogue, from plot to imagery. The student may be well advised to search for examples of these dramatic elements.

The language in 'A Game of Chess' both reflects and is part of the essential drama of the poem. The diction and syntax of the first section reflect the description of the room. Thus words used to describe the 'props' of the dramatic setting could well describe the style also – words such as 'burnished', 'synthetic', or 'rich profusion'. Archaic and artificial-sounding words such as 'Cupidon', 'unguent' and 'laquearia' add to this sense of an urgent, forced style. Overall, the feeling is one of claustrophobia, a sense of being trapped, or 'prolonged' in this gorgeous, cluttered room. The long sentences add to this feeling. (The first sentence is nine lines long.) Similarly, the various subordinate clauses within these long sentences contribute to the sense of being 'troubled, confused'. The lavish opulence of the room and the language in which it is described thus create a feeling of unease.

In the same way there is a glut of active verbs and participles from lines 14–34, almost hypnotising the reader and stifling a response.

At times, however, the language is wonderfully economic. 'Sad light' (line 20) and 'And still she cried, and still the world pursues' beautifully combine both description and emotion.

However, on other occasions the deliberate literariness of the lines hides the brutal reality. This is the case with the description of the rape of Philomel. The rather lofty, Miltonic tone of:

> Above the antique mantel was displayed
> As though a window gave upon the sylvan scene

tends to obscure what is actually happening in the picture. The euphemisms used, 'The change of Philomel' and 'So rudely forced', tend to lessen the enormity of the sexual violence. Thus the sense of sexual decadence is evoked.

The poet's scornful reaction to such opulent decadence is seen in lines 28–29:

> And other withered stumps of time,
> Were told upon the walls . . .

The cold brevity of these lines is in sharp contrast to the aureate earlier descriptions. This economy of expression continues in line 30:

> Leaned out, leaning, hushing the room enclosed.

Here the strained repetitiveness of the line prepares us for the strained emotions of the woman introduced in line 35, while the word 'enclosed' confirms for us the claustrophobia of the room.

The woman's speech reflects her neurotic state. The repetition of one word from earlier on in the line at the end of three of the lines – 'Speak.' 'What?' 'Think.' – emphasises the neurotic state.

The repetition of 'nothing' from lines 44–50 reflects not only the emotional vacancy of the man, but also suggests that this vacancy reverberates in her mind as well. An emotional stalemate is the result.

The unnaturalistic rhythm of the woman's speech, with its deadening, repetitive, nervous questioning, is counterpointed by the smooth rhythm of the quotation from Shakespeare's *Tempest* (line 49). However, the irony here is further compounded by the vulgar ragtime rhythm of 'that Shakespeherian Rag –'

The diction and syntax of the speaker in the pub scene is essentially that of urban English working class. In tone it is an abrupt shift from that of the woman in the room. The word 'said' is repeated some fifteen times in a gossipy fashion.

This not only realistically reflects the rhythms and patterns of speech of the working class, but also adds a certain prayer-like intonation.

The barman's sonorous 'HURRY UP PLEASE IT'S TIME' both breaks into and breaks up the speaker's narrative, adding levels of meaning not intended by the speaker. Its repetition contributes to the urgency of the narrative, even introducing a comic, quasi-apocalyptic tone.

The quotation from Shakespeare's *Hamlet*, which ends the passage, has Ophelia's lingering farewell remind us that the time is indeed out of joint. Ophelia's words, which rise out of the mêlée of farewells in lines 100–101, enhance the pathos of these people's lives and remind us again that the past does indeed haunt the present and that music may be made out of suffering.

MAIN THEMES
• The marvels of the past contrast with the squalid nature of the present.
• The past haunts the present.
• The stunting effect of improperly directed love/lust
• Lust without love
• Sexual corruption may be deceptively beautiful.
• The desire to fill the wasteland with song
• Modern people's failure to come to terms with their cultural heritage
• The emotional strain of modern life
• Sense of purposelessness in modern life
• Intimations of mortality.

MAIN IMAGES
• Opulent luxury of the room
• Rape of Philomel
• Nervous gestures of the woman
• The story of Lil and Albert
• The landlord crying 'Time'.

Journey of the Magi (1927)
Text of poem: New Explorations Anthology page 224

This is the first of the Ariel Poems, a set of poems which, beginning in 1927, the year in which Eliot joined the Anglican church, were published by Faber & Faber as a sort of Christmas card. Both this poem and 'A Song for Simeon' (1928) refer specifically to the birth of Christ.

The Magi were the three wise men or kings – commonly, but not scripturally, known as Balthazar, Caspar and Melchior – who journeyed from the east to pay homage to the newly born baby Jesus, according to the gospel of

St Matthew 11: 1–12. However, Eliot's inspiration comes not from this well-known gospel story alone but also from a sermon preached by Lancelot Andrews, Bishop in Winchester, on Christmas Day 1622, which Eliot quotes in his 'Selected Essays'. The first five lines of the poem are a direct quotation from this sermon by Lancelot Andrews.

The poem is essentially a dramatic monologue spoken by one of the magi, who is now an old man, recalling and reminiscing on the journey he and his companions made to witness a Birth. Thus the poem is concerned with a quest and those travelling must traverse a type of wasteland to reach the promised land. The Magi's journey is challenging, painful and difficult. It involved giving up old comforts, certainties and beliefs so that it became a 'Hard and bitter agony for us'. Reaching their destination doesn't lead to any great sense of achievement or celebration. Instead the narrator is unsure of the significance of what he has seen. 'It was (you may say) satisfactory.' The narrator remains disturbed and bewildered as he returns to the 'old dispensation' which he and his companions now find strange. He longs for death now, so that he can achieve new life.

The poem can be seen as an analogy of Eliot's own agonising spiritual journey. The quest for a new spiritual life involves rejecting the old life with its many attractions. Thus, the Birth also includes a death; the death of the old way of life. Such a journey involves doubt, regrets and lack of conviction. Maybe 'this was all folly.' This tone of uncertainty leads us to appreciate that rather than asserting his beliefs Eliot is expressing his willingness to believe, which is his present spiritual condition.

THEMES AND ISSUES

The poem is a dramatic monologue in which the magus, the narrator, tells of his and his companions' experiences in their journey to the birth of Christ. The opening five lines are an abbreviation of Andrew's sermon as mentioned above, which Eliot includes as part of the magus's narration.

The journey undertaken is one from death to life. It begins in 'The very dead of winter.' The hardships endured represent the sacrifice the magi must make in order to achieve new birth. Also, before there is a birth there must be a death of the old life.

The hardships undergone include not only the weather and trouble with their camels, but also major regrets for what is left behind:

> The summer palaces . . . the silken girls bringing sherbet.
>
> (lines 9–10)

These real attractions cannot be easily overcome.

Exactly how tough the journey was is seen in the sequence from line 11 to line 16. The increasing torment outlined in the matter-of-fact descriptive statements here is made all the more effective by the repetition of 'And . . . ' The hostility of various communities, symbolic of a disbelieving world, leads them 'to travel all night'. Adding to their discomfort is the realisation that the hostile unbelievers may be right – 'That this was all folly.' (line 20)

The next section, beginning at line 21, seems at first to confirm the death-to-life theme. It is 'dawn'; there is 'a temperate valley', 'a running stream and a water-mill beating the darkness' – all of which can be seen as birth images. However, ambiguity and uncertainty quickly return. The 'three trees' are reminders of the Crucifixion of Christ, as are the 'Six hands . . . dicing for pieces of silver' (line 28). These, coupled with the negativity of the horse galloping away, 'the empty wine-skins' and 'no information', can be seen as furthering the theme of death. However they may also suggest the interrelation between death and birth. Christ's incarnation leads inexorably to His Crucifixion, just as His Crucifixion leads to eternal life.

Ambiguity can also be seen in what should be the joyful climax of the journey and confirmation of belief. However, this is not so. The intense anticipation and anxiety of 'not a moment too soon' is immediately followed by the uncertain reticence of

it was (you may say) satisfactory. (line 32)

No description of the Birth or the One who was born is given.

This sense of uncertainty turns to a degree of confusion in the last section, as the magus tries to work out the meaning of what he saw. Maybe like the knight meeting the Fisher King in the Holy Grail legend, he has failed to ask the right question. While he is convinced that it was significant – 'And I would do it again' (line 34) – and is anxious that no part of his narrative should be overlooked:

. . . but set down
This set down
This: . . .
        (lines 34–36)

the Birth doesn't seem to have been what he expected. He 'had thought they [birth and death] were different', but 'this Birth was . . . like Death, our death.' (lines 39–40).

So the Magi return to their kingdoms but feel alienated among their own people. They must continue to live amidst the old way of life – 'the old dispensation' (line 42) – while not believing in it. So their Birth remains a bitter agony while they wait for 'another death' (line 44). Another death is required – the magus's own, or perhaps Christ's – before he can enter a new life.

IMAGERY AND SYMBOLISM

The whole poem is structured around a journey, both real and symbolic. The journey as recalled by the magus is one from death to birth, the imagery of which suggests the inner struggles of the narrator and his companions.

The journey begins at 'the worst time of year' with 'The ways deep and the weather sharp' and ends in 'a temperate valley . . . smelling of vegetation'. The symbolic movement from death to life is clear. Paradoxically, however, there is also a movement from life to death. Here 'The summer palaces . . . And the silken girls bringing sherbet' represent the old life. The travellers make their way through a wasteland of 'cities hostile and the towns unfriendly', until in the valley there is a symbolic death of the old life as the 'old white horse galloped away'. Some critics have seen references to the Fisher King myth in the journey and its symbols.

The second stanza contains a series of death and birth images. 'Dawn', 'temperate valley', 'vegetation' can be seen as birth images, while water is universally acknowledged as symbolising life. However, a flowing river or stream is also a traditional poetic symbol of the passing of time. The action of the 'water-mill' can be seen as beating the darkness of time.* There then follow a series of images foreshadowing the well-known imagery surrounding Christ's death. The 'three trees on the low sky' reflect the three crosses on the Hill of Calvary. The 'hands dicing' suggest the Roman soldiers dicing for Christ's clothes and the 'pieces of silver' remind us of the thirty pieces of silver that Judas was paid for his treachery.

The 'white horse' can be seen as an ambiguous image. It may symbolise the life-giving, triumphant Christ of the Book of Revelations (VI: 2, 19:11). However, as the horse is said to be 'old' and since it 'galloped away' it may also represent the collapse of paganism, 'the old dispensation' of line 42.

LANGUAGE AND TONE

As befits a dramatic monologue the language reflects not only natural speech patterns, which catch the rhythms of speech, but also a particular voice – the voice of the magus, at times both reminiscent and complaining:

> Then the camel men cursing and grumbling
> And running away, and wanting their liquor and women.

Here the emphasis falls into a natural pattern of speech and voice inflection. The prayer-like, incantatory tone also befits both the speaker and the theme. The strong repetition of 'And' in the first two sections reflects this. Overall the purposefully ambiguous symbols and images introduce a tone of uncertainty.

The opening paraphrased uncertainty of Lancelot Andrews' sermon sets the tone of desolation and the bitter environment of the first stanza. The quotation also serves a second purpose for Eliot. It incorporates the poem into a particular tradition. Thus it serves a similar function to the quotation from Dante at the beginning of 'Prufrock' and is part of his efforts to create a synthesis between past and present.

The remainder of the first stanza is quite vitriolic in tone, as the magus criticises both his predicament and his previous life. This criticism is coupled with a tone of regret,

> The summer palaces on slopes, the terraces,
> And the silken girls bringing sherbet.

The sensual sibilant 's' sounds of these lines underscore what is being regretted. A tone of contempt can be seen in the ever-expanding criticism of the remainder of the first stanza.

The second stanza suggests a tone of nostalgia as the magus remembers his arrival at 'a temperate valley'. Then the last three lines of this stanza culminate in an understatement: 'it was (you may say) satisfactory.'

The word 'satisfactory' as seen, reflects the ambiguity and uncertainty of the magi's reaction. Perhaps, they are not completely aware of its relevance. The word is given particular emphasis by the expression in parentheses preceding it and by its irregularity with the set rhythm of the line.

This tone of uncertainty is continued in the next stanza and develops into a tone of anxiety and of urgency:

> . . . but set down
> This set down
> This: . . .

The dislocation and repetition of these lines emphasise this residual tone of uncertainty and urgency. The run-on line:

> . . . this Birth was
> Hard and bitter agony for us, . . .

creates a similar tone of anxiety and perhaps even of self-pity.

The poem ends in a conditioned statement:

> 'I should be glad of another death',

perhaps expressing a tone of resignation.

MAIN THEMES
- The Birth of Jesus Christ
- A quest/journey as an analogy of spiritual searching
- Lack of conviction/uncertainty/alienation
- Birth entails death

- The need for suffering in order to attain a new Birth.

MAIN IMAGES
- A journey
- A wasteland of 'cities hostile'
- Death and birth images
- Biblical images.

Usk *(extract from* Landscapes III, *1935)*

Text of poem: New Explorations Anthology page 226

INTRODUCTION

This is one of Eliot's five 'Landscape poems', three of which are based in America, one in Wales and one in Scotland.

This poem resulted from a ten-day holiday taken by Eliot in Wales in 1935.

In keeping with the term 'Landscape', the poem is a suggestive or evocative sketch in which the poet can be seen as an artist/painter. Like the other 'Landscape' poems, this poem consists of scenes and perceptions of deep significance in the development of Eliot's thinking. In particular, the 'Landscape' poems are definitive pointers in terms of Eliot's developing religious and poetic sensibilities, which are further explored in the 'Four Quartets'.

In this sense, although listed under *Minor Poems*, there is nothing minor about the significance of these poems. Indeed, taken as a sequence of five poems, we can see that Eliot is again evoking drama here, as he did in 'The Wasteland' and in the individual quartets of 'Four Quartets'. The sequence of five is in keeping with the number of acts required by Aristotle for tragic drama. Shakespeare also adhered to this. So both 'Usk' and 'Rannoch' can be seen as two acts in a drama outlining the relationship between human beings and the natural world. As number III, Usk marks a climax in the sequence.

A READING OF THE POEM

'Usk' is a pastoral poem in both senses of the word, i.e. it is descriptive of the countryside and is also spiritually instructive.

The opening of the poem is abrupt, sudden and in the imperative mood. The reader is being instructed:

> Do not suddenly break . . . or
> Hope to find . . .
> . . . do not spell

We are being told *not* to seek images such as 'the white hart', 'the white well', the 'lance'. These are evocative of the classical Arthurian/Celtic legends. As such they are also evocative of the countryside.

Thus Eliot is suggesting that in such a landscape we should not conjure up the past or any notion of romantic fantasy. This he dismisses as 'Old enchantments.' He tells us to 'Let them sleep.' As a sort of second thought he allows us to '"Gently dip, but not too deep"'.

However, having been instructed *against* something, we are now instructed *towards* something. Our relationship with the landscape should not be escapist or full of romantic fantasy, but should be such as to lead us *towards* the spiritual.

In a prayer-like incantation, he tells us to 'Lift your eyes'. We are being sent on a more active spiritual journey – a pilgrimage – 'Where the roads dip and where the roads rise'.

Here we are to seek 'The hermit's chapel, the pilgrim's prayer' which, although conventional images of the spiritual, will not be found in any conventional setting but 'Where the grey light meets the green air'.

A spiritual home will be found in something that is neither human nor animal. Indeed it may not be found in the natural landscape at all, but in the eternal continuum of light and space, i.e. 'Where the grey light meets the green air'.

There is a note of hope here that is not found in 'The Love Song of J. Alfred Prufrock', 'Preludes' or 'A Game of Chess'. It echoes that tiny note of hope, which is to be found in 'The Journey of the Magi' and marks a shift towards a spiritual solution for Eliot in the face of life's difficulties.

USE OF LANGUAGE

The language suggests a certain sense of detachment on the part of the poet. The poem reads as advice to others from someone who has already reached a conclusion or discovered a position with which he is happy. Even though this is a description of a place, the poet is not part of the place. This can be seen as a type of metaphysical detachment.

The negative imperatives and the cacophonous alliterative sounds of the first line introduce us to the poet's attitudes towards the 'Old enchantments.'

These same imperatives also evoke that sense of self-assured, commanding authority we associate with metaphysical poets such as the seventeenth-century poet, John Donne.

In keeping with this robust style the rhythm is quick and irregular. This lively, almost bounding style is furthered by the use of alliteration and repetition in many of the lines. The rhythm, like the road, dips and rises. The use of enjambment, or run-on lines, in the second part of the poem in particular, and the quite intense rhyme, also add to the sense of insistent energy.

The incantatory tones of some of the imperatives have been alluded to already. In fact the tone of the whole poem can be found in the three dimeter lines:

> Hope to find . . .
> Lift your eyes . . .
> Seek only there . . .

The dramatic exhortational tone of an Old Testament prophet is clear and in keeping with one aspect of the pastoral theme.

Finally, the choice of colours in this landscape 'painting' suggests both a sense of peace and invigoration. 'White' is bright, while 'grey light' evokes images of a chill, bracing wind, and 'green' is traditionally seen as a natural, soothing colour. The sense of peace is also evoked by the choice of individual words such as 'sleep', 'gently', 'dip' and 'prayer'.

MAIN THEMES

- A pastoral poem in both senses
- Avoid the 'old enchantments'
- Seek the spiritual
- A journey.

MAIN IMAGES

- Medieval romantic fantasies – 'hart', 'well', 'lance'
- The road
- 'The hermit's chapel'
- 'Grey light', 'green air'.

Rannoch, by Glencoe (extract from Landscapes IV, 1935)

Text of poem: New Explorations Anthology page 228

[Note: *This poem is also prescribed for the Ordinary Level 2006 exam*]

'Rannoch' is the fourth in the five-poem sequence, 'Landscapes'. (See Introduction on 'Usk'.)

A READING OF THE POEM

The poem explores the relationship between human beings and the natural world. Like 'Usk' it is a pastoral, in the sense of being both a description of a countryside and also containing a message. It may suggest elements of a pastoral elegy to some readers.

In many ways this poem is a stripping away of the idyllic, idealised Golden Age pastoral to reveal a landscape of famine and war.

The poem opens with two death-in-life images – 'the crow starves', 'the patient stag | Breeds for the rifle.'

They are the distressing results of the capacity of humans to condition the landscape. This is a barren landscape full of death. Here all creatures feel constricted and oppressed:

> . . . Between the soft moor
> And the soft sky, scarcely room
> To leap or soar.

The softness here is not of ease or comfort, but a reflection of the sense of oppression. Sky and moor practically meet. If all relationships need space and time, then failure is inevitable here due to a distinct lack of space. This landscape is a burden.

Erosion is the norm here – 'Substance crumbles'; everything is suspended 'in the thin air' of the inexorable movement of time – 'Moon cold or moon hot.'

This psychological topography allows no means of escape. 'The road winds' without apparent purpose. Instead we are offered a journey through 'listlessness', 'languor' and 'clamour'. The sense of direction and invigorating movement evident in 'Usk' is totally absent here. We are stuck in the wretchedness of history and its endless cycles: 'ancient war', 'broken steel', 'confused wrong'. These are the relics of embattled lives, before which the only appropriate response is silence. These old rivalries will not be resolved because 'Memory is strong | Beyond the bone.'

In this landscape of memory where 'Pride snapped', the 'Shadow of pride is long'. In 'the long pass' of a lifetime, there will be no resolution, no reconciliation – 'No concurrence of bone.' This is because even though pride is humiliated (snapped), it holds onto its shadow.

Unlike 'Usk' this poem offers no religious perspective, no sense of hope and direction between life and death – only a sense of 'betweenness', where we are biologically fated to evoke old rivalries. They are of the bone and 'Beyond the bone'.

Living in a state of betweenness, the rational aspect of ourselves is lost amidst the 'Clamour of confused wrong', almost indifferent to suffering, including our own. As is common in Eliot's poetry, the human in its non-rational state is symbolised in animal imagery. Here the human is seen as 'crow' and 'the patient stag' awaiting their fate. They are as unable to understand what they had been reduced to as are the inhabitants of the city street in the 'Preludes'.

The existentialist awareness and its agony are to be found in the speakers and the readers of these poems.

The tragedy of 'Rannoch' may be alleviated by the hope of 'Usk'. However, 'Usk' is not a solution but an indication of the journey that must be taken. But 'Rannoch' is the tragedy that may prevent 'Usk'.

THE USE OF LANGUAGE

This is a dysfunctional landscape and the poet's use of language reflects that.

The end-of-line neatness of strong rhyme and natural pauses in 'Usk' is absent. Instead we are presented with a rather discordant structure. A line or lines run on, only to finish abruptly in the middle of the next line.

There is an emphasis on alliteration, in keeping with Eliot's admiration of medieval English.

This, however, does nothing to even out or smooth the lines. Rather the effect is insistent, if not altogether frenzied when combined with the stutter-like rhythm. This nervous, stutter-like effect is added to by actual close word repetition. All of this creates an unease and a tension in the reader.

Rhyme, where it does exist, is internal or slightly off end – e.g. 'wrong', 'strong' and 'long' and 'sour', 'war'. Again this adds to the sense of a discordant structure.

The sense of constriction explored in the imagery of the first four lines is also present in the language. In the second sentence:

> Between the soft moor
> And the soft sky, scarcely room
> To leap or soar.

there appears to be no room for a main verb.

We are also presented with an anagram as a type of rhyme, i.e. 'moor' and 'room'. The 'moor' turns on itself to become 'room', emphasising the constriction and oppression and becoming an analogy for the retracing and restating of grievances in a closed system of confused wrongs and strong memories.

MAIN THEMES
- Death in life
- Time
- Impact of human beings on the natural world
- War, destruction and erosion
- Unresolved rivalries.

MAIN IMAGES
- The crow and the stag
- Moor and sky

- Winding road
- (Images of) war
- Bone.

East Coker IV (extract from The Four Quartets, *1940)*

Text of poem: New Explorations Anthology page 230

INTRODUCTION

This short piece is part of 'East Coker', the second of 'The Four Quartets'.

'The Four Quartets' is seen by many critics as the most important work of Eliot's career. Helen Gardner has called them Eliot's masterpiece. The new forms and ideas with which he experimented in the 'Landscape' poems ('Usk', 'Rannoch') are developed fully in 'The Four Quartets'.

In keeping with the musical title, the structure of the 'Quartets' is symphonic and thus extraordinarily complex – a complexity which need not trouble the student here.

Time is again one of the central themes – in particular its constant change in contrast with unchanging eternity. The philosophical considerations of the contrast between the real and the ideal, the human and the spiritual, explored in his earlier poetry, are again evident here.

'East Coker' takes its name from the village in Somerset, England, from which Eliot's ancestors emigrated to America. 'East Coker' is concerned with the place of mankind in the natural order of things and with the notion of renewal. This theme of rebirth, which is also found in the 'Journey of the Magi', is part of the spiritual progress of the soul. The soul must yield itself to God's hands and die in order to be born again. Indeed the soul must first suffer in order to be capable of responding fully to God's love. St John of the Cross calls this 'the dark night of the soul'. The saint's writing on this has influenced Eliot here.

A READING OF THE POEM

The poem, written for Good Friday 1940, sees Eliot at his most symbolic and a reading of the poem is, in effect, an interpretation of this symbolism.

The poem is a metaphysical one, structured around metaphysical conceits and paradoxes similar to those which may be found in the poetry of the seventeenth-century poet, John Donne. It lies in the tradition of seventeenth-century devotional verse, such as that of Donne, Herbert and Vaughan.

The 'wounded surgeon' is Jesus Christ, whose suffering and death on the Cross, and whose subsequent Resurrection, ensured mankind's redemption.

The 'wounded surgeon' will cure the soul of its sickness: 'the distempered part'. The surgeon's knife, 'the steel', which operates, or 'questions', is God's love. This is in keeping with St John of the Cross's 'The Dark Night of the Soul', which has influenced Eliot here.

The soul is not unaware of God's love operating on it. It feels 'The sharp compassion of the healer's art'.

The oxymoron that is 'sharp compassion' suggests the idea of a necessary evil, i.e. in order to be cured the soul must suffer first. Suffering is a means of grace. This is 'the enigma of the fever chart'. A physical evil can be seen as a spiritual good. Thus the metaphysical paradox is 'resolved'.

The beginning of the second verse continues this notion of suffering as a means of grace. Thus, 'Our only health is the disease'.

The conceit of a hospital is continued with the image of 'the dying nurse'.

'The dying nurse' is the Church – 'dying' in the sense of the common fate of mankind. The Church's role is not to placate or please us, but to remind us firstly of 'Adam's curse', which is never-ending toil and suffering, similar to the vision of mankind's daily life in the 'Preludes'. The Church's second role is to remind us that, 'to be restored, our sickness must grow worse', meaning, that it is only through the fullest suffering that we can be fully cleansed or cleared of our sickness/evil.

The 'hospital' conceit is continued in the third stanza. 'The whole earth is our hospital' in the sense that it is here we can learn the value of suffering and can be cured of our sickness. The 'ruined millionaire' is Adam, whose endowment brought sin into the world – Adam's sin is Original Sin in Christian belief. The 'paternal care' is that of God, under Whose care we would be privileged to die, if we do well as 'patients' in this world. The word 'prevents' is used in its seventeenth-century sense, meaning to go before us with spiritual guidance. God will help us by guiding us towards repentance. The second and modern meaning of 'prevents', that is to stop or frustrate, is also appropriate. God stops our lives everywhere through death.

The notion of cure is continued in the fourth stanza. The cure is a fever one – because 'to be restored, our sickness must grow worse', as stated in the second stanza. The purgation, or cure, must move from a purgation of the flesh, burning away all the sickness and impurities of the flesh, until it ascends to a purgation of the mind:

> If to be warmed, then I must freeze
> And quake in frigid purgatorial fires

The essence of a breaking cold/hot fever, the body shivering and sweating as it rids itself of disease, is achieved here.

The flames of purgation Eliot calls roses, the symbol of both human and divine love. Roses and thorns are also the emblem of martyrdom. So suffering is seen as the basis of the cure – a thorough penitential suffering.

The fifth stanza opens with an image of the 'wounded surgeon' again. It is Jesus Christ on the Cross, whose suffering leads to our Redemption. The image also evokes the Eucharist, the central act of worship for Christians. It may also evoke the need for suffering in ourselves, so that we too will be cured.

The image of flesh and blood is continued in the next two lines in Eliot's criticism of our blindness. We like to think that there is no need for humility and penance with our ideas of our own importance – 'we are sound, substantial flesh and blood'.

The adjectives 'sound, substantial' suggest that we rely too much on the physical, the materialistic.

However, Eliot recognises that behind our materialism, we innately acknowledge our need for repentance and the grace of God. This is why 'we call this Friday good.'

USE OF LANGUAGE

In this poem Eliot has revived the metaphysical poem. He uses many of the features we associate with the seventeenth-century poetry of Donne, Herbert and Vaughan.

In line with metaphysical poetry there is a strong sense of argument throughout the poem. The argument, as outlined above in the READING OF THE POEM, is that we need to reject the demands of the body and achieve redemption through curing its ills. Pain and suffering are means towards achieving redemptive grace or enlightenment.

This argument is presented throughout a series of metaphysical paradoxes, e.g.

> The 'wounded surgeon' will cure us
> 'sharp compassion'
> 'the enigma of the fever chart'
> 'Our only health is the disease'
> 'to be restored, our sickness must grow worse.'
> 'if we do well, we shall | Die'
> 'If to be warmed, then I must freeze'
> 'frigid purgatorial fires'
> 'in spite of that, we call this Friday good.'

Many of these are examples of what is known as metaphysical wit, which is renowned for its clever but serious, incisive, challenging and intelligent puns and paradoxes. The wit of the last stanza in particular removes any sense of emotional religiosity and serves to intensify the devotional mood.

A conceit is an elaborate, sustained comparison. These were much used by the seventeenth-century metaphysical poets. Eliot, in keeping with this, uses conceits in this poem. The 'wounded surgeon' is an example, as are seeing the earth as a hospital and the notion of the fever cure.

The meaning of symbols used is explored above in READING OF THE POEM. However the student should be aware that symbolism is as much a use of language as it is an exploration of meaning. Such usage invigorates both language and meaning.

Similarly, Eliot's precision of language adds depth to the meaning of both individual words and the poem as a whole. His use of the word 'prevents' in the third stanza is an example of this.

Examples of metaphysical wit are seen in the last stanza, in the evocative fused imagery of the first two lines in particular.

Eliot 'reinvented' the alliterated four-stress line commonly found in medieval English. This poem generally follows their pattern, with quite strong medial pauses: e.g. 'The **wound**ed **surg**eon **plies** the **steel**' or '**Beneath** the **bleed**ing **hands** we **feel**'.

However, this kind of verse can become monotonous. Eliot's genius was to apply the pattern with sufficient flexibility to avoid monotonous rigidity.

W.B. Yeats once said that rhythm in poetry should be used 'to prolong the moment of contemplation'. Perhaps we can say this of both the rhythm and the strong, definite rhyme patterns in this poem.

MAIN THEMES
- The idea of necessary evil – a physical evil may be a spiritual good.
- Suffering as a means of attaining grace/redemption
- The purgation of evil
- The caring love of God
- Growth towards a new life.

MAIN IMAGES
- The wounded surgeon
- Conceit of a hospital
- The nurse
- The ruined millionaire – Adam
- Play of opposites – 'frigid fires'
- The Cross
- The Eucharist.

T.S. Eliot – An Overview

Not even the most learned critic has said that Eliot's poetry makes easy reading.

Yet of all twentieth-century poets he is perhaps the most rewarding. No other poet has better expressed the social condition and psychological state of modern man.

While Eliot's poetry can be read with pleasure at first sight, a full understanding will not come immediately. This is so because quite often, instead of the regular evocative images other poets use, Eliot presents us with a series of literary and historical references. Eliot himself insisted that the reader must be prepared to answer the call for knowledge which poetry demands. Indeed if the reader does persevere, then he/she will be rewarded with a use of symbolism and allusion, and an experimenting with the language and form of poetry, which deepen and intensify the experience of reading it. He/she will feel what Eliot himself called the 'direct shock of poetic intensity'.

INFLUENCES AND THE 'MODERN MOVEMENT'

The 'Modern Movement' is that which effected a revolution in English literature between 1910 and 1930. As the leading poet in the movement, Eliot brought about the break from the poetic tradition of the nineteenth century. Apart from some notable exceptions, such as Hopkins and Hardy, poetry in English had become degenerate in both taste and theme. It appealed to the imperialist prejudices of a smug, self-complacent audience, convinced of its own superiority in just about everything. Poetry flattered rather than educated.

Eliot's achievement, in both his poetry and his critical essays, was in founding new criteria of judgement on what constitutes poetry.

Similar revolutions were happening in the other arts. James Joyce revolutionised prose writing, as did Pablo Picasso painting and Igor Stravinsky music. The First World War (1914–1918) also helped. At first poetry was used for propaganda. Rupert Brooke's saccharine war sonnets were enthusiastically received. However, as the war dragged on public perception was forced to change, as Wilfred Owen and Siegfried Sassoon wrote of the revolting horrors of war. Owen insisted that poetry need not be beautiful, but it must be truthful.

One aspect of the revolution that Eliot effected was the introduction to English of a style of poetry that is known as 'Symbolism'. When he arrived at Oxford in 1914, Eliot brought with him a deep love and admiration for the French nineteenth-century symbolist poets. These included Charles Baudelaire and Jules Laforgue. Eliot's debt to these poets is extensive – from diction to creative remodelling of subject matter, from tone to phrasing.

Eliot adapted from Charles Baudelaire (1821–1867) the poetical possibilities of addressing 'the more sordid aspects of the modern metropolis'. Examples of these are seen in 'Preludes' and in 'The Love Song of J. Alfred Prufrock'.

From Laforgue (1860–1887) he adopted a tone of mocking irony and despair. Eliot said he owed more to Laforgue 'than to any poet in any language'.

Laforgue was a technical innovator. He pioneered 'vers libre', or free verse, which Eliot also adopted. 'Vers libre' is verse freed from rigid, conventional forms of regular rhyme and rhythm. Instead Laforgue, and Eliot, use odd or irregular rhyme with varying rhythms to enhance both the theme and tone of the verse. Examples of these can be found throughout Eliot's poetry.

Laforgue also developed a sort of dramatic monologue, a stream-of-consciousness or interior monologue, as it is better known. Eliot adapted this method also, as can be seen in 'The Love Song of J. Alfred Prufrock' and 'Journey of the Magi'. However, Eliot developed the method to a further degree in the distancing and the self-mockery of the dramatic personae of his poems.

Eliot also admired many of the seventeenth-century English poets, seeing in them the emotional intensity and intellectual precision he found in the French Symbolists. Eliot saw a similarity between the seventeenth and twentieth centuries, in that both centuries experienced the disintegration of old traditions and the arrival of new learning. He particularly admired what came to be known as the Metaphysical Poets and felt that John Donne was closer to him in spirit than most other English poets. Eliot shares with Donne an often robust style, with colloquial language mingling with intellectual language. Like Donne, Eliot's poems contain a sense of argument, unexpected juxtapositions and eclectic references, demanding an intelligent attention from the reader. Even a cursory glance at 'A Game of Chess' or 'The Four Quartets' will confirm this.

However, it was the Italian poet Dante (1265–1321) who was the greatest influence upon Eliot. He saw Dante as greater even than Shakespeare, seeing the Italian poet expressing 'deeper degrees of degradation and higher degrees of exaltation'. The presence of Dante in Eliot's verse extends beyond the epigraph in 'The Love Song of J. Alfred Prufrock' to a recreation of the whole experience of his verse. The hell or purgatory in which both Prufrock and the women in 'A Game of Chess' live reflects this.

Eliot first met Ezra Pound in 1915, another great American poet and critic, who subsequently had a profound influence on Eliot's development both as a poet and as a literary critic. It was through Pound that Eliot came to be influenced by the so-called imagist school of poetry. Imagism promoted the use of common speech in poetry, a complete freedom in subject choice, accuracy, concentration and precise description. The reader need only look at the 'Preludes', 'Rannoch, by Glencoe' or 'Aunt Helen' to see how true all of this is of Eliot's poetry.

THEMES

As said above, Eliot lived in a period that saw the disintegration of old traditions and beliefs and the arrival of new learning and new experiences. As a poet then, he had to find a different way of addressing the new. Pound's famous phrase

'Make it new' was a rallying cry to those who wished to tackle themes relevant to their own experience. For Eliot, this was as much a recovery of a lost tradition in poetry as it was a revolution. Thus we find in Eliot's poetry a *contemplation of the past and an examination of the new* in relation to the past. 'Journey of the Magi' is one such poem.

While Eliot made poetry new, it didn't mean that he approved of everything that was new in contemporary life. On the contrary, there was his belief that much in modern life was a betrayal of civilised values. His poetry is full of his sense of disgust for urban society. 'The Love Song of J. Alfred Prufrock' and 'Preludes' are two such poems. *Modern urban life*, for Eliot, *is an emotional and cultural wasteland*, a world of thoughtless self-gratification and deadening purposelessness. The modern city is a symbol of the nightmare of human decadence. This view is explored in particular in 'Preludes' and 'A Game of Chess'.

This particular notion of *meaningless existence* expands into the wider theme of *death-in-life* and *life-in-death*. Twentieth-century man may be condemned to a living death, but redemption can be achieved. For Eliot this is the answer to how we should live: that is, we need to die to the old life in order to be born into the new. Humanity needs to *journey in search of its spiritual well-being*. This may involve *suffering*, but the cure is at hand. The 'Journey of the Magi', 'Usk' and 'East Coker IV' explore these themes. To redeem itself and construct a new life for itself, humanity must face a painful readjustment of its values and attitudes. Death accompanies a new Birth. Joy follows.

Much of the above reflects Eliot's own *spiritual journey* and his conversion to Anglicanism in 1927. Anglicanism, or more particularly Anglo-Catholicism, appealed to his need for orthodox theological dogma and for an emotional, mystical spirituality.

His conversion to Anglicanism was also a consolation to him during the nightmare that was his first marriage. This too was a living death. His marriage with Vivienne Haigh-Wood may explain the most persistent *personal theme* underlying Eliot's poetry i.e. the *sexual*, whose erotic note is as often as not linked with regret, disappointment, frustration and longing. 'The Love Song of J. Alfred Prufrock' explores this theme most strongly. At the centre of Prufrock's purgatory is a *confusion between love and sexual gratification*. Prufrock is both attracted to and repulsed by women. The theme of *appearance and reality*, or the *real and the ideal*, is explored in Prufrock's love-song, where his fear of women who 'fix you with a formulated phrase' is contrasted with his idealised vision of womanhood as 'sea-girls wreathed with seaweed red and brown'.

Eliot's *portrayal of women* is said to be critically and tortuously realistic, reflecting his attitude towards *human relationships* in general. The girl in the 'Preludes' is physically repulsive and, while the woman in the first part of 'A

Game of Chess' may be attractive, she is an emotional wreck. The second part of 'A Game of Chess' explores the tragedy resulting from casual relationships. Miss Helen Slingsby, in 'Aunt Helen', is his 'maiden aunt', whose social foibles suggest a fastidious but repressed character and whose mores are flamboyantly rejected by the behaviour of the footman and maid after her death.

For Eliot, though, it is only the *beauty of divine love* that makes sense of all human relationships. In the 'Preludes' he declares:

> I am moved by fancies . . .
> The notion of some infinitely gentle,
> Infinitely suffering thing.

'The Journey of the Magi' too can be seen as an exploration of divine love or as a struggle to understand the Incarnation of Christ, that moment when divine love made itself manifest.

This theme of *divine love* is made all the more clear in 'East Coker IV', where Christ himself is seen as suffering and dying in order to be reborn. Divine love is linked inextricably with the theme of a journey through suffering to a rebirth.

The Incarnation took place in a moment of time, a moment when historical time and the timelessness of God's eternity met. Eliot's exploration of *time* is central to his poems. It is part of his effort to make sense of life. This is seen in 'Journey of the Magi'.

In 'The Love Song of J. Alfred Prufrock', time is seen as inexorably repetitive, a process which leads ultimately to decay. In the 'Preludes' time is a burden, whose rhythmic patterns beat out the tedium of urban life. Time destroys 'Aunt Helen's' passion for order and restraint, while the result of man's behaviour in times past is seen in 'Rannoch, by Glencoe', where both man and animals are stuck in the wretchedness of history.

IMAGERY, SYMBOLISM AND ALLUSION

While all of the above are dealt with in specific detail in the discussion of the individual poems, a few general points may be useful for the student also.

Eliot's use of *imagery is eclectic*, that is he drew inspiration from a wide tableau of human experience and did not limit himself to nature as a source, something which had become so much a part of the later Romantics. Under French influence and his admiration for seventeenth-century English poets, Eliot trawled widely to ensure an intellectual sharpness and an emotional intensity in his poems.

Much of the meaning and the power of Eliot's poetry lie in his use of images and symbols. *Sordid, seedy images of city life* appear again and again, from 'The Love Song of J. Alfred Prufrock' to 'Preludes' to 'A Game of Chess'. Even in

'Journey of the Magi', cities are seen as 'hostile'. Such use of significant imagery becomes, with repetition, a symbol. It evokes particular ideas and emotions. This is in keeping with Eliot's rather notorious view that poetry communicates before it is understood. Thus the suggestiveness of imagery and symbolism become part of the excitement of discovery when reading Eliot's poetry.

Similarly *journeys, a street or road are common images* throughout Eliot's poetry. These are seen in 'Journey of the Magi', 'Preludes', 'Usk' and 'Rannoch, by Glencoe', for example. These images also become symbolic, evoking Eliot's search or quest for meaning in life, culminating in his achievement of a satisfactory religious perspective.

However, individual images can also be symbolic. Eliot, for example, uses *animal imagery* to reflect the human in its non-thinking, non-rational state. Hence the use of the crab image/symbol in 'The Love Song of J. Alfred Prufrock'. The 'crow' and 'the patient stag' play similar roles in 'Rannoch, by Glencoe'.

Similarly, Eliot's use of *body parts as images*, as in 'Preludes', 'The Love Song of J. Alfred Prufrock' and 'A Game of Chess' becomes symbolic of the depersonalisation, stereotyping and conformity of modern urban society.

Similarly also, the *images of clocks* and the references to *time* from 'Aunt Helen', to 'Preludes' to 'A Game of Chess' and 'The Love Song of J. Alfred Prufrock', can become a symbol of individual transience and the urgency for renewal.

The student should be particularly aware of Eliot's abrupt transitions in imagery and of his use of images other than visual images. 'Preludes', for example, explores *aural, tactile and olfactory images* in quickly changing, cinematic-style sequences.

Eliot is the most erudite of poets. He was widely read in *everything from literature to history, from psychology to anthropology, from psychology to philosophy*. This is in keeping with his passion not only for self-discovery, but also for discovering the nature of twentieth-century man. Hence his use of allusion is his way of exploring intellectual traditions and expressing himself more precisely.

In this way, his use of allusion is not just an ostentatious *reference to literary history*, for example, but is a way of making a tradition alive again, while also focusing the present situation in that tradition. So, his epigraph in 'The Love Song of J. Alfred Prufrock' both recalls Dante's work and places Prufrock in an urban Hell. Thus, his allusions universalise his themes and the situations in which his characters' personae exist.

Sometimes his allusions come in the form of more *indirect quotation*, as in his reference in 'The Love Song of J. Alfred Prufrock' to Andrew Marvell's poem 'To His Coy Mistress', or in his references to Hamlet and Lazarus. *Direct quotation* of Shakespeare also takes place in 'A Game of Chess', while indirectly

Thomas Middleton, Virgil and Milton are alluded to. All such references and allusions help to build up the picture which tells us some universal truth.

The detailed notes on each poem explain the significance of these allusions and references.

VERSE STRUCTURE

In keeping with the French Symbolists' *'vers libre'*, or free verse, Eliot broke with the regular forms and structures of his immediate predecessors. The suggestiveness of his imagery and symbols demanded that the structures of his verse should be equally suggestive.

If Eliot's imagery often consists of *abrupt transitions*, so also does his verse structure. The structure often reflects both themes and imagery. Thus the *irregular juxtaposition of lines of different length* in 'The Love Song of J. Alfred Prufrock' reflects the agitated nature of Prufrock, while the regularity of lines 23–34, reflect the incantatory tone of the lines. Similarly, the *short lines 33–35* in 'Journey of the Magi' reflect the anxiety of the magus that no part of his narrative should be overlooked.

Eliot also composes his lines to suggest *the natural speech patterns and rhythms of contemporary speech*. This is particularly true of the pub scene, which opens in line 139 of 'A Game of Chess'. The direct speech rhythms of the female narrator give a sense of immediacy to the tone and themes. Into these speech patterns Eliot introduces *colloquialisms and even slang*. The lines do indeed reflect speech patterns, but they also satisfy a metrical pattern.

At times Eliot *repeats particular words and phrases to give a prayer-like or incantatory tone*. This may also effect a reflective mood. This is seen in 'Journey of the Magi' with the strong repetition of 'And'. The strained repetitiveness of lines in 'A Game of Chess' and in 'The Love Song of J. Alfred Prufrock' reflects the nervous tension of the speakers.

Rhyme is used for particular effects in Eliot's poetry. The jingling rhyme of the couplet referring to Michelangelo in 'The Love Song of J. Alfred Prufrock' reflects the shallowness of the women and the mock-heroic tone. Rhyme is used in the 'Preludes' to create a *lyrical effect* in keeping with its title. Both the rhythm and rhyme use in 'East Coker IV' are 'reinventions' of Medieval English verse, which W.B. Yeats, for one, believed helped 'to prolong the moment of contemplation'.

Eliot's interest in music is seen not only in many of the titles of his poems – e.g. 'The Love Song of J. Alfred Prufrock', 'Preludes', 'The Four Quartets' – but *in the very structures of the poems and his use of language*. Some of the verses of 'The Love Song of J. Alfred Prufrock' are composed of single sentences, whose repetitiveness not only reflects the tedium of Prufrock's life but gives a symphonic effect. The heavy stressed *rhythm* of the 'Preludes' suggests the fatigue of the city's inhabitants, while the lyrical sibilant 'S' sounds of lines 9 and 10 of 'Journey of the Magi' evoke the sensuality of the life being left behind. The robust rhythm of 'Usk' suggests the invigorating landscape and underscores the commanding authority of the imperative verbs. The musicality of 'East Coker IV' has been referred to already.

Eliot – a dramatic poet

As can be seen in his poems, Eliot excels in creating characters whose situations reflect the universal condition of man.

Eliot's greatest *verse drama* is, without doubt, 'Murder in the Cathedral', but many of his poems are verse dramas in themselves. The use of *internal monologue*, or stream-of-consciousness speech, is a particularly effective device in *creating drama* in verse.

'The Love Song of J. Alfred Prufrock' has all the elements of drama. The main character is in *conflict*, within himself and with society in general. In his monologue he develops his conflict and demonstrates his *character*, while also creating both the characters and speech of others. Characters are placed in *particular times and places* where the drama unfolds. A *plot*, or storyline, is developed and comes to a conclusion. The reader (or audience) becomes interested in the fate of this character – one who reflects the reader's own predicament, perhaps. Overall, *dialogue* is either direct or implied, advancing the plot and enhancing the reader's understanding of the character.

In this way, 'Aunt Helen', 'Preludes', 'A Game of Chess' and 'Journey of the Magi' are also verse dramas. The pub scene in 'A Game of Chess' is a dramatic reflection of the world in miniature. The student may enjoy reading it out loud in 'an appropriate accent'.

Many of Eliot's poems are 'spoken' by created personae or else detached observers. The latter, as in 'Preludes', has been called a cinematic style. For the student interested in film these may prove especially rewarding. It may also be worth noting how many of Eliot's characters are grotesque in the literary sense. In Prufrock, Miss Helen Slingsby and the women in 'A Game of Chess', Eliot has created characters as memorable as those of Shakespeare or Dickens.

Questions

1. Write a personal response to the poetry of T.S. Eliot. Support your answer by reference to the poetry of Eliot that you have studied.
2. 'The poetry of T.S. Eliot appeals to modern readers for various reasons.' Write an introduction to Eliot's poetry in which you suggest what these reasons might be.
3. Imagine you have been asked to give a reading of T.S. Eliot's poetry to

your class. What poems would you choose and why would you choose them?

4. Suppose someone told you that he/she found T.S. Eliot's poetry too obscure. Write a response to this person in which you outline your understanding of Eliot's poetry.

5. What impression did the poetry of T.S. Eliot make on you as a reader? In your answer you may wish to address the following:
   - your sense of the poet's personality
   - his major themes
   - the poet's use of imagery and language
   - the poem/poems that appealed to you most.

6. 'Eliot's major achievement is as a verse dramatist.'
   Write out a speech you would make to your class on the above topic.

Bibliography

Gardner, Helen, *The Art of T.S. Eliot*, Faber and Faber: London 1985.

Moody, A.David, (editor), *The Cambridge Companion to T.S. Eliot*, Cambridge: Cambridge University Press 1994.

Braybrooke, Neville, (editor), *T.S. A Symposium for His Seventieth Birthday*, Garnstone Press: London 1958.

Donoghue, Denis, *Words Alone: The Poet T.S. Eliot*, Yale University Press 2000.

Steed, C.K., *The New Poetic: Yeats to Eliot*, Pelican Books 1967.

Herbert, Michael, *T.S. Eliot Selected Poems*, York Notes, Longman York Press 1982.

Southam, B.C., *A Student's Guide to The Selected Poems of T.S. Eliot*, Faber and Faber: London 1968.

Press, John, *The Chequer'd Shade: Reflections on Obscurity in Poetry*, Oxford University Press: London 1963.

Leavis, F.R., *New Bearings in English Poetry*, Pelican Books 1972.

* If the 'water-mill' represents Christ then 'darkness' could represent death, which Christ conquers by the Resurrection. On the other hand the water-mill could represent the superior forces of those in the world who put Christ to death.

6 *Elizabeth* BISHOP

John G. Fahy

A *literary life*

Elizabeth Bishop was born on 8 February 1911 in Worcester, Massachusetts. Her parents, William Bishop and Gertrude Bulmer (the family name was variously spelt Bulmer, with a silent l, and Boomer), were both of Canadian origin.

Her father died when she was eight months old; her mother never recovered from the shock and for the next five years was in and out of mental hospitals, moving between Boston, Worcester, and her home town of Great Village in Nova Scotia, Canada. In 1916 Gertrude Bulmer's insanity was diagnosed as permanent and she was institutionalised and separated from her daughter, whom she was never to see again. She died in 1934. Elizabeth was reared for the most part by the Boomer grandparents in Great Village, with occasional long stays with the wealthy Bishop household in Worcester, which she did not enjoy. As a child she suffered severe lung illnesses, often having to spend almost entire winters in bed, reading. Chronic asthma became a problem for her all her life.

She describes her early days in Nova Scotia from a child's point of view in the autobiographical short story 'In the Village'. The elegy 'First Death in Nova Scotia' also draws on some childhood memories. 'Sestina' too evokes the sadness of this period. These, and snippets from unpublished poems and papers, point to an unsatisfactory relationship with an ill and transient mother. Yet in spite of these difficulties her recollections of her Nova Scotia childhood were essentially positive, and she had great affection for her maternal grandparents, aunts and uncles in this small agricultural village.

In 1927 she went to Walnut Hill School for girls, a boarding-school in Natick, Massachusetts. From 1930 to 1934 she attended Vassar College, an exclusive private university in Poughkeepsie, New York, where her fees were paid at first by the Bishop family and then by the income from a legacy left by her father. She graduated in English literature but also studied Greek and music, and she always retained a particular appreciation for Renaissance lyric poetry and for the works of Gerard Manley Hopkins. It was at Vassar that she first began to publish stories and poems in national magazines and where she met the poet Marianne Moore, who became an important influence on her career as a poet and with whom she maintained a lifelong friendship and correspondence. It was also at Vassar that she formed her first lesbian relationship, and here too, on her own admission, that the lifelong problem with alcohol addiction began.

Between 1935 and 1938 she made a number of trips to Europe, travelling to England, Ireland, France, North Africa, Spain and Italy in the company of her friends Louise Crane and Margaret Miller, the latter losing an arm in a road accident on the trip. Bishop dedicated the poem 'Quai d'Orléans' to Miller.

In 1939 she moved to Key West, Florida, a place she had fallen in love with over the previous years. 'The Fish' reflects her enjoyment of the sport of fishing at that time. She and Louise Crane bought a house there, now called the Elizabeth Bishop House. Later she lived with Marjorie Carr Stevens, to whom 'Anaphora' was dedicated posthumously after Stevens's death in 1959. Key West became a sort of refuge and base for Bishop over the next fifteen years.

In 1945 she won the Houghton Mifflin Poetry Award. In 1946 her first book of poetry, *North and South,* was published and was well received by the critics. 'The Fish' is among its thirty poems. At this time she met and began a lifelong friendship and correspondence with the poet Robert Lowell.

In 1948 she won a Guggenheim Fellowship, and in 1949–50 she was poetry consultant to the Library of Congress, supervising its stock of poetry, acquiring new works, and providing opinions and advice. The income from this work was important to her, as she had dedicated herself exclusively to her poetry, at which she was a slow and often erratic worker.

The years 1945 to 1951, when her life was centred on New York, were very unsettled. She felt under extreme pressure in a very competitive literary circle and drank heavily. 'The Bight' and 'The Prodigal' reflect this dissolute period of her life. In 1947 she began receiving medical support for her chronic depression, asthma, and alcoholism.

In 1951 she left for South America on the first stage of a trip around the world. She stopped first in Brazil, where she went to visit her old acquaintances Mary Morse and Maria Carlota Costellar de Macedo Soares. She was fascinated by the country and by Lota Soares, with whom she began a relationship that was to last until Soares's death in 1967. They lived in a new house in the luxurious Brazilian countryside at Petrópolis. 'Questions of Travel' and 'The Armadillo' reflect this period of her life.

A Cold Spring, her second volume of poetry, was published in 1955. It contains 'The Bight', 'At the Fishhouses', and 'The Prodigal'.

In 1956 she won the Pulitzer Prize. In 1957 *The Diary of Helena Morley* was published. This was a translation by Bishop of the diary of a girl aged between thirteen and fifteen who lived in the Brazilian village of Diamantina in the 1890s. In 1965 *Questions of Travel,* her third volume, was published. Among this selection, as well as the title poem, were 'Sestina', 'First Death in Nova Scotia' and 'Filling Station'.

In 1966–67 she was poet in residence at the University of Washington in

Seattle, where she met Suzanne Bowen, who became her secretary, human caretaker and, after Soares's death, lover. They lived in San Francisco (1968–69), where Bishop found the new culture bewildering, and then in Brazil, until the tempestuous ending of the relationship in 1970.

In 1969 the *Complete Poems* was published. In 1970 Bishop won the National Book Award for Poetry. She was appointed poet in residence at Harvard University, where she taught advanced verse writing and studies in modern poetry for her first year and, later, poets and their letters. She described herself as 'a scared elderly amateur prof'. It was here she met Alice Methfessel, an administrative assistant who became her minder and companion for the remainder of her life. She began to do a good many public readings of her poetry to make a living, as she had not been able to get much of her money out of Brazil. She continued to teach courses for the remainder of her years, though she found the work draining and it interfered with her already slow production of poetry. But she needed the money to maintain her style of life and travel.

In the summer of 1972 she went on a cruise through Scandinavia to the Soviet Union. From 1973 to 1977 she secured a four-year contract from Harvard to teach a term each year, until her retirement in May 1977. She continued to do public readings, punctuated by spells in hospital caused by asthma, alcohol and depression. She managed to visit Mexico in 1975 and went on a trip to Europe in 1976.

In 1976 *Geography III* was published. Among this slim collection of nine or ten poems are 'In the Waiting Room' and 'The Moose'. The poems in this volume show a new, more directly personal style and a return to her past and her sense of self in search of themes. Competing with failing health, including a bleeding hiatus hernia, she continued her usual round of readings, travel and some writing. She died suddenly of a brain aneurysm on 6 October 1979.

The Fish

Text of poem: New Explorations Anthology page 261

[*Note: This poem is also prescribed for Ordinary Level 2006 exam*]

In the late 1930s, Bishop discovered Florida and a love of fishing. Based on real fishing experiences, her notebooks of the time show images and line fragments that were later developed in 'The Fish'. She worked on the poem during the winter of 1939 and sent a finished draft to Marianne Moore in January 1940, and the poem was first published in the *Partisan Review* in March 1940. It is included in her first published collection of 1946, *North and South*.

THE SPEAKER: THE I AND THE EYE

The poem is narrated in the first person, so we get to meet the poet – the 'I' in the poem – directly, as we do in quite a few of Bishop's poems. This gives the experience of the poem an immediacy and an intimacy for the reader. But while the reader may feel closely involved in the drama, there is a hint that the speaker herself is something of an outsider, not a native of the place, the inhabitant of a 'rented boat'. Perhaps this lends a certain objectivity to the drama and the description of it.

We are also introduced here to the famous Bishop 'eye', which sees both the beautiful and the grimy, describes not only surface detail but even imagines the interior:

> the dramatic reds and blacks
> of his shiny entrails,
> and the pink swim-bladder
> like a big peony.

Minute descriptions and calculated use of detail are a feature of Bishop's poetry. This is how she apprehends the world and comes to grips with experience: through aesthetic re-creation. Detail is important as a basis for understanding.

Bishop re-creates the fish in minute detail. This is how she 'interiorises' it, comprehends it. At first she domesticates it in the imagery, making it familiar by linking it to details of faded everyday living (he is 'homely', 'brown skin hung in strips like ancient wallpaper,' 'shapes like full-blown roses', 'rags of green weed'). Yet something of its essential wildness, the otherness of its creative being, is retained in some of the descriptions:

> – the frightening gills,
> fresh and crisp with blood,
> that can cut so badly . . .

This is also rendered in war imagery:

> . . . from his lower lip . . .
> grim, wet, and weaponlike,
> hung five old pieces of fish-line . . .
> Like medals with their ribbons
> frayed and wavering . . .

But perhaps the most crucial moment in the poet's comprehension of the fish is when she examines the eyes,

which were far larger than mine
but shallower, and yellowed,
the irises backed and packed
with tarnished tinfoil
seen through the lenses
of old scratched isinglass.

The detail is re-created poetically, using all the echoes and sound effects of alliteration and assonance reminiscent of a Hopkins 'inscaping', re-creating in words the essence of the thing observed ('shallower', 'yellowed', 'backed and packed', 'tarnished tinfoil'). The detailed re-creation leads to the poet's realisation that these eyes are unresponsive: the fish is oblivious to her, there is no real sentient contact between human and animal.

They shifted a little, but not
to return my stare.

There is no question here of humankind's heroic struggle against Nature, such as we find in Hemingway's *The Old Man and the Sea*. The experience is not glorified or mythologised, but rather rendered as she saw it. She is reported as saying to her students (quoted by Wesley Wehr):

I always tell the truth in my poems. With 'The Fish', that's exactly how it happened. It was in Key West, and I did catch it, just as the poem says. That was in 1938. Oh, but I did change one thing: the poem says he had five hooks hanging from his mouth, but actually he only had three. Sometimes a poem makes its own demands. But I always try to stick as much as possible to what really happened when I describe something in a poem.

We notice that, even as she is asserting the absolute integrity of her eye and the accuracy of the descriptive process, she is also aware of the creative demands of the poetic process. The poem is an accurate record, but only up to a point.

A DRAMATIC POEM

The critic Willard Spiegelman, reflecting on the dramatic quality of Bishop's poetry, said: 'We do not normally think of Bishop as a poet of struggle; the tension in her poems is mostly internalised, and confrontations, when they occur, are between the self, travelling, moving or simply seeing, and the landscape it experiences.' This is particularly applicable to this poem. The first and last lines ('I caught a tremendous fish' and 'and I let the fish go') frame this drama. There is little external conflict, though there are hints of military antagonism and danger from the fish. The confrontation framed by these lines is mainly internal.

So why does she release the fish? Was it because of the lack of heroic struggle?

> He didn't fight.
> He hadn't fought at all.

Does the lack of contact in the eyes disappoint her? Or does she release him out of respect for his history of previous successful encounters, a record emblazoned on his lip ('a five-haired beard of wisdom trailing from his aching jaw')? Perhaps these are part of the decision, but the real moment of truth occurs because of the sudden appearance of the accidental industrial rainbow when the bilge oil gleams in the sun ('where oil had spread a rainbow around the rusted engine'). Fortuitous this may be – a grim parody of natural beauty, an ironic comment on humankind's relationship with nature – but it provides for the poet a moment of aesthetic unity with the grandeur of the world, and everything is transformed ('everything was rainbow, rainbow, rainbow!'). It is a moment of revelation, in which this new image of the fish colours the environment and alters her relationship with nature. No longer antagonistic, confrontational, she has metaphorically tamed, re-created and understood the fish.

The ending of the poem is very similar to a Wordsworth nature poem such as 'The Daffodils': the hypnotic vision ('I stared and stared'), the wealth accruing to the viewer ('victory filled up the little rented boat'), and feelings of inspiration and joy through creating a connection with the world, a world that has been transformed by the vision, this moment of epiphany,

> where oil had spread a rainbow
> around the rusted engine
> to the bailer rusted orange,
> . . . until everything
> was rainbow, rainbow, rainbow!

The Bight

Text of poem: New Explorations Anthology page 264

GENESIS OF THE POEM

'The Bight' was probably written in early 1948. In a letter to Robert Lowell dated January of that year Bishop tells of the excavations at Garrison Bight, Key West. 'The water looks like blue gas – the harbor is always a mess here, junky little boats are piled up, some hung with sponges and always a few half sunk or splintered up from the most recent hurricane – it reminds me a little of my desk' (Brett Millier, *Elizabeth Bishop: Life and the Memory of It*). She wrote to Lowell again the following month, saying that she was trying to finish two poems about Key West, 'and then I hope I won't have to write about the place any more.'

BISHOP'S IDIOSYNCRATIC DESCRIPTIONS

This is a typical example of the poet's technique of description, minutely detailed and accurate yet coloured in a personal way, either by her wit or by the view implicit in the imagery. The extraordinary quality of the water is emphasised by the poet wittily turning the accepted view of things on its head. It is made to look strange, so that we look at it afresh.

> Absorbing, rather than being absorbed,
> the water in the bight doesn't wet anything.

She presents the water to us through a number of sense perspectives: touch, sight, smell, and sound:

> the color of the gas flame turned as low as possible.
> One can smell it turning to gas; if one were Baudelaire
> one could probably hear it turning to marimba music.

To Bishop, the world of the bay seems predominantly mechanical – not just the dredge at work, but 'pelicans crash . . . like pickaxes,' 'man-of-war birds' have 'tails like scissors,' and 'glinting like little plowshares, the blue-gray shark tails'. There is even a hint that the scene is dangerous, potentially explosive ('the pilings dry as matches' and the water 'the color of the gas flame'). The helpless, ineffectual aspect of creatures and things is displayed (pelicans 'rarely coming up with anything to show for it,' boats 'stove in, and not yet salvaged, if they ever will be'). Altogether there is presented a detailed picture of life chugging along in the midst of disorder and ineffectuality.

VIEW OF THE WORLD

Bishop's world here is a tired, run-down, worn-out one, her view completely unromantic. It is a world of mechanical reactions, of trained responses.

> The frowsy sponge boats keep coming in
> with the obliging air of retrievers.

There may be routine, but there is little sense of spirit, of wholeness or of perspective in the picture. The usual mechanical, monotonous pulse of life goes on ('Click. Click. Goes the dredge') but against a background of 'untidy activity', 'unanswered letters', 'old correspondences' and a general lack of cohesion. This atmosphere is created, at least partly, by the disparate nature of the imagery: picture follows unconnected picture, and there is no sense of any linkage or pattern (water, dredge, birds, frowsy sponge-boats, fence of sharks' tails for the Chinese-restaurant trade, little white boats stove in, and again the dredge). Yet the prevailing attitude is one of stoicism: life goes on, 'awful but cheerful'.

A PERSONAL POEM?

The subtitle 'On my birthday' really colours the entire poem. Despite the absence of the first-person voice, the sub-title forces us to acknowledge the shadowy presence of the poet, like the ghost at the feast. Why does she mark her birthday in this unusual way, viewing this particular scene? What special significance has the scene for her?

It has been suggested that the 'disorder and latent violence in the vehicles convey the disorder in Elizabeth's mind' (Millier) as she thinks about her own life. 'Thirty-seven and far from heaven,' she noted. The comparison between the confusion in the bay and the clutter of her own desk, as recorded in her letter to Lowell, together with the extraordinary simile or conceit of the 'little white boats . . . like torn-open, unanswered letters', would indicate a high degree of personal meaning in the poem, even though the description of the bay has been universalised. Indeed, often in Bishop's poems, private significance is revealed out of apparently objective description.

Does she identify with the frowsy sponge-boats, the little white boats piled up against each other, or the wrecked ones 'not yet salvaged'? Perhaps she is celebrating the survival against the storms of many small craft, as much of her own life was spent at the mercy of the tides of alcohol and depression. It is difficult not to read 'awful but cheerful' as a personal statement.

At the Fishhouses

Text of poem: New Explorations Anthology page 266

GENESIS OF THE POEM

Elizabeth Bishop travelled to Nova Scotia in the summer of 1946. It has been suggested that she undertook the trip in order to be out of the way when her first collection, *North and South,* was published. At any rate, it was her first visit to Great Village in fifteen years. She had spent the previous two years undergoing counselling, trying to understand the origins of her alcoholism and bouts of depression. Now she was returning to her physical origins, the scenes of her less-than-idyllic childhood.

From her notebook entries of the time we know that the trip was disturbing, but it gave rise to a number of poems. 'At the Fishhouses' was published in the *New Yorker* on 9 August 1947.

SUBJECT MATTER AND THEMES

This poem could be read as a meditation on the significance of the sea and its influence on humanity and landscape.

The poem is set at the convergence of sea and shore and at a place of important interaction between humankind and the sea. Human enterprise depends on the sea and is subservient to it. Symbolically, the 'cleated gangplanks' lead up out of the water to the storerooms, but the 'long ramp' also descends into the water, 'down and down'. This symbiotic relationship is also alluded to in the 'talk of the decline in the population I and of codfish and herring'. The sea's influence permeates and colours everything, having the power to transform magically ('all is silver . . . the silver of the benches, I the lobster pots, and masts, scattered I among the wild jagged rocks, I is of an apparent translucence'), or to bring decay and ruin ('an ancient wooden capstan . . . where the ironwork has rusted'). Humankind is surrounded by the sea and dwarfed by it. One has the sense of the sea as some forbidding power encircling humanity ('element bearable to no mortal'), indeed indifferent to humanity's fate, as suggested in the incantatory evocation of the tides:

> the same sea, the same,
> slightly, indifferently swinging above the stones

Yet the sea provides that crucial moment of epiphany for the poet, when she gains insight into the nature of knowledge: that it is temporal and transient.

Our knowledge is historical, flowing, and flown.

THE POET'S METHOD

The speaker slowly draws us into the picture in the opening sequence, with vivid details of sight (the 'old man . . . a dark purple-brown,' the description of the fish-houses: 'all is silver'), sense ('a cold evening', 'the air smells'), and sound (the talk, the presumed sounds of wheelbarrow and scraping). The specific detail augments this sense of realism in the opening (five fish-houses, steeply peaked roofs, narrow, cleated gangplanks, etc.) The present tense of the narrative gives it immediacy.

The reader is invited to share in the speaker's 'total immersion' in both the uncomfortable reality ('it makes one's nose run and one's eyes water') and the mesmeric fantasy ('if you should dip your hand in . . . your hand would burn | as if the water were a transmutation of fire').

Once again the poet uses detail as a way of possessing. Only by describing and imagining the mysterious movements and powers of the sea does the speaker win some control over them.

Through total immersion and conjuring up, she finally wins some insight and understanding. Her method, as usual, is a combination of straightforward description and poetic imagining. In the latter, she often transforms the scene or the object in the retelling: she deliberately makes it strange in order to force us to see it afresh ('your hand would burn | as if the water were a transmutation of fire | that feeds on stones and burns with a dark gray flame').

The process of winning through to her final visionary insight is marked by fits and starts, reflecting perhaps the difficulty of achieving any kind of self-knowledge. The poetic contemplation of the silvering of the landscape is interrupted by the mundane conversation on population decline. The renewed contemplation of the sea in the third section ('cold dark deep') is interrupted by the humorous episode with the seal.

> He was interested in music;
> like me a believer in total immersion,
> so I used to sing him Baptist hymns.

But it finally manages to build to that rhythmic incantation of the climax ('indifferently swinging above the stones . . .').

This stop-start method employed in the narrative is also used by Bishop in the rhythm of the language, in order to control the emotion in the poem. She uses the metre, and repetition of words and phrases (*anaphora*), to convey the hypnotic power of the sea.

> I have seen it over and over, the same sea, the same,
> slightly, indifferently swinging above the stones,
> icily free above the stones,
> above the stones, and then the world.

But she breaks this atmosphere with the everyday language of the conditional clause ('if you should dip your hand in'). The flow of the verse builds again, and is again brought down to earth by 'if you tasted it, it would first taste bitter,' before it is allowed to build to that intense and rhythmic conclusion.

THE VISIONARY INSIGHT EXPERIENCED BY THE POET

This entire poem is devoted to the strange and inexplicable power of the sea, a subject revealing Bishop's romantic impulses. The sea in this poem takes on qualities of the other elements, particularly of air and fire, thereby establishing itself as the primal force in nature. More significantly for the poet, the sea is equated with knowledge, and it is the realisation of this, achieved gradually through her total immersion and re-creation process of poetry, that forms the climax of the poem.

Knowledge is broken down into its elements ('dark, salt, clear, moving, utterly free'). Could these epithets be translated as disturbing, preserving, transparent, ever-changing, and outside our control? The description of knowledge might be read as a view of human knowledge in general, but it is difficult not to read it also as personal. The reference to its darker side, as well as to its objectivity and transparency, could be seen as a personal note, in view of Bishop's psychological search and journey back to the roots of her depression and alcohol problems. The nature of the knowledge in the poem is overtly sexual, with maternal overtones:

> drawn from the cold hard mouth
> of the world, derived from the rocky
> breasts . . .

This hard, forbidding maternal image might be taken as a reference to her unsatisfactory relationship with her mother and to the human and genetic knowledge derived from her. This knowledge is temporal and transient, no lasting inheritance, rather 'flowing, and flown' – quite a bleak view of life, with its suggestion of the isolated individual, unconnected to the past, at the mercy of the tide.

The Prodigal

Text of poem: New Explorations Anthology page 270

GENESIS OF THE POEM

Elizabeth Bishop said that this poem originated from her thoughts when one of her aunt's stepsons offered her a drink of rum in the pigsty at about nine o'clock in the morning during her trip to Nova Scotia in 1946. Perhaps that was the final spark that engendered the poem, but the theme could never have been far from her thoughts, as she herself struggled with alcoholism all her life.

About the time of her thirty-eighth birthday, on 8 February 1949, she fell into a deep trough of depression. In an effort to rally out of it she went on a holiday to Haïti, from where she wrote to Marianne Moore to say that she had finished some poems, including 'The Prodigal'. Ironically, on her return from

Haïti she went into a long and heavy drinking bout.

'The Prodigal' was published in the *New Yorker* on 13 March 1951.

THEME AND DEVELOPMENT

This poem deals with the exile of the alcoholic. Like all good poetry, it functions at the level of the individual in the narrative but also at a universal level, exploring the metaphorical exile of alcoholism: the isolation, the skulking, the deception and hiding, the lack of control, aspirations rather than action. (Where do these feature in this poem?)

There is enormous human understanding in this poem. Despite the physical dirt of odour and ordure, the heart can still lift to the religious impulse ('the lantern – like the sun, going away – I laid on the mud a pacing aureole') or thrill to the romantic beauty of nature ('the sunrise glazed the barnyard mud with red; I the burning puddles seemed to reassure'). In fact the prodigal seems to retain a particularly benign relationship with nature, appreciating the delicacy of even these animals ('light-lashed . . . a cheerful stare') and maintaining a comfortable domesticity between animal and human ('The pigs stuck out their little feet and snored'). Nature here is a bringer of wisdom. The bats' 'uncertain staggering flight' is the spur to his self-awareness, his moment of 'shuddering insights', and so his eventual turning back.

The poem is depressingly realistic in its evocation of filth and human abasement:

> even to the sow that always ate her young –
> till, sickening, he leaned to scratch her head.

But it is noble and uplifting in its awareness of the spark of soul that still flickers even in the most abject circumstances.

FORM

The poem is structured as two sonnets of a rather loose nature. They each have the requisite fourteen lines, and the first one maintains the conventional octave–sestet division, but the rhyming schemes are eccentric, if not absent altogether. The rhythm is a mixture of iambic pentameter and four-stress lines.

Questions of Travel

Text of poem: New Explorations Anthology page 272

GENESIS OF THE POEM

In 1951 Bishop left for an intended journey around the world, travelling via

South America. But she stopped off in Brazil, where she remained, with brief intervals, for the next fifteen years or so. This poem reflects her fascination with travel and with Brazil in particular. 'Questions of Travel' is the title poem of her third volume of poetry, published in 1965, though it had been worked on for a good while before that. There are at least seven earlier drafts in existence.

SOME OBSERVATIONS ON THEMES

- This is a travel poem with a difference. True, it features the expected descriptions of the unusual and the exotic, as Bishop views, with a traveller's curiosity, 'the crowded streams', 'the trees . . . like noble pantomimists, robed in pink', 'the sad, two-noted, wooden tune of disparate wooden clogs', the 'music of the fat brown bird', the 'bamboo church of Jesuit baroque', the 'calligraphy of songbirds' cages', and the silence after rain – all the elements of a superior imaginative letter home.

- Her observations are given a particularly temporal significance as they are made against the great dwarfing background of the ages of time. But it is a time that, with typical Bishop quirkiness, has a disorderly aspect:

  – For if those streaks . . .
  aren't waterfalls yet,
  in a quick age or so, as ages go here,
  they probably will be.

- Bishop goes deeper than the postcard façade in order to acknowledge the limitations of our knowledge and understanding of a foreign culture.

  To stare at some inexplicable old stonework,
  inexplicable and impenetrable . . .

She really doesn't expect it all to add up in the visitor's mind ('to have pondered, I blurr'dly and inconclusively').

- Even more basically, Bishop examines and questions the very need to travel. Partly motivated by traveller's exhaustion ('think of the long trip home'), she rises above this to engage the question at a philosophical level.

  What childishness is it that while there's a breath of life
  in our bodies, we are determined to rush
  to see the sun the other way around?

Is it lack of imagination? she wonders. She presents the idea as a philosophical debate between movement and travel ('Should we have stayed at home and thought of here?' and 'could Pascal have been not entirely right | about just sitting quietly in one's room?'). She seems to attribute the travel urge to the human need to achieve our dreams.

> Oh, must we dream our dreams
> and have them, too?

- The conclusion of her musings, expressed at the end of the poem, is that the human being is not absolutely free to choose: the necessity for travel is often forced upon a person ('the choice is never wide and never free'). She seems to see travel or homelessness as part of the condition of humankind ('should we have stayed at home, | wherever that may be?').

SETTING

The setting is the interior, away from the coast, the more usual scene of Bishop's conflicts. But even here she is ever-mindful of the sea, and her geographical mind-frame continues to make connections ('the crowded streams | hurry too rapidly down to the sea'), as if the sea is associated with oblivion and annihilation, and even the beauty here is threatened and transient.

POETIC METHOD

- She uses the now familiar method, combining precise observation with her idiosyncratic descriptions, where objects are made to look entirely strange so that we view them in a new light. She draws the reader in with detail and then challenges us visually to look hard and understand.

We can see this at work in the first section of the poem. Using all the conventional poetic devices of alliteration, assonance and sibilance, she re-creates the fluid continuity of the waterfalls as they 'spill over the sides in soft slow-motion'. With graphic, clever imagery she evokes the gigantic scale of the scene, giving it an aura of sadness ('those streaks, those mile-long, shiny, tearstains'). Then, shockingly, we are invited to this upside-down view of the mountains:

> the mountains look like the hulls of capsized ships,
> slime-hung and barnacled.

She has domesticated them by reference to human machinery, yet allowed them to retain their strangeness by the imagery associations with the secret depths of the earth.

- The poem is structured as a dramatic monologue, a dialogue with herself, which is an appropriate form given the philosophical approach to the subject. Having asked if it would not have been better to stay at home, she proceeds, by a series of negative questions, to reach that indefinite conclusion.
- The poem is written in free verse.
- Flashes of humour sparkle here and there, as a welcome relief from the gentle complaining and insistent questioning. We notice the comparison of equatorial rain with politicians' speeches ('two hours of unrelenting oratory | and then a sudden golden silence').

> And have we room
> for one more folded sunset, still quite warm?

Should this be read as a genuinely Romantic urge or as a sardonic swipe at acquisitive and sentimental tourists?

The Armadillo

Text of poem: New Explorations Anthology page 276

GENESIS OF THE POEM

This poem was published in the *New Yorker* on 22 June 1957 and falls among the later of the first batch of poems about Brazil that Bishop published. She had been working on various components of it – imagery etc. – for a number of months, if not years. The fire balloons, the armadillo, the owls and the rabbit feature in her letters of the previous year.

DEDICATION TO ROBERT LOWELL

Lowell had said that his famous poem 'Skunk Hour' was indebted to 'The Armadillo'. So, when she finally published it, Bishop dedicated the poem to him. But there may be more significance than just personal sentiment in the dedication, as Lowell had become a conscientious objector to the Second World War when the Allies fire-bombed German cities. The gesture of defiance of destruction from the skies finds an echo in the last stanza of the poem.

A PHILOSOPHICAL READING OF THE POEM

What view of humanity informs this poem? Does she see humankind as deliberately destructive? No; but unthinking and primitive, yes. The balloons are a manifestation of primitive worship. They are also illegal and dangerous. But they are beautiful, romantic – likened to hearts, stars, and planets, with the planets developed as the main association in the poem. There is also a hint of the fickleness of the human heart ('light that comes and goes, like hearts'). Humankind aspires to the beautiful and to a religious spirit but is unthinking, and the consequences of our actions bring destruction on human beings and the environment, threatening the balance of nature.

So it is really an ecological outlook of Bishop's that is at play here. Lacking a religious outlook on life, what is the big question for humanity? It must be, how do we best preserve for the future what exists here? One of the options is to return to a world that existed before man began to 'impose his egotistical will' on it, to try to recover childhood's innocence, structure and security. It might be suggested that this is what Bishop is attempting in 'First Death in Nova Scotia' and 'Sestina'; but here all she can do is make an uncertain gesture of defiance, as in the last stanza.

POETIC METHOD

- The usual detailed observation is evident, accurately catching, for example, the frantic movement of the owls, or the stance of the armadillo. Sometimes the descriptions are poetic ('It splattered like an egg of fire').
- Bishop's eye is that of the observer rather than the expert. 'The pale green one,' she says of a star. Rather like 'the fat brown bird' of 'Questions of Travel', this creates an easy familiarity with the reader.
- She is adept at leisurely, detailed portraiture, as when describing the balloons that take up the first five stanzas. But she is good also at swift drawing that catches the essential image – of the armadillo, for example.

> a glistening armadillo left the scene,
> rose-flecked, head down, tail down . . .

- But she is no longer able to dupe herself into believing that her descriptions are accurate. She does realise that she has re-created the scene poetically.

> Too pretty, dreamlike mimicry!

In this final stanza she stands outside the poem, reflecting on the poetic process and on the opposition of her two modes: accurate description versus poetic re-creation in order to understand.

TONE: HOW BISHOP CONTROLS FEELINGS

The last stanza provides what is for Bishop a most unusual emotional outburst. The critical cry 'too pretty, dreamlike mimicry!' can be read as aimed at the poetic method but also at the fire balloons' imitation of the destructiveness of war. The gesture of defiance is vulnerable, for all its posturing ('weak', 'ignorant'). It is little better than a hopeless, passionate, vain gesture, which further emphasises the poet's emotional involvement.

> a weak mailed fist
> clenched ignorant against the sky!

This is an unusual outburst from Bishop, whose poetry is tightly controlled even when dealing with an emotive subject. This technical control over her verse keeps it from sentimentality and gives it 'an elegant, muted, modernist quality', as Penelope Laurans put it (in *Elizabeth Bishop: Modern Critical Views*, edited by Harold Bloom). Laurans examines in detail how the poet shapes the reader's response to this beautiful and cruel event:

    (1) **by a factual presentation**, as we have seen;

    (2) **by metrical variation** – in other words, continually changing rhythm so as not to allow the reader to become lost in the lyrical music, stopping the momentum of the verse. A detailed study of the first four stanzas will show how this operates. Stanzas 1 and 2 have a regular metrical pattern: lines 1, 2 and 4 are all of three stresses, with the five-stress third line emphasising the descriptions of the balloons, their frailty, beauty and flashing romanticism. Then stanzas 3 and 4 change to varying three-stress and four-stress lines. Even in the first two regular stanzas there are irregularities. For example, the first sentence of stanza 1 ends in the third line, so the sense is against the flow of the metre. The *abab* rhyme of the first stanza changes in the second. The rest of the poem has three-stress and four-stress lines, but they vary from stanza to stanza. Technically, the overall effect is to arrest any flow or musical momentum that might allow the verse to become sentimental;

    (3) **by using metre and other technical strategies** to draw back from moments of emotional intensity, just at the point where a Romantic poet would let it flow. Stanzas 6 to 9 provide a good example of this. In particular, the flow and enjambment from the end of stanza 6 to 7 conjure up the fright of the owls.

> We saw the pair
> of owls who nest there flying up
> and up, their whirling black-and-white
> stained bright pink underneath, until
> they shrieked up out of sight.

But this moment of intensity is broken up by a change in the metre from tetrameter to irregular three-, four- or five-stress lines. We also find single-unit end-stopped lines, which break the flow:

> The ancient owls' nest must have burned.

The poet now focuses on the detailed description of the animals – the armadillo and the baby rabbit. We are caught up in this and brought back to reality.

Sestina

Text of poem: New Explorations Anthology page 278

Four poems from *Questions of Travel* – 'Manners', 'Sunday 4 a.m.', 'First Death in Nova Scotia' and 'Sestina' – deal with Bishop's return to her origins. 'Sestina' (originally entitled 'Early Sorrow') works on all the significant elements of her childhood. The poem probably evokes the time and atmosphere after her mother's last departure from Great Village to the mental hospital. It also reflects a great deal of thinking and reading about child psychology. In reality, despite the privations and tensions reflected in the poem, Elizabeth Bishop always maintained that she was happy in Great Village.

THE SESTINA FORM

A *sestina* is a poem of six, six-line stanzas in which the line endings of the first stanza are repeated, but in different order, in the other five. The poem concludes with an *envoy*, which is a short address to the reader (or the person to whom the poem is addressed). So the elements here are: house, grandmother, child, stove, almanac and tears; and they are rearranged in the other stanzas like a sort of moving collage.

Some of the elements carry greater symbolic weight, such as the almanac, which has been construed as representing the poet's lifelong anxiety about the passing of time. The house is a pictorial representation of her childhood, and the little Marvel stove seems to provide a counterbalance of domesticity, heat and comfort.

A PSYCHOLOGICAL READING OF THE POEM

The poem deals with memories of childhood uncertainty, loss and a pervasive sense of sorrow. Interesting psychological readings of the poem have been offered by Helen Vendler (in *Elizabeth Bishop: Modern Critical Views*, edited by Harold Bloom), among others. Her reading focuses on tears as the strange and crucial component of this childhood collage. The grandmother hides her tears. The child senses the unshed tears and displaces them elsewhere: in the kettle, the rain, the teacup. The child must translate the tears she has felt, so she transfers them to the 'man with buttons like tears'.

The absence of parents is the cause of all these tears. By the end of the poem, in the tercet that draws together all the essential elements, tears are planted, or sorrow implanted, in the child's life cycle.

The drawing of the house also attracts the interest of psychologists. Its rigid form is taken to represent the insecurity of the young child's makeshift home, her path and flowerbed seen as an attempt to domesticate and put her own stamp on it and so give her some tenuous grasp on security. Helen Vendler asserts: 'The blank center stands for the definitive presence of the unnatural in the child's domestic experience.' Of all things, one's house should not be inscrutable, otherwise there is a great void at the centre of one's life. This becomes one of Elizabeth Bishop's recurring themes: that nothing is more enigmatic than the heart of the domestic scene.

The tercet achieves a resolution of sorts, offering a more balanced view of the human condition. It asserts that grief, song, the marvellous and the inscrutable are present, perhaps necessarily, together in life. But we are left with the impression that the inscrutable, the strange, is the most powerful element in human development.

First Death in Nova Scotia

Text of poem: New Explorations Anthology page 280

BACKGROUND NOTE

Apart from her short story 'In the Village', the poem is one of the few published memoirs of Bishop's childhood. It is also the only time her mother is featured in a published poem. The elegy is based on an actual funeral, probably in 1914, of a cousin named Frank. 'First Death in Nova Scotia' was published in the *New Yorker* on 10 March 1962.

POINT OF VIEW

This is another of Bishop's poems in which she attempts to recover her childhood. With an astute and sensitive psychological understanding, she is very successful at re-creating the consciousness of a child and establishing the point of view of the very young.

She manages to suggest the feelings of confusion through the blurring of colour distinctions. Red and white, the national colours, seem to permeate the entire scene, or at least colour the meaning of it. As well as of the national flag, they become the colours of little Arthur, of the dead bird, of the royal robes, and even of the coffin timbers. The child has held on to just one set of familiar colours.

Also, the child's memory seizes and holds objects (the chromographs, the stuffed loon, the lily of the valley). The child's memory recalls desires, desires for objects ('his breast . . . caressable', 'his eyes were red glass, I much to be desired').

The child has difficulty coping with the difference of death, so the 'reality 'hold' slips. The familiar becomes unreal, the bird is alive again, just uncommunicative (he 'kept his own counsel | on his white, frozen lake'). There is an effort to make the unfamiliar – death – real in the child's terms, with surreal consequences.

> Arthur's coffin was
> a little frosted cake.

The adults too cope with death by participating in a sort of fantasy:

> 'Come,' said my mother,
> 'Come and say good-bye
> to your little cousin Arthur.'

The child fantasises that the 'cold, cold parlor' is the territory of Jack Frost and that the royal couple have 'invited Arthur to be | the smallest page at court.' The child has created a fantasy world in which reality and fantasy, present, past and future, and the national colours all fuse together. But the strain of credibility is too great, and doubt begins to enter her head. The doubt is not an adult doubt about Arthur's ultimate destiny but, in typical child fashion, a doubt about the means of transport.

> But how could Arthur go,
> clutching his tiny lily,
> with his eyes shut up so tight
> and the roads deep in snow?

The use of the child's point of view has allowed a very dispassionate treatment of death. Emotion does not get in the way, and the entire focus is on the unknowable strangeness of death.

THEMES AND ISSUES

- **Memories of childhood.** If this poem can be taken to reflect Bishop's recollections of childhood as a whole, then it is a bleak view. It encompasses death, both of people and creatures; a confused inability to comprehend the reality of the world; a world lacking in warmth or the normal human comforts of childhood ('cold, cold parlor', 'marble-topped table'); a world devoid of emotion; and a shadowy mother figure who is associated with the rituals of death rather than any maternal comfort.
- **A child's first exposure to death and her attempts to comprehend it** ('domesticate' it, in Bishop's terms).
- **Death – its unknowable strangeness.**
- **A secular view of death** (Arthur goes to court rather than Heaven!) – yet not

completely secular, as it recognises another reality beyond this.
- **The frailty of life** ('he was all white, like a doll I that hadn't been painted yet').

Filling Station

Text of poem: New Explorations Anthology page 282

[*Note: This poem is also prescribed for Ordinary Level 2006 exam*]

A CELEBRATION OF THE ORDINARY

Many of Elizabeth Bishop's poems show a fascination with the exotic: with travel, with the mysterious forces in nature, and with the extremes of human experience; but she is also a poet of the ordinary, the everyday, the mundane and banal. She is interested in both the extraordinary and the ordinary.

And the scene we are introduced to at the beginning of this poem is not just the antithesis of beauty, it is unmitigated 'grot': 'oil-soaked, oil-permeated', 'crushed and grease-I impregnated wickerwork,' 'a dirty dog,' etc. What Bishop does is focus her well-known curiosity on this everyday dull scene and probe its uniqueness and mystery. She finds its meaning through her usual poetic method: accumulation of detail and a probing beneath the surface of the seen.

THE DOMESTIC GIVES MEANING TO LIFE

What is revealed as the details pile up is evidence of domesticity, even in this greasy, grimy world of oil and toil: the flower, the 'taboret I (part of the set)', the embroidered doily; and even the dirty dog is 'quite comfy'. In a parody of metaphysical questioning,

> Why the extraneous plant?
> Why the taboret?
> Why, oh why, the doily?

the poem searches for answers, for reasons why things are so, for some harmony or coherence at the heart of this grimy scene. The answer appears in the last stanza, where there are indications of an anonymous domestic presence:

> Somebody embroidered the doily.
> Somebody waters the plant.

For Bishop, domesticity is the greatest good, and establishing domestic tranquillity is what gives meaning to life. She has elevated this into a philosophy of life in place of a religious outlook. Indeed this last stanza has been read as a parody of the great theological Argument from Design used as an indication of the existence of God.

In Bishop's 'theology', is the Great Designer feminine? Certainly we could argue that the world of work described here operates on the male principle. The 'several quick and saucy | and greasy sons' and even the 'big hirsute begonia' all evoke a male world of inelegant, rude and crude health. In contrast, the domesticity is achieved mainly through the female principle:

Embroidered in daisy stitch
With marguerites, I think,

and it is this principle that provides order and coherence and meaning ('arranges the rows of cans') and is a proof of love ('somebody loves us all').

TONE

There are some complicated and subtle shifts of tone throughout this poem. From the somewhat offhand tone of the opening line ('Oh, but it is dirty!') she first takes refuge in descriptive detail. Some critics have read the beginning of the poem as condescending ('little filling station,' 'all quite thoroughly dirty'). The flashes of wit may give some credence to that interpretation ('Be careful with that match!' and the comic book of 'certain color').

But the poet is gradually drawn into the scene and becomes involved. The stance of detached observer no longer provides complete protection for her. She is engaged intellectually at first ('why, oh why, the doily?'), and, as she uncovers what gives coherence and meaning to the scene, an emotional empathy is revealed ('Somebody loves us all'). Perhaps this is as much a *cri de cœur* of personal need as it is an observation. But the wit saves the poem from any hint of sentimentality:

Somebody waters the plant,
or oils it, maybe.

Could we describe the tone of the poem as wryly affectionate? Or do you read the tone of the ending as bemused, as the poet is left contemplating the final irony that love is a row of oil cans?

In the Waiting Room

Text of poem: New Explorations Anthology page 284

A READING OF THE POEM

This poem depicts a traumatic moment of awareness in the child's development. It occurs when the young girl first experiences the separateness of her own identity and simultaneously becomes aware of the strangeness of the world of which she is a part. She fails to find a satisfactory, intelligible relationship between her now conscious 'self' and this 'other' world, a failure so emotional for her that it causes a momentary loss of consciousness, a temporary retreat into that black abyss.

At the beginning of the poem the child sees the world as safe, domestic, familiar: the world of her aunt, a waiting-room, overcoats, lamps and magazines. But the magazines expose her to the primal power of the earth, volcanic passion erupting out of control, the primitive destructive urges of humans (cannibalism), and the barbarous decorations of the naked women. Clearly this newly revealed primitive and exotic world is frighteningly 'other' to the child, and she can comprehend it only by domesticating it through a household simile:

> black, naked women with necks
> wound round and round with wire
> like the necks of light bulbs.

The unfamiliarity of this broader world is shocking to the child ('Their breasts were horrifying'.) Yet it is a world she shares, as she empathises with her aunt's cry of pain.

> What took me
> completely by surprise
> was that it was *me:*
> my voice, in my mouth.

The conflicting claims of self and of the world are cleverly conveyed by Bishop through a constantly changing inside–outside perspective maintained throughout the poem. At first we are in Worcester but outside the room, then inside the room ('sat') while it grew dark outside. Next we are back in the waiting-room while the aunt is further inside. The child looks inside a volcano but outside the cannibals and the naked women. The cry ('from inside, I came an oh! of pain') first drives the child inside herself ('my voice, in my mouth'). This sends her into a fainting dive ('I – we – were falling, falling'), until she is driven right off the world, and the perspective changes radically to a view from space ('cold, blue-black space').

These radical changes in perspective – from the people in the waiting-room to inside herself, to the African women, from inside to outside the waiting-room and the world, from 'I' to 'them' and back again – convey the child's confused apprehension of this widening world and bring on the fainting spell.

And it is in this atmosphere of shifting perspectives that she asserts her individuality, naming herself for the first time in a poem ('you are an *I*, | you are an *Elizabeth*'), yet immediately the claims of the 'other' world are manifest ('you are one of them'). She has great difficulty integrating the recently discovered elements of this world, unifying the exotic and the familiar, the naked women with the aunt and the people in the waiting-room in the familiar trousers and skirts and boots. She has even greater difficulty accepting any kind of personal unity with this other world, particularly at a time when she feels most alone, having just discovered herself.

> What similarities –
> boots, hands, the family voice
> I felt in my throat, or even
> the *National Geographic*
> and those awful hanging breasts –
> held us all together
> or made us all just one?

Even though the fainting spell passes, the moment of visionary insight fades and the child is relocated in actual time and place, the issue is not resolved ('the War was on'). This war is both political and personal for the child. Outside, the world is hostile ('night and slush and cold'), and her uneasy relationship with it continues.

These twin realisations of being an individual and yet somehow being uneasily connected to this strange and varied world form the central wisdom of this poem, what her biographer Brett Millier has described as 'the simultaneous realisation of selfhood and the awful otherness of the inevitable world'. It is interesting that Bishop chooses the age of seven to mark this onset of adult awareness, an age traditionally seen as initiating moral responsibility. She herself has dated the onset of many of her own most important attitudes from the age of six or seven, including a feeling of strangeness or alienation from the world. She also dates the beginnings of her feminist philosophy from that age.

ELIZABETH BISHOP AND CONSCIOUSNESS OF SEX ROLES

'In the Waiting Room' describes the poet's first encounter with consciousness of sex roles. Through the magazine the child learns, though perhaps at a sub-rational level, that women practise mutilations on themselves and their babies to make them more sexually attractive. They themselves perpetuate their role as sex objects, encourage this vanity, accept this type of slavery. Aunt Consuelo's 'oh! of pain' suggests the weakness and vulnerability of women. And Bishop identifies with woman's pain.

Yet her attitude to women is somewhat ambivalent. While she identifies with the cry, she is disparaging about the woman's weakness.

even then I knew she was
a foolish, timid woman.
I might have been embarrassed,
but wasn't.

She recoils in horror from female sexuality, from 'those awful hanging
breasts.' This ambivalence about the value of femininity affected her view of
herself, her sexual orientation, and gave rise to a complicated treatment of
questions of sex roles in her poetry.

POETIC STYLE: SOME COMMENTS

A private poem

'In the Waiting Room' is somewhat unusual in that it is such a self-contained
poem. Usually in Bishop's poems the private experience described mushrooms
into a universal truth. While we might draw some universal conclusions about
childhood and the development of self-awareness, the truths this poem
essentially conveys reflect idiosyncratic Bishop attitudes to life: the
estrangement, the pain, the confusions of life, the view of woman, etc.

Descriptive accuracy

The fabled truth of Bishop's descriptions lets her down here. Research has
shown that there are no naked people in the *National Geographic* of February
1918, and Osa and Martin Johnson had not yet become famous at that time. So
for once her realism is a product of poetic licence!

Use of metre

The poem is written in very short, sometimes two-stress but more often three-
stress lines. Trimeters are quite a limiting line formation, not often used for the
communication of complicated ideas or deep emotions (though Yeats manages
to convey deep irony and anger through the regular thumping trimeter beat of
'The Fisherman'). The use of trimeters here by Bishop is probably deliberate, to
limit the reader's emotional engagement with the poem. Not that the poem is
devoid of emotional impact: the moments of revelation are intensely felt. But, as
the critic Penelope Laurans (in *Elizabeth Bishop: Modern Critical Views*, edited
by Harold Bloom) demonstrates in her scanning of some passages, Bishop
deliberately varies the metre to prevent a lyrical build-up that might invite an
emotional investment by the reader. Instead, the reader is forced to think and
reflect, in this example on the word 'stranger', which is stressed both by its
placement and by the metre:

‿ ‐ ‿ ‐ ‿ ‐ ‿
I knew | that nothing | stranger

‿ ‐ ‿ ‐ ‿ ‿ ‐ ‿
had ever | happened, | that nothing

‐ ‿ ‿ ‐ ‿ ‐ ‿
stranger | could ever | happen

The less usual *amphibrach* foot (˘ ˉ ˘) creates a certain ponderousness, which forces the reader to reflect on, rather than be caught up in, the experience.

At another key moment, the variation of feet is used to create the effect of puzzlement.

‐ ‿ ‐ ‿ ‐ ‐ ‿
How – | I didn't | know any

‐ ‿ ‿ ‐ ‿ ‐ ‿
word for it | – how 'un|likely' . . .

‿ ‐ ‿ ‐ ‿ ‿ ‿
How had I | come to | be here

Again, the effect is to limit the emotional appeal. Bishop uses her technical skills to keep the reader at bay, at a safe distance.

An overview of Elizabeth Bishop

The purpose of this section is to assist the reader in forming an overview of the poet's work. For this reason the material is structured as a series of 'thinking points', grouped under general headings. These cover the poet's main preoccupations and methods, but they are not exhaustive. Neither are they 'carved in stone', to be memorised: they should be altered, added to or deleted as the reader makes his or her own notes.

These thinking points should send the reader back to the poems, to reflect, to reassess, to find supporting quotations, etc.

THEMES OF BISHOP'S POETRY

Childhood
- Many of her poems have their roots in childhood memories, indeed are based on her own childhood ('Sestina', 'First Death in Nova Scotia', 'In the Waiting Room').
- The perspective is mostly that of adult reminiscence ('Sestina', 'In the Waiting Room'), but occasionally the child's viewpoint is used ('First Death in Nova Scotia').
- The lessons of childhood are chiefly about pain and loss ('Sestina', 'First Death in Nova Scotia', 'In the Waiting Room') and about alienation from the world ('In the Waiting Room'), but there is also the comfort of grandparents ('Sestina').

- There is a strong tension between the need to return to childhood and the need to escape from that childhood ('In the Waiting Room', 'At the Fishhouses', 'The Moose'); she even returns in dreams in a poem called 'The Moose'.
- Perhaps this is based on the notion of childhood as the completion of the self, and the poems are a search for the self?
- We know that she attended counselling to find the origins of her alcoholism and depression. Yet her reconstructions of childhood do not seem to function as Freudian psychoanalytical therapy. She doesn't seem to alter her direction or attitudes as a result of drawing her past into the conscious, though she does seem to find a deal of comfort and a greater acceptance in the later poem, 'The Moose'. She is not trying to apportion blame, neither is she trying to be forgiving or sympathetic. In general she seems neutral and detached ('First Death in Nova Scotia', 'Sestina').
- She also deals with the end of childhood and the awakening to adulthood ('In the Waiting Room').

Her life was her subject matter

Bishop was 'a poet of deep subjectivity', as Harold Bloom said. She wrote out of her own experience, dealing with such topics as:
- her incompleteness ('Sestina', 'In the Waiting Room')
- her disordered life and depression ('The Bight')
- alcoholism ('The Prodigal')
- her childhood – of loss, sorrow and tears ('Sestina'), absence of parents ('Sestina'), balanced by grandparents' sympathy and support ('Sestina')
- achieving adulthood and the confusion of that ('In the Waiting Room')
- travel, her wanderlust ('Questions of Travel'), her favourite places ('At the Fishhouses')
- even her hobbies, such as fishing ('The Fish').

The poet and travel

- As her own wanderings show, she was a restless spirit, constantly on the move: Nova Scotia, Florida, Brazil, Europe, New York, San Francisco, Harvard.
- Many of the places she visited (Nova Scotia, the Straits of Magellan, the Amazon Estuary, Key West, Florida) stand at the boundary between land and sea. There is a tension between land and sea in her poems ('At the Fishhouses', 'Questions of Travel'), with the sea viewed as a strange, indifferent, encircling power ('At the Fishhouses'). Perhaps this is a metaphor for the conflict between the artist and life. Quite a few of her poems are set at this juncture between land and sea ('The Fish', 'The Bight', 'At the Fishhouses').

- She seemed to be fascinated by geographical extremities: straits, peninsulas, wharves; mountains, jungle, outback ('Questions of Travel', 'The Armadillo', 'At the Fishhouses', 'The Bight'). Perhaps she was attracted to the near-isolation of these places. They are almost isolated in her poems. One critic viewed these as the sensual organs of a living earth, 'fingers of water or land that are the sensory receptors of a large mass'. The poet is seen as making sensuous contact with the living earth.
- Bishop has an eye for the exotic and the unusual ('Questions of Travel', 'The Armadillo') but also for the ordinary ('Filling Station').
- She dwells on the difficulty of ever really knowing another culture ('Questions of Travel'), but this did not prevent her trying.
- Travel and journeying can be seen as a metaphor for the discovery of truth in some poems ('Questions of Travel').
- Could this preoccupation with travel be seen as exile from the self?

Bishop and the natural world
- Nature is central to her poetry, either as an active element central to the experience of the poem or by making an intrusion into the domestic scene (in a minority of poems such as 'Filling Station', 'Sestina', 'First Death in Nova Scotia', 'In the Waiting Room').
- An ecological world view is at the core of her philosophy – replacing religion, some would say ('The Armadillo'). Her view of humankind's relationship with nature involves a dialectical process of interdependence rather than humankind dominating or subjugating nature. But we see both extremes in the poems: humankind's destructiveness ('The Armadillo') but also the achievement of a comfortable domesticity with nature, even at the primitive animal level ('The Prodigal').
- The experience of really looking at and encountering the natural is central to her poetic process ('The Fish', 'Questions of Travel').
- Our ability to understand the natural is sometimes limited, yet there are great moments of awe and insight in our encounters with the other-worldly spirit of nature ('The Fish').
- Bishop is always aware of the sheer beauty of nature ('The Bight', 'Questions of Travel', 'The Armadillo').
- This is tied in with her fascination with travel and her interest in the exotic ('The Armadillo', 'Questions of Travel').
- She attempts to domesticate the strangeness of nature through language and description.
- Consider also some points already discussed, such as how geographical extremes fascinate her, her beloved places, and the significance of journeys for her.

The domestic and the strange

- The importance of the domestic is also a central ground in her poetry. Domesticity is one of the unifying principles of life. It gives meaning to our existence ('Filling Station').
- The comfort of people, of domestic affections, is important ('Filling Station', 'Sestina').
- Yet the heart of the domestic scene can sometimes be enigmatic. This strangeness, even at the centre of the domestic, is a powerful element in human life ('Sestina', 'First Death in Nova Scotia', 'In the Waiting Room'). One can be ambushed by the strange at any time, even in the security of the domestic scene ('In the Waiting Room').
- The process of domesticating is a central activity of humanity: domesticating the land, domesticating affections, domesticating the non-human world.

Bishop's philosophy as revealed in the poems

- Bishop's is a secular (non-religious) world-view: there is no sense of ultimate purpose, and in this she relates to modernist American poets like Frost and Stevens.
- Hers is very much a here-and-now, existential philosophy: the experience is everything. There is some sense of tradition or linear movement in her life view, but tradition is just an accumulation of experience. The transience of knowledge ('At the Fishhouses') and the limits to our knowing ('Questions of Travel') contribute to this outlook.
- Her ecological outlook is at the basis of her philosophy, as we have seen: humankind in dialectical action with nature, discovering, encountering, not domineering ('The Fish').
- She demonstrates the importance of the domestic ('Filling Station').
- Her view of the human being is as fractured and incomplete ('Chemin de Fer'). This duality has been described by Anne Newman (in *Elizabeth Bishop: Modern Critical Views,* edited by Harold Bloom) as follows: 'She sees the ideal and the real, permanence and decay, affirmation and denial in both man and nature'; a sort of 'fractured but balanced' view of humanity. Examine 'Filling Station' and 'In the Waiting Room' for signs of this.
- A person may not always be entirely free to choose her location ('Questions of Travel'), yet she can make a choice about how her life is spent. Life is not totally determined ('The Prodigal').
- The bleaker side of life is often stressed, the pain, loss and trauma ('The Prodigal', 'Sestina', 'First Death in Nova Scotia', 'In the Waiting Room'), yet she is not without humour ('At the Fishhouses', 'Filling Station').
- She believes we need to experience our dreams ('Questions of Travel').
- Is the overall view of humankind that of the eternal traveller, journeying? And

is the journey all? Would you agree with Jerome Mazzaro's view (in *Elizabeth Bishop: Modern Critical Views,* edited by Harold Bloom): 'Like Baudelaire's voyagers she seems instead to be accepting the conditions of voyaging as the process of a life which itself will arrive meaninglessly at death with perhaps a few poems as a dividend'?

- She expresses the unknowable strangeness of death ('First Death in Nova Scotia').
- Yet there is a sort of heroism evident in her poems. Many of the poems feature a crisis or conflict of some sort, with which the narrator deals courageously, often learning in the process ('The Fish', 'In the Waiting Room').

Bishop and women's writing

- Are you conscious of the femininity of the speaker in Bishop's poems? Some critics have argued that the importance of the domestic principle in her philosophy ('Filling Station') and the attitudes of care and sympathy in the poems (for the fish, the prodigal, the animals and birds) and even the occupational metaphors, for example of housemaking ('Filling Station', 'Sestina') and dressmaking and map colouring in other poems, all indicate a strong feminine point of view in her poetry. Other critics have argued that her rhetoric is completely asexual, that the poet's persona is neutral, the Bishop 'I' is the eye of the traveller or the child recapturing an innocence that avoids sex roles altogether, an asexual self that frees her from any sex-determined role. Examine 'Questions of Travel' and 'First Death in Nova Scotia' in this regard.
- We have already encountered something of her treatment of her own sexuality and her attitude as a child to female sexuality ('In the Waiting Room'). She also deals with sexuality in other poems, such as 'Crusoe in England', 'Santarém', 'Exchanging Hats', and 'Pink Dog'.

Bishop's links to the Romantics

The following are some of the distinguishing features of Romanticism. Consider Elizabeth Bishop's poetry in the light of some or all of these statements.

1. Romanticism stressed the importance of the solitary individual voice, often in rebellion against tradition and social conventions.
2. The subjective vision is of great value in society.
3. In place of orthodox religious values the individual looks for value and guidance in intense private experience.
4. Nature often provides such intense experience, hence the notion of nature as the great teacher and moral guide.
5. Romanticism can show a divided view of the individual. The individual is often pulled in opposite directions – for example solitariness versus sociability, lonely pursuit of an ideal versus community fellowship.

6. It is anti-rational. Feelings, instinctive responses, unconscious wisdom and passionate living are valued more than rational thought.

7. Dreams and drug-enhanced experiences are especially valued. Children, primitive people, outcasts, even the odd eccentric figure are regarded as having special insight and wisdom.

- 'Bishop explored typical Romantic themes, such as problems of isolation, loss, and the desire for union beyond the self.' Explore the poetry in the light of this statement.
- It has been said that Bishop's practice of poetry follows Wordsworth's advice that poetry should embody controlled passion, should deal with powerful feelings but with the restraint of hindsight: 'spontaneous overflow of powerful feelings', 'emotion recollected in tranquillity'. Would you agree?
- Examine 'At the Fishhouses' as a great Romantic poem.

STYLE AND TECHNIQUE

Variety of verse forms
- Though she was not often attracted to formal patterns, a variety of verse forms is found in Bishop's poetry: sonnet, sestina, villanelle, etc. ('The Prodigal', 'Sestina').
- She used a variety of metres, but often favoured trimeter lines ('The Armadillo'). This sometimes resulted in those long, thin poems.
- She was happiest using free verse ('Questions of Travel', 'The Bight', 'At the Fishhouses', etc.).

Her descriptions
- The surface of a Bishop poem is often deceptively simple.
- A favourite technique is 'making the familiar strange' ('The Bight', 'Questions of Travel').
- Her detailed descriptions function as repossession or domestication of the object by the artist. This is how she gradually apprehends her subject, through the accumulation of detail ('The Fish').
- Bishop often insisted on the truth of her descriptions, but the reality is more complex than that. Her descriptions are both re-creation and creation, creating veracity but also using poetic licence ('The Armadillo'; also 'In the Waiting Room').
- Her similes and metaphors are often surprising, like conceits. They can be both exciting and exact.

Control of feeling
- Many of her poems deal with emotive subjects ('In the Waiting Room').
- There is an element of spontaneity and naturalness in the tone. Consider the

opening of 'In the Waiting Room' and 'Filling Station'. 'The sense of the mind actively encountering reality, giving off the impression of involved immediate discovery, is one of Bishop's links to the Romantics,' as the critic Penelope Laurans put it.

- Yet spontaneity and feelings are firmly controlled by technique, in particular by variation of metre (see critical commentary on 'The Armadillo', among others). 'It is sometimes assumed that the cool surfaces of Bishop's poems reveal their lack of emotional depth; in fact Bishop often uses such reticence as a strategy to make a deeper, more complex emotional appeal to the reader' (Penelope Laurans). (Examine 'The Armadillo' and 'In the Waiting Room' and their critical commentaries.)
- The matter-of-fact tone avoids sentimentality. The use of understatement controls feeling ('In the Waiting Room').

The absence of moralising
- Her dislike of didacticism is well documented. She disliked 'modern religiosity and moral superiority', and so she avoids overt moralising in her poems. The scenes offer up their wisdom gradually, as the descriptions help us to understand the object or place ('At the Fishhouses', 'Questions of Travel').

Bishop as a dramatic poet
Consider:
- scenes of conflict or danger
- moments of dramatic encounter
- dramatic monologue structure in many of the poems.

Making the strange familiar: forging a personal understanding of Bishop's poetry
Think about the following points, and make notes for yourself or discuss them in groups.
- Which poems made the deepest impression on you? Why?
- Which passages would you wish to read and reread? Why?
- In the selection you have read, what were the principal issues that preoccupied the poet? What did you like or dislike about the way she treated these issues?
- Did you find that reading Bishop gave you any insights into human beings or the world? What did you discover?
- From your reading of the poems, what impression did you form about the personality of the poet herself? What do you think made her happy or sad? What did she enjoy or fear? What values or beliefs did she have? Or is it difficult to answer these questions? If so, what does that tell you about the voice of the poet in these poems?

- Think about the landscapes and places that attracted her. What do they suggest about the poet and poetry?
- Think about the people featured in her poetry. What do you notice about them?
- Describe your overall response to reading her poetry: did you find her voice disturbing, frightening, challenging, enlightening, comforting, or what? Refer to particular poems or passages to illustrate your conclusions.
- What do you like or dislike about the style of her poetry?
- Do you find her poetry different in any way from other poetry you have read? Explain.
- Why should we read Bishop? Attempt to convince another pupil of the importance of her poetry, in a letter, speech, or other form.
- What questions would you like to ask her about her poetry?

Questions

1. 'The human being at a moment of crisis is the central concern of much of Bishop's poetry.' Discuss this statement, with reference to two or more poems you have read.
2. The child's relationship with the world is a major theme in Bishop's poetry. What aspects of this theme do you find developed in the poems?
3. 'Bishop's poems may be set in particular places, but the discoveries made are universal.' Discuss this statement, with reference to any two poems.
4. 'The real focus of Bishop's poetry is inside herself. Her poems are primarily psychological explorations.' Discuss.
5. 'The view of the poet that comes across from these poems is of an isolated eccentric who nevertheless has a keen interest in human beings.' Discuss.
6. 'A keen eye for detail and a fascination with the ordinary are distinguishing features of Elizabeth Bishop's poetry.' Discuss.
7. 'A deep sense of interior anguish lies at the heart of many of her poems.' Discuss this view, with reference to at least four of the poems you have read.
8. 'She is a poet who lives in a painter's world in which shapes and colours are enormously significant' (Anne Stevenson). Discuss, with reference to a selection of her poems.
9. 'For all the unhappiness of the themes she deals with, we often find a note of humour, even of fun, in Bishop's poems.' Discuss.
10. 'Bishop has the oddest way of describing things; she sometimes makes the ordinary appear strange.' Explore the effects of this technique in at least two of the poems you have studied.
11. 'We find a distinct lack of emotion in Bishop's poetry.' (a) How does she achieve this? (b) Is it always true of her poetry? Explain.

12. 'Man, for her, appears as a figure in a landscape, flawed, helpless, tragic, but capable also of love and even of happiness' (Anne Stevenson). Discuss this aspect of Bishop's poetry, with reference to the poems you have studied.

Bishop's writings

Complete Poems, London: Chatto and Windus 1991.
Collected Prose (Robert Giroux, editor), London: Chatto and Windus 1994.
One Art: The Selected Letters (Robert Giroux, editor), London: Chatto and Windus 1994.
Exchanging Hats: Paintings, Manchester: Carcanet 1997.

Bibliography

Bloom, Harold (editor), *Elizabeth Bishop: Modern Critical Views,* New York: Chelsea House 1985.
Harrison, Victoria, *Elizabeth Bishop's Poetics of Intimacy,* Cambridge: Cambridge University Press 1993.
McCabe, Susan, *Elizabeth Bishop: Her Poetics of Loss,* Pittsburgh: Pennsylvania State University Press 1994.
Millier, Brett, *Elizabeth Bishop: Life and the Memory of It,* Berkeley: University of California Press 1993.
Spiegelman, Willard, 'Elizabeth Bishop's natural heroism' in *Centennial Review,* no. 22, winter 1978, reprinted in *Elizabeth Bishop: Modern Critical Views,* edited by Harold Bloom.
Stevenson, Anne, *Elizabeth Bishop,* New York: Twayne 1966.
Wehr, Wesley, 'Elizabeth Bishop: conversations and class notes' in *Antioch Review,* no. 39, summer 1981.

6 *Sylvia* PLATH

Ann Hyland

Introduction

Sylvia Plath was born in Boston, Massachusetts, on 27 October 1932 to Aurelia Schober Plath and Otto Plath. Shortly after his son Warren's birth in 1935, Otto Plath fell ill. His condition was treatable, but he refused to consult a doctor. In 1940, following an operation, he died. Neither of the children attended the funeral.

These events had a huge effect on Sylvia's life. Her father's illness deprived her of both parents' attention for much of her early life. His death, which she sometimes saw as suicide because of his refusal to seek medical help, left her feeling bereft. She never came to terms with her grief and anger at his loss, and these feelings resurfaced in her last poems.

Sylvia's childhood taught her the value of being a 'good girl'. Her mother's approval was gained by being quiet, not disturbing her invalid father, reading and writing, and also doing well in school. This she achieved with little difficulty: remarkably intelligent and very ambitious, she always earned high grades. Her writing life began early, and her first poem was published when she was only eight.

She was a brilliant pupil in secondary school, consistently earning A grades. Attractive, vivacious, and active in school clubs, she led a busy social life. She worked hard but loved clothes, dancing, music and dating.

One problem that she refers to in her letters to her mother and in her journals was her anxiety to conceal her academic ability from the boys she dated: she felt (probably rightly) that her popularity would suffer if she upstaged them academically. In the conservative 1940s and 50s girls were meant to be 'nice': that is, genteel, polite, and above all feminine – certainly not ambitious and intellectual, publicly questioning the status quo. There was an all-pervasive pressure to conform to society's expectations.

By the end of her secondary school career she had achieved some success as a writer and artist. A number of her stories had appeared in *Seventeen*, a popular teenage magazine, while some poems and drawings were published in the *Christian Science Monitor*. She had also been introduced to the works of authors who were important influences on her writing: D. H. Lawrence, Virginia

Woolf, Emily Dickinson, Dylan Thomas and W.B. Yeats. In 1950 she entered Smith College, Massachusetts, a prestigious women's university, where her academic and writing success continued. At the end of her third year, in June 1953, she won a guest editorship with a young women's magazine, *Mademoiselle*. This involved living in New York for the month. Her work schedule there was demanding, and she was also expected to fulfil endless social engagements. The whole experience was exhausting.

On her return home to Wellesley she became severely depressed. She was treated with electro-convulsive shock therapy, which seems to have been disastrous: far from curing her, it propelled her into a serious suicide attempt. Her life was saved only because her brother discovered her hidden in the cellar three days after she disappeared. She entered a psychiatric hospital, where she recovered with the help of a sympathetic psychiatrist. This experience formed the basis for her novel *The Bell Jar*, published in 1963.

She resumed her studies in Smith College in January 1954, graduating with first-class honours the following year. She won a Fulbright Scholarship to study literature in Cambridge, England, where she met Ted Hughes, a young English poet ('that big, dark, hunky boy, the only one there huge enough for me'). They fell in love, and they married in June 1956.

On completing her studies in Cambridge she accepted a teaching job in her old university, Smith College, and moved to America with her husband for two years. 'Black Rook in Rainy Weather' and 'The Times are Tidy' date from this period.

Shortly after the couple returned to London, in December 1959, her first collection, *The Colossus and Other Poems*, was published. Their daughter, Frieda, was born in April. The following year they moved to Devon, a move that increased her work load. She devoted much energy to turning their old manor-house into a home and to working the extensive garden that surrounded it, in addition to acting as her own and her husband's literary agent and caring for Frieda.

Her son, Nicholas, was born in January 1962. During this time, despite her many domestic tasks and the work involved in looking after two small children, she was writing. Poems from this period include 'Morning Song', 'Finisterre', 'Mirror', 'Pheasant', 'Elm' and 'Poppies in July'. She also completed *The Bell Jar*.

For some time Sylvia and Ted's relationship had been growing troubled, and they separated in August 1962. She remained in Devon, caring for the children and writing, but suffered poor health and recurring depression. Yet this period saw the flood of creativity that produced the poems that made up her second book, *Ariel*, including 'The Arrival of the Bee Box'. She herself was amazed at what she was writing: ' I am . . . writing like mad – have managed a poem a day before breakfast. All book poems. Terrific stuff, as if domesticity had choked me' (*Letters Home,* 12 October 1962).

In December she moved to London with her children. To her great joy she succeeded in renting a flat where W. B. Yeats had once lived. The winter of 1962/ 63 was one of the coldest on record in England, which added to the trauma of setting up a new home alone. She had problems with heating, power failures, and getting a telephone. She and the children suffered from severe colds, and she had trouble finding a reliable child-minder. These difficulties exacerbated her depression. Despite this, she continued writing; 'Child' dates from January 1963.

However, her difficult circumstances eventually overwhelmed her. Early on the morning of 11 February she left some milk and food by their beds for the children and sealed the door to their room to ensure their safety. She then took an overdose of sleeping pills, sealed herself in the kitchen and gassed herself.

Sylvia Plath's fame has grown steadily since her death. At first this was mainly because of the dramatic circumstances of her suicide: the fame she had always longed for became hers for the wrong reasons. However, the publication of *Ariel* and the *Complete Poems* showed that she was indeed a poet of genius, whose work deserved recognition for its own sake.

The facts of Sylvia Plath's life are easily told. Less simple to assess is the mass of material that has been written about her since (and because of) her suicide. She is variously seen as
• a brilliant but fragile genius
• an ungrateful daughter who hated her mother
• a loving daughter whose loyalty and affection are reflected in her letters home
• an over-ambitious manic depressive
• a controlling and jealous wife who pushed her husband into a love affair
• a loving wife and mother whose life was destroyed by her husband's betrayal
• a virulent feminist whose marriage break-up and suicide expressed her outrage at the ties of domesticity.

In fact it seems that those who write about Sylvia Plath can use her life story to prove almost anything. One reason for this is that she was married to, and just separated from, a famous poet who went on to become Poet Laureate. Another is the quantity of material she wrote. Apart from the poems there are many short stories, essays, and articles for magazines. She also did radio broadcasts and was the subject of a number of interviews. But perhaps most widely quoted – to support points of view that can be utterly contradictory – are the journals she kept from her earliest days almost to the time of her death, and her thousands of letters to family and friends. And indeed these *Letters Home* (published in 1975) and the *Journals* (1982) tell a lot about her. They reflect her 'exaggerated, high-voltage, bigger-than-life personality and imagination'. They show a young woman who thought about everything, and longed to live life to its fullest. Here is a tiny sample of her opinions:

• On writing: 'It is as necessary for the survival of my haughty sanity as bread is to my flesh.'

• 'And by the way, everything in life is writable about if you have the outgoing guts to do it, and the imagination to improvise. The worst enemy to creativity is self-doubt.'

• On herself: 'I want, I think, to be omniscient . . . I think I would like to call myself "the girl who wanted to be God".'

• On life: 'God is this all it is, the ricocheting down the corridor of laughter and tears? of self-worship and self-loathing? of glory and disgust?'

• On depression: 'I have been and am battling depression. It is as if my life were magically run by two electric currents: joyous positive and despairing negative – whichever is running at the moment dominates my life, floods it.'

• On children: 'Graduate school and travel abroad are not going to be stymied by any squealing, breast-fed brats.'

• On being a woman: 'Learning of the limitations of a woman's sphere is no fun at all.'

• On marriage: 'I plan not to step into a part on marrying – but to go on living as an intelligent mature human being, growing and learning as I always have.'

• 'I am afraid of getting married. Spare me from cooking three meals a day – spare me from the relentless cage of routine and rote. I want to be free.'

• On having children: 'Children might humanise me. But I must rely on them for nothing. Fable of children changing existence and character as absurd as fable of marriage doing it.'

• On poetry: 'A poem can't take the place of a plum or an apple. But just as painting can re-create, by illusion . . . so a poem, by its own system of illusions, can set up a rich and apparently living world within its particular limits.'

• 'Technically I like it to be extremely musical and lyrical, with a singing sound.'

• On the issues that mattered to her: 'The hurt and wonder of loving; making in all its forms – children, loaves of bread, paintings, buildings; and the conservation of life of all people in all places.'

• On politics: 'I do believe I can counteract McCarthy . . . by living a life of honesty and love . . . it is in a way serving my religion, which is that of humanism, and a belief in the potential of each man to learn and love and grow.'

Regardless of where people stand on her personality and life, all are agreed on Sylvia Plath's unique and distinctive voice, and on the impact she has had on the poetry of the end of the twentieth century. The inscription on her headstone could be read as a metaphor for her life: *Even in the midst of fierce flames, the golden lotus may be planted.*

Black Rook in Rainy Weather

Text of poem: New Explorations Anthology page 290

> 'If only something would happen!' Something being the revelation that
> transfigures existence; works a miraculous presto-chango upon the
> mundane mortal world – turning the toads and cockroaches back into
> handsome fairy princes. (*Journals,* April 1953)

Sylvia Plath was always aware of the need for inspiration to trigger her creative
impulse: she hoped for a moment of insight, a 'miracle', to work a change on
the 'mundane mortal world', enabling her to create. She wrote 'Black Rook in
Rainy Weather' at a time when she was finding it a struggle to write, despite her
conviction that writing was her life's work.

A READING OF THE POEM

The growing acceptance of identity as a writer is one theme. The year is at the
'stubborn season of fatigue' – late autumn or winter. The speaker is warily
walking, 'trekking' in the rain, when her eye is caught by a black rook hunched
above her on a twig. Everything around is dull and low-key: bird, rain, 'spotted
leaves', 'mute sky', 'ruinous landscape'. Despite this, the speaker is vaguely
expectant: a miracle may occur, a trick of light may 'hallow' (make sacred)
something as ordinary as a kitchen table or chair, causing it to glow with
heavenly radiance. The muse or inspiration may appear as a 'miracle', a 'celestial
burning', transforming what might otherwise be an uneventful life, giving

> A brief respite from fear
> Of total neutrality.

She doesn't know what inspiration may surprise her, or

> . . . flare
> Suddenly at my elbow.

The black rook in the rain may even shine and force her to give it her full
attention – 'seize my senses'. Therefore she is watchful: such a miracle has
happened before.

One such miracle would be the inspiration to create something
extraordinary from her dull surroundings, to

> Patch together a content
> Of sorts.

She might write, create something wonderful. The 'mute sky' may not grant the desired 'backtalk', but the speaker knows that 'miracles occur'. Waiting for the muse is like

> The long wait for the angel,
> For that rare, random descent.

She is prepared to wait.

LANDSCAPE

Plath's poetry is often highly subjective, focusing on her inner self, her feelings and thoughts – even when she appears to be writing about the outside world. She uses her immediate surroundings as a metaphor for her feelings and ideas.

This is evident in her treatment of landscape. One critic has described how her poetic landscapes embody associations between scene and mood; she calls them 'psychic landscapes'. She notes Plath's 'ability to transform realistic objects and scenes into consistent sets of metaphors for her thoughts and emotions'. These concrete objects, however, are clearly realised – made real – by Plath's skilful use of language and imagery.

'Black Rook in Rainy Weather' creates a clear picture: the speaker is out walking doggedly on a wet day when she sees a black rook hunched on a bare tree. Everything around is dull and lifeless: sodden fallen leaves, the dark, rainy day, the 'ruinous landscape'. Having set the scene, the speaker quickly moves to her own fears and limited expectations. She is hopeful that (with luck, maybe, perhaps . . .) even such a dull scene may be transformed. The cause of this transformation – miracle, descent of an angel – would seem to be something that might fire her imagination.

Essentially, the bleak place is a metaphor for the speaker's own bleakness. Her mood, like the scene, might be suddenly transformed by a sudden radiance, a miracle, a flash of inspiration. The mute sky may grant her the 'backtalk' she desires.

THEMES

- Hope – the expectation of a sudden change for the better
- Despondency – the grim dullness of 'neutrality'
- Creativity – the miracle of a sudden inspiration
- Miracles – the rareness and randomness of life-enhancing moments of brilliance.

TECHNIQUE
Use of contrast

There is a strong contrast between the dullness of the landscape and the radiant miracle that may occur. The speaker knows that the most 'obtuse object' – black rook, bleak day, dullness, kitchen chair – can be transformed by a miracle, a 'celestial burning', the 'descent of an angel'.

The difference between actual dullness and possible radiance is strongly marked. Plath underlines the blackness by her choice of adjectives: wet, black, desultory, mute, sceptical, minor, obtuse, wary, dull, ruinous. The verbs too convey dispiritedness: hunches, fall, complain, trek, haul, wait. The repetition of the sound 'rain' in line 3 adds to the general bleakness. In complete contrast to this, the hoped-for change is conveyed in terms of brightness: light, fire, incandescence, radiance, flare, shine. It is linked with the divine: miracle, hallowed, angel.

Language

The language of 'Black Rook in Rainy Weather' includes a mixture of the colloquial and the formal. Almost slangy expressions are used side -by- side with archaic words (words that have fallen out of use). Particularly striking are the semi-Biblical words: 'hallowed', 'bestowing largesse', 'portent'. These contrast strongly with the everyday sound of 'I can't honestly complain,' 'with luck', 'of sorts'. In your opinion, what is the effect of this?

How convincing do you find the possibility of this miracle? Do you feel that the speaker has already experienced such a moment? Look at her description of the moment – the words used to describe it. Be aware also of the many parenthetical statements: 'although', 'I admit', 'may', 'it could happen', 'with luck', 'of sorts', 'if you care to call' . . . . There is certainly no doubt of her wariness.

Rhyme and rhythm

Throughout Plath's career she worked painstakingly on technique, rewriting and reworking her poems until they were as close to perfect as she could make them. In earlier poems her attention to technique is sometimes too obvious, almost overshadowing the subject matter, the theme.

'Black Rook in Rainy Weather', one of her earlier poems, is carefully crafted. Before reading the comments below, re-read it, paying attention to rhyme (end-rhyme, half-rhyme), consonance (rhyming consonants), assonance, alliteration and rhythm. Note down any patterns you observe.

Perhaps the most striking feature of this poem is the carefully patterned rhyming scheme. There are five end-rhymes, repeated in each stanza: in other words, the rhyming scheme is *abcde, abcde, abcde*. In every stanza there is also internal rhyme: stiff twig; arranging – rearranging – rain; desultory – design; table – chair.

The rhythm is also skilfully worked out. Mostly the poet uses three-beat lines, but in each stanza this is broken by a four-beat or (occasionally) a five-beat line. The variation avoids monotony, and also gives some interesting effects. Look at the opening lines and notice the effect of the pattern: the grouping of stresses –

On the stiff twig up there

Hunches a wet black rook

Arranging and rearranging its feathers in the rain

– slows down the voice, drawing attention to the rigidity of the bird, emphasising the bleakness of the scene.

Commenting on 'Black Rook in Rainy Weather' in a letter to her mother, Plath criticised its 'glassy brittleness'. What do you think she might mean?

The Times Are Tidy

Text of poem: New Explorations Anthology page 294

'The Times Are Tidy' was written in 1958, at the height of the socially, politically and materially self-satisfied era of President Eisenhower. It was a time of complacency, when any challenge to the *status quo* – the way things were – was quickly silenced. The 'establishment' – the powerful elite – viewed change as unnecessary and as a threat to its survival. The smug satisfaction of this decade in the United States was all-pervasive. Artists in general suffered under the oppression of a culture that saw anything that differed from the norm as a threat. This was the McCarthy decade, when those suspected of socialist or communist sympathies were blacklisted. According to one commentator,

> in 'The Times Are Tidy', Plath uses irony and humour to deflate . . . behaviour she finds questionable. The poem focuses on the collapse of moral standards and the all-pervasive addiction to comfort and conformity which so strongly characterised the 1950s.

SOME IDEAS

The 1950s – the 'tidy times' – are contrasted with the very 'untidy' times of the world of legend, an era when heroes fought dragons, and witches cast spells and brewed magic potions, risking burning at the stake for their practices.

The 'stuck record' of stanza 1 suggests the tendency of the needle on a worn record to go 'ruh-ruh-ruh' when it sticks. It may symbolise the social boredom and monotony of the time.

The 'watchful cooks' were probably the critics of corrupt political values, who were often dismissed and blacklisted. The corruption or (at best) damaging inactivity of politicians could therefore continue without being too closely observed, allowing the 'mayor's rôtisserie' to turn around 'of its own accord': there was no interference in the continuous political graft and favour-giving.

HUMOUR AND IRONY

Plath used humour in all her writings, sometimes light and amusing, bringing a smile to the reader's face; more often black and biting. She particularly ridiculed what she found self-important or pompous. Her humour is seen in her use of wordplay, entertaining images, and sound effects that sometimes echo nursery rhymes or popular jingles. Very often her humour underlined a serious message.

In 'The Times are Tidy' the decade of smug comfort ('cream an inch thick') and boredom ('stuck record') in which she lived is described ironically. No self-respecting hero would want to live in it: there is 'no career' in adventure; dragons have 'withered to leaf-size'. Witches, with their magic herbs, love potions and talking cats, have been burnt up. Plath sets the present age against the world of legend, of fabulous creatures and mythical heroes.

The final lines are deeply ironic: the very elements that have thrilled children of all ages have disappeared or been forced out. But yet they 'are better for it'. Life may be flat, boring, uneventful, 'a stuck record' – but it is suggested that the 'cream an inch thick' is more than compensation for the lost excitement. The imagination is starved, adventure is dead; but life is rich and comfortable, predictable and safe. Plath seems to suggest the ironic question: what else could children (or even adults) want?

Think of the connotations of 'cream'; note down some of the phrases in which it is used. What point is the poet making here? Do you consider it an apt image with which to conclude this poem?

THEMES

- The political corruption of an era that sees material gain as all that counts
- The collapse of moral standards in public life, where self-seeking, greed and corruption dominate
- Self-righteousness – the justification of the status quo because it benefits the elite

- The death of the spirit of adventure, the failure to challenge the 'dragon' of political smugness and corruption, which threaten to suffocate society.

Morning Song

Text of poem: New Explorations Anthology page 296

Plath wrote 'Morning Song' ten months after the birth of her first child, Frieda, on 1 April 1960. She intended it to be the opening poem of a new collection entitled *Ariel*. The first word of the poem, and therefore of the book, is 'Love', setting a warm, positive tone for the collection. It is one of a number of poems she wrote to or about children and motherhood.

Her attitude towards performing the duties of motherhood was often ambivalent. She was aware of the repetitiveness of the work involved in caring for babies, and the inroads it would make on her time; however, this was the negative side of being a mother: it did not cloud her deep love for her children, which is always clear and unequivocal.

A READING

The opening image creates a warm, loving mood. The speaker addresses the child directly, affirming that she was conceived in love, set in motion 'like a fat gold watch'. The tone is tender and humorous. The mother then recalls the infant's birth, her first cry establishing her place 'among the elements'.

The new parents talk of her arrival, magnifying it; but they also feel threatened by it. The world is a 'draughty museum' and this 'statue' in its 'nakedness' is vulnerable – making them aware of their own vulnerability – 'shadows our safety'.

The 'bald cry' brings a change of scene, from the intimacy of lines 1 and 2 to the chilly world – the 'museum' – where the parents feel their safety is shadowed. The mother feels displaced, unimportant. Even though her love helped to create this child, she now feels that she is no longer necessary. She compares herself to the cloud that brings rain, creating a pool of water: the cloud is momentarily reflected in the pool before the wind slowly blows it on:

> . . . slow
> Effacement at the wind's hand.

This seems to suggest that she is briefly reflected in her child but is then displaced, effaced. It is as if the mother has nothing more to give: the child is autonomous.

However, this troubling idea gives way to the present reality of the child's need of its mother, the mother's attentiveness to the child. The child's 'moth-breath' is almost imperceptible, but the mother hears it. At the first cry she 'stumbles' from bed, heavy and cow-like in her flowery pink nightdress – a note of self-mockery here. She moves towards the child, whose open mouth is 'clean as a cat's.' This startling image suggests the delicate pinkness of the child's mouth.

As morning breaks, the single cry changes to a 'handful of notes' – echoing the 'bald cry' of stanza 1. The image of the 'vowels [rising] like balloons' suggests the beauty of the sounds, and adds a note of playfulness.

IMAGERY

Plath's images are remarkable for their clarity and unexpectedness. Highly concrete, often drawn from ordinary, everyday things, they catch the reader unawares. The 'fat gold watch' of stanza 1 is simple but vivid, witty and unusual. Its marked rhythm is emphatic:

     – ‿ – – –

   like a fat gold watch.

The description of the world as a 'drafty museum' and new babies as 'naked statues' is a most unusual image, one that makes the reader think. It is an image she has used before: it suggests a world that has held on to its past, storing events, people, everything that makes up our life – not a very comfortable place, but perhaps not unsafe for the new 'statue'.

Imagery is effective in contrasting the infant's lightness and delicacy and the mother's clumsiness and heaviness: the baby's 'moth-breath | Flickers' (notice the lightness of the sounds as well as the delicacy of the image), her 'clear vowels rise like balloons'. The mother, however, is portrayed as homely and a little clumsy: she stumbles 'cow-heavy', swathed in a 'floral . . . Victorian nightgown.'

Imagery is also central to the contrast between the first three stanzas and the last three. There is a conscious development in animation: watch, statue, walls, mirror and even cloud are inanimate objects, just things, incapable of independent activity; moth, cat, singer (child) and cow (mother) are living creatures, capable of acting alone. Can you suggest a reason for the change from inanimate to animate? What is the effect on the reader?

FEELINGS

'Morning Song' evokes a number of moods. There seems to be a placid acceptance in stanza 1 ('fat gold watch', the midwife's matter-of-fact action, the 'bald cry [taking] its place among the elements'). However, this changes in stanza 2: the world is now cold – 'a drafty museum' – and the adults seem dwarfed by the place. Their 'voices echo', they are 'blank as walls', and their safety is threatened. Why? Does the baby's nakedness make them feel more vulnerable? Or perhaps the new arrival reminds them that they are now an older generation, facing death?

The sense of unease becomes even stronger in stanza 3. The speaker seems to feel that she has nothing to offer the infant: she is mirrored in the child for a while, before being slowly effaced by the passage of time.

These feelings of dislocation, unimportance and impermanence are quickly dispelled by the present moment, evoked vividly in stanza 4. The baby's gentle breath, the rose-patterned room and the watchful mother in her old-fashioned nightdress create a scene of warmth and intimacy.

The remaining stanzas reflect the growing feeling of connectedness between mother and child: one cry brings her to the child, whose mouth is wide open. The dawn breaks to the baby's clear 'handful of notes'. Intimacy, love, joy and pleasure dominate these stanzas. What do you think Plath may be saying here about motherhood?

What is your final impression of this morning song?

Finisterre

Text of poem: New Explorations Anthology page 298

'Finisterre' (Finistère) is the French name for a region in the west of Brittany. It means 'land's end' – the point where land gives way to sea.

PLATH AND NATURE

Plath wrote many poems that describe a scene or a place – landscape poems. In these she creates a vivid picture of the place described, conveying a strong sense of the atmosphere and mood of the place at a particular time. Also, she frequently uses the scene described to draw the reader into the mood of the speaker. A number of critics have used the term 'psychic landscapes' to describe such poems.

In 'Finisterre' a seemingly ordinary – though wild and remote – place is described in graphic terms that reflect fear, hopelessness and death. The scene actually becomes secondary to the feelings, despite the speaker's detailed, realistic descriptions. The rugged black cliffs extend into the sea, which pounds them with explosive force. The comparison with 'knuckled and rheumatic' hands 'cramped on nothing' is striking. This is quickly followed by a series of unusual metaphors for the rocks: 'faces of the drowned', 'old soldiers', 'messy wars', 'hidden grudges'. The poet personifies them, creating a powerful metaphor for anger, destruction, and death. The mood evoked is sinister and grim.

Stanza 2 opens with a lovely picture of the small, delicate flowers – trefoils, stars, and bells – edging the cliff, almost like embroidery. But the lightness is quickly dispelled: such flowers might have been embroidered by 'fingers . . . close to death'. And this strikes the note for the remainder of the stanza: death is omnipresent. The mists are described as

> Souls, rolled in the doom-noise of the sea.
> They bruise the rocks out of existence, then resurrect them.
> They go up without hope, like sighs.

The speaker walks through them, and they almost suffocate her: 'They stuff my mouth with cotton,' and leave her 'beaded with tears.'

In 'Black Rook in Rainy Weather' Plath also used nature as a vehicle for feelings. What is the impact of this approach?

THE MONUMENT

Our Lady of the Shipwrecked, as described in stanza 3, would certainly be one reason why the souls of stanza 2 go up without hope! She is aloof, self-important, and self-absorbed,

> . . . three times life size,
> Her lips sweet with divinity.

She strides towards the horizon, in love with the sea. Far from ignoring those at her feet, she doesn't even appear to know of their presence. The marble sailor is distraught, but gets no attention; the black-clad peasant woman appears to feel that directing her prayers to the praying sailor may be more effective than trying to establish contact with Our Lady of the Shipwrecked.

The monument described here is of a kind not uncommon in Brittany, once a deeply religious region: a kneeling figure looking up to an upright figure, which is looking up to heaven. (Think of the popular statues of Our Lady of Lourdes.) What impression do you form of Plath's response to this monument?

IRONY

There is considerable irony in the description of Our Lady of the Shipwrecked. The statue to whom people pray understands nothing. Her love is for the 'beautiful formlessness of the sea', the source of the shipwrecks she was erected to protect against. She dominates the scene, taking the narrator's – and therefore the reader's – attention away from the underlying horrors of the earlier stanzas. Her pink-tipped cloak, her sweet appearance and her love for the sea seem wildly inappropriate when compared with the doom-laden bay. And how can she love something that has such hideous secrets, hides grudges?

Plath is setting up an ironic contrast here. How effective do you think this is?

There is humorous irony in the final stanza also: in the contrast between the chatty peasants with their commercial stalls and the ancient grudging rocks of stanza 1. The only reference the stallholders make to the headland is rather off-hand: 'The Bay of the Dead down there'. The name, however, alerts the reader to one possible explanation for the gloom of the opening stanzas. It also conveys how ordinary it is to those who make their living from tourists. The trinkets on the stall – flapping laces, postcards, necklaces, toy ladies – add to the feeling of ordinariness. It almost seems that, in creating such a homely picture, the narrator is mocking her own over-reaction to the scene in stanza 1.

Another ironic – and humorous – contrast is that between the 'toy ladies' and Our Lady of the Shipwrecked. They are miniature ladies, made from fragile shells – 'trinkets the sea hides' – with no claim to anything other than prettiness. She, on the other hand, is gigantic, made from marble, and is associated with God – 'lips sweet with divinity.' However, she offers no comfort to those who pray to her; whereas the shell ladies are pretty – and available to those who wish to buy them.

The conclusion seems to be deliberately jaunty: 'These are our crêpes. Eat them before they blow cold.' What it the impact of the tone here?

Imagery

The strong visual imagery that is a feature of Plath's poetry is evident in 'Finisterre'. Her ability to create 'startling, beautiful phrases and lines' (Ted Hughes) is rightly celebrated. Here the promontories of rock are

> . . . the last fingers, knuckled and rheumatic,
> Cramped on nothing. Black
> Admonitory cliffs

Dark underwater rocks 'hide their grudges under the water.' The notion that mists 'bruise rocks out of existence, then resurrect them' is a remarkable description of the effect of fog.

Can you identify images that you find particularly striking? What is their impact?

The poem is written in nine-line stanzas, a heavy formal structure that is particularly appropriate for conveying the weighty terrors of the opening stanzas.

The language too is heavy and forceful, with harsh sounds: 'admonitory', 'knuckled', 'gloomy', 'dump of rocks', 'sea cannons', 'budge', 'grudge'. Harsh '*k*' and '*g*' sounds echo through it, as do long vowel sounds: 'exploding', 'faces', 'drowned', 'gloomy', 'old'. The pounding rhythm of these lines echoes the pounding of the cannoning sea.

Contrast this with the lightness of stanza 4. The same nine-line stanza is used, but the effect is quite different. How does the writer achieve this? Look at colour, sound effects, rhythm, line length, use of dialogue.

THEMES

- A rather grim seascape
- The failure of formal religion to answer people's needs
- Hidden unhappiness and hopelessness
- Fear of the unknown.

CONCLUDING NOTE

In general, 'Finisterre' is a remarkable re-creation of a scene and of a mood. The narrator's progress through the place is reflected in what she sees, hears and feels: sea, sounds, weather, rocks, flowers, monument, stallholders. All of it is coloured by Plath's unique imagination.

Mirror

Text of poem: New Explorations Anthology page 302

Commentaries on 'Mirror' are immensely varied. At one extreme it has been described as 'silly adolescent scribbling which simply informs the reader that Plath is like everyone else, searching the reaches for what she really is' – an unusually dismissive attitude. At the other extreme it is considered to be a wonderfully complex meditation on the conflict between woman as creative writer and woman in the socially acceptable role of wife, homemaker and mother. In between there is a wealth of opinions.

The variety of interpretations shows how 'Mirror' touches the life experience of many people. Ironically, the poem has become a mirror in which each reader sees his or her concerns reflected – making one wonder if this was Plath's intention.

Before you read the following notes it would help you if you were to arrive at your own understanding of what Plath is saying. It might be useful to make notes about your response to the poem as a whole, or to individual images or ideas.

BACKGROUND NOTE

In her personal life, Sylvia Plath frequently questioned who she was. Expectations for a young woman in the late 1950s were limiting: appearance was important, as was marrying suitably and being a good wife, homemaker and mother. For Plath, with her fierce ambition to be a successful writer, such a world was deeply threatening. She certainly loved to look well, enjoyed dating, wanted to marry, have a home and have children – but not at the cost of her writing.

From early in her life she returns frequently in her *Journals* to her fear that marriage would oblige her to bury her creative genius in order to attend to the daily round of housework and baby-minding, which was the lot of most married women in that era.

> Will I be a secretary – a self-rationalising housewife, secretly jealous of my husband's ability to grow intellectually & professionally while I am impeded – will I submerge my embarrassing desires & aspirations, refuse to face myself, and go either mad or become neurotic?

Women writers had an even harder struggle than most: their work was often seen as 'nice', a neat accomplishment – but not necessary. These concerns may have helped to inspire this poem.

A READING OF 'MIRROR'

The 'I' persona of stanza 1 is identified as a mirror only through the title and the named functions. Without the title, this stanza would read like a children's riddle poem. The reader, however, has little difficulty in guessing the identity of 'I'. How much of the poem would you need to read to identify it?

Having identified itself as a mirror, it then informs the reader in stanza 2 that it is a lake. The shift in meaning forces the reader to question the other elements of the poem. This *duality* (doubleness) is echoed in many places and adds to the difficulty of giving a definitive reading.

Stanza 1 seems clear and unambiguous at first reading. Short, simple statements set out the precision, truthfulness and objectivity of 'I'. However, these statements raise many questions when examined closely. Why does a mirror need to explain that it is without preconceptions? 'unmisted by dislike'? 'not cruel, only truthful'? If it is as objective and exact as it claims, why does it 'think' (an inexact statement) that a wall could be part of its heart? Can a mirror have a heart? How does this fit in with its own notion that it is exact?

Perhaps because of these contradictions and the almost childlike certainties, the tone of this stanza is light and breezy. The wittiness of the riddle format, the precise details, the simplicity and the fast rhythm all add a humorous note. Even the self-importance of the mirror – a little god – is amusing, as is the wordplay on 'I' and 'eye'.

The opening statement of the second stanza – 'Now I am a lake' – adds a new dimension, causing the reader to revise the first reading of stanza 1. Is the mirror choosing an image to describe itself as it is in the mind of the woman 'who bends over me'? This woman is not just looking at the superficial reflection: she is 'searching my reaches for what she really is.' A silver, exact, four-square mirror has no reaches: it is flat, two-dimensional. It can only reflect back the surface image: there is no depth, no murkiness, no darkness. Yet the woman sees there something that makes her turn away, escape what she sees or suspects by looking 'to those liars, the candles or the moon.'

The 'truth' follows her – 'I see her back and reflect it faithfully' – and her tears and agitation are the mirror's reward. Despite this she returns: the truth she finds in the mirror is important to her. 'Each morning' in the mirror she sees her face, sees that

> she has drowned a young girl, and in me an old woman
> Rises towards her, like a terrible fish.

One simple interpretation of this is that she sees her youth 'drowning', and watches with horror the approach of old age – which she views as monstrous, a terrible fish.

This raises other questions. Why 'drowning'? This implies suffocation, sudden loss, not the gradual fading of youth. The old woman and the terrible fish are terrifying – and certainly don't come from the mirror. They rise up from the murky depths of the lake, the darkness, the reaches of the woman's sub-conscious.

The frightening truths that rise from the depths are what the woman meets when she searches for 'what she really is' – her true identity. This is not the pretty, docile, smiling, youthful woman that society admires: it is something frightening, dark, ugly, terrible – and true.

THEMES

- Knowing oneself
- Ageing
- Identity: the double self

- Fear
- The human condition.

TWO-SIDEDNESS

A poem is not necessarily part of the life story of the poet, nor of those around her; the 'I' persona is not the poet narrating her life experiences. However, those experiences inform the poet's work; they are the raw material from which she shapes her poetry.

You may find it helpful, therefore, when studying this poem to look back at Plath's life. Of particular relevance to 'Mirror' is the fact that she spent long years striving to achieve high ambitions: a consistent 'alpha' (A grade) pupil through school and university, she always strove to give of her best. It often appears, though, that she judged her best not just by her own very high standard but also by the far more unpredictable standard of winning the recognition and approval of others. This was true of her work and of her life: she seemed to need constant affirmation of her worth. One consequence of this was a pleasant, smiling appearance, the 'all-American girl' image – 'a maddening docility', according to Robert Lowell, whose writing class she attended – which often concealed so-called negative emotions such as anger, disappointment, resentment, jealousy and hatred.

In several of Plath's poems she presents a double image, two sides of a person: in 'In Plaster' (1961), for example, the speaker – the body encased in plaster, a metaphor here for the inner self – talks about the plaster cast that she has had to wear and recognises its whiteness, its coldness, and its utter dependence on what it encases. When the clean white plaster is removed this ugly, hairy, old, yellow person within will be revealed; but the speaker is determined to 'manage without' the plaster. In this way what appears clean, bright and pleasant is in fact only cheap plaster; the true self may be ugly – but it is the real self.

> I used to think we might make a go of it together –
> After all it was a kind of marriage, being so close.
> Now I see it must be one or the other of us.
> She may be a saint and I may be ugly and hairy,
> But she'll soon find out that doesn't matter a bit.

What similarities do you see between this and 'Mirror'?

REVEALING ONE'S TRUE IDENTITY

A committed poet, Plath knew the importance of speaking from the heart. But speaking from the heart means saying things others might not approve of, expressing socially unacceptable feelings. It means revealing one's true identity, and risking rejection. 'Mirror' could be read as an expression of this conflict. At this time in her life Plath's style and subject matter were undergoing a change, which eventually gave birth to her most powerful and controversial poems, many of which voice sentiments that a lot of people experience but don't talk about.

The mirror could be seen as a metaphor for her 'golden girl' image – silver, exact, reflecting back what others projected, not creating any controversy. But the lake has hidden depths, and when these are searched, murkiness, darkness, terror and ugliness are revealed – and the demure young lady is drowned. This mirror therefore has a bright side and a dark side, like Plath herself – like all who share the human condition.

Pheasant

Text of poem: New Explorations Anthology page 304

'Pheasant' is a wonderful evocation of the beauty and vitality of a bird that is under threat of death. Read it through a few times just for enjoyment.

Get a sense of the speaker's attitude to the bird (note how this is conveyed). Her relationship with 'you' also colours the poem; the tension generated by the opening lines is sustained to the end, and underlined by the closing plea. Pay particular attention to her use of clear images, precise detail, language, colour and contrast to paint a picture of what she sees now, and remembers from last winter.

A READING

The opening line is the narrator's heartfelt plea to 'you' not to kill the pheasant this morning, as he had said he would.

The pheasant is pictured in strong, visual language: the narrator is startled by

> The jut of that odd, dark head, pacing
> Through the uncut grass on the elm's hill.

She values it for its sheer beauty, its vitality. The bird seems to her to be at home on the hill – 'simply in its element.' It is kingly – visiting 'our court' (possibly a play on the name of Plath's home, Green Court). Last winter it had also visited during snowy weather, leaving its tail-track and its large footprint, which differed from the 'crosshatch' of smaller birds.

Returning to the present, she captures its appearance in a few graphic words – 'green and red', 'a good shape', 'so vivid', 'a little cornucopia', 'brown as a leaf' – as it 'unclaps' its wings and flies up into the elm, where 'it is easy.'

The narrator feels that she is the trespasser: she disturbed the pheasant as it sunned itself in the narcissi. She turns again to 'you', pleading once again for its life: 'Let be, let be.'

VOICE

One strength of this poem lies in the personal voice of the narrator. It is as if the reader is looking in on a moment of her life – eavesdropping on her words to 'you'. The tone is intimate, immediate. Her plea is clear and unambiguous: 'Do not kill it.'

Her response to the pheasant is equally immediate: it rings absolutely true; there is no doubting the sincerity of her admiration. Can you pinpoint how this effect is achieved?

The pheasant is described in a concrete, detailed manner. There is indeed nothing 'mystical' about it: it is so vivid, so alive that this alone should be reason enough to let it be. Plath captures the vividness in a few well-chosen details: movement (jut, pacing, unclaps), colour (dark, green, red, brown), and shape (print of its big foot, tail-track). Its very sense of being at home here gives it a kingliness: it paces the hill, 'in its element', 'visits us', settles in the elm where it 'is easy', making the narrator feel she trespasses 'stupidly.'

Her statement that

> . . . it isn't
> As if I thought it had a spirit

suggests the idea that it has indeed a spirit, that she feels some mystical connection with it. Everything she says gives the impression that it has a superior claim to this place, and a right to live.

MOOD

The pleas that open and close the poem suggest tension between 'I' and 'you'. Her spirited defence of the pheasant is sparked by her recollection that 'you said you would kill it this morning.' The abruptness makes the statement sound like an accusation.

These words, and her defensiveness, suggest another scene, not described here. Why has 'you' threatened to kill the bird? Why are they in conflict about it? Do the final words suggest defeat or victory? While there are no answers to these questions in the poem, looking at the possibilities can help you to determine the tone of the poem.

- Tension
- The rights of wild creatures
- The mystery of beauty.

TECHNIQUE

Verse form

The verse form of this poem is *terza rima,* a form that Plath used frequently. This is an Italian term meaning 'third rhyme', and it is based on three-line stanzas, where the first and third lines rhyme. Often the end-sound of the second line becomes the rhyme of lines 1 and 3 in the next stanza, and so on, creating the sound-pattern *aba, bcb, cdc* . . . The stanzas are therefore interlaced.

This verse form is an effective one for building a narrative: it creates a series of short, interlaced vignettes. In this poem each stanza traces some aspect of the pheasant's appearance or its actions, with the grammatical sentence often carrying the thought through the break into the next stanza. This creates an almost casual flow, despite the formal structure of the poem.

Rhyme

A glance through the poem will show that *terza rima* is used consistently, though the rhymes often depend on *consonance* (rhyming final consonants) rather than on the more traditional and more obvious end-rhyme.

The effect of this muted rhyming pattern is a subtle music, an effect Plath strove to achieve in all her poetry. The singing quality of the poem is helped by her use of assonance and repetition. Again a quick look at any stanza reveals examples. In stanza 1, for example, there is

> . . . kill it this morning.
> . . . kill it. It startles . . . still.

Can you find other examples?

Rhythm

Pay attention also to the 'voice-rhythm' of the lines, the way many lines echo the rhythm of normal speech. While this creates an impression of ease and simplicity, it is in fact a highly skilful achievement, requiring mastery of technique.

STYLE

While Plath's attention to technique is evident when one studies 'Pheasant' closely, it does not stand out or impose itself on the reader. Form here serves the content: it draws attention to what the poet is saying, or adds to the beauty of the poem. It is not simply an end in itself.

Compare this with her technique in earlier poems, such as 'Black Rook in Rainy Weather'. Can you explain the difference? A look at the poet's level of engagement with her topic might be a good starting-point.

Elm

Text of poem: New Explorations Anthology page 306

Sylvia Plath dedicated 'Elm' to her friend Ruth Fainlight, an American poet. This is one of the first poems in which the distinctive voice of Plath's later poetry is heard. She always drew on her own experiences for material for her poems; but these late poems reflect a level of intensity not found in 'Finisterre' or 'Black Rook in Rainy Weather'. They also have a freedom, a lack of constraint and natural flow quite unlike the careful patterning of her earlier poems.

Some critics have linked the deep fear and rage expressed in 'Elm' with the growing tensions in Plath's marriage at the time of writing. These possibly triggered a renewal of the unresolved grief caused by the loss of her father at the age of eight, and of the depression that had caused her to have a nervous breakdown at the age of twenty. Part of the treatment for depression at that time was electric shock treatment, most probably the source of the image of scorching burning filaments used here and in other poems.

But it is important to emphasise that while these factors clearly influenced Plath's choice of theme and style, she is not writing about her life. A poem is an artistic creation, a work of art, which may be inspired by external events but is not a documentary about those events.

'Elm' is a complex poem. It is best perhaps to listen attentively to it several times to tune in to its deeply felt emotions, its energy. Try not to concentrate too much on understanding or interpreting individual lines or stanzas: respond rather to the general effect, the rich images, the sounds, the rhythm and, above all, the feelings that infuse it.

A READING

The speaker seems to be quoting the words she imagines the elm is directing to her. The elm – speaking as 'I' throughout – taunts 'you', the speaker, the source of the fear released in the poem, for her fear of the unknown. 'I know the bottom . . . I do not fear it,' she claims – unlike 'you', who fears it. 'You' hear the sea – or perhaps the voice of nothingness, a voice she is familiar with since her madness.

'You' foolishly seeks love – a 'shadow' that has galloped away. The elm will mimic that galloping sound all night, driving you to near-death: 'Till your head is a stone, your pillow a little turf'.

The taunting voice of the elm then describes some of the nightmarish horrors she knows, horrors that suggest a nervy, exhausted state:
• the sound of poisons, rain, 'this big hush', and its fruit, 'tin-white like arsenic'
• sunsets – atrocities that 'scorch to the root', making its 'filaments burn and stand'
• the wind, a destructively violent force that leaves nothing unharmed, will 'tolerate no bystanding', causing the elm to shriek
• the merciless moon, a symbol of barrenness, whose cruel radiance burns; when freed from the elm, this moon is flat – like a woman who has had radical surgery.

The frenzied violence of the verbs – scorch, burn, stand, break up, fly, shriek, drag, scathe – eases off in the next stanzas. The elm challenges 'you' for releasing the bad dreams that now 'possess and endow me.' The distinction between 'you' and the elm – so clear at first – is blurred. 'You' now seems to inhabit the elm – perhaps it is the dark, fearful side of the elm.

The elm turns from external violence to inner terror – a 'cry' that

> . . . flaps out
> Looking, with its hooks, for something to love.

She feels a terrifying 'dark thing', with its 'soft, feathery turnings', that sleeps in her, something that is also wicked, malignant. These 'soft feathery turnings' sound even more sinister than the wild violence of the earlier stanzas.

Silent inward terror gives way to a less claustrophobic tone. Looking outwards again, the elm watches 'clouds pass and disperse.' They may be the 'faces of love', and – like the love that went off like a horse in stanza 2 – they are irretrievable, gone for ever. The taunting voice that earlier mocked 'you' for her need for love has changed. The elm too seems to feel bereft (or possibly angry?): '. . . I agitate my heart'.

She now changes from the confident, knowing, fearless voice of the early stanzas to a fearful, petrified being, 'incapable of more knowledge.' This sounds as if she knows at some level what she could learn (does in fact 'know the bottom') but does not want to truly understand.

The cry, the dark thing, is now a face, 'so murderous in its strangle of branches', a creature whose 'snaky acids hiss' and freeze the will. The elm is now struggling with 'slow, isolate faults', which are self-destructive, potentially fatal, 'that kill, that kill, that kill.'

LANGUAGE

Plath's language in this poem is extraordinarily rich. The opening is simple and direct. 'I know the bottom, she says. I know it with my great tap-root'. Indeed many lines in the poem are written in the same simple, unvarnished style:

> 'Love is a shadow'.
> 'I let her go. I let her go'
> 'This is rain now, this big hush.'
> 'I am terrified by this dark thing | That sleeps in me;'
> 'Its snaky acids hiss.'

It is this directness that strikes the reader most forcibly on a first reading.

The tactile quality that is so often noted in Plath's poetry is evident here: words like 'stone', 'turf', 'arsenic', 'burn and stand', 'scathes', 'soft, feathery turnings' evoke things we can feel or hear or touch or taste. Every line of the poem contains concrete language – words, phrases and images that pile up to create a vibrant and powerful effect. It is as if each sensation, each feeling, each moment described is etched out. This has a powerful impact on the reader; the effect is cumulative until the final

> . . . isolate, slow faults
> That kill, that kill, that kill.

IMAGERY

While her experience is conveyed through metaphors, these are not used for their cleverness. The images used are powerful, conveying depth of feeling in richly evocative terms.

Re-examine the images that you find most striking. Notice the sparseness of the language: many of the statements are simple and clear, depending on strong verbs and nouns for their impact.

The central metaphor, the elm, is drawn from her immediate surroundings. 'The house in Devon was overshadowed by a giant wych-elm, flanked by two others in a single mass, growing on the shoulder of a moated prehistoric mound' (Ted Hughes). It features in a number of her poems, including 'Pheasant'; the bird settled in it, 'easy'. In 'Elm', however, there is no ease. Indeed the first draft of this poem opened with the lines 'She is not easy, she is not peaceful.'

Many of the images used here recur in other Plath poems: sea, horse, moon, scorching, clouds, acid, colours. By reusing the same images throughout her work she has created a series of symbols that echo and link up with each other, gaining an additional force from repeated use.

THEMES

Like 'Mirror', 'Elm' has been read and interpreted in innumerable ways. Some themes are:

- the 'stigma of selfhood' (Plath wrote these words at the top of the first draft of this poem) – the awful fear of being oneself
- despair and frustration
- the paralysis of fear
- the loss of love
- jealousy
- dissatisfaction
- the threat of madness
- exhaustion.

TECHNIQUE

Form

The close observance of writing rules – technique or form – sometimes made Plath's poems seem over-controlled. As her work developed she moved away from such tight control towards a freer style. 'Elm' is a good example of her success in overcoming what she herself called a 'clever too brittle and glassy tone', a move that enabled her 'to speak straight out, and of real experience, not just in metaphorical conceits'. It is remarkably open and intense, reflecting feelings that come from the deepest self.

Rhythm and rhyme

Written in *tercets* (three-line stanzas), this poem flows with the poet's feelings. There is no attempt at a rhyming scheme. What difference do you think this makes? The lines are free-flowing and varied in length. Can you suggest why this is?

There is, however, consistent use of internal rhyme: assonance, alliteration, repetition. Even in its wildest moments, this poem sings. Commenting on her later poems, Plath said: 'I speak them to myself . . . I say them aloud.' Can you find any evidence of this attention to sound effects in 'Elm'? Listen to it again, and pay close attention to the impact of sound effects, sentence length, one-liners and direct speech.

NOTE

This poem benefits from repeated readings. Trying to make sense of each individual line or stanza will only confuse you. Listening to it and re-reading it several times will enable you to tap in to the energy and the powerful emotions that infuse it.

Poppies in July

Text of poem: New Explorations Anthology page 310

A READING

The first part of 'Poppies in July' presents the physical appearance of the poppies: their intense red colour, the wrinkly petals, their light, flickering movement in the wind, their 'little bloody skirts!' However, the metaphors used go well beyond simple description: the poet is indirectly telling a 'story', rather than merely describing flowers.

Firstly, the poppies are associated with fire – usually a metaphor for vitality or life force in Plath's poetry. Here the fire is like 'hell flames', normally connected with intense pain. However, the speaker does not know whether they hurt her: 'Do you do no harm?' They do not burn the speaker – or if they do, she doesn't feel the pain. This suggests a state beyond pain, a sense of numbness.

She is exhausted; this may be caused by the sheer vividness of the poppies. They are fully alive, but she is apparently unable to experience life. They seem to plunge her into despair at something that is happening to her in her life. Her pain is underlined by the references to blood: they look like

> . . . the skin of a mouth.
> A mouth just bloodied.

or 'little bloody skirts'. The flowers are personified, given human characteristics.

The 'I' persona can't be like the poppies, it seems: she can't feel their burning, share their vitality. She is not fired by any life force or vitality. She can't bleed: 'If my mouth could marry a hurt like that!' Even her state of not feeling pain seems to distress her. It's not that she is not in pain: she just can't feel it, which brings its own anguish.

She turns from the appearance to the hidden properties of the poppies in the second part of the poem – their 'fumes', their 'opiates' (opium is extracted from the seeds of the white poppy), which can cause sleep, oblivion. She longs for the 'dulling and stilling' state they could induce in her.

The red poppies, a symbol of life, colourful and vivid, could help the speaker to escape into the dull, colourless world of oblivion, away from the exhaustion caused by the intensity of life, by the agony of just being. She longs for non-being.

TONE

There is a strong contrast between the vividness and vitality of the poppies and the dull, lacklustre mood of the speaker. She watches them, sees their 'flames', but 'cannot touch' them; even though she puts her 'hands among the flames', 'nothing burns.' She feels exhausted simply watching them: her mood seems directly opposite to the mood she attributes to the poppies.

She gives the impression that she can't participate in life – can't bleed, can't sleep, can't 'marry a hurt'. These lines suggest the feeling of desperation that leads her to yearn for oblivion;

> Dulling and stilling.
> But colorless. Colorless.

BACKGROUND

'Poppies in July' is one of a series of poems where the 'I' persona turns in on herself, dealing with some deep-seated grief; she does not disclose the source and nature of this, but the feeling is strongly conveyed. She longs for oblivion, but does not explain why. However, on reading the poem we get the sense that life itself is too much for her.

A companion poem to this one, called 'Poppies in October', written some months later, is quite different in tone. Here the blazing red of the poppies – 'brighter than sunrise' – is

> a gift
> A love gift
> Utterly unasked for.

This underlines the sense that it is not the poppies that generate the sense of grief and hopelessness, the desire for oblivion: it comes from within the speaker; but it is only temporary.

COMPARING THREE POEMS

'Pheasant', 'Elm' and 'Poppies in July' were written around the same time (in April and July 1962). In each poem the speaker is engaging in a struggle with some threatening force beyond herself. Each seems to re-create or suggest a scene in the drama of tensions within her life – a scene involving suspicion, hurt, jealousy and anger.

Re-read the three of them together, and note how the mood of the speaker seems to progress. In 'Pheasant' she is quite rational, though fearful for the pheasant. Her plea is logical and ordered and based on very ordinary claims: the beauty of the pheasant, its kingliness, colours, right to be in this place. At the same time the reader is aware of her tension right through the poem, and of the note of possible surrender in the final line: 'Let be, let be.'

In 'Elm' the speaker has lost love; it has galloped away and is irretrievable. The anguish experienced is expressed in a series of harsh, brilliant metaphors, conveying deep feelings of rage, terror, anguish and finally exhaustion.

'Poppies in July' reflects that same exhaustion: the vividness and movement of the flowers make the speaker feel exhausted. There is a sense of deep pain: 'hell flames', 'mouth just bloodied', 'bloody skirts'. She longs for oblivion, for non-being.

The Arrival of the Bee Box

Text of poem: New Explorations Anthology page 312
[*Note: This poem is also prescribed for Ordinary Level 2006 exam*]

THE BEE POEMS

Over one week, in October 1962, Sylvia Plath wrote a cycle of five poems, generally called the 'bee poems', set in the world of bee-keeping. All five are written in five-line stanzas, and they form a unit in that they move logically through the various phases of bee-keeping.

These poems grew from her own experience. Her father's speciality was bees: he studied them throughout his life, and wrote two highly regarded books on the subject. Given her lifelong obsession with her father, it is not surprising that Plath should have found it an interesting topic. Indeed, one of her earlier poems was entitled 'The Bee-Keeper's Daughter'.

After the birth of her son, Plath decided to keep bees, and she turned to the local bee-keepers' society for help in setting up her hives. Each of the poems in the cycle deals with a practical element of bee-keeping, drawing on the poet's initiation into this skill. But each one is also a metaphor for something in life: it is as if through these poems she found a way of defining her identity, coming to terms with elements of life.

THE STORY OF THE POEM

The story of 'The Arrival of the Bee Box' is straightforward: the narrator has taken delivery of a bee box ordered some time before. She describes its appearance, and also the appalling noise that comes from it. This she finds threatening, but also fascinating: she 'can't keep away from it.' Looking through the little grid, she sees only 'swarmy' darkness. She considers sending them back, or possibly even starving them. These considerations don't sound very convincing, however; she quickly goes on to wonder how hungry they are, and whether they will attack her when she unlocks the box. There are flowers in the garden that should attract them away from her when they fly out. She concludes by apparently deciding to free them tomorrow: 'The box is only temporary.'

THEMES

- Freedom and repression
- Self-expression

- Being oneself
- Control.

METAPHOR

Metaphor is the use of a word or phrase that describes one thing with the purpose of explaining or giving an understanding of something else. In describing the arrival of the bee box and her reactions, Plath explores a number of themes through a series of rich metaphors.

The bee box

The bee box itself is presented as something solid, ordinary: a 'clean wood box', 'square as a chair' and very heavy. The language here is direct and wholesome: even the rhyme of 'square' and 'chair' seems to underline its homely quality. However, this ordinariness quickly changes. The next line brings in a sinister note – or possibly it is merely humorous: this could be the coffin of a midget or a square baby were it not for the noise coming from it.

The box clearly means more to the speaker than a practical way of transporting bees. It immediately suggests death ('coffin') and threat ('dangerous'). Discovering that a familiar object is sinister and threatening is truly frightening: it seems to remove the feeling of safety one has around everyday things. She is fascinated and frightened. It contains, locks in, something she wants to keep in but also wants to release.

The bee box can be seen as a metaphor for containment, imprisonment or repression; this repression could come from concern for outward appearances, form, doing the right thing, trying to be what others expect, to behave in an acceptable way, saying the correct words, not being yourself, denying your true self. This is a form of repression, of boxing in something so that others will accept what they think you are. Remembering Plath's concerns about her life and her art, can you see why this seems an apt interpretation?

The bees

The sense of something sinister is heightened in stanza 2. The threat comes from the contents of the box – the bees, their noise, their clamour, their apparent anger.

Plath uses three metaphors to describe the hidden bees, each of them an image of power and oppression:
- They are like tiny shrunken African hands, packed for export: black, clambering – like slaves in a slave-ship. She has power over them: she could free them, but wonders how.
- They are like a Roman mob, safe individually but 'my god, together!' The exclamation mark (unusual in Plath's poems) suggests many possibilities. Not

being an autocrat, a Caesar, she feels she can't control them.

• They are just maniacs – thus also locked away, mad, a threat to others unless controlled by someone else.

Some critics see these as metaphors for the narrator's voice. If the box is external appearances, the bees may be seen as the speaker's inner life, feelings, real self or core of identity. This true self, her authentic voice, is locked in by convention. Her repressed words are 'a din', 'a noise that appals', 'unintelligible syllables', 'furious Latin.' Suppressed by rigid outer form or convention, they are unintelligible, formless and fearsome.

Her dread of releasing these words and ideas is so great that she wonders about getting rid of them, starving them: 'I need feed them nothing'; but the idea is half-hearted. Can you see anything in the structure of this statement that might imply that she doesn't fully mean it?

She fears that she herself may suffer if she releases the bees (or words):

'It is the noise that appals me . . .'
'I have simply ordered a box of maniacs.'
'I wonder if they would forget me'
'They might ignore me immediately'

In what way do you think she would be hurt by her own words? by her own poetry? by releasing her imaginative powers?

Tree

The narrator then imagines herself turning into a tree to avoid their anger. The reference to Daphne connects her (the speaker) with other women – she is not alone in her fear. The references to the 'blond' flowers of the laburnum and the 'petticoats of the cherry' also connect her with women.

How might her silence, her repression of her real self be echoed in the lives of other women at that time?

INTERPRETING THE POEM

This is only one interpretation of this rich metaphorical poem. There are others: look back at 'Mirror' and 'Elm'. Do you see anything that connects with them? Note the resemblances and the differences. As with many poems, 'reading in' one meaning can be simplistic, blocking the way to other possible interpretations and ideas.

TECHNIQUE

Wordplay and sound effects

There are several examples of Plath's clever wordplay and witty sound effects in this poem: the short '*i*' sound of 'din in it' combined with the repeated '*n*' seems to mimic the bees' buzzing; the almost unpronounceable 'unintelligible syllables' echoes the meaning of the words.

She also uses internal rhyme (square – chair – square – there), and also repetition (grid . . . grid – dark . . . dark – black . . . black). These are effective: sometimes they underline a point or highlight a word; always they make the poem sing.

The five-line stanza used in 'The Arrival of the Bee Box' is similar to that used in all five bee poems. There is, however, one difference in this poem: there is an additional single line at the end of the poem:

The box is only temporary.

It is almost as if it has escaped – has been freed – from the form of the poem.

NOTE

This is a complex and rich poem, one that will benefit from several readings. As it is part of a cycle of five poems, reading it together with the other four may add to your understanding.

Child

Text of poem: New Explorations Anthology page 315
[*Note: This poem is also prescribed for Ordinary Level 2006 exam*]

A READING

This simple poem is almost like a lullaby. The mother addresses her child, wanting to fill his eye,

the one absolutely beautiful thing

with wonders.

The tone at first is clear and bright. She longs to fill his vision with colour, ducks, newness and flowers. He is like a flower-stalk without wrinkle, or a pool that reflects the beauty of the world. However, the tone changes in the final stanza; the narrator turns away from the child and his world to

this troublous
Wringing of hands.

She sees another world that is the direct opposite of the light and flower-filled world of the child,

> . . . this dark
> Ceiling without a star.

This could perhaps be a reflection of her fears for the child in a world that is often antagonistic to beauty and dangerous for the helpless. It might also refer to her own feelings of unhappiness and depression. There is a marked contrast between the joyful, limpid quality of the first three stanzas and the dark, unlit, enclosed space of the last line. What effect has this on the reader? What is your response to the poem?

PLATH AND CHILDREN

'Child' is one of a number of poems that Plath wrote about children, in particular her own children and her relationship with them. It is an eloquent love poem, reflecting a strong connection with them and with the world she would like to show to them. However, in most of these poems the poet turns from the tender joy and lightness of her child's world to anxiety; the conclusion here creates a strong sense of darkness, chilliness. There is a suggestion that she fears threatening forces that may hurt the child.

STYLE

'Child' is written in the three-line stanza form, one that Plath used often in her later poems. Here it seems particularly appropriate. The sort stanzas are clear and uncluttered, the rhythm quick and light. Most lines have two or three beats, giving the poem an easy, flowing movement.

The theme is simple: love, childhood joys, motherhood, and also fear and anxiety about the bleakness that may threaten the child, the 'troublous wringing of hands'.

The language is concrete: the narrator lists simple objects that bring joy to children: colours and ducks, the zoo of the new, flowers and water. Her fear too is worded in concrete terms: 'wringing of hands', 'dark ceiling without a star.'

Compare this poem in tone, theme and style with 'Morning Song'.

Overview of the poems

This is a brief look at the selection of poems by Sylvia Plath that you have studied. The points made here represent one interpretation of her work. It is important that you develop your own response to each poem; where this differs from the suggestions given here, trust your own judgment. Re-read the poem, and validate your opinion.

BACKGROUND

Plath wrote incessantly during her short life: poetry, short stories, articles, essays and one semi-autobiographical novel. Her writings were first published in magazines on both sides of the Atlantic; later they appeared in book form.

She considered poems written before 1956 as 'juvenilia'. Her first published book, *The Colossus,* includes only poems written after this date, among them two of the poems you have studied, 'Black Rook in Rainy Weather' and 'The Times are Tidy'. Her remaining poems were published after her death in three collections: *Ariel and Other Poems, Crossing the Water* and *Winter Trees.*

Her last poems are generally seen as Plath's outstanding achievement. Here she truly found her voice, expressing herself in a distinctive, unique style. She was aware of this herself: while writing them, she informed her mother:

> I am a writer . . . I am a genius of a writer; I have it in me. I am writing the best poems of my life; they will make my name . . . (*Letters Home,* 16 October 1962).

Her husband describes these poems equally glowingly:

> Her real self showed itself in her writing . . . . When a real self finds language and manages to speak, it is surely a dazzling event. (Ted Hughes, foreword to *The Journals of Sylvia Plath,* 1982)

READING PLATH'S POEMS

There is a widespread tendency to interpret Plath's work as autobiographical, to read her poems as if they tell her life story. While it is quite obvious – and probably inevitable – that a writer's life will influence what she writes, it is important to understand that poetry is art. Writing about this issue, Ted Hughes pointed out that the reader must learn 'to distinguish between a subjective work that was trying to reach an artistic form using a real event as its basis, and a documentary of some event that did happen'.

Some critics read her later poems exclusively in the light of her suicide. They argue that she signals her suicide (intentionally or otherwise) in a number of her last poems, through various references to despair, rage, loss, separation or death. This is by no means as obvious as these critics claim. Many of these poems are the work of a woman who is coming into her own, recognising her own needs, using her own voice, finding her true self. Look back, for example, at 'The Arrival of the Bee Box'. This is about facing and releasing the fears that are hidden beneath the surface – not about a woman who is contemplating death.

It is important to read the poems as they stand. Looking for signs of what was to happen afterwards in her life is to predetermine how the poems should be read, not actually attending to the poem itself.

THEMES AND ISSUES IN THE PRESCRIBED POEMS

The writer's identity

In 'Black Rook in Rainy Weather' (1956), one theme is the poet's identity as a writer. The speaker, surrounded by wintry bleakness, longs for the miracle that will transform this into something radiant. That miracle is the creative impulse, the imagination that will change an otherwise uneventful period. For the speaker, this miracle was of vital importance.

Motherhood

Plath wrote many poems dealing with all aspects of pregnancy, childbirth and motherhood, at a time when writers, especially poets, rarely touched on such topics. Her best-known work on the theme, 'Poem for Three Voices', evokes powerfully the variety of emotions experienced by women around pregnancy, miscarriage, motherhood and adoption. Her poems on this theme are remarkable for their lyricism (song-like quality), depth of feeling, and tenderness.

> What did my fingers do before they held him?
> What did my heart do, with its love?

However, being a realist, she also reflected the other side of being a mother: the drudgery, the anxieties, and the level to which a mother is bound to her child.

> I have never seen a thing so clear . . .
> It is a terrible thing to be so open: it is as if my heart
> Put on a face and walked into the world.

Both attitudes are seen in 'Morning Song'. The mother's life is shadowed by the child's arrival, but is enriched by the joy of love. 'Child' also reflects the simple pleasure she derives from her child; his eye is the one absolutely beautiful thing that she longs to fill with the beauty of the world. But there is also an underlying threat to the child's safety, which distresses her.

Identity

Plath frequently returned to the issue of double identity in her writing. The subject of her undergraduate dissertation in Smith College was 'The Magic Mirror: A Study of the Double in Dostoevsky Novels'. Her interest in what appears on the surface and what is hidden is reflected in 'Mirror'. Here, the depths hide something frightening and sinister something the woman would prefer to avoid but cannot escape.

'Elm' also deals with doubleness: the apparent calm of the elm in the opening stanzas, and the hidden terrors that surface as she talks.

A similar preoccupation is at the heart of 'The Arrival of the Bee Box'. The practical, square box is a simple container: apparently there are no mysteries here. However, it conceals something sinister, but also fascinating.

Nature
Plath's abiding interest in the world around her, her interest in nature, is reflected in many poems. Her descriptions are remarkable for their concrete, precise detail.

'Finisterre' paints a graphic picture of the scene before her eyes, conveying the harshness of the sea, the bleakness of the rocks, the delicacy of the flowers on the cliff and the effect of the mist.

'Black Rook in Rainy Weather' is strong in visual details, accurately portraying a scene on a wet, wintry day.

Her painterly style creates graphic images in 'Pheasant': the bird itself, the flowers, the hill and elm in the background, the earlier scene where the snow was marked with the 'crosshatch' footprints of various birds.

Through unusual images, 'Poppies in July' captures the vivid colour and fluid movement of the poppies' petals.

'Pheasant' reflects her stance against the destruction of nature, a concern that features in many of her poems.

Psychic landscapes
While Plath's descriptions of landscapes and seascapes are striking, the scene is at times simply the backdrop to the mood of the speaker.

'Black Rook in Rainy Weather' is strong in visual detail, but the place does not really matter. What comes across as significant is the mood of the speaker, the sense of tentative expectancy. The landscape is almost a backdrop.

In 'Finisterre', the place is identified by the title. The landscape is captured in a series of wonderful images. Many of these are personified: cliffs are 'admonitory', rocks hide their grudges, the sea wages war and mists are without hope. The place assumes an atmosphere that is oddly human.

TECHNIQUE

Style
Plath's style changed considerably during her career, but there are certain features that mark all her work:
- remarkable use of language
- unusual and striking imagery
- humour.

Language

Plath's 'crackling verbal energy' is apparent in her poems' biting precision of word and image. Her writing has been variously praised for its tactile quality, power, incisiveness, control, taut originality and luminosity. Joyce Carol Oates observed that 'the final memorable poems ['Elm', 'Poppies in July' and 'The Arrival of the Bee Box', among others] . . . read as if they've been chiselled with a fine surgical implement out of arctic ice.' In her *Journals*, Plath constantly urges herself to develop a 'diamond-edged', 'gem-bright' style. This she certainly achieved. Part of her technique was to reuse certain words in many poems, which thus took on an almost symbolic meaning: smiles, hooks, element, dissatisfaction, vowels, shriek, horse, sea.

'Black Rook in Rainy Weather' is a good example of her earlier control of language and form. In it the language is clear and precise, creating a series of carefully worked out pictures.

'Pheasant' is a later example of her skilled control of descriptive language. The form here is less dominant, and the poet's feelings are reflected in the personal voice that speaks throughout. The words are simple, the descriptions are vivid, and the poem is crystal clear. It is a good example of Plath's descriptive powers at their best.

'Elm' shows her powerful response to loss, pain and terror. The feeling of despair, for example, is conveyed through a number of highly charged nouns and verbs.

Imagery

Certain images recur in Plath's poetry, taking on a symbolic meaning that gains added force through repeated use.
• The moon symbolises barrenness, coldness and the negation of life. In 'Elm' it is merciless, cruel and barren, associated with pain and suffering.
• The mirror often symbolises the hidden alter ego (the 'other self'), as in 'Mirror'.
• The horse is a symbol of vitality. In 'Elm', love gallops off like a horse.
• Blood symbolises vitality, life force and creativity, as in 'Poppies in July'. In a later poem, Plath states:

> The blood jet is poetry,
> There is no stopping it

• The sea is often associated with undefined menace or hidden threat, as is so graphically evident in 'Finisterre'.

She uses many other images, however, that are not symbolic, images that add to the vividness and immediacy of what she is describing. One of the most distinctive features of her work is her use of metaphors, many of which are visual. Examples abound:

• Mists are 'souls', which 'bruise the rocks out of existence' ('Finisterre').
• The pheasant is 'brown as a leaf', a 'little cornucopia' ('Pheasant').
• Poppies are 'little hell flames', 'wrinkly and clear red, like the skin of a mouth | A mouth just bloodied', 'little bloody skirts' ('Poppies in July').
• The bee box is 'square as a chair', a 'midget's coffin' ('The Arrival of the Bee Box').
• Bees are like 'African hands, | Minute and shrunk for export' ('The Arrival of the Bee Box').
• A life of boring regularity is like a 'stuck record' ('The Times are Tidy').
• The baby's mouth opens 'clean as a cat's' ('Morning Song').
• Her crying is 'a handful of notes', which rise 'like balloons' ('Morning Song').

Plath attached great importance to colours, often identifying them with specific attributes. The repeated use of colour to suggest certain qualities links her poems to one another, giving added force to her meaning.

• Red signifies vitality, life force: the red poppies are animated, vital, unlike the colourless life of the narrator. The pheasant's vitality is envisaged largely through its vivid colouring.
• Green too signifies the positive, creativity, life force: the pheasant is red and green.
• Black is associated with death, anger, depression, aggression and destruction: the black headland that opens 'Finisterre' underlines the sinister mood.
• The depressed mood of the speaker in 'Black Rook in Rainy Weather' is conveyed through the repetition of black and the dominating presence of the rook.
• Surprisingly, white too is sinister: the white faces of the dead, the white mists in 'Finisterre'.

Humour

Running through her work is Plath's humour, sharp and ironic at times, at other times mocking and black. She uses ironic humour to challenge self-importance, to mock what she found ridiculous and pompous, and often to mock herself.

'The Times are Tidy' ridicules the politicians and the life of the 1950s. The smug satisfaction of this decade was all-pervasive. Plath ironically contrasts this era with that of dragon-slayers and witches (created by myth-makers). The rich cream – wealth and material possessions – is an ironic substitute for adventure and excitement. The inch-thick cream suggests fat cats 'creaming' it.

In 'Finisterre' the ironic description of the monument shows how remote formal religion is from the concerns of ordinary people. The giant statue of Our Lady of the Shipwrecked ignores the plight of the little people at her feet. The introduction of the shell-toy women makes the reader wonder whether they don't offer more comfort than their gigantic marble sister.

In 'Morning Song' she uses gentle self-irony, creating an amusing picture of the mother in the small details given: she stumbles from her bed, cow-like in her flowery nightdress.

'Mirror' opens with the mirror's unintentionally comic description of itself, giving the poem an ironic twist.

PLATH'S ROMANTICISM

Sylvia Plath was a lyric poet in the Romantic tradition. She wrote poems that drew on her own experience of life and explored a range of emotions from love and joy to terror and despair. Like the Romantics, she looked inwards rather than outwards; her experience is gauged by what she has lived through.

'Elm' is perhaps the most striking example of this. It is one of a number of poems she wrote around the same time, expressing agonising emotions. Some of these emotions were quite 'acceptable', provided they were not shown too openly: the grief and loneliness expressed in 'Elm', for example. However, less acceptable was the intensity with which she voiced these; it was considered 'over the top', too revealing. She also voiced the other, far less 'acceptable' feelings (those not talked about in public) here and in other poems: gleeful destructiveness and hatred ('Daddy') or intense resentment ('The Zoo-Keeper's Wife').

The writer and critic Joyce Carol Oates sees in these poems the seeds of Plath's eventual suicide.

> Her poems have that heart-breaking quality about them that has made Sylvia Plath our acknowledged Queen of Sorrows, the spokeswoman for our most private, most helpless nightmares; her poetry is as deathly as it is impeccable; it enchants us almost as powerfully as it must have enchanted her.

Not everyone agrees with this estimate, however. Janice Markey sees Plath's writings as life-affirming.

> The enduring success and greatness of Plath's work lies in its universal appeal and in an innovative, effective presentation. Plath was the first writer in modern times to write about women with a new aggressive confidence and clarity, and the first to integrate this confidence and clarity in a sane, honest and compassionate vision.

Forming a personal view or response

1. What did you like best about Sylvia Plath's poems?
2. Choose one poem that you enjoyed and identify what appealed to you about it.
3. In what way is Plath different from the other poets on your course?
4. Plath's poetry reflects many facets of life. Which of these did you find most interesting?
5. What did you learn about Plath as a person from studying her poetry?
6. Is there anything you particularly like or dislike about her poetry?
7. Are the themes and issues in her poetry relevant to young people today?
8. Plath's unique and distinctive voice has often been praised. Do you find her voice – her way of writing, of expressing her ideas – unique?
9. Is there any particular image or description that remains with you from reading Plath's poetry? If so, identify why it impressed you.

Questions

1. 'Sylvia Plath created a language for herself that was utterly and startlingly original.' How true is this statement of the poems by Plath that you have studied?
2. Discuss Plath's treatment of nature in her poems. Support your discussion by quotation from or reference to the poems by her that you have studied.
3. 'Plath's poetry is a reflection of the era in which she lived.' Discuss this statement, supporting your discussion by quotation from or reference to the poems by Plath that you have studied.
4. Write a short essay on the aspects of Sylvia Plath's poems (content or style) that you found most interesting. Support your discussion by reference to or quotation from the poems by Plath that you have studied.
5. 'Sylvia Plath: a personal response'. Using this title, write an essay on the poetry of Plath, supporting your points by quotation from or reference to the poems on your course.
6. 'Sylvia Plath's taut language and startling images make her poems unique.' Discuss this statement, supporting your discussion by quotation from or reference to the poems by Plath that you have studied.
7. 'Sylvia Plath's poetry reflects a wide range of emotions.' Discuss this statement, concentrating on at least two different emotions that are evident in her poetry.
8. 'Despite the seriousness of her themes, Plath uses humour to devastating effect at times.' Discuss this statement, supporting your discussion by quotation from or reference to the poems by Plath that you have studied.

9. 'Recurring themes of loneliness, separation and pain mark the poetry of Sylvia Plath.' Discuss this statement, supporting your discussion by quotation from or reference to the poems by Plath that you have studied.
10. 'The use of brilliant and startling imagery gives a surreal quality to the poems of Sylvia Plath.' Discuss this statement, supporting your discussion by quotation from or reference to the poems by Plath that you have studied.

8 *Michael* LONGLEY

John G. Fahy

Life and writings

ichael Longley was born in Belfast on 27 July 1939, of English parents.
His father, Richard – who features in the poems 'Wounds', 'Wreaths'
and 'Last Requests' from this selection – fought in the First World War
and was gassed, wounded, decorated, and promoted to the rank of captain.
Between the wars the Longleys moved to Belfast, where Richard was a commercial
traveller for an English firm of furniture manufacturers. He enlisted again in the
Second World War, ending with the rank of major.

In *Tuppenny Stung*, a short collection of autobiographical chapters, you can
read of Michael Longley's childhood: of his twin brother, Peter, and older sister,
Wendy; of his ingenious and versatile war-veteran father ('that rare thing, an
Englishman accepted and trusted by Ulstermen'); of his crippled and
temperamental mother ('It has taken me a long time to forgive her that
atmosphere of uncertainty, its anxieties, even fears'); of his irrepressible English
grandfather, 'Grandpa George'; and the usual menagerie of eccentric relatives
we all accumulate. You can read of his primary and secondary education and the
forces on his early cultural formation: Protestant schoolboy fears of the dark
savageries supposedly practised by Catholics; an English education system
dismissive of Irish culture and history; Protestant Belfast's fear and resentment
of the Republic. His early education and local socialisation made him aware of
conflicting classes and religions and of the duality of Irish identity.

Later he was educated at the Royal Belfast Academical Institution and in
1958 went to Trinity College, Dublin, where the student population at that time
consisted in the main of Southern and Northern Protestants, middle- and upper-
class English, and a scattering of Southern Catholics who defied the Catholic
Church's ban on attendance. Longley studied classics and wrote poetry but felt
very under-read in English literature until taken in hand by his friend and young
fellow-poet Derek Mahon:

> We inhaled with our untipped Sweet Afton cigarettes MacNeice, Crane,
> Dylan Thomas, Yeats, Larkin, Lawrence, Graves, Ted Hughes, Stevens,
> Cummings, Richard Wilbur, Robert Lowell, as well as Rimbaud,
> Baudelaire, Brecht, Rilke – higgledepiggledy, in any order. We scanned
> the journals and newspapers for poems written yesterday. When

Larkin's 'The Whitsun Weddings' first appeared in Encounter, Mahon steered me past the documentary details, which as an aspiring lyricist I found irritating, to the poem's resonant, transcendental moments. He introduced me to George Herbert who thrilled me as though he were a brilliant contemporary published that very week by the Dolmen Press. Herbert, thanks to Mahon, is a beneficent influence in my first collection and provides the stanzaic templates for two of its more ambitious poems.

Longley first worked as a teacher in Dublin, London and Belfast. From 1964 he was one of the group of young writers fostered by Philip Hobsbaum at Queen's University, though Longley felt that his poetry didn't fit in particularly well.

From the beginning Hobsbaum made it clear that his stars were Séamus Heaney and Stewart Parker, who was teaching in the States at this time. Hobsbaum's aesthetic demanded gritty particularity and unrhetorical utterance. Heaney's work fitted the bill especially well: at the second or third meeting which I attended a sheet of his poems was discussed – 'Digging' and 'Death of a Naturalist' (it was called 'End of a Naturalist' then).

By this time I was beginning to enjoy what was for me as a lapsed Classicist a new experience – practical criticism. But I didn't much care for the Group aesthetic or, to be honest, the average poem which won approval. I believed that poetry should be polished, metrical and rhymed; oblique rather than head-on; imagistic and symbolic rather than rawly factual, rhetorical rather than documentary. I felt like a Paleface among a tribe of Redskins. Although I have since modified my ideas, I still think that despite the rigours of practical criticism and the kitchen heat of the discussions, many Group poems tended to be underdone.

Longley worked for the Arts Council of Northern Ireland between 1970 and 1991, when he took early retirement. His work for the arts was driven by a number of guiding principles, among which were the nurturing of indigenous talent (he used to ask, 'How much of what we are doing differentiates us from Bolton or Wolverhampton?'), support for the artists, not just the arts, and the need to transcend class barriers and bring the arts, at an affordable price, to the working class.

He was always a champion of cultural pluralism, fostering the artistic expression of both sides of the religious and political divide. In fact the first event Longley organised for the Arts Council was 'The Planter and the Gael', a poetry-reading tour by John Hewitt and John Montague, in which each poet read poems exploring his particular experience of Ulster. So it was not surprising that Longley should be invited to join the Cultural Traditions Group at its launch in 1988. Its aims are, as he has written, 'to encourage in Northern

Ireland the acceptance and understanding of cultural diversity; to replace political belligerence with cultural pride'.

His vision of Ulster culture has always sought to include its many different strands and influences and so encourage a unique hybrid rather than separate, antagonistic cultures. As he has said elsewhere, 'Imaginative Ulstermen (and by extension, Irishmen) could be the beneficiaries of a unique cultural confluence which embraces the qualities of the Irish, the Scottish, the English and the Anglo-Irish' (quoted by Michael Parker).

Longley fostered a great range and diversity of artists, from traditional singers and fiddlers to painters, photographers and drama groups. For the last nine years of his career with the Arts Council he was combined arts director, overseeing traditional arts, youth arts and community arts, while concentrating on his chief preoccupation, literature. Here he directed Arts Council money towards publication, attempting to ensure that as many writers as possible got into print.

Michael Longley is a fellow of the Royal Society of Literature and a member of Aosdána. He is married to the critic and academic Edna Longley.

No Continuity City (1969), Longley's first volume, is known for its technically accomplished and learned poetry. Among its concerns are poets and poetry and nature, but it is best known for the learned, witty and sophisticated love poetry, almost in the metaphysical tradition. *An Exploded View* (1973) continues to deal with poetry and poetic issues. Nature is also a preoccupation. 'Badger' is from this volume. This book does respond briefly to the upsurge of violence around this time; in 'Wounds' the violence is seen from the broad perspective of international conflict. A great number of the poems focus on an alternative life in the west of Ireland; 'Carrigskeewaun' and 'Poteen' are among these. This attachment of Longley's for County Mayo also forms the focus of his third volume, *Man Lying on a Wall* (1976).

The Echo Gate (1979) demonstrates Longley's now established bifocal view: on Belfast and Mayo. He confronts the political violence in its stark, everyday settings in 'Wreaths' and explores the war experiences of his father as a perspective on this violence in 'Last Requests'. He also explores the folklore, ethos and culture of the west of Ireland and finds a bleak, unconscious parallel between its crude violence and that of Belfast in 'Self-Heal'.

Gorse Fires (1991) is centred on Longley's adopted second home of Carrigskeewaun in County Mayo. But it also includes poems on the Holocaust, the Second World War and the Spanish Civil War. Interspersed with these are some free translations from Homer's *Odyssey,* focusing on Odysseus's return to his home and interpreted by some critics as having strong if oblique references to Longley's own home province. 'Laertes' is from this sequence.

In *The Ghost Orchid* (1995) Longley continues to write perceptively and sensitively about the delicacy of nature: the long grasses by the lake like autumn lady's tresses; sandpipers; the sighting of otters and dolphins; birdsong; and of course the flowers that give the volume its title. These are not so much nature studies in the usual sense as intimate encounters that are shared with the reader in the style of a personal diary. And the locations are wide-ranging, from the west of Ireland to the stone gardens of Japan.

This volume not only celebrates the natural beauty of the world but also affirms the sexuality of life, whether manifested in nature's flowers or in artwork, from sheela-na-gigs to Japanese erotic art. A variety of styles of language is employed, ranging from the simplicity and precision of Haiku-style description to the phonic thunder of Ulster dialect.

In this volume also Longley continues with his very creative free translations, from the Roman love poet Ovid, from Virgil, and also from Homer. 'Ceasefire' is one of these, featuring the meeting between King Priam and Achilles at the end of Homer's *Iliad*.

Tuppenny Stung (1994) is a collection of autobiographical chapters, previously published in periodicals or delivered as lectures from 1972 to 1992.

POETRY COLLECTIONS

	In this selection
No Continuing City (1969)	
An Exploded View (1973)	'Badger'
	'Wounds'
	'Poteen'
	'Carrigskeewaun'
Man Lying on a Wall (1976)	
The Echo Gate (1979)	'Wreaths'
	'Last Requests'
	'Mayo Monologues 3: Self-Heal'
Gorse Fires (1991)	'An Amish Rug'
	'Laertes'
The Ghost Orchid (1995)	'Ceasefire'
Broken Dishes (1998)	

Badger

Text of poem: New Explorations Anthology page 346

A READING OF THE POEM

This nature poem celebrates that nocturnal woodland creature, the badger, but it also questions humankind's interference in nature.

The badger's legendary strength is evoked both in the descriptions ('the wedge of his body') and by his activities ('He excavates . . . into the depths of the hill'), which personify him as a muscular miner. There is a sense of uncompromising directness and dependability about his 'path straight and narrow' that contrasts with the deceptiveness of the fox and the giddiness of the hare. That ruggedness is also evident from his indiscriminate diet: he can cope with the poisonous dog's mercury and the tough brambles as well as the gentler bluebells.

But it is his relationship with the earth that is most interestingly portrayed. Longley sees the badger as a sort of horticulturalist: he 'manages the earth with his paws'; he facilitates the growth of great oak trees ('a heel revolving acorns'). The picture comes across of an animal at one with the earth, the caretaker of the hill, which in turn takes care of him in death. The animal's close association with prehistoric tombs lends him an even greater aura of significance. Somehow he becomes a symbol of the earth's ancientness, its longevity and mythological power. Longley himself has said that he thinks of animals as spirits. He tries to have an animal in each of his books.

The poem also deals with humankind's destructiveness and cruelty, our interference in the natural world. The poet's criticism of this is communicated through the bleak ironies of section III: digging out the digger, the bitter euphemism of this process being described as a forceps birth, the irony of being 'delivered' to his death:

> It is a difficult delivery
> once the tongs take hold.

There is sympathy for the 'vulnerable . . . pig's snout' and implicit condemnation of the brutal treatment ('his limbs dragging after them') and also of the environmental disturbance:

> So many stones turned over,
> The trees they tilted.

This treatment is in marked contrast to the badger's careful management of the earth, unaided by machines or 'tongs' of any kind! A clear environmental statement is made here, but it is subtly put across through the contrast rather than by any kind of didactic statement.

TONE

This is a tough, unsentimental poem, recording the perennial secret workings of nature. True, it does romanticise the badger somewhat:

> Night's silence around his shoulders,
> His face lit by the moon.

But it also records the violence, the suffering and the destruction of nature and creatures.

Behind that wealth of observed details and naturalist knowledge we can detect a tone of admiration for the animal's strength and its management of the woodland ('His path straight . . . not like the fox's zig-zags . . .') and we can certainly feel the poet's sympathy for the vulnerable animal in section III.

Wounds
Text of poem: New Explorations Anthology page 348

BACKGROUND NOTE

In his autobiographical book *Tuppenny Stung*, Longley elaborates on his father's wartime experiences:

> Having lived through so much by the time he was thirty, perhaps my father deserved his early partial retirement. At the age of seventeen he had enlisted in 1914, one of thousands queuing up outside Buckingham Palace. He joined the London-Scottish by mistake and went into battle wearing an unwarranted kilt. A Lady from Hell. Like so many survivors he seldom talked about his experiences, reluctant to relive the nightmare. But not long before he died, we sat up late one night and he reminisced. He had won the Military Cross for knocking out single-handed a German machine-gun post and, later, the Royal Humane Society's medal for gallantry: he had saved two nurses from drowning. By the time he was twenty he had risen to the rank of Captain, in charge of a company known as 'Longley's Babies' because many of them were not yet regular shavers. He recalled the lice, the rats, the mud, the tedium, the terror. Yes, he had bayoneted men and still dreamed about a tubby little German who 'couldn't run fast enough. He turned around to face me and burst into tears.' My father was nicknamed Squib in the trenches. For the rest of his life no-one ever called him Richard.

A READING OF THE POEM

The figure of his father features prominently in Michael Longley's poetry. The father is graphically and sympathetically realised and the father–son bond asserted in such poems as 'In Memoriam', 'Wounds', 'Last Requests', and 'Laertes'.

The poet's relationship with his father in 'Wounds' is characterised by intimacy and tenderness. There is an intimacy about their style of communication. 'Two pictures from my father's head' suggests a perfect non-verbal understanding, which the poet has kept 'like secrets'. The caress is tender, repetitive and comforting: 'I touched his hand, his thin head I touched.' The father's sense of humour, even if a little grim, indicates the easiness of the relationship: 'I am dying for King and Country, slowly.' (This refers to the link between his final illness and the old war wounds; see 'In Memoriam': 'In my twentieth year your old wounds woke | As cancer.')

In these repeated father–son exchanges Longley is probing his own identity and defining his background. Much has been written about the supposed identity crisis of the Ulster Protestant writer, shakily situated between the conflicting claims of the English and Irish literary traditions and outlooks. As Terence Brown points out in another context, Longley is a lyric poet nurtured in the English and classical traditions 'attempting to come to terms with the fact that he was born in Ireland of an English father and that he now lives in a Belfast shaken almost nightly by the national question, violently actualised.' This family experience of immigration might be seen to mirror the experience of the Ulster Protestant as immigrant. We catch some of this confusion, this incomprehension of the local view in the father's bemused reaction to the Ulster soldiers' sectarian battle cries:

> 'wilder than Gurkhas' were my father's words
> of admiration and bewilderment.

He expresses admiration, presumably for their courage, but complete bewilderment at the sectarian sentiment. Something of the same bewilderment is evident in the poet's own reaction to present-day violence when he describes the murder of the bus conductor:

> . . . shot through the head
> By a shivering boy who wandered in
> Before they could turn the television down

The air of incomprehension, this slight sense of distance from local realities, which may be the inheritance of the immigrant, is shared by father and son.

In summary, the poet is establishing his identity as the son of a courageous English soldier. There is no direct discussion of an identity crisis, either literary or political; but we do register a sense of bewilderment, something of the outsider's air of detachment in the attitudes of both father and son towards Ulstermen at war.

Longley is using his father's First World War experiences as a perspective on present-day atrocities. Patricia Craig says that the violence of the trenches is 'brought up smack against the dingier violences of present-day Belfast'. Whether it is more or less dingy in the poet's eyes is debatable. The grotesqueness of the slaughter and the indignities of violent death are emphasised in both the world war and the present-day killings. The 'landscape of dead buttocks' that haunted his father for fifty years is hardly less bizarre than the recent image of

Three teenage soldiers, bellies full of
Bullets and Irish beer, their flies undone.

What is different and shocking about the portrayal of modern violence in the poem is its invasion of the domestic scene:

Before they could turn the television down
Or tidy away the supper dishes.

It is casual, perpetrated by a boy who 'wandered in'. The shocking ordinariness of the violence is underlined by the ridiculous apology, 'Sorry, missus.' It is as if he had just bumped into her in the street. Death is delivered to your home with a casual, polite apology.

ISSUES RAISED IN THE POEM

Longley's sense of identity
- The poet is defining himself by describing his family background.
- The English military background is an important and accepted facet of the poet's identity.
- The sensitive and humorous portrait of his father communicates an easy and tender father–son relationship.
- The importance of that father-figure generally in the poet's life: the long-dead man is still a powerful reality.
- The violent city is part of his identity also.

Violence
- The 'wounds' of the title refers to old war wounds, lingering psychological wounds (haunting images), and new wounds.
- The universality of killing: the world of the poem is a world of violence, whether legitimised as war or condemned as illegal. Does the poem differentiate between war violence and present-day atrocities?
- The less-than-glorious reality of war
- The indignity of violent death
- The increasing ordinariness of violence: terror at the heart of the domestic scene
- The wanton nature of present-day violence.

Tone
The opening is conversational, personal. The speaker is sharing a confidence, inviting us in: 'Here are two pictures . . . secrets.' There is evidence of a certain wry humour, which successfully deflates any possible attempt at glorifying either his father or the war ('I am dying for King and Country, slowly'; 'A packet of Woodbines I throw in, | A lucifer').

Is there a note of critical irony detectable in the parson's fussiness about dress in the face of death, and a hint of religious cynicism in the apparent indifference of God to human suffering and evil ('the Sacred Heart of Jesus | Paralysed')? The emotional impact is frequently disguised behind the relentless listing of details, but it is there, for example in 'heavy guns put out | The nightlight in a nursery for ever'. And the understatement of the last line packs quite an emotional punch.

Visual impact

This particularly visual style relies heavily on Longley's eye for incongruous details, such as the sectarian battle-cries as the soldiers go over the top; the chaplain with the stylish backhand; the domestic details of the three teenage soldiers, lured to their deaths by the promise of sex; the bus conductor who 'collapsed beside his carpet-slippers,' etc. And they all make the point about how brutally unglorious death is.

Poteen

Text of poem: New Explorations Anthology page 351

A READING OF THE POEM

The description of illicit whiskey-making turns into a statement about national identity. The primitive, superstitious act of 'one noggin-full | Sprinkled on the ground' as a sort of votive offering to the spirits opens up other atavistic echoes and race memories. It conjures up images of other illegal activities, rebel plottings, also carried on in remote bogland and similar inaccessible areas. Poitín-making becomes a symbol of historical Ireland, the Ireland of the dispossessed, of the rebel, with all the paraphernalia of secret societies, stored weapons, and furtive plottings (souterrains, sunk workshops, cudgels, guns, the informer's ear, blood-money).

So it becomes a poem about 'the back of the mind' (suppressed race memory), and the racial consciousness evoked is one of furtive living, blunt violence ('cudgels, guns'), and seamy betrayals ('the informer's ear'). It is not exactly an idealised picture, but rather a bleak and realistic psychological portrait where greed and romantic aspiration go hand in hand ('Blood money, treasure-trove').

Carrigskeewaun

Text of poem: New Explorations Anthology page 353

A READING OF THE POEM

We notice that Longley's view of County Mayo is certainly not the romanticised one of the tourist or holiday weekender, but more like the realistic perception of the native who sees the landscape in all its harshness and its beauty. He presents its arid face to us, a landscape of boulders and dry-stone walls, a harsh territory inimical to human and animals alike, the graveyard of many.

> This is ravens' territory, skulls, bones,
> The marrow of these boulders supervised
> From the upper air:

But he also presents the serene beauty of nature, in the image of the lake 'tilted to receive | The sun perfectly'. His interest is primarily in the physical landscape and the flora and fauna rather than in the people; in fact he seems to enjoy his solitary, Crusoe-like existence, dislodging mallards, discovering cattle tracks, etc., in this sparsely populated place.

He has a keen naturalist's eye, as we can see from his perceptive descriptions of the birds in 'The Path'. Kittiwakes 'scrape' the waves; mallards' necks 'strain' over the bog; and the 'gradual disdain' of the swans is captured. He understands both their movements and their psychology. And his treatment of them is gentle, as evidenced by the verbs used to describe his actions: 'dislodge', 'to nudge', etc. There is a sensitive and perceptive naturalist at work here.

For all the harshness of the scene, Longley is at ease with it. In a primitive and slightly crude way he shares a sense of identity with the people's forebears, who also 'squatted here | This lichened side of the dry-stone wall'. He feels that he is part of the life cycle of the place, part of the process of erosion, as when he notices the effect of his footprints in the strand:

> Linking the dunes to the water's edge,
> Reducing to sand the dry shells, the toe –
> And fingernail parings of the sea.

And he enjoys the atmosphere of serenity and acceptance in 'The Lake', as if he too were one of the 'special visitors'.

Family and the human community are but a shadowy presence here. Ghost-like memories of his children are conjured up ('my voice | Filling the district as I recall their names'), or they are registered merely as footprints in the sand. Images of family domesticity he carries in his head, as one might carry a photograph of loved ones:

> Smoke from our turf fire
> Recalls in the cool air above the lake
> Steam from a kettle, a tablecloth and
> A table she might have already set.

So, in some ways, the image of the poet here is the traditional romantic one of the figure alone in the landscape, communing with nature. Yet this poet's home and family are never far away, a constant presence in his mind. Peter McDonald sees Carrigskeewaun as Longley's home from home and says that here Longley is 'bringing one home into contact with another through naming the elements that are missing. Here, it is the family "home" that is named in the stern solitude of a mountain landscape.'

THEMES

- The poet's appreciation of this western landscape, its elemental harshness and its quiet welcoming beauty, its solitude, its abundance of wildlife, etc.
- An exploration of the relationship between humans and nature: the calm sense of belonging, etc.
- Yet an awareness that humankind is but a tiny part of the process of nature's cycle, helping to dispose of 'the dry shells, the toe | And fingernail parings of the sea.' This generates a sense of philosophical perspective.
- The love of family, children and domesticity that is somehow inspired by this wild place.

THE SIGNIFICANCE OF THE WEST OF IRELAND IN LONGLEY'S POETRY

Longley's preoccupation with the west of Ireland can be traced throughout his poetry. 'Carrigskeewaun' and 'Poteen' are from his second collection, *An Exploded View*, which contains poems from 1968 to 1972. So even as he was focusing on the erupting violence of the times (in such poems as 'Wounds') he was also contemplating an alternative. His attachment to the west grew as a result of long summers spent in County Mayo, and this is evident from Longley's third volume, *Man Lying on a Wall* (1976). And his fifth volume, *The Gorse Fires* (1991), is centrally focused on Carrigskeewaun, which had become his second home.

Critics have interpreted this fascination with the west in various ways. Terence Brown asks: 'Which is the poet's Ireland – Belfast or Mayo?' He believes this relates to the poet's confused sense of national identity, in attempting to be an Ulsterman and an Anglo-Irishman. Brown believes that the problem of confused identity 'can partially be solved in an identification with the Irish landscape'. And he notes how unusual 'Carrigskeewaun' is in Longley's work for the sense it creates of a person 'at ease with himself and his fellows'.

Peter McDonald takes a slightly different approach, regarding the west as an issue of perspective rather than identity. He feels that the west is in fact a way of undoing the settled nature of the poet's identity and that what it does is provide a new sense of perspective, an angle from which home can be reappraised, 'can be reapproached without the encoding of tribal claims to certain territories'.

Gerald Dawe argues that while Longley accepts his northern roots, the ties of family, home, class and country, he is also searching for an alternative, imagined ideal, 'a compensatory order to transcend these'. He says: 'For Longley, the west of Ireland is seen as an embodiment of some kind of alternative life, a fictional life that compensates for certain values and attitudes missing in the real, given, historical world . . . Longley itemises that vision into the simple sights of landscape and nature which, common to the west of Ireland, take on in his work a symbolic potency all of their own.'

What values and attitudes are embodied in 'Carrigskeewaun', and what is symbolised by the landscape? What values are missing from Longley's real, historical world?

Wreaths

Text of poem: New Explorations Anthology page 357

A READING OF THE POEM

In 'Wreaths' Longley deals directly with what is euphemistically described as the 'Troubles'. He describes the violent killings, in graphic detail, in their ordinary, everyday settings: a kitchen, a shop, the roadway. In each case his focus of attention is the human consequences of this violence, the loss of life, the deranged grief of relatives, or the psychological effect on the general population as it forces people to relive memories of family deaths.

'The Civil Servant' was written in memory of Martin McBirney QC, a lawyer and friend who was murdered by the IRA. This poem shows violence invading the heart of domestic life: the kitchen. It is the contrast between the ordinariness and intimacy of the setting and the incongruity of the violence that makes the greatest impact in this poem.

> He was preparing an Ulster fry for breakfast
> When someone walked into the kitchen and shot him . . .
> He lay in his dressing gown and pyjamas
> While they dusted the dresser for fingerprints

The language rhythms too record that incongruity. The prosaic, conversational rhythms of the first line leave us unprepared for the violence of lines 2 and 3. The insignificance of life is recorded. It is regarded as of temporary and symbolic importance only, like the transitory outing of a red carpet, walked on and forgotten:

> They rolled him up like a red carpet and left
> Only a bullet hole in the cutlery drawer;

The emotional control of the narration adds to the strangeness of this piece. The killing is described in a matter-of-fact tone, in the neutral and precise language of a police witness ('A bullet entered his mouth and pierced his skull'). The loss is recorded in cultural terms only ('The books he had read, the music he could play'). The only indication of feeling comes in the disturbed actions of the widow, who 'took a hammer and chisel | And removed the black keys from his piano.' And even that is narrated in measured, controlled language: 'Later his widow . . . and removed . . .' It is this control of feeling that is one of the most chilling aspects of this poem.

Matter-of-fact descriptions and conversational rhythms of language also characterise the narration of 'The Greengrocer', written about a local shopkeeper, Jim Gibson. Yet the tone here is laced with a bleak irony:

> He ran a good shop, and he died
> Serving even the death-dealers
> Who found him busy as usual . . .

The ironic timing of the violence is emphasised. The Christmas wreaths, celebrating a birth, become his burial wreaths and also provide the general title for the pieces. We register the inappropriateness of this death amid the Christmas fare and the exotic fruit ('Dates and chestnuts and tangerines'). It is ironic too that the killing is overtly linked to the Christmas story ('Astrologers or three wise men'). Is there a bitterness towards the powerlessness of religion here?

'The Linen Workers', based on the Bessbrooke sectarian murders, has a more psychological focus, exploring how public political violence impinges on private thoughts and memories. Strangely, it is also the most personal of the three poems, written in the first person and dealing with the poet's personal memories.

The setting for the massacre of the linen workers is once again an ordinary everyday venue: the roadside. Death is seen as the scattering of the personal bric-a-brac of living:

> . . . spectacles,
> Wallets, small change, and a set of dentures:
> Blood, food particles, the bread, the wine.

While some of these images have symbolic value (for example the bread and wine, symbolic of self-sacrifice, renewal and eternal life), it is the set of dentures that resonates in the poet's mind, triggering bizarre memories of his dead father. The effect is surreal: the Christ figure, like some giant hoarding, 'fastened for ever | By his exposed canines to a wintry sky' in a parody of the Crucifixion. The father, once a victim of world-war violence, is disinterred to witness the fruits of violence yet again ('Before I can bury my father once again | I must polish the spectacles . . . And into his dead mouth slip the set of teeth'). The images are of victims, religious and familial. Also we see the ubiquitous nature of violence, stretching through history, erupting in the modern community and reaching into the individual psyche, where it shakes up disturbing past and private memories.

THEMES

- The casual 'ordinariness' of violent death in the community
- The ubiquitous nature of violence, in kitchen, shop or street, in the mind
- Human insignificance in the face of violence ('The Civil Servant')
- The bitterness of unseasonal death ('The Greengrocer')
- The psychological effects of violence, reaching right through people's lives, invading the psyche, interlacing public horror and private memory ('The Linen Workers')
- The ineffectiveness of religion in the face of this onslaught ('The Greengrocer'; 'The Linen Workers').

IMAGERY

For the most part the images consist of background details of domestic living, of insignificant private possessions: an 'Ulster fry', dressing-gown, pyjamas, dresser, cutlery drawer, holly wreaths for Christmas, spectacles, etc. They evoke ordinariness, urban banality, and the insignificance of ordinary lives.

Details of the killings are restrained, devoid of horror or gory detail. They are either rendered in stark simplicity ('A bullet entered his mouth and pierced his skull') or conveyed in general terms ('he died,' 'they massacred'). The impact is always in the consequences, conveyed through the telling details, such as the pathetic list of personal bric-a-brac ('spectacles | Wallets, small change, and a set of dentures'). The surreal images of a gap-toothed Christ and a long-dead bespectacled father convey the psychological disturbance of violence.

TONE

The deadpan, largely unemotional tone of the narration, particularly in 'The Civil Servant' and 'The Greengrocer' (see 'A READING OF THE POEM' above), serves to emphasise the air of unreality and the incongruity of violent death in these everyday settings. 'The Linen Workers' is less controlled. For example, 'massacred' has overtones of horror and revulsion. In this poem there is more evidence of the poetic voice involved in the drama, commenting, not just recording details but interpreting also. 'Blood, food particles' are seen as 'the bread, the wine'.

But Longley does not approach this violence from any sectarian or political point of view, or indeed with any moral attitude. Certainly there is no sympathy for the violence, no attempt to explain or understand the killings. Neither is there outraged condemnation, just a patient recording of the facts. And through these facts, this list of intimate consequences, we see the pointlessness of the violence. Longley's slightly disengaged attitude and neutral tone allow the reader a clear view.

Last Requests

Text of poem: New Explorations Anthology page 360
[*This poem is also prescribed fro Ordinary Level 2005 exam*]

A READING OF THE POEM

This poem focuses on death and once again on the death of his own father. The two parts are complementary, part I dealing with the father's earlier brush with death in the trenches and part II focusing on his actual death-bed scene. Perhaps the earlier scene is meant to serve as a comfort: he could have died so many years before.

The death-bed scene is treated with a mixture of pathos and humour. The sense of separation, the impenetrable distance of death is physically illustrated: 'I . . . Couldn't reach you through the oxygen tent.' The onlooker's feeling of helplessness and inadequacy is recorded in the wry comment by the poet: 'I who brought you peppermints and grapes only'. Yet there is humour occasioned by the speaker's misinterpretation of the father's hand movement. The poet needs to interpret it as a last romantic gesture, a kiss, whereas it signifies the dying man's more prosaic need for nicotine, like the need for that last sacramental cigarette before a battle. Perhaps this can be read as yet another sign of the separation wrought by death: a mental as well as a physical distance from loved ones.

Despite the humour, we are in no doubt of the effect of the scene on the poet. Every detail is etched into his mind: 'the bony fingers that waved to and fro'. The memories carry not only the gesture but the mood of the moment.

> The brand you chose to smoke for forty years
> Thoughtfully, each one like a sacrament.

There is real feeling here behind the façade of wit. The seamier side of war is also adverted to ('Your batman . . . Left you for dead and stole your pocket watch'). Once again Longley views military exploits with a jaundiced eye.

Mayo Monologues – Self-Heal

Text of poem: New Explorations Anthology page 362

CONTEXT OF THE POEM

This is one of the sequence of four poems – 'Brothers', 'Housekeeper', 'Self-Heal' and 'Arrest' – collectively entitled 'Mayo Monologues' from the volume *The Echo Gate* (1979). They deal with the pathetic and flawed relationships of some isolated and lonely people.

A READING OF THE POEM

The poem deals with the tragic consequences of an inherently flawed relationship between the young female narrator, a teacher, and a mentally retarded boy. At first the relationship was one of innocent education, centring on the communication of beauty.

> I wanted to teach him the names of flowers,
> Self-heal and centaury; on the long acre
> Where cattle never graze, bog asphodel.

But it is an unequal pairing, incompatible intellectually and physically, the delicacy of the flowers contrasting strangely with the grotesque figure of the boy-man whose 'skull seemed to be hammered like a wedge | Into his shoulders, and his back was hunched, | Which gave him an almost scholarly air.'

The intellectual frustration is described in the natural image of the butterfly:

> Each name would hover above its flower
> like a butterfly unable to alight.

But the only delight he can comprehend and reach for is sexual. A community taboo is broken, and enormous and brutal consequences, out of all proportion to the deed, fall on him with the weight of a Greek tragedy, souring beauty and stunting humanity further. The savage treatment meted out to him unleashes a terrible savagery within himself.

THEMES

- A view of the dark undercurrents in rural society, involving sullied innocence, thwarted sexuality, ignorance and prejudice, and the crude violence and brutality just beneath the surface
- Insensitive treatment of the mentally retarded
- The almost insignificant origins of tragedy.

A POEM OF PRIMITIVE ENERGIES

This poem is highly charged with elemental human passions. The female narrator, exhibiting a dangerous innocence, was taking risks. Though innocent of any complicity, she is sensitive enough to question her motivation –

> Could I love someone so gone in the head
> And, as they say, was I leading him on?

– and, discounting what was a reasonable reaction on her part, she does not completely exonerate herself from her role in precipitating the consequences:

> I wasn't frightened; and still I don't know why,
> But I ran from him in tears to tell them.

So there is a traumatic, sexually charged moment, a sense of sullied innocence, and a hint of regret that perhaps things could have been handled differently.

We are confronted with the basic animal nature of humankind, lurking just beneath the surface; the unexpected sexual advance is later represented in animal imagery: 'I might have been the cow . . . and he the ram'. The primitive animal brutality, coupled with ignorance and lack of any tolerant insight into this condition, is shocking.

> He was flogged with a blackthorn, then tethered
> In the hayfield.

The belief that violence is effective begets a cycle of wanton cruelty: the cow's tail docked with shears and 'The ram tangled in barbed wire | That he stoned to death when they set him free.' And one cannot help but be overawed by the disproportionate nature of the consequences, as if one were viewing a world out of control.

As a view of the west of Ireland

The poem paints an unflattering picture of the dark undercurrents, the barely tamed savagery, the pain of ignorance and prejudice just beneath the surface of rural society.

Tone

Sympathy, revulsion and anger all swirl beneath the surface of this poem. Yet all feelings are controlled by Longley's matter-of-fact descriptions, by the quiet, conversational rhythms of the language and the balanced point of view of the narrator. The narrator herself is the victim of sexual advances, yet in many ways she is a detached and sympathetic observer. She both questions her own motives and understands the actions of the retarded man. So we are drawn in to sympathise with both parties. We understand her sense of regret and her bewilderment at it all: 'and still I don't know why, | But I ran . . .' We cannot help but be revolted by the brutality, narrated in matter-of-fact, unadorned language: 'He was flogged . . . tethered . . . dock with shears . . . the ram tangled . . . he stoned to death . . .'

But overall we register the deep irony of these events. A worthy desire to educate, enlighten and beautify has created instead a dark, brutal monster. And we note the irony of the title: the plant produces no healing properties on this occasion; there are no immortal flowers for his mind, or indeed for hers.

Longley relates these dark deeds not with condemnation and bitterness but with a quiet understanding that this is how things are.

RELEVANCE TO NORTHERN IRELAND?

Séamus Heaney's comment on this poem follows a psychological approach in Jungian terms and argues that poetry is the symbolic resolution of lived and felt conflict. He accepts that Longley had no deliberate notion of writing a poem relevant to the 'Troubles'; yet he suggests that the innocent and yet not quite detached female voice in the poem might be the voice of poetry, understanding the victim and the violence and embellishing it with her vision. This is the role of the poet in a violent society; this is how the poet deals with the conflict.

> So she might be an analogue for the action of the poetic imagination as we have been considering it: by comprehending and expressing the violent reactions of the victim in relation to the violent mores of the community, by taking all this into herself and embalming it with flowers and memory, she turns a dirty deed into a vision of reality.

The action of poetry, he says,

> is a self-healing process, neither deliberately provocative nor culpably detached.

An Amish Rug

Text of poem: New Explorations Anthology page 364

[*Note: This poem is also prescribed for Ordinary Level 2005 exam*]

A READING OF THE POEM

The Amish rug, a gift from the speaker to his lover, carries with it his memories of that culture and community and so enriches the poet's life and love.

The Amish experience of the world is deliberately limited ('a one-room schoolhouse') and calls for simplicity and lack of adornment ('as if . . . our clothes were black, our underclothes black'). Mechanisation and industrialisation are avoided ('boy behind the harrow,' etc.) and marriage is signified by its religious element and its simplicity rather than any ostentation ('Marriage a horse and buggy going to church'). Children are a natural, elemental part of the landscape ('silhouettes in a snowy field'). The predominant black-and-white colouring emphasises the simplicity of the culture and the uncompromising nature of the moral values.

The rug, symbol of cultural encounter, and very different from indigenous Amish artefacts, yet transmits the Amish values of naturalness and religious belief. Its colours are described in images from nature, 'cantaloupe and cherry'. Depending on its placing in the room it can be either 'a cathedral window' or 'a flowerbed'. The unspoken wish seems to be that it may bring something of its natural beauty into their lives.

This is a love poem of great charm and elegance. The lover's gift is a simple patchwork quilt. The lovers' desire is for a simple life and uninhibited naturalness in their relationship:

> So that whenever we undress for sleep or love
> We shall step over it as over a flowerbed.

Laertes
Text of poem: New Explorations Anthology page 366

BACKGROUND NOTE

This poem is based on an episode from Homer's Greek epic poem 'The Odyssey'. Odysseus, king of the island of Ithaca and one of the Greek heroes of the Trojan war, was for ten years prevented from returning home, blown hither and thither by the storms of Poseidon. Many in Ithaca presumed him dead. Suitors seeking to marry his faithful wife, Penelope, gathered at his palace and wasted his estate in continuous feasting.

Odysseus returned, disguised to all at first except to his son, Telemachus, and killed all the suitors in a great and bloody slaughter. As these were the sons of local princes and prominent nobles, there were likely to be repercussions. Before facing these, Odysseus slipped out to the hill country to visit his father, Laertes, who had retired to his vineyards. And this is where the poem is set.

Longley rendered a number of episodes from the *Odyssey* in a fairly free translation, as he explained in the notes with *Gorse Fires*:

> In differing proportions and with varying degrees of high-handedness but always, I hope, with reverence, I have in seven of these poems combined free translation from Homer's 'Odyssey' with original lines.

A READING OF THE POEM

Here Longley returns to his recurring theme of father–son relationships, this time in the classical context of Homer's *Odyssey*. The poem offers interesting psychological insights into the roles people fulfil in a relationship and how these roles alter over time. Odysseus's memories of his childhood centre on a dependent, persistently questioning child–parent relationship, 'traipsing after his father | And asking for everything he saw'. Despite the fact that he now returns as the conquering hero, his first instinct is to revert to his child role and run to the parent for comfort, blurting out his tale. But now the roles have been reversed. The father is now a fragile old man ('So old and pathetic'), and the erstwhile child has become the protector and comforter:

> Who drew the old man fainting to his breast and held him there
> And cradled like driftwood the bones of his dwindling father.

Another interesting aspect of the encounter is the son's need to be recognised. The dramatic delaying tactic practised by Odysseus – the drawing out of the old man to see if he remembered – may seem pointlessly cruel to a modern reader. 'So he waited for images . . . Until Laertes recognised his son'. But, psychologically, Odysseus seems to need to be recognised, at least in the outward physical aspect. Perhaps this could be read at a deeper level also and seen to refer to the son's need for a father's recognition of his deeds, his achievements, his independent separate self. In Homer's original version, as we can see from the extract, old Laertes is made to undergo a more formal, rigorous testing, and so the recognition becomes highly significant.

The father–son relationship in this poem, as in the other Longley poems on the same theme, is emotional and tender:

> Odysseus sobbed in the shade of a pear-tree for his father
> So old and pathetic that all he wanted then and there
> Was to kiss him and hug him and blurt out the whole story,

The need for comfort, for emotional closeness, for recognition, for protection and the joy of meeting are at the heart of this father–son relationship.

The poem also makes a statement about home. Home here is a place of familial love, psychological and emotional support and affirmation. But, taking the broader context of the Homeric allusion into account, we cannot evade the awareness that home is also a place of strife and intrigue, civil wars and bloody retribution. And we can hardly avoid drawing parallels between the Homeric world of Ithaca and Northern Ireland. Perhaps this is the greatest value of the allusion. It allows Longley to contemplate the perplexing realities of background, obliquely and from a distance.

Odyssey

BOOK 24 (EXTRACT)

(Translated by E.V. Rieu)

> When they reached the spot, Odysseus said to Telemachus and his men: 'Go into the main building now and make haste to kill the best pig you can find

for our midday meal. Meanwhile I shall try an experiment with my father, to find out whether he will remember me and realise who it is when he sees me, or fail to know me after so long an absence.'

As he spoke, he handed his weapons of war to the servants, who then went straight into the house, while Odysseus moved off towards the luxuriant vineyard, intent on his experiment. As he made his way down into the great orchard he fell in neither with Dolius nor with any of the serfs or Dolius' sons, who had all gone with the old man at their head to gather stones for the vineyard wall. Thus he found his father alone on the vineyard terrace digging round a plant. He was wearing a filthy, patched and disreputable tunic, a pair of stitched leather gaiters strapped round his shins to protect them from scratches, and gloves to save his hands from the brambles; while to crown all, and by way of emphasising his misery, he had a hat of goatskin on his head. When the gallant Odysseus saw how old and worn his father looked and realised how miserable he was, he halted under a tall pear-tree and the tears came into his eyes. Nor could he make up his mind at once whether to hug and kiss his father, and tell him the whole story of his own return to Ithaca, or first to question him and find out what he thought. In the end he decided to start assuming a brusque manner in order to draw the old man out, and with this purpose in view he now went straight up to his father.

Laertes was still hoeing round his plant with his head down, as his famous son came up and accosted him.

'Old man,' said Odysseus, 'you have everything so tidy here that I can see there is little about gardening that you do not know. There is nothing, not a green thing in the whole enclosure, not a fig, olive, vine, pear or vegetable bed that does not show signs of your care. On the other hand I cannot help remarking, I hope without offence, that you don't look after yourself very well. In fact, what with your squalor and your wretched clothes, old age has hit you very hard. Yet it can't be on account of any laziness that your master neglects you, nor is there anything in your build and size to suggest the slave. You look more like a man of royal blood, the sort of person who enjoys the privilege of age, and sleeps on a soft bed when he has had his bath and dined. However, tell me whose serf you are. And whose is this garden you look after? The truth, if you please. And there's another point you can clear up for me. Am I really in Ithaca? A fellow I met on my way up here just now assured me that I was. But he was not very intelligent, for he wouldn't deign to answer me properly or listen to what I said, when I mentioned a friend of mine and asked him whether he was still in the land of the living or dead and gone by now. You shall learn about this friend yourself if you pay attention to what I say. Some time ago in my own country I befriended a stranger who turned up at our place and proved the most attractive visitor I have ever entertained from abroad. He said he was an Ithacan, and that Arceisius' son Laertes was his father. I took him in, made him thoroughly welcome and gave him every hospitality that my rich house could afford, including presents worthy of his rank. Seven talents of wrought gold he had from me, a solid silver wine-bowl with a floral design, twelve single-folded cloaks, twelve rugs, twelve splendid mantles and as many tunics too, and besides all this, four women as skilled in fine handicraft as they were good to look at. I let him choose them for himself.'

'Sir,' said his father to Odysseus, with tears on his cheeks, 'I can assure you that you're in the place you asked for but it's in the hands of rogues and criminals. The gifts you lavished on your friend were given in vain, though had you found him alive in Ithaca he would never have let you go before he had made you an ample return in presents and hospitality, as is right when such an example has been set. But pray tell me exactly how long ago it was that you befriended the unfortunate man, for the guest of yours was my unhappy son – if ever I had one – my son, who far from friends and home has been devoured by fishes in the sea or fallen prey, maybe, to the wild beasts and birds on land. Dead people have their dues, but not Odysseus. We had no chance, we two that brought him into the world, to wrap his body up and wail for him, nor had his richly dowered wife, constant Penelope, the chance to close her husband's eyes and give him on his bier the seemly tribute of a dirge.

'But you have made me curious about yourself. Who are you, sir? What is your native town? And where might she be moored, the good ship that brought you here with your gallant crew? Or were you travelling as a passenger on someone else's ship, which landed you and sailed away?'

'I am quite willing,' said the resourceful Odysseus, 'to tell you all you wish to know. I come from Alybas. My home is in the palace there, for my father is King Apheidas, Polypemon's son. My own name is Eperitus. I had no intention of putting in here when I left Sicania but had the misfortune to be driven out of my course, and my ship is riding yonder by the open coast some way from the port. As for Odysseus, it is four years and more since he bade me farewell and left my country – to fall on evil days, it seems. And yet the omens when he left were good: birds on the right, which pleased me as I said goodbye, and cheered him as he started out. We both had every hope that we should meet again as host and guest and give each other splendid gifts.'

When Laertes heard this, he sank into the black depths of despair. Groaning heavily, he picked the black dust up in both his hands and poured it onto the grey hairs of his head. Odysseus' heart was stirred, and suddenly, as he watched his dear father, poignant compassion forced its way through his nostrils. He rushed forward, flung his arms round his neck and kissed him. 'Father,' he cried, 'here I am, the very man you asked about, home in my own land after nineteen years. But this is no time for tears and lamentation. For I have news to tell you, and heaven knows there is need for haste. I have killed the gang of suitors in our palace. I have paid them out for their insulting gibes and all their crimes.'

Laertes answered him: 'If you that have come here are indeed my son Odysseus, give me some definite proof to make me sure.'

Odysseus was ready for this. 'To begin with,' he said, 'cast your eye on this scar, where I was wounded by the white tusk of a boar when I went to Parnassus. You and my mother had sent me to my grandfather Autolycus, to fetch the gifts he solemnly promised me when he came to visit us. Then again, I can tell you all the trees you gave me one day on this garden terrace. I was only a little boy at the time, trotting after you through the orchard, begging for this and that, and as we wound our way through these very trees you told me all their names. You gave me thirteen pear trees, ten apple, forty fig trees, and at the same time you pointed out the fifty rows of vines that were to be mine. Each ripened at a different time, so that the bunches on them were at various stages when the branches felt their weight under the summer skies.'

Laertes realised at once that Odysseus' evidence had proved his claim. With trembling knees and bursting heart he flung his arms round the neck of his beloved son, and stalwart Odysseus caught him fainting to his breast. The first words he uttered as he rallied and his consciousness returned were in reply to the news his son had given him. 'By Father Zeus,' he cried, 'you gods are still in your heaven if those suitors have really paid the price for their iniquitous presumption! But I have horrible fear now that the whole forces of Ithaca will soon be on us here, and that they will send urgent messages for help to every town in Cephallenia.'

'Have no fear,' said his resourceful son, 'and don't trouble your head about that; but come with me to the farmhouse here by the orchard, where I sent on Telemachus with the cowman and swineherd to prepare a meal as quickly as they could.'

Ceasefire
Text of poem: New Explorations Anthology page 367

Background note
This poem was first published in the *Irish Times* on 3 September 1994, two days after an IRA ceasefire was announced. It is another 'free translation' of an episode from Homer's classic poem *The Iliad*, which tells the story of Troy's

siege by the Greeks. *The Iliad* begins in the tenth year of the Trojan conflict and ends with the burial of Hector, shortly after this episode.

During the conflict, Achilles sulked in his tent and refused to fight, because of a dispute with Agamemnon over a woman. However, with the Greeks in danger of being routed by Hector, Achilles allowed his close friend Patroclus to borrow his armour and his men to defend the Greek ships. But Patroclus was killed by Hector. In a fit of grief, rage and guilt, Achilles went back to the battle and after great slaughter pushed the Trojans back and killed Hector. In a frenzy of vengeance he dragged Hector's body in the dust behind his chariot, round the walls of Troy, and for eleven days thereafter round the tomb of Patroclus. Finally, old King Priam, prompted by the gods, came to the Greek camp bearing a huge ransom to redeem the body. He clasped the knees and kissed the hands of Achilles, urging him to remember his own father of similar age and also separated from his son.

You can read a translation of the original scene below.

THEMES

This poem deals with the aftermath of war. It explores the sadness of mourning, the feelings of those left behind to pick up the pieces, the emotions of the victors as well as the bereaved. It faces squarely the compromises people make when necessary, the self-abasement that even proud people will suffer for love and grief. And it signals the building of a reconciliation of a sort. So it relates quite aptly to the needs of a post-conflict Northern Ireland. Indeed, Longley himself has said that he kept Gordon Wilson's face as Priam in front of him while he wrote this poem.

VISUAL GESTURES

This dramatic episode is built around extravagant visual gestures: the kneeling; kissing hands; pushing the old king gently away. The set-piece meal also acts as a visual tableau, performed with eyes and looks, more reminiscent of a romantic scene than of a meal between deadly enemies. Much of the poignancy of this poem is communicated through gestures and looks.

IMAGERY

The most exciting thing about the imagery is the unusual nature of the similes. 'Wrapped like a present' is shockingly inappropriate. Yet the very lightheartedness of that image seems to heighten the pathos of the scene, the awfulness of that old man's burden, just as an insensitive comment would increase the sympathy felt in such a situation. The hint of eroticism in 'To stare at each other's beauty as lovers might' is equally inappropriate for the recently mortal enemies. Indeed the reversal of roles in the image of the king's self-abasement – on his knees, kissing the hand of his son's killer – is visually shocking.

All this disturbing imagery punctures the heroic concept of war and conveys something of the true discomfort of the moment, the uncertainty and tension of this scene.

The Iliad

BOOK 24 (EXTRACT)

(Translated by Robert Eagles.)

Priam found the warrior there inside . . .
many captains sitting some way off, but two,
veteran Automedon and the fine fighter Alcimus,
were busy serving him. He had just finished dinner,
eating, drinking, and the table still stood near.
The majestic King of Troy slipped past the rest
and kneeling down beside Achilles, clasped his knees
and kissed his hands, those terrible, man-killing hands
that had slaughtered Priam's many sons in battle.
Awesome – as when the grip of madness seizes one
who murders a man in his own fatherland and flees
abroad to foreign shores, to a wealthy, noble host,
and a sense of marvel runs through all who see him –
so Achilles marvelled, beholding majestic Priam.
His men marvelled too, trading startled glances.
But Priam prayed his heart out to Achilles:
'Remember your own father, great godlike Achilles –
as old as I am, past the threshold of deadly old age!
No doubt the countrymen round about him plague him now,
with no-one there to defend him, beat away disaster.
No-one – but at least he hears you're still alive
and his old heart rejoices, hopes rising, day by day,
to see his beloved son come sailing home from Troy.
But I – dear god, my life so cursed by fate . . .
I fathered hero sons in the wide realm of Troy
and now not a single one is left, I tell you.
Fifty sons I had when the sons of Achaea came,
nineteen born to me from a single mother's womb
and the rest by other women in the palace. Many,
most of them violent Ares cut the knees from under,

But one, one was left to me, to guard my walls, my people –
the one you killed the other day, defending his fatherland,
my Hector! It's all for him I've come to the ships now,
to win him back from you – I bring a priceless ransom.
Revere the gods, Achilles! Pity me in my own right,
remember your own father! I deserve more pity . . .
I have endured what no-one on earth has ever done before –
I put to my lips the hands of the man who killed my son.'

Those words stirred within Achilles a deep desire
to grieve for his own father. Taking the old man's hand
he gently moved him back. And overpowered by memory
both men gave way to grief. Priam wept freely
for man-killing Hector, throbbing, crouching
before Achilles' feet as Achilles wept himself,
now for his father, now for Patroclus once again,
and their sobbing rose and fell throughout the house.
Then, when brilliant Achilles had his fill of tears
and the longing for it had left his mind and body,
he rose from his seat, raised the old man by the hand
and filled with pity now for his grey head and grey beard,
he spoke out winging words, flying straight to the heart:
'Poor man, how much you've borne – pain to break the spirit!
What daring brought you down to the ships, all alone,
to face the glance of the man who killed your sons,
so many fine brave boys? You have a heart of iron.
Come, please, sit down on this chair here' . . .
But the old and noble Priam protested strongly:
'Don't make me sit on a chair, Achilles, Prince,
not while Hector lies uncared for in your camp!
Give him back to me, now, no more delay –
I must see my son with my own eyes.
Accept the ransom I bring you, a king's ransom!
Enjoy it, all of it – return to your own native land,
safe and sound . . . since now you've spared my life.'

A dark glance – and the headstrong runner answered,
'No more, old man, don't tempt my wrath, not now!
My own mind's made up to give you back your son.
A messenger brought me word from Zeus – my mother,
Thetis who bore me, the Old Man of the Sea's daughter.
And what's more, I can see through you, Priam –

no hiding the fact from me: one of the gods
has led you down to Achaea's fast ships.
No man alive, not even a rugged young fighter,
would dare to venture into our camp. Never –
how could he slip past the sentries unchallenged?
Or shoot back the bolt of my gates with so much ease?
So don't anger me now. Don't stir my raging heart still more.
Or under my own roof I may not spare your life, old man –
suppliant that you are – may break the laws of Zeus!'

The old man was terrified. He obeyed the order.
But Achilles bounded out of doors like a lion –
not alone but flanked by his two aides-in-arms,
veteran Automedon and Alcimus, steady comrades,
Achilles' favourites next to the dead Patroclus.
They loosed from harness the horses and the mules,
they led the herald in, the old king's crier,
and sat him down on a bench. From the polished wagon
they lifted the priceless ransom brought for Hector's corpse
but they left behind two capes and a finely woven shirt
to shroud the body well when Priam bore him home.
Then Achilles called the serving-women out:
'Bathe and anoint the body –
bear it aside first. Priam must not see his son.'
He feared that, overwhelmed by the sight of Hector,
wild with grief, Priam might let his anger flare
and Achilles might fly into fresh rage himself,
cut the old man down and break the laws of Zeus.
So when the maids had bathed and anointed the body
sleek with olive oil and wrapped it round and round
in a braided battle-shirt and handsome battle-cape,
then Achilles lifted Hector up in his own arms
and laid him down on a bier, and comrades helped him
raise the bier and body onto the sturdy wagon . . .
Then with a groan he called his dear friend by name:
'Feel no anger at me, Patroclus, if you learn –
even there in the House of Death – I let his father
have Prince Hector back. He gave me worthy ransom
and you shall have your share from me, as always,
your fitting, lordly share.'
                              So he vowed

and brilliant Achilles strode back to his shelter,
sat down on the well-carved chair that he had left,
at the far wall of the room, leaned toward Priam
and firmly spoke the words the king had come to hear:
'Your son is now set free, old man, as you requested.
Hector lies in state. With the first light of day
you will see for yourself as you convey him home.
Now, at last, let us turn our thoughts to supper' . . .

They reached out for the good things that lay at hand
and when they had put aside desire for food and drink
Priam the son of Dardanus gazed at Achilles, marvelling
now at the man's beauty, his magnificent build –
face-to-face he seemed a deathless god . . .
and Achilles gazed and marvelled at Dardan Priam,
beholding his noble looks, listening to his words.
But once they'd had their fill of gazing at each other,
the old majestic Priam broke the silence first:
'Put me to bed quickly, Achilles, Prince.
Time to rest, to enjoy the sweet relief of sleep.
Not once have my eyes closed shut beneath my lids
from the day my son went down beneath your hands . . .
day and night I groan, brooding over the countless griefs,
grovelling in the dung that fills my walled-in court.
But now, at long last, I have tasted food again
and let some glistening wine go down my throat.
Before this hour I had tasted nothing' . . .

Some themes and issues in the poetry of Michael Longley

NOTE 1

For the purpose of acquiring an overview, it might be useful to re-read the poems
in thematic groupings rather than in chronological order. For example:

(1) 'Wounds', 'Last Request' and 'Laertes' deal with the poet's father and
thereby with his sense of his own identity and family background.

(2) 'An Amish Rug' features intimate love and home and family values and
contributes to our understanding of the poet and his identity.

(3) 'Wreaths', 'Wounds' and 'Ceasefire' deal with violence, past and present,
with violent myths, official war, and the present 'Troubles'.

(4) 'Carrigskeewaun', 'Poteen', 'Badger' and 'Self-Heal' feature the Mayo landscape, Longley's second home and alternative culture.

NOTE 2

Consider each general point made, and return to the relevant poems for supporting evidence and quotation. If you disagree, make your argument with supporting reference also. Either way, build up a knowledge of the poetic detail. Make notes for yourself, perhaps in spider-diagram form.

EXPLORATION OF IDENTITY: POEMS OF SELF-DEFINITION

We can interpret a number of the poems in this selection as pieces exploring the poet's own background, environment, and values. These areas are not covered in any broad and systematic way, but selected subjects serve as anchor points of his identity.

- Family identity is anchored on the figure of his father in these poems. Acknowledgment of his soldier father helps clarify his own identity. As the critic Edna Longley summarised it, 'The father focuses questions of belonging rather than longing: an Englishman who fought twice for his country.'
- Honouring and remembering the dead is a part of this identity: see 'Last Rites', 'Wounds' and 'Laertes'. (The father–son relationship is examined separately, page 304).
- The violent society also is part of that identity: see 'Wounds' and 'Wreaths'.
- Family values, intimate love and a yearning for simplicity are part of this tapestry of identity: see 'An Amish Rug'.
- An alternative culture, the native Irish identity, is explored in 'Poteen', with its emphasis on the rebel race memory: see the critical commentary of 'Wounds' (pages 279–82) for a discussion of conflicting identities.

VIOLENCE

- A stark treatment of violence in its ordinary, everyday reality: see 'Wreaths'.
- The pervasive nature of violence in society; death invades the home: see 'The Civil Servant' and 'The Greengrocer'; it even invades the psyche: see 'The Linen Workers'.
- Human insignificance and powerlessness in the face of this violence: see 'Wreaths' and 'Wounds'.
- The 'Troubles' are dealt with against a background of wars and other human conflicts; this gives a sense of perspective to present-day violence: see 'Wounds', 'Wreaths', and 'Last Request'. 'He is able to analogise between different kinds and theatres of human conflict in a personal and historically informed and mediated treatment of the troubles' (Peacock).

- Longley presents the pictures of violence in a neutral, non-partisan way and with a slight air of detachment. He concentrates on presenting detailed pictures rather than conveying emotions: see 'Wounds' and 'Wreaths'.
- Examine what Longley himself has to say (in *Tuppenny Stung*) about the relationship between a poet and the 'Troubles':

> I find offensive the notion that what we inadequately call 'the Troubles' might provide inspiration for artists; and that in some weird *quid pro quo* the arts might provide solace for grief and anguish. Twenty years ago I wrote in Causeway: 'Too many critics seem to expect a harvest of paintings, poems, plays and novels to drop from the twisted branches of civil discord. They fail to realise that the artist needs time in which to allow the raw material of experience to settle to an imaginative depth where he can transform it . . . He is not some sort of super-journalist commenting with unflattering spontaneity on events immediately after they have happened. Rather, as Wilfred Owen stated fifty years ago, it is the artist's duty to warn, to be tuned in before anyone else to the implications of a situation.'
>
> Ten years later I wrote for the Poetry Book Society about what I was trying to do in my fourth collection, The Echo Gate: 'As an Ulsterman I realise that this may sound like fiddling while Rome burns. So I would insist that poetry is a normal human activity, its proper concern all of the things that happen to people. Though the poet's first duty must be to his imagination, he has other obligations: and not just as a citizen. He would be inhuman if he did not respond to tragic events in his own community, and a poor artist if he did not seek to endorse that response imaginatively. But if his imagination fails him, the result will be a dangerous impertinence. In the context of political violence the deployment of words at their most precise and most suggestive remains one of the few antidotes to death-dealing dishonesty.']

OTHER CONFLICTS

- War: he deals with the seamier side of war, the grave-robbing, anti-heroic view in 'Last Request'; see also 'Ceasefire'.
- Violence in society: see 'Self-Heal'.

THE WEST OF IRELAND

- A different landscape, another ethos, alternative values
- Is he claiming kinship with an alternative national identity, as in 'Poteen'; merely fleeing home; or finding a good place of perspective from which to look north? See the critical commentary on 'Carrigskeewaun'.

- Identifying with the Irish landscape? See 'Carrigskeewaun'. 'The sense of a man at ease with himself and his fellows' (Brown)
- The sheer enjoyment of nature, feeling part of the process: see 'Carrigskeewaun'.
- A genuine naturalist's pleasure, the preoccupation with creatures: see 'Badger'.
- The lonely, isolated nature of his western experience, the absence of community, family, and people: see 'Carrigskeewaun'.
- Not a romantic view of the west; he records the harshness, the pain, the violence and the ignorance as well as the beauty: see 'Badger', 'Carrigskeewaun', and 'Self-heal'.
- Again the precise description, the keen eye for detail: see 'Carrigskeewaun', 'Badger'.
- A view of the west as a place of compensatory values: 'a community of realisable values that are personally authentic and yet generally available, such as there seems to be present in nature: particularly in the redemptive landscapes of the west of Ireland' (Dawe).

THE FATHER FIGURE
- Honouring and acknowledging the dead is part of the process of self-definition: see 'Wounds' and 'Last Requests'.
- But Longley seems preoccupied with the father's dying, his almost-dying in the trenches and then his actual death: see 'Last Requests' and 'Wounds'. Then his psychological disinterment happens in 'The Linen Workers'. Is this becoming a fixation?
- Images of his father are of a frail old man, such as in 'Laertes' and 'Ceasefire', or focus on his teeth and glasses, images of his imperfection: see 'The Linen Workers'. But they are of a man with endearing human frailties, such as the cigarette addiction. And he has a sense of humour: see 'Wounds'.
- Intimacy of the father–son relationship: see the imagery of 'Wounds': 'I touched his hand, his thin head I touched.'
- Interesting reversal of father–son roles in 'Laertes': the hero slipping back into the child's role, the adult still needing recognition or affirmation from the father.
- A father's love and the lengths to which he will go to reclaim a son are evident in 'Ceasefire'.

THE ELUSIVE 'HOME' IN LONGLEY'S POETRY
- Very few concrete images of home feature in these poems. A bedroom features in an 'An Amish Rug'.

- The father figure, used by the poet to define his identity, is never pictured at home but only in the trenches, in his grave, in the hospital bed: see 'Wounds' and 'Last Requests'.
- Carrigskeewaun is the poet's home from home, yet it produces no concrete home, merely an imagined image: 'Recalls . . . a tablecloth and | A table she might have already set.'
- The passages from Homer that struck a chord with Longley are about a man longing for home, prevented for years from returning and on his return finding it taken over by others.

THE SENSE OF PERSPECTIVE IN LONGLEY'S POETRY

- Peacock talks of Longley's ability to look beyond the immediate issues of his own society and personal circumstances to other historical times and literary traditions. Notice the range of settings and times: present-day Ulster; the west of Ireland; the trenches in Europe, 1914–18; the classical Greece of Homer. The result is 'a catholicity of culture and political outlook which fosters objectivity, non-partisan human sympathy and historically informed understanding' (Peacock).
- The past and present are placed in juxtaposition to achieve a sense of perspective: violence in the First World War and present-day Belfast; the classical past of Ithaca has parallels with modern Ulster ('Laertes' and 'Ceasefire').
- Is present-day violence dingier? Or is all killing pointless?
- Past and present, life and death are no longer distinct: the dead father is ever present in 'The Linen Workers'.

A GENERALLY UNROMANTIC VIEW OF LIFE

- Dominated by war and violence: see 'Wounds', 'Last Requests', 'Wreaths', and 'Ceasefire'.
- Country life is rendered in all its realistic harshness ('Carrigskeewaun'), its brutality and pain ('Badger'), its ignorance and prejudice ('Self-Heal').
- The exception in this selection is 'An Amish Rug', with its yearning for simple values and loving intimacy.

YET THERE IS SYMPATHY IN HIS POETRY

- For the human condition: see 'Self-Heal'
- For grieving parents and dead heroes: see 'Ceasefire'
- For nature's creatures: see 'Badger'
- For victims of violence, ancient and modern: see 'Wounds' and 'Ceasefire'.

Style and technique: some points

FIRST-PERSON NARRATIVE

- The personal voice lends an air of intimacy to many of the poems: see 'Self-Heal', 'Carrigskeewaun', and 'An Amish Rug'.
- He uses a female voice in 'Self-Heal'.
- There is a strong autobiographical element in some of the poems: see 'Last Requests' and 'Wounds'.

DETAILED DESCRIPTIONS

- The use of precise detail creates the realism, whether dealing with violence or the beauties of nature: see 'Wreaths' and 'Carrigskeewaun'.
- Longley has an eye for incongruous detail. Often the point of the poem is made through this visual style rather than through any explicit comment: see 'Wounds' and 'Ceasefire'. For example, he views violence in the context of world wars and other violent contexts, and he views love in the context of the Amish culture.

TONE

- The tone is unemotional for the most part, neutral and slightly detached: see 'Wreaths'.
- The concentration is on precise, matter-of-fact descriptions, objectively rendered: see 'Wreaths' and 'Self-Heal'.
- Yet the tone is not callous; he is full of sympathy for the human condition: see 'Self-Heal'.
- The indications of emotion occur in the poems dealing with his father: see 'Wounds' and 'Last Requests'.
- The balanced tone is achieved through this wide perspective he takes up. For example, he views violence in the context of world wars and other violent contexts, and he views love in the context of the Amish culture: see 'Wounds' and 'An Amish Rug'.

INDIRECT TECHNIQUE

- He approaches subjects obliquely at times: for example, he uses his father's war experience to forge a perspective on Northern violence: see 'Wounds'. Or he uses classical Greek poetry to explore the psychological and emotional relationship with his father: see 'Laertes' and 'Ceasefire'.
- This attempt at contrast and comparison is sometimes reflected in the structuring of the poem in two halves, resonating off each other: see 'Wounds'.

SHAPE

- Shape and form are important in Longley's poems. See, for example, the thin, longish poem 'Poteen', resembling a tube; the rectangular picture-postcard sections of 'Carrigskeewaun'; or the rock-like, unbeautiful oblong of 'Self-Heal', immovable as ignorance. Explore the relationship between shape and meaning in the poems.

Forging a personal understanding of Longley's poetry

1. Which poems do you remember most sharply?
2. Which images have remained in your mind?
3. Choose any poem of Longley's. Place yourself in the scene; view it with the poet's eye. What do you see, hear, smell, etc.? How are you feeling? Why write that poem?
4. What are the poet's main preoccupations? What does he love, hate, fear, etc.? What interests him?
5. What do you discover about the personality of the poet? What do you think are his attitudes to life?
6. What does he contribute to your understanding of Ireland and of human nature?
7. What would you like to ask him?
8. What do you notice that is distinctive about the way he writes?
9. Compare his work with that of Séamus Heaney. What similarities and differences do you notice with regard to themes and styles of writing?
10. Why read Michael Longley?

Questions

1. Outline the main issues dealt with in this selection of Longley's poetry.
2. 'Violent events are seen in all the pathos of their everyday settings' (Peacock). Would you agree?
3. 'Longley views all military exploits with a jaundiced eye.' Comment on this statement, with reference to at least two poems from the selection.
4. 'The truth of human relationships is an important issue in the poetry of Michael Longley.' Comment on this aspect of his poetry.
5. 'One of the strengths of Longley's poetry is its descriptive detail.' Examine this element of his style, with particular reference to at least two of the poems.
6. Examine the treatment of death in the poetry of Michael Longley.
7. 'The west of Ireland is seen as the embodiment of some kind of alternative life' (Dawe). What aspects of this alternative life does Longley deal with in the poems you have read?

Michael Longley: writings

No Continuing City, London: Macmillan 1969.
An Exploded View, London: Victor Gollancz 1973.
Man Lying on a Wall, London: Victor Gollancz 1976.
The Echo Gate, London: Secker and Warburg 1979.
Poems, 1963–1983, London: Secker and Warburg 1991.
Gorse Fires, London: Secker and Warburg 1991.
Tuppenny Stung: Autobiographical Chapters, Belfast: Lagan Press 1994.
The Ghost Orchid, London: Jonathan Cape 1995.

Bibliography

Allen, Michael, 'Rhythm and development in Michael Longley's earlier poetry' in *Contemporary Irish Poetry: A Collection of Critical Essays*, edited by Elmer Andrews, London: Macmillan 1992.

Brown, Terence, *Northern Voices: Poets from Ulster*, Dublin: Gill and Macmillan 1975.

Craig, Patricia, 'History and retrieval in contemporary Northern Irish poetry' in *Contemporary Irish Poetry: A Collection of Critical Essays*, edited by Elmer Andrews, London: Macmillan 1992.

Dawe, Gerald, *Against Piety: Essays in Irish Poetry*, Belfast: Lagan Press 1995.

Eagles, Robert (translator), *Homer: The Iliad*, New York: Viking Penguin 1990.

Heaney, Séamus, 'Place and Displacement: Reflections on Some Recent Poetry from Northern Ireland' (first Pete Laver Memorial Lecture, Grasmere, 1984) in *Contemporary Irish Poetry: A Collection of Critical Essays*, edited by Elmer Andrews, London: Macmillan 1992.

McDonald, Peter, 'Michael Longley's homes' in *The Chosen Ground: Essays on the Contemporary Poetry of Northern Ireland*, edited by Neil Corcoran, London: Seren Books 1992.

Parker, Michael, 'Priest of the masses' [a review of Longley's Poems, 1936–83], *Honest Ulsterman*, no. 79, autumn 1985.

Peacock, Alan, 'Michael Longley: poet between worlds' in *Poetry in Contemporary Irish Literature* (Irish Literary Studies, 43), edited by Michael Kenneally, Gerrards Cross (Bucks.): Colin Smythe 1995.

Ordinary Level, 2006 EXAMINATION

Explanatory note

Candidates taking the Ordinary (Pass) level exam in 2006 have a choice of questions when dealing with the prescribed poems. They can answer either (a) a question on one of the poems by a poet prescribed for Higher Level for the 2006 exam, or (b) a question from a list of other prescribed poems (i.e. the alternative poems discussed on pages 311–33).

(a) The poems by Higher level poets that may also be answered by Ordinary level candidates in the 2006 exam are as follows:

Donne	The Flea (p. 11)
	Song: Go, and catch
	  a falling star (p. 14)
		Eliot	Preludes (p. 164)
			Rannoch, by Glencoe
			  (extract from
			  Landscapes IV)
			    (p. 185)

Hardy	The Darkling Thrush
	    (p. 39)
	During Wind and Rain
	    (p. 45)
		Bishop	The Fish (p. 202)
			Filling Station (p. 220)

Hopkins	Spring (p. 67) Inversnaid (p. 83)	**Plath**	The Arrival of the Bee Box (p. 261) Child (p. 264)

Yeats	The Lake Isle of
	  Innisfree (p. 116)
	The Wild Swans at
	  Coole (p. 121)
	Swift's Epitaph
	    (p. 144)
		Longley	Last Requests (p. 288)
			An Amish Rug
			    (p 291)

(b) The alternative poems that Ordinary level candidates sitting the exam in 2006 may choose to study instead are discussed on pages 311–33.

CONTRIBUTORS
Carole Scully
John McCarthy
John G. Fahy
David Keogh
Bernard Connolly

Robert Herrick
Whenas in silks my Julia goes

Text of poem: New Explorations Anthology page 431

A READING OF THE POEM

The opening line of this poem immediately sets the scene for the reader. Herrick watches Julia, who is dressed in silken clothing, move about in front of him. However, despite her name being mentioned in the first line of the poem, we learn nothing more about her.

The following five lines are concerned with Herrick's reaction to what he sees, particularly the silk fabric. His thoughts are 'sweetly' filled with the 'liquifaction of her clothes'. His eyes are captivated by the 'brave vibration'. He is spellbound by the 'glittering'.

For Herrick, the image of Julia 'in silks' is a sensual and erotic one. However, the sensuality and eroticism do not come from Julia or the silken fabric, but rather from Herrick's perception of the fabric. In this way, they originate from within Herrick himself. It is Herrick's response to the silk that makes it sensual and erotic. He finds it erotically suggestive, arousing and full of sensual promise, while another may simply see it as a piece of cloth. So, in the first three lines, he is engulfed by the sensuality of the silk, likening it to liquid flowing smoothly and 'sweetly'. His own excitement increases in the second three lines, where the 'brave vibration' of the moving fabric sweeps over his internal being.

It is evident from such words and phrases as 'methinks', 'I cast mine eyes' and 'taketh me' that the emphasis of the poem is firmly placed on Herrick himself and his reactions. In this respect, Julia becomes little more than a shadowy object in the background, a mechanism to produce movement in the silken fabric.

THEME

Although at first this poem appears to be about Julia, in reality it focuses on Herrick's personal responses. He is attracted and aroused, not by any of Julia's unique features or qualities, nor by the fineness of the silken fabric; they are simply objects that trigger a series of reactions within him. Herrick finds the intensity of these reactions both enjoyable and disturbing.

LANGUAGE

Herrick chooses his words carefully, so that the actual sounds of the words help to reinforce the images he creates. So, lines 2–3 are filled with the letters 'l' and 's' to suggest a sense of liquid. The very sounds of these letters help the reader to 'feel' something of the sensory quality of liquid. Similarly, the letters 't', 'i' and 'e' in the final line create brittle words that convey the sparkling, reflected light of the moving silk, encouraging the reader to 'see' the fabric.

Herrick uses rhyme in a similar way. The first three lines end in 'goes', 'flows' and 'clothes', all 'liquid' in their sounds, while the second three lines end with the shorter 'see', 'free' and 'me', echoing an increase in excitement and the 'brave vibration'.

By using these techniques, Herrick creates vivid images that help the reader to understand the sensual nature of his response.

TONE

The tone of this poem is filled with a sense of tension. On the one hand, Herrick is attracted by, and clearly enjoys, the movement of the silk, using phrases such as 'how sweetly flows'. On the other, he seems to feel overwhelmed by the intensity and depth of his reaction. The final line: 'O how that glittering taketh me!' expresses his awareness that this is an irresistible and disturbingly uncontrollable response that consumes him.

Henry Vaughan
Peace
Text of the poem: New Explorations Anthology page 438

A READING OF THE POEM

The poet addresses his soul and describes heaven as 'a Countrie | Far beyond the stars', guarded by a sentry 'All skilfull in the wars'. Peace sits 'crown'd with smiles' above the clamour and danger that characterise life on Earth. Christ is portrayed as a military commander commanding the angelic troops. He is the soul's friend, who for motives of 'pure love' descended to the earth to die 'for thy sake'. If the soul could 'get but thither' to Christ, in heaven 'there growes the flowre of peace'. Peace is symbolised by the 'Rose that cannot wither' and as a fortress offering security. The soul is exhorted to cease its wanderings: 'Leave then thy foolish ranges' and to embrace Christ, who 'never changes' and is 'Thy God, thy life, thy Cure.' This poem is perhaps best understood as a dramatic sermon in which Christ offers mankind peace. Peace is defined in terms of military security with Christ as the warrior prince, and offering an end to aimless wandering. In his poem 'Man' Vaughan refers to the human condition: 'Man is the shuttle . . . God ordered motion but ordained no rest'. In 'Peace', rest – 'ease' – replaces restlessness – 'foolish ranges' – in the poet's view of heaven, protected by 'one who never changes'.

IMAGERY

Vaughan's use of imagery in the poem is striking, as heaven is 'a Countrie | Far beyond the stars'. Christ is presented as a warrior; he 'Commands the Beauteous files', offering protection; he is 'skilfull in the wars'. Associated with this warlike image is 'the flowre of peace', which is 'The Rose that cannot wither'.

Christ/peace is a 'fortresse', offering an end to aimless wandering: 'thy foolish ranges'. Vaughan weaves the various strands of imagery together to dramatic effect, to convey a moral lesson, as the soul is exhorted – 'O my soul awake!' – to embrace Christ's peace.

MUSCULAR LANGUAGE

Vaughan writes with vigour, as the brisk rhythm of the short lines, with their forceful beat, builds up to the pause at the semicolon in line 16. The following line is in the imperative, as the soul is instructed to act on the knowledge gained: 'Leave then thy foolish ranges;'. Triplication in the final line enhances the rhetorical effect of the punctuation, with pauses after the key words 'Thy God, thy life, thy Cure.' The poem possesses a hymn-like quality, with its alternate lines rhyming and its simplicity of language.

Samuel Taylor Coleridge
The Rime of the Ancient Mariner (part IV)
Text of the poem: New Explorations Anthology page 443

A READING OF THE POEM

Part IV of the 'Rime of the Ancient Mariner' opens with the wedding guest in fear of the old sailor's appearance: 'I fear thee . . . I fear thy skinny hand . . . thy glittering eye'. The mariner assures him that he is not a ghost: 'This body dropt not down.' He describes, in the third stanza, his terrible loneliness and suffering: 'Alone, alone, all, all alone . . . My soul in agony.' In the following stanza he describes 'That many men so beautiful!' who are all dead. The mariner feels guilt at his own survival: 'a thousand thousand slimy things | Lived on; and so did I.' His spiritual despair is suggested by his inability to pray: 'and made | My heart as dry as dust.' He closes his eyes so as not to see the disapproving looks of his shipmates: 'The look with which they looked on me | Had never passed away.' The mariner wishes he was dead, 'And yet I could not die.' It is the appearance of the water-snakes that marks a turning point for the mariner: 'I watched their rich attire: | Blue, glossy green, and velvet black'. The dormant heart of the sailor is touched: 'A spring of love gushed from my heart, | And I blessed them unaware'. In the final stanza there is a highly symbolic action – 'The Albatross fell off, and sank | Like lead into the sea.' By blessing the water-snakes the mariner has begun his spiritual regeneration.

THE ROLE OF THE SUPERNATURAL

Supernatural events are at the centre of the poem's narrative; the killing of the albatross – 'a bird of good omen' – unleashes the sequence of events leading up to part IV of the poem. In the extract the mariner is surrounded by the bodies of his dead shipmates: 'Nor rot nor reek did they'. They still stare contemptuously at the mariner: 'The look with which they looked on me | Had never passed away.' The becalmed ship casts a ghastly supernatural shadow: 'The charmed water burnt alway | A still and awful red.' Overcome with the joy of watching living creatures, the mariner blesses them 'unaware'. He attributes this action to the work of 'my kind saint' and repeats, 'I blessed them unaware'. The final supernatural event in part IV is 'And from my neck so free | The Albatross fell off'. In the marginal gloss Coleridge wrote, *'The spell begins to break.'*

THE BALLAD FORM

Coleridge uses the conventions of the ballad form and its idiom to create an architecture of poetic sound. The *ballad rhythm* gives the narrative drive and entices the reader into the poem – see lines 255–258, with the description of the moon. *Direct speech* is used dramatically: 'I fear thee, ancient Mariner! | I fear thy skinny hand!' Coleridge varies the length of the lines to achieve particular effects. Look at the penultimate stanza, where six lines, instead of the usual four or five, describe the climactic moment of blessing the water-snakes. *Repetition* occurs for functional purposes as well as being part of the ballad format: 'And I blessed them unaware' (lines 277 and 279). *Assonance* combines with repetition to remarkable effect in 'Alone, alone, all, all alone, | Alone on a wide wide sea!' There is a primal *simplicity in the language* that reflects the elemental simplicity of the subject matter: 'The Albatross fell off, and sank | Like lead into the sea.' 'The Rime of the Ancient Mariner' retains the direct *storytelling*, characteristic of all ballads, but does so at greater length. Development of *character* and motivation is as *underdeveloped* and *superficial* as in the traditional form. Coleridge adds a depth of spirituality and symbolism that is more characteristic of the Romantic movement than the traditional ballad.

Edward Thomas
Adlestrop
Text of poem: New Explorations Anthology page 450

A READING OF THE POEM

The opening of this poem is quietly understated. Thomas simply speaks to the reader, explaining how the name 'Adlestrop' triggers a memory for him.

His description of his brief stop at Adlestrop is communicated with a deceptive simplicity. In the first stanza, he relates how he came to be in Adlestrop: 'the express-train drew up there | Unwontedly', adding that it was 'late June'. In the second stanza, we hear how his gaze lingered first on the station: 'No one left and no one came | On the bare platform.' Idly, Thomas noted the name of Adlestrop on the signpost. But then, his gaze moved beyond the station out to the English countryside surrounding it and, suddenly, 'Adlestrop' was no longer 'only the name'. The third stanza gives a wonderful sense of the view that stretched out before Thomas. Our eyes move with his from the 'willows, willow-herb, and grass' in the foreground, to the 'haycocks' further beyond, and then farther still, up to the 'high cloudlets in the sky.' In the fourth stanza, we learn that the beauty and harmony of the moment were increased, for Thomas, by the singing of a blackbird 'Close by' and 'Farther and farther, all the birds | Of Oxfordshire and Gloucestershire.'

THEME

Although Thomas can be classed as a 'War Poet', in that he wrote his poetry around the time of the First World War, he did not concentrate on writing about the war. Rather, he wrote of the unique beauty of the English countryside and of his great love for it.

In 'Adlestrop', Thomas describes a brief moment when he encountered this natural beauty and responded with admiration and appreciation. The fact that the First World War, with all its horrors, had begun, simply served to make such a view and such a feeling all the more precious.

LANGUAGE AND RHYME

Thomas uses the language of everyday speech in this poem. However, this in no way limits the effectiveness of his images. For instance, in the second stanza, we see how his skilful arrangement of familiar words in familiar patterns successfully communicates the experience of stopping unexpectedly and briefly on a train journey. Similarly, the third stanza graphically conveys the breathtaking view that was stretched out before him.

Such simplicity should never be regarded as commonplace or easily achieved.

It is somewhat surprising to realize that Thomas' poem has a rhyme scheme, as the words seem to flow naturally. He has succeeded in managing the conversational language with such expertise that the rhyme is subtle and in no way interrupts the flow of the words and thoughts.

IMAGERY

Thomas creates a series of images that evoke the scene so distinctly, it is as if we too are sitting on the train. He achieves this by building a strong sensory element into his images. His reference to the 'heat' appeals to the sense of touch. He brings hearing into play with the hissing steam, the person clearing his throat and the songs of the birds. Finally, sight ranges from the 'bare platform' to the Adlestrop sign and, then, to the 'willows, willow-herb', the 'haycocks' and 'the high cloudlets'.

D.H. Lawrence
Piano
Text of poem: New Explorations Anthology page 455

A READING OF THE POEM

The poem opens quietly, 'Softly in the dusk', as a singer is performing. Childhood memories are called to mind as the poet sees a picture of himself as a child, sitting at his mother's feet as she plays the piano. Line four uses significant detail to suggest the mother's character: 'And pressing the small, poised feet of a mother who smiles as she sings.' She is presented as accomplished, 'poised' and warm – 'who smiles'. In stanza two the poet describes how he is overcome with nostalgia 'till the heart of me weeps to belong | To the old Sunday evenings at home'. Lawrence finds the memory so painful that it is 'In spite' of himself that the singing 'Betrays me back'. A cosy idyllic picture is painted: 'And hymns in the cosy parlour' with 'winter outside'. In the third stanza the poet describes that no matter how loudly the singer sings or the accompanist plays, the music of the present will always be lost as he is taken back to the past. He says, 'The glamour | Of childish days is upon me'. His control of his emotions is loosened: 'my manhood is cast | Down in the flood of remembrance'; there is a terrible intensity in his feelings of loss and grief: 'I weep like a child for the past.'

SOUND EFFECTS

In this poem Lawrence achieves a verbal music, as the singing and accompaniment is reflected in the language. Assonance – 'Softly, in the dusk, a woman (echoing the u in dusk) is singing to me' – combines with a sibilant 's' to create a musical pattern. Rhyme enhances the musical effect: 'me – see, string – sings'. Sound echoes sense (onomatopeia) in the description of the piano sounds from the child's perspective: 'in the boom of the tingling strings'. The harshness of the contemporary singer's voice, when compared to the memory of the Sunday evening hymns as his mother played, is suggested by the choice of the word 'clamour'.

A NOVELIST'S EYE IN CREATING SCENES AND SUGGESTING CHARACTER

Lawrence has the capacity to describe scenes vividly with an economy of detail. The opening line paints a highly atmospheric picture with the minimum of information: 'Softly, in the dusk, a woman is singing to me'. In the same stanza a family scene of great warmth and charm is described, as the deep love between mother and child is apparent: 'A child sitting under a piano . . . And pressing the small, poised feet of a mother who smiles and sings.' In these two lines Lawrence has portrayed his mother as a confident, accomplished woman who gave joy and love to her children. The second stanza has a strongly atmospheric description of Sunday evenings, singing hymns in 'the cosy parlour'. Physical cold on the outside – 'with winter outside' – serves to highlight the emotional warmth inside, with a loving family and a sense of religious certainty.

Edwin Muir
The Horses
Text of poem: New Explorations Anthology page 459

A READING OF THE POEM

Muir quickly establishes the background to his poem in the opening three lines. There had been a 'seven days war' that, despite its brief duration, produced such a terrible effect on the world that it was put 'to sleep'.

Muir develops this concept of a sleeping world by describing the changes that occurred in the emotional lives of the ordinary people. They were catapulted into a state of shock, unable to communicate and haunted by a sense of terror: 'We listened to our breathing and were afraid.' Muir uses the vivid image of nations 'Curled blindly' in the foetal position, a recognized response for a traumatized person, to convey the extent of this terror. It is clear that the enormity of the war was such that those who survived it were forced, for their own sanity, to close down their emotional and psychological responses, to put these parts of their beings asleep. Even though time has passed, the people are still unable to cope with this worldwide emotional and psychological devastation, it 'confounds' them 'with its strangeness'.

In the aftermath of the 'seven days war' the world, as a whole, retreats away from the technology on which it had once depended. Muir unfolds a series of images that show the prewar machinery gradually becoming less relevant. The radios no longer work; the warships are useful only for transporting dead bodies; a plane crashes into the ocean; the tractors 'lie about our fields' unused. The world that was once filled with the humming of engines is now a silent one. This silence indicates that the world, too, has had to close down a part of its existence, to put it 'to sleep'.

The people come to regard machinery and technology as representing the 'old bad world' that had given birth to the war, the war that 'swallowed' their children. Radios had been used to circulate news of the war so, Muir tells us, even if they were once more 'to speak', they would be ignored because they would speak of a world the people 'would not have . . . again.'

Into this sleeping world come 'the strange horses'. They signal their arrival with a cacophony of sound that shatters the world's silence. The 'distant tapping' grows into a 'deepening drumming' and then into a 'hollow thunder'.

They move with a noisy energy that frightens the people who have become used to listening to their own breathing. Nevertheless, the horses stir up old memories, leading the people to recall the way in which the technology of the prewar world had totally changed the lives of the horses. The horses had been willingly sacrificed to 'buy new tractors', just as the human children had been sacrificed in 'one great gulp'. Muir makes a clear contrast between the vibrancy and strength of the horses and the lifeless tractors that lie like 'dank sea-monsters', to emphasize how this movement towards technology had been a grave error.

Gradually, the horses reawaken the sleeping people. Images of 'fabulous steeds' and 'knights' fill the minds that had been shocked into closing down. The horses offer a 'long-lost archaic companionship' that warms emotions for so long repressed. They bring with them a way of connecting with the life that the people once had, before technology and machinery took over. The horses carry something of the purity of 'Eden', the perfect world that God created for Adam and Eve. They remind the people that there is a life-force that will persist even in the 'wilderness of the broken world'. In this way, the arrival of the horses changes everything and signals a 'beginning'.

IMAGERY

Muir uses a series of vivid images to convey the world that has been brought about by the 'seven days war', and to help the reader to share in the emotions felt by the people who experience it. There is real horror in the image of the children being 'swallowed' in 'one great gulp', and a terrible sadness in the 'nations' huddled like terrified babies.

He conveys the energy and the healing power of the horses with a series of extremely effective images. They engulf the people like 'a wild wave', washing away the effects of the war. They enable the people to break away from a world of inescapable drudgery, suggested by the 'oxen' with the 'rusty ploughs'. The image of the 'half-a-dozen colts' being born in 'some wilderness of the broken world' captures the unyielding urge of the horses to survive, and it is this that inspires wonder and hope in the people.

TONE

Muir controls the tone of this poem with great skill. His conversational tone creates a great sense of immediacy, as if we are actually talking to a survivor of a terrible war.

The emotions of the speaker are raw and real, as with the resignation in the line 'By then we had made our covenant with silence', and the desperate determination filling 'We would not listen' and 'We would not have it again.'

After the arrival of the horses the tone changes to one of hope: 'Our life is changed; their coming our beginning.'

Dylan Thomas
Do Not Go Gentle Into That Good Night
Text of poem: New Explorations Anthology page 478

A READING OF THE POEM

Dylan Thomas wrote this poem about his father's impending death. The poem uses a fusion of imagery and sound to suggest how the poet feels.

In line one Thomas uses the imperative, as he appeals to his father not to embrace death too readily. Death is represented as 'that good night'. He asserts that 'Old age should . . . rage against the dying of the light' – another symbol of the extinction of life. It may also be significant that Thomas's father went blind as his health failed. The second stanza reflects on the fact that sensible men know that death is inevitable and that it must be accepted: 'know dark is right', but still cannot practise what they preach. Thomas uses the dramatic enigmatic image of 'forked no lightning' to represent how this accepted wisdom does not inspire real resignation. The image of not going 'gentle into that good night' is repeated as a refrain reiterating the poet's appeal to his father. Stanza three refers to how good men at the end, 'the last wave by', conscious of the good they might do – 'how bright | Their frail deeds might have danced in a green bay' – would not willingly embrace death, which is once again symbolised as 'the dying of the light'. In stanza four Thomas describes how 'Wild men', who lived life with great intensity – 'who caught and sang the sun in flight' – and become aware 'too late' of their reckless ways, also do not go easily into the 'good night' of death. In stanza five Thomas puns on 'Grave men' who paradoxically see with 'blinding sight', and whose 'Blind eyes could blaze like meteors'. These men too 'rage against the dying of the light.' In the final stanza Thomas reaches a pitch of even greater emotional intensity, as he prays for his father: 'And you, my father,' to 'Curse, bless, me now with your fierce tears'. The stanza is extended to accommodate both refrains in a remarkably passionate conclusion.

USE OF SOUND EFFECTS

Dylan Thomas uses the sound of the language to suggest the dramatic intensity of his emotions.

Alliteration: The repetition of 'g' and 't' sounds adds to intricate patterns of sound in line one, 'Do no_t_ go gen_t_le in_t_o tha_t_ _g_ood nigh_t._'

Alliteration is used for emphasis throughout the poem: '_d_ee_d_s . . . _d_ance_d_' and '_bl_ind . . . _bl_aze'.

Assonance: Verbal music is created with the patterns of repeated vowel sound in the poem; '_a_ge | r_a_ve | d_a_y', 'd_y_ing | l_i_ght' and 'Bl_i_nd _eye_s . . . l_i_ke . . . bl_a_ze . . . g_ay_'.

Rhyme: The first and final line in each stanza rhyme. In an unusual rhyme pattern the second lines of each stanza rhyme: 'day | they | bay | way | gay | pray'.

Repetition: Lines and phrases are repeated to achieve a chant-like effect (lines 1, 6, 12 and 18 are identical, as are lines 3, 9, 15 and 19).

Colloquialisms: The choice of 'gentle' rather than the more grammatical adverb 'gently' reflects a colloquial quality that is often present in the work of Dylan Thomas.

Antithesis: 'Curse, bless' is an example of opposite ideas being placed side by side to express the intensity and conflicting nature of the poet's overwrought emotions.

Puns: 'Grave men' has a black humour that is unexpected, given the poem's theme.

Paradox: 'See with blinding sight' is an apparent contradiction that highlights the clarity of thought of those who are near death.

IMAGERY

Many of the images Dylan Thomas uses cannot easily be paraphrased, but have immense powers of suggestion. The central images of 'that good night' and 'the dying of the light' are immediately comprehensible, but 'have forked no lightning' and 'how bright | Their frail deeds might have danced in a green bay' are more problematic. These two metaphors are drawn from the natural world and testify to the poet's imaginative vision and sensibility.

It is the interplay of symbolism and language that give the poetry of Dylan Thomas its unique appeal.

Edwin Morgan
Strawberries
Text of poem: New Explorations Anthology page 483

A READING OF THE POEM

Morgan begins his poem by focusing on the strawberries that were eaten by the couple on this remembered afternoon. He regards the strawberries as special: 'There were never strawberries | like the ones we had | that sultry afternoon', just as 'that sultry afternoon' was special.

His description of the two people is one of intimacy and closeness. They sit on a step 'facing each other', knees interlocked. There is a feeling of commitment and belonging in the phrase 'your knees held in mine'. The eating of the strawberries reinforces this sense of physical intimacy. The actions of the couple mirror each other: 'we dipped them in sugar'. They look not at the strawberries as they eat, but at each other.

The sensuality of the strawberries, evident in such phrases as 'strawberries glistening' and 'we dipped them in sugar', captures the simmering sensuality that crackles between the lovers. It becomes clear that the eating of the strawberries is, in reality, an introduction to another type of sensual intimacy that the couple anticipates sharing. They eat the strawberries 'not hurrying', drawing out this anticipation, savouring the expectation and the promise of this moment. The tension builds with each mouthful until the plates are empty and 'laid on the stone'. The image of the 'two forks crossed' is reflected in the poet's moving towards his companion 'and I bent towards you'. The sweetness of the strawberries dipped in sugar becomes the sweetness of his companion's presence, and both merge in the taste of his lover's lips. The hot sunlight that shone on the 'strawberries glistening' now shines on the couple in their sensual 'forgetfulness' as they create a 'heat intense'. The remembered moment is so intense for Morgan that it comes out of the past and into the present, as he urges his lover 'lean back again let me love you'.

The poem closes on the spectacular images of 'summer lightening' flashing on the 'Kilpatrick hills' and a rain-storm cleaning the forgotten plates. These could be seen as representing the intensity of the couple's loving. However, there is an undercurrent of destruction and danger about the 'lightening'. Could Morgan be suggesting that although this sensual, intense love shared by the couple was incredibly special, it also carried danger with it, because it made the lovers emotionally vulnerable to each other? Does the storm that washed the plates represent the ending of their love?

THEME

Morgan writes about the theme of love in an intensely sensual and physical way. He uses the eating of the strawberries to suggest a sense of anticipation and close intimacy. Similarly, the heat of the sun indicates the intensity of their relationship. However, he seems to sound a cautionary note about such love with the images of the lightning and the storm.

STRUCTURE

Interestingly, this poem is written as one unpunctuated piece. Morgan tries to represent, on the page, the continuous movement of his memories of 'that sultry afternoon'. His words and phrases glide smoothly from one image to another, capturing the way in which remembered thoughts of an incident flow, without full stops or commas.

Morgan's use of the past and present tenses cleverly communicates the way in which past memories can become so vivid that they take over the present moment. So the past tense, used for eating the strawberries, suddenly becomes the present as he holds his lover and says, 'lean back again let me love you' and urges that they surrender to 'forgetfulness'.

Patricia Beer
The Voice
Text of poem: New Explorations Anthology page 488

A READING OF THE POEM

Patricia Beer's poem opens conversationally: 'When God took my aunt's baby boy, a merciful neighbour | Gave her a parrot.' The reference to the parrot is unexpected and sets the tone for some wry observations from the poet. A dramatic turning point in the unnamed aunt's life is referred to matter-of-factly: 'And turned her back on the idea of other babies.' Her difficult financial circumstances are suggested by the fact that she 'could not have afforded' the parrot. In her house the parrot 'looked unlikely' because of his bright coloration; the only other colour there was the old-fashioned, cheap 'local pottery' with quaint dialect inscriptions, 'Du ee help yerself to crame, me handsome'. Beer describes how the parrot 'said nothing', while speculating entertainingly on what sounds might have issued from him, 'From pet-shop gossip or a sailor's oath . . . tom-tom, war-cry or wild beast roaring.' The aunt teaches him 'nursery rhymes morning after morning'; he learns to speak in a Devon accent. Beer associates the parrot with the aunt's lost child: 'He sounded like a farmer, as her son might have.' In a telling phrase, 'He fitted in.'

Beer mixes humour and pathos, as the parrot becomes ill: 'he got confused, and muddled up | His rhymes. Jack Horner ate his pail of water . . . I wept'. There is some of Beer's characteristic wry humour to be observed in 'He had never seemed puzzled by the bizarre events | He spoke of' and clever phrasing in 'And tumbled after.' Ironically when the aunt died, 'widowed, childless, pitied | And patronised', the poet is left with no memory of her voice, 'But I can still hear his'.

LANGUAGE

Beer captures the rhythms and idioms of colloquial speech: 'When God took my aunt's baby boy' and 'And turned her back on the idea of other babies.' Her style is direct: 'But I can still hear his', while displaying a playful sense of humour as she echoes the nursery rhyme: 'Said 'Broke his crown' and 'Christmas pie'. And tumbled after.' Her use of dialect helps to suggest the character of the aunt's house and decorations: 'With the local pottery which carried messages | Like "Du ee help yerself to crame, me handsome"'. Beer sums up the aunt's life most succinctly: 'My aunt died the next winter, widowed, childless, pitied | And patronised.' The alliterating *w* and *p* sounds help make the line memorable, like the *h* sounds in the final line: 'I can still hear his.'

TONE

As the poem opens the poet seems detached 'When God took . . . a merciful neighbour gave her a parrot.' There are flashes of humour as she describes the aunt's pottery and 'her jokes; she used to say turds and whey'. The parrot's confusion in his final illness is humorously illustrated; she also suggests her feelings: 'I wept'.

The final stanza allows a rather different perspective, as Beer reflects on the unnamed aunt's life, 'widowed, childless, pitied | And patronised.' She is far more sensitive to the woman's suffering and concludes ironically with the poignant observation, 'She would not have expected it to be remembered | After so long.' In a poem about voices the aunt has no voice and no name. The colourful parrot's voice is still heard.

Richard Murphy
The Reading Lesson
Text of Poem: New Explorations Anthology page 493

Critical commentary
'The Reading Lesson' is based on a dialogue between two people. The speaker in the poem is a reading teacher who is trying to help a fourteen-year-old

traveller boy to read. The poem describes the boy's struggle to come to grips with the world of letters and the teacher's frustration at his lack of progress, and it also shows the rest of society's reaction to their attempts. The poem uses images that are part of the boy's world to describe the struggle that goes on between them.

The boy either doesn't want to read or he is finding it so hard that he has almost given up. The first metaphor that is introduced by the poet to describe the situation is the dog hunting the hare. This gives the reader an image of a great wild chase – that he is trying to trap and tie down the boy's wild nature and bring it to a passive trap. There is a sense here, understood by both the teacher and the boy, that if he is 'tamed' he may lose something in the trade-off between them. The hunt is brought up to a climax when the teacher finally becomes so frustrated that he challenges the boy with a stern question. The teacher may think he is being rhetorical, but the boy takes him very literally and gives an equally stern reply:

> 'Don't you want to learn to read?'
> 'I'll be the same man whatever I do.'

The teacher compares this riposte to an animal that has been cornered and comes out with his teeth bared on his release.

The second verse continues with the nature imagery. The poet uses a mule, a goat and a snipe to describe the way the boy looks at the page. He explains that the atmosphere is tense and says that if there is

> 'A sharp word, and he'll mooch
> Back to his piebald mare and bantam cock.'

He finishes by explaining that his task is as difficult as catching mercury.

The third verse shows us that they have all but given up; the boy will not be using his fingers to follow words on a page, but he will use them to go hawking scrap or even going pickpocketing. The teacher says that the boy could easily revert to the stereotype that the chuckling neighbour ascribes to him. The neighbour says that the boy is untameable, that he will always have a yearning to escape and go back to being his natural, wild self as soon as he has the chance.

The final verse finishes with some images that are specific to travellers. He says that books are something that the boy feels will restrict him and stop him from making his own way. They are as restrictive and separate from him as the idea of settling on a small farm to live for the rest of his life. He says that his life will be one of petty theft and poaching. He ends by comparing this book learning to the wren. The wren became The King Of All Birds by being clever enough to sit on the back of an eagle and therefore fly the highest in the sky. To the boy, that is how unobtainable to him books are.

U. A. Fanthorpe
Growing Up
Text of poem: New Explorations Anthology page 501

A READING OF THE POEM

Growing up was a difficult process for U. A. Fanthorpe, and in this poem she traces her feelings of alienation at the various stages in her life. Babyhood is described in the first stanza: 'I wasn't good | At being a baby.' She learned to conceal her feelings and perspective on the world at an early age: 'Masking by instinct how much I knew | Of the senior world'. Her refusal to conform to the stereotypical norms of infant behaviour is demonstrated humorously in 'Shoplifting daintily into my pram'.

As a child she realised that she did not fit in with children: 'Children, | Being childish, were beneath me'; nor with adults: 'Adults I despised or distrusted.' Grown-ups considered her '*Precocious, naïve*'; her defence was 'to be surly'.

Adolescence made her feel even more 'out of step'. Her physical development 'nudging me . . . To join the party', she found puberty especially traumatic, 'With hairy, fleshy growths and monthly outbursts'. Her feelings are powerfully summed up in 'Was caught bloody-thighed, a criminal | Guilty of puberty.' Emily Dickinson was her role model; she admired her for being 'intransigent' and because she 'Never told anyone anything'.

In the fourth stanza she relates how difficult she found social interaction: 'Never learned | The natives' art of life.' She developed a strategy for social survival by staying 'mute', except for 'the hard-learned arcane litany | Of cliché'. She concludes that she was 'Not a nice person'.

There is a change of mood in the final stanza, even though the art of social life is still mysterious: 'Masonic', she has found 'A vocation even for wallflowers.' She observes 'the effortless bravura | Of other people's lives'. Fanthorpe cannot take for granted what she describes in the simile 'like well-oiled bolts, | Swiftly and sweet, they slot into the grooves | Their ancestors smoothed out along the grain.' Her feelings of alienation are lifelong, but she has found a niche as an observer of other people's lives.

STYLE

Fanthorpe's style is conversational – 'I wasn't good | At growing up' – and direct. She manipulates sound cleverly, as her use of alliteration for emphasis testifies: 'Called to be connoisseur, I collect'. The smoothness of other people's lives is suggested by the 's' sounds in 'Swiftly and sweet, they slot into the grooves'. Fanthorpe has a mischievous sense of humour: 'Biting my rattle, my brother (in private), | Shoplifting daintily into my pram.' Her images are drawn from the familiar world: 'cliché, my company passport', and the 'well-oiled bolt'. Her allusion to 'Emily' tells much about her own character and the qualities she aspires to: 'intransigent . . . Struggled to die on her feet . . . Never told anyone anything.'

Ted Hughes
There Came a Day
Text of poem: New Explorations Anthology page 506

A READING OF THE POEM

The first stanza of this poem instantly captures our attention with its vivid and unusual image. Hughes describes how the Autumn day catches Summer with the same practical efficiency as a farmer catching and killing a hen for his dinner. Although amusing, there is an underlying 'black humour' in his use of the image of the unfortunate hen to describe the season of Summer. Hughes deliberately rejects the idealised, romantic language generally used in poetry about the seasons. He wants us to recognise and acknowledge that the changing of the seasons represents the ruthlessness that, he feels, is at the heart of the world of Nature. So, Autumn is shown destroying Summer with the same cold determination as the farmer killing a hen.

Hughes illustrates this ruthless determination in the following four stanzas. The Autumn day strips the trees 'bare' with a careless delight, in order to see 'what is really there.' Again, the humour is rather grim: one can imagine the trees gripping their leaves like embarrassed Victorian ladies, while Autumn, an insensitive fellow, attempts to pull them away. The sun is treated with similar contempt as Autumn rolls him away like an old beach-ball. The excuse given that the sun will 'come back rested' does not hide the ruthlessness of this action. In truth, Autumn does not care 'if he comes at all.' Even the birds that fill the summer skies are frightened away by this bully. Only the 'brave tomtit' has the courage to remain and by so doing gains Autumn's respect. Similarly, the tiny seeds are forced down into the soil, just to see if they have the strength to survive such treatment.

It is only when Autumn turns to 'the people' that his attitude seems to become less ruthless. He will 'Stuff them with apple and blackberry pie – '. However, there is something unpleasant about this image. Perhaps it has echoes of the poor hen being prepared for dinner in the first stanza; or perhaps it is the feeling of contempt implicit in Autumn's attitude to 'the people'. Simply by providing an abundance of apples and blackberries for these greedy humans, Autumn knows that he can distract them from his destruction of Summer and make them love him 'till the day I die'.

The poem closes with a particularly disturbing image. Autumn is shown approaching like a terrible monster with a mouth 'wide' and 'red as a sunset'. The 'red' is suggestive of heat and ripeness, but also of blood and destruction. Behind all this heat lies a tail that is 'an icicle', just as the season of Autumn begins with warmth and ends with the frozen chill of Winter.

RHYTHM

Hughes cleverly uses rhythm to add to the overall impact of this poem. There is a 'sing-song' rhythm, rather like that of a nursery rhyme, running through the second to the fifth stanzas. This contrasts with the images of destruction that are described in these stanzas, and reinforces the carelessness with which Autumn lays waste to the world of Summer.

HUMOUR

The 'black humour' evident in this poem arises out of Hughes' awareness of the ruthlessness underlying the world of Nature. He creates vivid images to communicate the relish and enjoyment that, he feels, Autumn gets from destroying Summer and all its features. The trees, the sun, the birds and the seeds are simply to be toyed with before their inevitable destruction, while the people are to be manipulated and fooled. Hughes believes that with the ruthless monster of Nature stalking the Earth there is no option but to take refuge in a humour that can only be grimly 'black'.

Eamonn Grennan
Daughter and Dying Fish
Text of poem: New Explorations Anthology page 520

In this poem Grennan describes the death of dogfish and his daughter's innocent non-reaction to it. The poem is a good example of how a poet can use sound to convey what he wants almost as much as he can use the words themselves. This is never more obvious than when the poet dominates the poem with alliterative 's' sounds. They almost smother the poem, resonating with the sliding along of the fish as they contort their way towards death.

Take the third stanza as an example:

> sliding the slow length of one another
> as spines stiffen, scales shimmer, glaucous
> sea-eyes pop with shock and resignation.

The reader can feel the water slurp around as the fish splashes against the rock pools. It is a worthwhile exercise to trace the 's' sounds all the way through this poem and to notice how dominant they are in each stanza.

The first three stanzas just show the fish as they lie, about to die. The poet describes all elements of them from their mouths to their tails. In the fourth his daughter enters. As she walks across the pier she bends to pet the fish, and then continues on her way as if this were an everyday thing. The poet is surprised at this, especially as he is fascinated by the final death dance of the dogfish.

He returns to what they were like when they were alive, and how their movement then was so smooth compared to their graceless state now: 'How they would glide, barely brushing | one another, bodies all curve and urgency'.

Now they are reduced to 'a hapless | heap of undulant muscle'. When life finally leaves them, the poet feels that he can compare them to the stone of the pier and they are as dead as that.

His daughter, meanwhile, goes on about her business, undisturbed by the death that has surrounded her that day. He revels in her innocence and in her 'cheerful small voice | still singing.'

Sharon Olds
The Present Moment
Text of poem: New Explorations Anthology page 525

This thoughtful meditation concerns issues of ageing and of how we perceive the ageing process. A daughter sees her father in hospital, where he is terminally ill, and she tries to reconcile the image she once had of her father as somebody who was strong physically and mentally with the frail figure who lies before her. Through the poem she gives a powerful description of what illness does to people, of how it can ravage the body and the mind at the same time in a ruthless manner.

She combines the body and the mind at the start of the poem. She shows how the father has gone in such a short time from being someone who was active to being just a passive entity on the edge of existence. The first instance comes when she sees him just lying on his hospital bed. He is now motionless, facing towards the wall. This is becoming her dominant image of him now, instead of the image that she had of him before he entered the hospital and he 'sat up and put on his reading glasses'. At that stage he was actively reading, taking things in, his eyes alive as the 'lights in the room multiplied in the lenses.'

She uses the image of food to show the changes he has gone through. He now is dependent on food that will pass through him for energy, not for taste. He eats 'dense, earthen food, like liver', which is pure tasteless fuel – not something more unusual and aesthetic, like pineapple with its exotic connotations.

She follows this by noticing the changes to his body over the years. He is none of the more appealing figures that he used to be. She goes in reverse chronological order through his phases of life. She describes him as a portly man with a 'torso packed with extra matter'. As a young man he was a 'smooth-skinned, dark-haired boy'.

She admits to not knowing him obviously when he was a baby, but she notes his dependence back then, when he would 'drink from a woman's | body'. Once again he is being fed. And his 'steady | gaze' now is again like when he was just born: where sleep brings only relief to him now, just as it did then.

She finishes with a metaphor of a swimmer, only her father is swimming towards death: and want as she might to help him, she is helpless. She can only look on while he continues in his struggle.

Paddy Bushe
Jasmine
Text of poem: New Explorations Anthology page 532

Critical commentary
This poem is about the decay of a father as he gets older and starts losing his memory, possibly through Alzheimer's Syndrome or maybe just through senility. The father has been taken from his children by his illness. The poem discusses how that makes the children feel.

The father asks the simple question, 'What colour is jasmine?' The question does not pose a difficulty for his son. What does cause a difficulty is the idea of how that question raised itself to the mind of the father in the first place. They are not sure how the question made its way to their father's mind, or where it was going to next:

> . . . we couldn't recognise the road
> your question had travelled, nor sound the extent
> of the blue void to which it would return.

We get the feeling that the question stopped them in their tracks as the ward had to come back to normality and the 'hum | of conscientious care.'

They decide that thinking about that question in a literal way isn't an option. So they 'took the long way home'.

In the final couplet the poet ties the metaphor to the rest of the poem. He asks that the question may bring his father to a kind of peace, just as a climbing plant such as jasmine can pull a broken piece of trellising together. It can climb among the broken pieces and allow them to stay tied to the wall even if they have come away. This is what he wishes for his father: that he will be able to keep himself together.

The poet creates the mood in this poem by using sensuous language. The language is designed to appeal to the senses by using soft s sounds. There is an atmosphere of compassion and of wonder.

Colour is also used to give life to the poem; as well as the colours in the flower itself, he also uses the 'blue from your wheelchair' and the 'blue void' to this end most effectively.

The poem ends in an upbeat fashion. The poet is toasting his father by beginning the couplet with a salutary 'And may . . .'

Overall this is a poem that is searching for understanding. It is one that is still asking questions about the significance of what occurred. There is almost a sense of hope from not knowing the answers, yet knowing that there is still activity in the father's mind.

Paul Muldoon
Anseo
Text of poem: New Explorations Anthology page 534

Critical commentary
'Anseo' describes how things happen in cycles and how the abused can often become the abuser.

The initial scene is a typical Irish primary school. The poet describes the roll-call system by which everybody would answer 'Anseo' as their name was called out. This word 'was the first word of Irish I spoke', as was the case and possibly still is for many Irish schoolchildren. The poet remembers what would happen at the start of every class, when the teacher would call out the last name on the roll – which belonged to Joseph Mary Plunkett Ward. This name is significant for a number of reasons. Joseph Mary Plunkett was one of the leaders of the Easter Rising in 1916. The Mary part of it is also significant, in so far as it is usually a name associated with girls rather than boys, and certainly not with a military leader – which the 1916 leader was and that this boy was about to become.

Finally, the name is also important because it gives the teacher a chance to make a pun on the boy's name. Every day he would ask the same question: 'And where's our little Ward–of–court?' There was a sense of expectancy around this question; the other students would look at each other to see the reaction to it. The teacher was obviously having fun at Ward's expense.

In the second verse we see the twisted nature of the teacher, as he would send Ward out to find his own stick to be beaten with. The teacher would refuse different options, until he got the right one to beat him with. This is the sort of ritual that Ward was seeing and, as we see later on, he was learning from it as well. The poet gives us fine detail as he outlines exactly the trouble that Ward would go to when he was preparing his own tormentor. We can almost imagine Ward taking pride in his work or being given a lecture about it from the teacher. We can see the engraving being like a commemoration on a gift:

> Its twist of red and yellow lacquers
> Sanded and polished,
> And altogether so delicately wrought
> That he had engraved his initials on it.

The poet then brings us further along in time. Joseph Mary Plunkett Ward is now doing what his part namesake had also done. He is leading a secret IRA battalion and had obviously risen through the ranks. There are many contradictions in his life when we see that

> He was living in the *open*,
> In a *secret* camp

He is no longer the boy who is being bullied and victimised. Instead he is 'Making things happen.' He has become an important person in a vicious world. He has also learned from his old schoolteacher. He calls a roll, just like in primary school. One feels the punishment for not answering the roll call this time could be much more severe than getting beaten by a hazel-wand.

He is now the one in the position of authority. He is able to put people in their place and tell them what to do. People have fear of him now.

Muldoon makes a simple point in a clever way and uses the simple Irish word 'Anseo' to illustrate it. He says that power must be used carefully. He also says that if not cared for properly, the bullied can become the bully.

Carol Ann Duffy
Warming Her Pearls

Text of poem: New Explorations Anthology page 540

Critical commentary

This is one of Duffy's most famous poems. It is a love poem of sorts, but more unusually it is a love poem written from the point of view of one woman for another.

The poem is set many years ago, and from some of the textual hints it may be set in Victorian times or even before. It is clear that the speaker in the poem is a maid. She has been given the simple task of warming her mistress's pearls. She has been asked to wear them for a few hours so that when the mistress needs to wear them later on they will not be cold on her skin.

The poem begins with a sentence that has no verb. This already creates an intimacy and seamlessness between the characters that permeates throughout the poem. The use of the word 'mistress' in a contemporary context also creates an intimate element to their relationship. This relationship is central to the progress of the poem. It is vital in terms of what it is and what the maid hopes it could become. The soft *w*s give a sense of reverie and wishfulness: 'wear them, warm then', 'white throat'.

This airy atmosphere continues with colours and textures: 'Yellow', 'white' and 'silk or taffeta'. Even the fanning action and the 'slow heat' combine to produce a sensuous feeling to the poem. The two women are brought together by the pearls which are 'Slack on my neck, her rope.'

The third verse shows the maid's true feelings. She admits to how she feels for her mistress:

> She's beautiful. I dream about her
> in my attic bed.

She feels as though she is with her through the pearls. She feels that the pearls allow a sort of symbiosis. She enjoys the effect that she has on the 'tall men', making them curious about the mixture of

> . . . my faint persistent scent
> beneath her French perfume.

The maid is as hesitant as a shy lover when she looks at her mistress through the mirror, as she prepares her for her night out. She is ready to ask her something or to tell her how she feels as 'my red lips part as though I want to speak'.

This tension exists between them without ever coming to the surface.

When the night ends, the maid still feels that she is with her mistress. The penultimate verse is the most erotic in the poem, as the maid dreams of her mistress undressing in her room. She is dreaming of her as she goes through the process of getting ready for bed. It is obvious that the maid wishes that she were getting into the bed with her.

There is a real sense of disappointment when the night comes to an end and they are finally divided, as the pearls are taken off. There is a disconnection between them. The intimate energy that has transferred between them wears off as the pearls cool down.

Paula Meehan
Would You Jump Into My Grave As Quick?

Text of poem: New Explorations Anthology page 542

A READING OF THE POEM

This extremely short poem starts as a folksy reminiscence about the narrator's granny and her ways. It begins as a cliché but then develops into being anything but. It is a dramatic monologue. The narrator is talking to some other woman, who has been making eyes at her man. The narrator is possessive and aggressive: she refers to her lover as 'my man'. She is condescending and snobbish: she talks about her enemy as being cheap. She threatens her that she'll end up 'six feet under'.

At one time it would have been unthinkable for a woman to write poetry on this subject. If we accept some people's perceptions of what poetry should be about, one of the last things that many people expect would be such an obvious act of aggression and threatening behaviour. Meehan brings poetry far beyond any preconceptions like these.

Meehan is also a playwright and is an expert in finding a character and writing in that person's voice. This poem is a good example of how this skill gives her freedom that other poets may struggle to find. To the reader's ear she seems to get perfectly inside the head of the person speaking. She does not restrict herself to saying how she feels about a subject: she engages other personae. This allows her to give voice to people who might otherwise not be heard.